On the Road to Mr Right

Belinda Jones is the bestselling author of *Divas Las Vegas*, *I Love Capri* and *The California Club*.

Praise for Belinda Jones

'A hilarious riot' *Company*

'The perfect antidote to the holiday blues' *Independent*

'A riotous page-turner, full of witty observations on life and love' *She*

'A deliciously entert͟a͟i͟n͟i͟n͟g͟ ͟b͟e͟a͟c͟h read' *heat*

'Mixing ͟.͟.͟.͟ ͟g͟r͟e͟a͟t gags but undercut ͟.͟.͟.͟,͟ this is a cut above m͟ ͟W͟oman's Own*

'A wise and witty read about the secret desires within us all' *Marie Claire*

'A sparkling read' *OK!*

'Riotously funny . . . an "un-put-down-able" book . . . You'll be reaching for the holiday brochures in no time' *Real*

'This will get you in the holiday spirit' *Company*

'As essential as your SPF 15' *New Woman*

'The perfect uplifting beach read' *B*

Also by Belinda Jones

Divas Las Vegas
I Love Capri
The California Club

BELINDA JONES
On the Road to Mr Right

arrow books

Published by Arrow Books in 2004

3 5 7 9 10 8 6 4 2

First published in the United Kingdom in 2004 by Arrow Books

Arrow Books
Random House UK Ltd
20 Vauxhall Bridge Road, London, SW1V 2SA

Random House Australia (Pty) Limited
20 Alfred Street, Milsons Point, Sydney, New South Wales 2061, Australia

Random House New Zealand Limited
18 Poland Road, Glenfield
Auckland 10, New Zealand

Random House South Africa (Pty) Limited
Endulini, 5a Jubilee Road, Parktown 2193, South Africa

The Random House Group Limited Reg. No. 954009

www.randomhouse.co.uk

A CIP catalogue record for this book is avilable from the British Library

Papers used by Random House
are natural, recyclable products made from wood grown in
sustainable forests. The manufacturing processes conform to
the environmental regulations of the country of origin

ISBN 0 09 944549 2

Typeset by SX Composing DTP, Rayleigh, Essex
Printed and bound in the United Kingdom by
Bookmarque Ltd, Croydon, Surrey

For my father – Trefor Jones

(for the wanderlust within)

Happy 70th Birthday

Acknowledgements

Road raves to: Emily O'Neill – my premier sidekick! (It all began with you, babygirl!), James Breeds for insisting on a red convertible, Kerry for snake-charming, Nina for attracting such beautiful sunsets and all the other gorgeous Thelmas in my life – Lara, Min, Sam, Emma, Tony, Tanya, Becci, Chee, Tahira and mother Pamela – for all the magical memories we have shared on our travels.

Cactus kisses to: all the hot rods I met along the way, especially Michael Neil (a man of wonderful words) and Grand Canyon Ken. Also the unsung weathermen and firemen of Wilmington, RBM, grammar-tastic Gareth and Jerry & Nathan for tolerating (just about) the sprawl of maps and guidebooks.

Bumper thanks to: Anna and Vicky at Orient Express, Sarah Harvey at Starwood, Stephanie & Co at Vista Verde and all the other accommodating hoteliers en route. Plus the tourist boards of Texas and North Carolina, in particular the stellar Connie Nelson – every town should have one of you!

Miles of gratitude to: my ultimate navigator Kate Elton – once again you have guided me with incredible skill and patience. You have a gift and I wish you every twinkly pink thing your heart desires! Also, to all the driving forces at Random House who gave this project a green light: Susan, Robert, Ron, Mark, Kate W, Georgina, Lizzy and Alison – you're fabulous and I'm so grateful for all your hard work and enthusiasm.

Champagne pit-stop for: Eugenie Furniss and Lucinda Prain at William Morris Agency (UK) Ltd. I am so excited to be working with you pro-racers! Let's floor it!

Finally, to Callie Khouri for giving the world *Thelma & Louise*, you are an inspiration.

'If adventures do not befall a young lady in her own village she must seek them abroad.'
Jane Austen

REVVING UP . . .

Picture the scene: It's late at night and my best friend Emily and I are heading home after a weekend of life-affirming hedonism in Las Vegas. We've always found it a profound wrench leaving that vibrant neon fantasy to face the grey reality of our lives back in England, but this time we're in a particularly despondent slump.

'I feel like we're going back to sit in this big, bland, sensory-deprived waiting room until our next visit,' I sigh, eyes blurring the white lines on the freeway. Over the last couple of nights we've come to realise there's not nearly enough dancing involved in journalism.

Not that our jobs are really the problem. If anything we have it pretty good scribing for a couple of the UK's top women's magazines. We can also put a substantial tick in the boxes marked FRIENDS and FAMILY. No horrors there. But the one big blank in both our lives is SIGNIFICANT OTHER, and 'His' absence is starting to take its toll. Lately, everything is looking a bit lacklustre and old. Without the spark that love brings, we're finding our energy depleted and our optimism at an all-time low. Only Vegas seems to get us going, tempting us back to a state of vitality with all its unexpected pleasures. That's what I relish – the thrill of not knowing who or what is coming next. As a consequence leaving to go back to our Groundhog Day existence feels so wrong I'm actually nauseous.

'Isn't there something we can *do*?' Emily pleads, getting so impatient with the accelerator that I think for a minute she's going to pull a U-y and head straight back to The Strip.

If only.

Instead she switches off the radio and looks at me with troubled eyes. 'I really don't think I can go back to normal this time.'

The quaver in her voice moves me. There's more to this than après-holiday blues. I feel it too. Ordinarily we get on the plane, zombiefied with resignation, fly home and do what we have to do. We're not gracious about it. We moan constantly, finding pleasure only in planning our next trip. But we always go home. This time there's a wall of resistance building and it's getting stronger and higher with every tyre rotation. Pretty soon we're going to slam into it and come to a complete halt. But what then? What choices do we really have?

Antsy with frustration, I wind down my window and lean out so the wind can bluster and buffet my face. It feels good, invigorating. I lean out further.

'You get back in this car!' Emily demands, tugging at my shoulder.

4

I slump back in my seat and laugh in exasperation. 'What are we going to do?'

'I don't know, you're the one with all the ideas,' Emily shrugs. 'Can't you have one of your barn-raising sessions?'

'Brainstorming,' I correct her, darting a glance at the dashboard clock – still a good five hours' drive ahead of us.

Five hours? My heart jolts. Suddenly I feel like I've been presented with a window of opportunity: five hours' 'safe time' to come up with a solution – some ingenious way to refocus our lives so we can let all the unnecessary distractions fall away and put all our energy into a spontaneous pursuit of love and vodka-cranberry.

A-jitter with determination I take a deep breath and announce, 'I think it's time for us to go over the rainbow.'

'Gosh, that was quick,' Emily startles. 'What's the plan?'

'I don't know yet,' I admit, taking out a notepad and pen in preparation for inspiration. 'But we have to act fast – once we're on that plane the portal that can lead us to a magical new world will close forever!' Nothing like a bit of drama-queening to rev up the adrenalin.

'Do you want the reading light on?' Emily offers.

'Not yet,' I decline, happy for now to be in a cocoon of darkness. I do all my best thinking at night; that's when anything seems possible.

'So, do we go about this in the usual way?' Emily enquires, psyching herself up for The Process.

'Absolutely. It's always worked in the past.'

This is how it goes: Emily takes the role of muse, I do the musing. I run a million options in my brain and when one gets me sufficiently agitated I tell Emily. She then squeaks excitement back at me, we start babbling over each other, whipping ourselves into a frenzy of possibility and wild expectation and then eventually we simmer down and construct a practical plan.

We've been operating like this for the past twelve years, ever since fate arranged for us to meet at the offices of *Just 17* magazine. She was on a week's work experience and I was filling in until they employed a full-time features writer. Prior to her arrival I'd been uncharacteristically subdued and paid little attention to the young blonde girl who walked in that Monday morning other than to give her something small to write, fully expecting to have to redo it. But in one short paragraph she made me snort with mirth.

I gave her more pieces to work on. Every one was a rib-tickling winner. From then on we'd spend the day rolling our wheelie chairs back and forth between each other's desks getting increasingly giggly and deranged. (Really, you have to see Emily laughing to believe it: it takes over her whole body – she convulses, bending double, clutching at her belly, face goes fuchsia, eyes and nose dribble . . . It's fantastic!) Unfortunately the production editor didn't feel it was appropriate to be having this much fun in a work environment and barked at us to quit our ridiculous snickering and get a grip! It felt like being back at school. I bit my lip but I couldn't wipe the smile from my face.

Even when Emily's week was up, she used to wait for me outside the Carnaby Street entrance and I would whisk her off to whatever shoot or assignment I'd been given. She was just such fun to have around. And so *game*. In the past friends had often responded to my hair-brained schemes with a tentative, 'Oh I don't know, it might go wrong, what if . . .' but Emily was always so gung-ho about things.

It wasn't long before our capers extended into après-office activities: wheedling our way backstage to befriend Chippendales, stalk boybands and, on one triumphant night, get down on the dance floor with Tom Jones, one thigh apiece. Things seemed to happen when we were together. It was like I'd been blessed with a soulmate and sidekick. We both felt life should be a giddy pleasure with the occasional dreary stint to offer contrast and make you realise how lucky you were, not one long chore with the occasional hysterical break-out. It became our shared goal to make the switch and live the fantasy. And here we are today, on the verge of a breakthrough. Or so I like to think.

I tug at the seatbelt so I can twist around and get a good look at my muse, currently powering through the Nevada desert on full-beam. You'd never think someone as sassy and confident and, let's face it, as busty as Emily would have a crap lovelife but man-misery has always been one of our key bonding issues. Despite countless summit meetings to discuss new ways of alerting Mr Right to our whereabouts, the condition persists. We've even started to predict worst-case scenarios for ourselves – me age seventy with a twitch and twelve cats, Emily engaged to Darren Day. That's something I intend to address with this life-changing masterplan.

I look at my notepad. Blank. I look at the clock. Four hours. That's OK. Plenty of time.

But first things first. I have to factor in our radically different tastes in men: Emily likes older, witty, doting types; I always go for the young, pretty, disinterested ones. She likes them rich and fragrant, I like them poor and fashionably skanky. She favours a clean shave and a closely-cropped bonce. I go weak at the sight of Catweazle whiskers and a ponytail. (I truly wish I could get over this fixation for men with long hair – it's brought me nothing but trouble! – but I've been skewed this way since I was a teenager so I don't hold out much hope.) I should also take into account our different styles of approach – Emily is bold and blatantly seductive whereas I tend to cop out and hide behind work, cooing: 'I'd love to put you in a magazine article!' On the plus side I've never fancied someone in a bar and not gone up to them – it's not that I'm brave, I just couldn't live with the 'what might have been' factor – but the downside is that it's always me doing the running. Just once I'd like to catch someone's eye and have them come up to me.

That's less of an issue for Emily. She's like a pro-active honeypot throwing men into a state of punch-drunk love and then moving on. As she recently confided: 'If you took away that feeling – you know, when you first meet someone and there's that stomach-flip, knee-buckle, urgent attraction – I wouldn't want to live.'

She means it. It's like an addiction to her. I, however, appear to be going cold turkey. I haven't been out with anyone in years and now I'm in my thirties I think of a relationship as something that happens to other people. The other week I totted up how many days I was in someone's arms last year and came up with six. Which basically means that for 359 days of the year I wasn't. And that was a good year. Even though I never wanted to get married, not even as a little girl – divorce runs in our family, and something about the motif of a ball and chain struck home rather too keenly – sometimes I get so swamped with loneliness I can hardly breathe. I love my friends, but it's like I'm missing someone I haven't even met yet. Only Emily can talk me round, fire me up and make me believe that if we just make one more concerted effort, we'll meet our matches. But lately I've stopped believing. People talk about losing heart and I think somewhere along the line, I've lost mine . . .

I didn't get off to a great start romantically: the first guy I slept with finished with me the next day, and I was so traumatised I didn't sleep with anyone for two years, until I found myself a nice grateful virgin who seemed to view me as a wordly Mrs Robinson figure whereas of course, in reality, I didn't have a clue. I'd kissed more pop posters than real lips. (I still slightly rue the day I made the transition from Adam Ant to the DJ's friend at the local Under-18 discothèque.)

After the virgin came the only quality guy I've ever dated – a debonair American art student named Don. More friends than lovers, we parted on good terms. Then, following a series of unwise crushes, my heart became well and truly ensnared by an enigmatic hippy-stoner with flame-dipped dreadlocks, a thrice-broken nose and the most alluringly gurgly laugh I'd ever heard. Christian – the only man in my life who has ever said 'I Love You' out loud, to my face, while actually going out with me. (As opposed to those pitiful, after-the-fact lamentations that pepper my history.) To this day he's still The One.

Rather unpromisingly, his first words to me were: 'Can you lend me 30p?' We were in Exeter's premier sticky-floored dive and he'd found himself caught short at the bar.

I looked into his huge, densely-lashed, brown eyes and it was love at first pint. I really was stupefied by him. I'd never before felt such a dreamy, swimmy sensation in someone's presence. By the end of the night we'd exchanged hairbands as a symbol of our love and arranged to meet on the cathedral green the next afternoon.

He was a mere three hours late. I forgave him. We lay on the grass sharing relationship revelations until the sun went down, then he walked me home. While I nervously dunked teabags in the kitchen he was clunking away at the typewriter in the study. After he left I pulled out the paper and found the words 'I think you're cool!' typed in the centre of the page. I was hooked. I couldn't believe someone as sexy and alternative as him could like someone as square and un-Crazy-Coloured as me.

To cut a long story short, we ended up moving into a flat together in London's Finsbury Park, and aside from the arguments, accusations and miscommunications it was heaven. He even asked me to marry him but instead of being overjoyed I had this sickening feeling in my gut that if I did, I would miss out on the chance of becoming the person I was really meant to be – our jealous insecurities were restricting us both. Then one day at work I burst into unstoppable tears in the ladies' loo and a woman I'd never met before said, 'You know, if it hurts this much, it isn't love.'

I knew what had to be done but splitting up from Christian was by far the most confusing and harrowing experience of my life. I went back to him on more than one occasion, only to make things worse, and one (bad) day he even told me that I would never be happy because I'd never let anyone truly love me. It's been like a curse that haunts me still.

You'd think that would be the end of that, but about eight years ago I was helping my mum with a big house-moving clear-out and I rediscovered his old love letters. They slayed me. Three hours later, on my way back to London, I was still in a daze on the train platform, still clutching them when, in a puff of soot, he appeared by my side – same platform, same train, same destination. It was as if I'd summoned him up.

On the journey we played Travel Mastermind, drank beer and talked. He'd had a baby but split with the mother of his bambino and appeared to have mellowed into a wiser, calmer, more content individual. It just felt so natural to be with him, as though fate was giving us a second chance, and my mind raced with possibilities. At Paddington he and his bike went one way, me and my cab went another. But not before one of the most heartfelt, swoon-inducing kisses ever.

'Do you remember –' I began, smiling at an incident from our past.

'I remember everything, Belinda,' he breathed, stroking my hair from my face.

I nearly passed out with the combination of emotion and desire.

We arranged to meet later that week but come the day, he didn't show. I practically threw up with disappointment – it was like losing him all over again. I never did find out why he changed his mind and to this day I get a loop in my stomach if I see someone who remotely resembles him. It's as though part of me is still hoping he'll magically appear like he did on that train platform. I wonder if I'll ever really be able to let him go and move on . . .

'What are you thinking about?' Emily prods me. 'You look a bit forlorn.'

'Ex-boyfriends,' I mumble, reaching for the bag of Starbursts.

'Nasty,' Emily winces.

'I know.' I pop a lime square in my mouth. 'Hey – do you know what's just occurred to me?'

She shakes her head.

'I've met every one of your boyfriends.'

Emily takes a moment to check the veracity of my claim then confirms, 'You're right! All five of them. And I've met all yours since . . .' Emily frowns. 'Who was it after Christian?'

'That medical student who was a little too thorough in his pill research,' I grimace, adding: 'The one with the long hair.'

'They've all got long hair,' Emily tuts. 'Anyway, I don't mean him – that only lasted a few weeks. The blond.'

'What blond? I don't like blonds.'

'You know, the one with the banshee ex-girlfriend

12

who chased you out of the house with a broken bottle?'

'Ohhhh!' It's all coming back to me. 'You mean The Carpenter.'

'Not exactly your intellectual equal, was he?'

Accordingly to Emily that's two giveaway clues that I'm a complete commitment-phobe right there – firstly I never choose anyone where there could be a chance of a future, and secondly I refer to them by their profession rather than their name in a bid to de-personalise them, so it's always The Carpenter, The Projectionist, The Drummer, The Taxidermist. Actually I never went out with a taxidermist though taxi drivers (specifically Algerian taxi-drivers) do have quite a thing for me.

'Of course, the next one was smart,' Emily remembers. 'If only he'd had a heart.'

She's referring to The Musician. At twenty-six, concerned that I was being too swayed by good looks, I deliberately found someone I didn't think was very attractive (although everyone else *did* which somewhat negated my personal triumph). He was sexy and funny but moany in excelsis, hell-bent on becoming The Most Bitter Wannabe In The Music Industry. During the nine months or so I wasted on him I did myself some serious damage in the self-esteem department. I genuinely felt I was missing the X-factor that compels people to fall head over heels with you – back then I didn't realise people had 'issues', I thought it was all a lack on my part. I would have sunk into a hideous depression were it not for the recurring saving grace in my life: gay men. Or more specifically at that point, my brand-new flatmate James Breeds.

Six-foot tall with David Schwimmer looks and David Beckham style, James cut a dashing figure. He was also extremely protective and ruled our household with an iron handbag, on occasion disconnecting the phone and locking it in a cupboard to prevent me from making shameful drunken calls to you-know-who.

James was everything I'd never had in a boyfriend – he'd open car doors for me, cook me dinner, surprise me with Belgian chocolates, fix my computer, take me to the theatre, he even shared his Eve Lom face mask with me. Finally I had 'someone to watch over me', and in return he says I injected some glamour into his world. I'd take him to showbiz parties where he'd be a wow, sneak him on press trips to Italy where everyone from the manager of the Excelsior Vittoria to the journo from the *Yorkshire Post* fell in love with him. Best of all I didn't have to feel jealous, just proud. And behind closed doors we had the best sofa life – a shared passion for reality TV, faux fur throws and cream cakes. Life was good.

Meanwhile Emily had put her wayward ways on hold and was living a homely life with a heterosexual. We'd hardly seen each other in months so one day I invited her to dinner at the flat, with James doing the catering, of course. It was the first time she'd seen our unconventional living arrangement – the whole place was open-plan with only a screen to separate our beds – and the set-up stopped her in her tracks.

'What happens when you want to bring someone back?' she spluttered.

'Well, it's only been a year,' I replied. 'It's yet to prove a problem.'

Emily was aghast. I just shrugged – sex had ceased to be a concern to me, and with the phobia I have about anyone seeing my thighs unsheathed, the current situation offered a convenient avoidance technique. Besides, far from feeling I was missing out, I actually suspected I'd got the better deal.

But Emily wasn't the only one to find fault with the arrangement. 'You'll never meet a straight man while you're with James,' various friends and work colleagues opined. I couldn't disagree – James had raised the bar so high, what straight man could compete?

Ultimately, it took a whole nation to tempt me away from him. I was sent to America on a work assignment and fell profoundly in love – with the country. And when I returned with Emily the Man Magnet – newly single and raring to go – it started loving me back. We walked into a bar on Sunset Boulevard and watched our lives change right before our eyes: after years of being invisible and dateless in the UK, I felt as though I'd been sprinkled with love dust. Suddenly men were looking my way and they wanted to talk to me, they even wanted to kiss me. Meanwhile Emily's already impressive suitor quota went through the roof. It seemed all we had to do was talk loudly in a British accent and the guys would flock and swoon.

We returned as often as we could, thriving on the attention. Sure there were a few disasters – a sinewy ex-soap star who'd been so mortally wounded by his last girlfriend he claimed his body had 'shut down', and then conveniently found an incredibly rich, thin blonde as soon as I'd reawoken his faculties. And Nick

– the only man in twenty years of dating I would actually have married.

'Now I never did like him,' Emily confesses. 'Spineless.'

'Moody too,' I add. 'And tight with his money – I hate that.'

'And he was twice the age of the men you usually date.'

Emily's right. He actually had a twenty-year-old son, who was far more my usual style. So what was it that won me over?

'He always reminded me of a young Al Pacino,' I muse. 'And he did look better in red than any man I've ever met.'

'I'm not sure that's a valid reason to give someone your heart,' Emily voices her concern.

'So that's where I've been going wrong all these years,' I sigh.

It's been three years since he dumped me for a spin instructor (like I don't have enough of a complex about my thighs) and now here I am, pedalling like crazy inside my head, trying to come up with a life-changing man plan. I look at my notepad – still blank bar some distracted doodles. I need some input from my muse.

Remembering an old Live The Life You Love quiz, I ask Emily, 'If money wasn't an issue, how would you spend your time?'

'Chasing men,' she says, matter-of-factly restating her *raison d'être*. 'It's the only thing that gives me a thrill.'

I nod in acquiescence, jotting down the words 'men' and 'thrill'.

Well, it's a start.

'What about you?' Emily returns the question. 'What would you do if you got paid regardless of what you did with your time?'

'Go travelling,' I reply. 'Like now, I wish we could just keep going – drive right the way across America, from one adventure to the next!' That would be my dream. The states are so diverse it would be like visiting fifty countries and a thousand movie sets in one.

I write 'travel' and 'adventure' and circle them maniacally. Again I look at the dashboard clock. Three hours and counting. Our mission to make escapism a way of life is starting to feel less attainable by the second. Giving in to a blah of despondency, I stare out of the window tapping the glass with my pen. We're the only car on the road in a black, black night, creeping through a mountain pass, straining as the gradient increases. I'm just wondering what the eerie silhouettes surrounding us might look like in daylight when I spy a road sign for Xxyzx.

Huh?! I do a double-take – surely that has to be some kind of joke?

'Emily – can you back up?'

Never one to let an illegal move put her off her stride, she obliges with a speedy reverse. I look for an addendum saying, 'We're trying to come up with a five letter word to name our town – don't worry, this is just a temporary filler' but there is none.

Consumed with curiosity, I scramble for the road atlas and attempt to locate Xxyzx in the index, but it's not listed under either Nevada or California. What I do find, however, is a collection of place names more absurd than I could ever have imagined.

17

'Hygiene, Colorado . . . Flasher, North Dakota . . . Moody, Missouri,' I read them out loud with increasing incredulity. 'Oh no – Cucumber, West Virginia!'

'You're kidding!' Emily cackles. 'Can you imagine trying to get people to take you seriously when you live in Cucumber?'

'I wouldn't mind being a resident of Cookietown, Oklahoma – isn't that adorable? Or wait – better yet – Bliss, Idaho.'

'I want to live in Bliss!' Emily whines.

'Don't we all,' I concur.

'More!' Emily demands.

I hold the road atlas closer to the reading light as my eyes strain to make out the smaller type: 'Spread Eagle, Wisconsin; Smackover, Arkansas.' I pause to chuckle in disbelief. 'And just when you think it can't get any more bizarre – Smut Eye, Alabama.'

'Smut Eye?' Emily hoots. 'I'm sorry. How is that possible?'

I shake my head, absolutely at a loss.

'I mean really – what kind of drugs are these people on?'

I laugh, forgetting our plight. This is the best car game ever! I decide to start scouring the map pages themselves and ask Emily to choose a number between 1 and 120.

'Ninety-seven!' she chirps.

I take a moment to study the page. 'Oe-ee!' I cry. 'You picked a cracker.'

'Where am I?'

'Pennsylvania. Are you ready?'

Emily nods gleefully.

'Peach Bottom, Bird-in-Hand, Blue Ball, Intercourse, *Lickingville* . . .'

'Nooo!' We narrowly avoid a metallic embrace with a passing BMW as Emily swerves at the mercy of one of her laughter-convulsions.

'Panic!' I yelp.

'We weren't that close!' she tuts.

'No,' I snigger, 'there's a village in Pennsylvania called Panic.'

'Why?' Emily despairs. 'Who on earth would want to live in Panic? It makes me anxious just thinking about it!'

'Maybe you'd feel more at home in Hooker!' I tease.

Emily snuffles in delight. 'Can you imagine if you went there and it really was entirely populated with hos!'

'And then you went to Pansy, Ohio and they were all gay!'

'Stop!' Emily shrieks.

'Or Shoulderblade, Kentucky and the streets were lined with contortionists doing dislocation tricks!'

We're getting increasingly hysterical.

'I've got to pee!' Emily complains. 'No more!'

We set aside our name-calling and concentrate on visualising a gas station. When one materialises, Emily scoots inside and I go back to flicking through the pages. It's then I start to notice a potential love theme – Boys Town, Nebraska; Fidelity, Illinois; Romeo, Michigan; Cazenovia, New York; Kissimmee, Florida . . . I want to wow Emily with as many places as possible so flick back to the A's so I can move through them

19

methodically. When she returns I've done Alabama and Arizona and I'm roving around Arkansas. It's here I spy the rudest place name so far.

'Gosh,' I cringe as she settles back behind the wheel. 'I wonder what the guys are like in Bald Knob.'

Giving my question undue consideration she suggests, 'Circumcised?'

'Emily!' I balk.

'You started it.'

Suddenly my brain vrooms into overdrive.

'What if, what if . . .' I splutter, bouncing in the passenger seat, unable to get my words out for all the hyperactive ideas ricocheting around inside my head.

'What if what?' Emily laughs at my hyperventilations.

'What if we went there and found out?'

Emily looks mildly disgusted. 'You want to go to Bald Knob and—'

'No, no!' I cut her short. 'Not there, *definitely not there*, but Cazenovia and Kissimmee – what if we went to these places looking for love?'

Emily blinks, trying to get her head around my proposition.

'Can you imagine if we found our future husband in Weddington, North Carolina, or some big strapping fella in Manly, Iowa?'

'Oh my God!' She's suddenly up-to-speed and charged with enthusiasm. 'It's brilliant!'

'It would be so much more fulfilling than another quick-fix Vegas weekend. We'd be gone for months!'

'Our search for the American Dream Guy!' Emily coos, entranced.

'*Thelma & Louise* with a happy ending!'

'Oh my God!'

'I'd make the travel arrangements, you'd attract the men, it's the perfect plan!'

A small cloud passes over Emily's face. 'I don't mean to be a downer but how would we fund this escapade?'

Her hesitation may be out of character but she has a valid concern – we've just blown most of our savings in Vegas.

I think for a moment. Curses – there's always a catch. But equally, where there's a will there's a way.

'We could write articles as we went along,' I decide. (We're now both freelance so there's no issue with us taking the time off work.) 'Or . . . Or we'd go to a couple of places, go home, do a bit of work, save the cash and then shoot off again!'

That's all she needs to hear. Emily grins over at me. 'When do we start?'

I grin back, getting a rushing in my chest and a surge of hope in my heart. This feels good on every level – travel, romance and my best friend, what could be better? We'll start by picking ten or so locations then go and check out the men who live there. It's so appealingly random – who knows who we might meet!

'Imagine if we fell in love with a redneck!' I titter. 'Our very own Kid Rock.'

'Or a hillbilly!' Emily volunteers.

'Or a piece of trailer-park trash.'

'Or a jock.'

'Or a native New Yorker.'

'Or a Southern gentleman.'

'Oh yes ma'am!' I laugh.

21

'Or a genuine article cowboy!' At this we sigh in unison.

'That's where we should start. Texas, the most American of American states,' Emily affirms.

I couldn't agree more and turn to page 106 so I can trace the map with my finger, looking for an appropriately romantic name. 'Dime Box, Fairy, Ben Hur—'

'*What?*' Emily screeches.

'I'm not making this stuff up,' I assure her, continuing my search over to the West. 'Noodle—'

'Noodle?' Emily gives me a look that says she's heard everything now.

'Tuxedo, Wink . . . I've got it,' I look up at her, triumphant. '*Eden!*'

'*Perfect!*' Emily cheers. 'It'll take us right back to Adam and Eve.' Then she smiles in wonder. 'It's like we're getting a second chance to make our love lives right!'

And in that moment all the relationship disappointments I've ever endured are wiped from the slate. There'll be no more cowering in my bed afraid of getting hurt again. I'm going to get out there – from the deserts of Arizona to the swamps of Louisiana – and I'm going to charge at life, and love! It's goodbye (and a raspberry) to 'he'll come along as soon as you stop looking for him' and hello to 'seek and ye shall find'.

'This is going to be so much fun,' Emily whoops.

'It's going to be more than fun,' I assure her. 'It's going to be Bliss, Idaho.'

EDEN, TEXAS

'Fig leaf?'

'Check!'

'Forbidden fruit?'

'Check!'

'Spare rib?'

'Check!'

'OK, we're all set for Eden!'

I wish I could say we're rattling along in a convertible Thunderbird, wind whisking our hair into a Gonk-like up-do, but the truth is we're hermetically sealed in a rented Buick. It was the high-tech steering wheel that suckered us – with buttons for cruise control, acceleration, air-con, station-seek and volume adjustment all just a finger-tap away it feels more like playing a video game than driving.

'I'm not sure we should be in a car at all,' I fret as we exit Austin airport. 'I mean, this being cowboy country

25

'n' all, shouldn't we be making our approach on horseback?'

'Eden is one hundred and fifty miles from here,' Emily tuts. 'I can think of better ways of getting that John Wayne walk.'

I chuckle to myself, then take a deep breath, marvelling at what lies ahead: 'We're really doing this, aren't we?'

'I know – can you Adam and Eve it?' Emily quips.

I sit up in my seat, suddenly alert. 'What if our dream is real?' I ponder out loud. 'What if we arrive in Eden and discover this idyllic oasis of lush vegetation and vibrant blooms and there, lounging at the base of an apple tree, are a pair of lonesome cowboys . . .'

'. . . stetsons tilted forward so that at first all we see is the long piece of grass manoeuvring around their mouths,' Emily takes up the fantasy.

'As we approach they scramble to their feet, extend a calloused hand and lead us to their magnificent stallions . . .'

'. . . coats gleaming gold in the setting sun,' I murmur.

'In one swift move they hoist us aboard . . .'

'. . . and we ride off into the horizon on a saddle built for two!'

We sigh in unison. It may be a tad premature to write ourselves a happy ending before we've even begun, but with so much riding on this trip we have to be optimistic. Emily and I have given ourselves just a week to find an Adam in Eden or a nice man in Nice. After that we'll assess whether our quest has legs (and arms, and a torso and all the other vital bits and pieces that will make up our Mr Right). It's a lot of pressure but even more anticipation – personally I like nothing better than to feel I'm on the verge of a major life change. And you can't get more major than Texas.

'I had no idea what a big-ass state this is,' I say, flexing the spine of the guidebook. 'It's actually larger than France, Belgium, Holland, Switzerland and Luxembourg *combined*!'

'No way!' Emily gasps.

'It's true! Twenty million people call the Lone Star State home.'

'While others simply call it prison,' Emily declares.

'What do you mean by that?' I scrunch my brow at her.

She directs my gaze to the barbed-wire-garlanded building before us.

'Eden Detention Center,' I read the official plaque. Oddly there was no mention of this in the travel guide. And yet it's hard to overlook considering there is nearly one inmate per Eden resident. (1300 prisoners to a town population of 1600.)

We step out of the car and shuffle up to the gate for a closer look.

'I bet the lifers could do with a bit of female company.' I squint, trying to make out the faces in a distant herd of orange jumpsuits.

'I thought we were supposed to be raising our standards on this trip!' Emily tsks, turning away. 'Besides, this is a minimal security prison which sounds a bit pansy to me.'

'You want to say that a bit louder?' I challenge as I hustle her on her way. That's all we need – a welcome lynching.

'I just hope this isn't a bad omen,' Emily bites her lip as we return to the car. 'Our first destination and we're greeted by a bunch of convicts.'

'Don't you worry,' I soothe her. 'I've already lined us up a date with someone squarely on the right side of the law.'

'We've got a date?' she balks, tripping on the grassy verge.

I catch her arm to steady her – I don't know why she's acting so shocked, it's what we've come away on this trip for.

'Yes. Lunch.' I try to sound casual, though secretly I'm rather chuffed with the head-start I have planned.

'Who with?' Emily demands.

'It's a surprise,' I trill, ducking into the car.

'Outrageous!' Emily protests, following swiftly behind. 'I thought the whole idea is that we rock up to these places unannounced and see what happens.'

'It is. Absolutely,' I assure her. 'It's just that when I was doing a little research on the internet, the only real link for Eden was for this shop called Venison World so I rang up to get some advice on where we could stay locally and got chatting to the proprietor—'

'Is that who our date is with?' Emily cuts in.

'No, she's a woman, Nancy Green. Anyway, she said there's really only one eligible bachelor in town—'

'Hold on! Hold on! What about the lonesome cowboys under the apple tree?!' Emily splutters, looking distraught.

'Hold your horses,' I tut. 'I'll come to them in a minute.'

Emily grips the steering wheel with such fervour

that the radio starts manically scanning channels and our ankles get blasted with an icy vapour.

'All right, all right! I'll tell you everything!' I give in.

'First tell me who the date's with,' Emily commands.

I give a resigned huff. I was hoping for a trumpet fanfare when I revealed his identity but I guess a radio ad for laxatives will have to do.

I clear my throat and proclaim, 'The Mayor of Eden!'

Emily is incredulous. 'Eden has a Mayor?'

'Yup. His name is Tommy Kelso.'

'Is he like an English mayor – all whiskery and portly?' Emily wants to know.

'I really have no idea,' I confess.

'Well how old is he?'

'Forty-something, I think.'

'So he's mine!' Emily brightens. 'Hmmm. Lady Mayoress. I like that.' She practises her most regal wave. 'Tell me more about what could be my new realm!'

Relieved that she's temporarily appeased, I bombard her with all the info I've collated on our little love hamlet.

'Eden is almost exactly at the centre of Texas and thus known as The Gateway City. Head east or south and you enter fabled Hill Country, north or west and you'll be greeted by a sprawl of rolling plains and cotton fields.'

'What about Eden itself?' Emily badgers me.

I turn to my next sheet. 'It says here the residents dwell among the tall grasses, pecan trees and prickly pear.'

We look up and see nothing but a bank and a Dairy Queen etched on the parched scrubland. Over to our right there's a gas station with a scruff of suspicious youths loitering outside like they are participating in a Hold-up Training Programme.

'Eden – The Garden of Texas?' snorts Emily. 'Are they having a laugh?'

'Perhaps they're being ironic,' I offer, equally disappointed by the lack of succulent greenery but keen to stay positive. It's only when I read on that I discover Eden is in fact named after a postmaster called Fred Ede, as opposed to a flourish of biblical flora.

'So why didn't they just call it Ede?' Emily complains. 'Nothing wrong with that, at least there wouldn't be any danger of getting done under the Trade Description Act.'

'You're right. That would have been a much better Edea!'

'That's not funny,' Emily grumbles as I guide her to the designated meeting point – the reality of presiding over an assortment of tatty bungalows, tangled tumbleweeds and a hair salon called Cowlicks clearly has diminished appeal.

'On the bright side it says that the people here are "downright friendly",' I try to pep her up.

'I would have thought that was compulsory – didn't you say that Texas means "friend" in some Native American tongue?'

'You were listening!' I beam. 'Yes – it comes from the word *tejas*. OH!' I flush as a rather more alarming sentence leaps out at me.

'Now what?' Emily gulps fearfully.

'It says here, "Our roots are in agriculture and *animal husbandry*"!'

But before we have time to get into any 'Do you take this goat?' imagery, we spot the Mayor.

So much for regal finery and a chunky-link chain, Tommy Kelso has a suitably ruddy complexion but he's opted for denim instead of ermine and arranged to meet us at the now legendary Venison World – a speciality shop entirely devoted to deer products and deer-themed gifts. (And pretty much the only reason why out-of-towners might stop in Eden.) Not exactly the mahogany-clad private chambers one might hope from a mayor.

'Welcome!' he greets us with a firm handshake but strictly averted eyes. 'You know, you're the first English women I've ever met!' he confides, as if paying his respects to friendly aliens.

'You're our first mayor,' Emily winks.

'Oh!' he gulps, thrown. 'Of course, y'all already know Nancy from your phone calls,' he quickly defers to the striking dame by his side. 'She's going to be our chaperone for the day.'

'Chaperone?' Emily mouths in disbelief.

I shrug back at her. I can't help but wonder where Tommy's got his information about English females – on the one hand, this propriety is all very *Room With A View* but then again, the perturbed look on his face suggests he's come straight from a screening of *Rita, Sue and Bob Too*.

'Can I interest you in an appetiser before lunch?' Nancy relieves the mayor of the burden of hospitality by leading us to the shop's deli counter where Emily is coaxed into ingesting various slithers of Bambi.

31

'You know, venison jerky is a powerful aphrodisiac,' Nancy announces, oblivious to the fact that the a-word has caused Mayor Tommy to drop behind the counter in sheer mortification. 'Ever since my daughter took some to college she's had teams of boys chasing her – now all her friends are placing orders!'

'How does it work?' Emily eagerly studies her sample. 'I mean, do you rub it behind your ears before a big night out?'

'There's a thought – maybe you should look into the perfume market!' I jest. 'One sniff and the world would cry, "Eau Deer!"' I look to the mayor, hoping for an approving laugh but find he's now lurking over by the deer-hide purses, feigning fascination with the stitching of a clutch bag. This isn't good. I can't imagine what's got him so jittery but I suspect the current conversation may be a little girlie for him so while Emily places a large jerky order with Nancy, I attempt to project a little small talk his way. Zero response. It comes to something when you can't even get the attention of the man you're on a date with.

'Come join us!' I resort to exaggerated arm signals, beckoning him over like I'm doing a move in an aerobics class.

'I don't want to get too close,' he shouts back, still keeping an overly reverential distance. 'You know how hot they are on stalking these days!' he adds, darting a furtive glance at the security camera.

What *is* going on? Do we really look that prissy or is living so close to a detention centre taking its toll? Even when we pile into his enormous maxi-van for a pre-lunch deer safari he shoos us away from a front seat that could accommodate a baseball team and suggests we hop in the back. Now there's such a stretch between us we feel like we're conversing with the driver from the back of the school bus.

Emily shakes her head in bemusement. 'If one of us did marry him, would he insist on separate chapels?'

'What was that?' Tommy hollers from the front seat.

'Nothing,' I chirrup, clamping my hand over Emily's mouth. 'Let's go!'

Following a short tour of the live and furry version of what Emily just ate, it's time for lunch proper. Now, to me, 'Lunch with the Mayor' conjures up certain images of grandeur, etiquette and cutlery dilemmas, all of which are markedly absent from the dining experience awaiting us at the Red Baron Restaurant – basically a wooden hut with an interior grubby enough to make the most hardened health inspector want to Jacuzzi in Domestos. I brave the toilets and find a jar of what looks like used cotton wool balls cowering under a layer of dust. Eden may have five churches but the 'cleanliness is next to Godliness' catchphrase hasn't caught on here.

I scoot out of the Ladies at speed, shuddering slightly and find Emily hovering awkwardly over the salad bar, torn between withered lettuce, blackened cauliflower florets and saggy tomatoes. Knowing she has to pick something she settles on a dry, cracked carrot and then moves on to the hot food section where, in a feat of daring the like of which I've never seen before, she grabs an unidentifiable chicken body-part and heads for the table. Meanwhile my enthu-siasm for mashed potatoes gets the better of me and I recreate Hill Country on my plate. I've never been one for saying grace before a meal but today I find myself in ardent prayer. (Lord, lead us not into the kitchen and deliver us from stomach pumps etc.) Now I know why Nancy declined the offer to join us.

'Enjoy!' Tommy cheers, boldly tucking in to his platter.

We look on in amazement as an assortment of bones splinter between his teeth, then find ourselves further agog as he reveals that he part-owns this eatery and lunches here practically every day. I use my psychic powers to transfer the word 'constitution' to Emily, she returns the word 'ox'.

As we attempt a convincing impression of someone chewing and swallowing, I can't help but wonder if Tommy's portion has been tampered with – he appears to be getting more confident and chatty with every bite. Maybe it wasn't us making him quake before, just low blood sugar. Either way, Emily decides it's time to risk getting a little personal.

'So, Tommy, what's the dating scene like here?' she enquires, sluicing down a mouthful with a gallon of lemonade.

He sets down his fork and sighs. 'I can probably count the eligible women of Eden on one hand and they're all like sisters to me,' he explains. 'If I wanna date someone I have to go out of town.'

'I feel the same way,' Emily makes a muffled aside.

I give her a discreet smack and ask what he thinks Texan women are looking for in a man.

'I believe the winning combination is tight-fitting jeans and a cute butt!' he chortles.

We gasp at his newfound playfulness then huddle up. 'So tell us,' we whisper. 'How should a girl go about wooing a Texan man?'

'Well, round here we're salt-of-the-earth country folk, not like those city slickers,' he sneers in the direction of Houston. 'You'll find real Texans are more macho – they like to initiate. It's the man who goes over in the bar and he's the one who'll buy the drinks. They don't like forward women,' he warns. 'And they don't respect women who go to bed with them on the first date.'

The sentence hangs in the air like a threat. Emily and I flush a synchronised pink – we feel so personally accused we're unable to compose a suitable response or segue.

'So you girls want dessert?' he asks, mercifully moving things along.

Unable to break the habit of a lifetime, I accidentally accept. To this day I don't know what I ate. But there is a reward at the end of our culinary endurance test.

'I've got a little present for you,' Tommy announces reaching into a paper bag and handing us each a copy of *The Taste of Eden Cookbook*.

'Oooh!' I choke. 'How lovely! And look – there's a dessert called "Next Best Thing To Tom Selleck"!'

'I think you were right about the irony factor here,' Emily mutters as our host takes a moment to congratulate the cook. 'Can we go now?' she whimpers.

I look over at Tommy – he's definitely someone's Mr Right, just not ours.

'OK,' I concede defeat. 'We'll get him to drop us

back at the car as soon as he's done.' (Well, it was worth a try – it's not every day you get to date a mayor.)

Amazingly this time we're invited to ride upfront in his truck. ('Does this mean we're engaged?' Emily giggles as she slides in next to me.) He even offers to take us for an early evening beer at Castanuela's Mexican restaurant.

'Unfortunately we've got to be at our accommodation by 4 p.m.,' I let him down gently. 'We're staying on a local ranch and that's the latest they can show us to our quarters.'

'Is that true?' Emily hisses while Tommy dallies to chat to a friend.

I nod. 'It's called the X-Bar!' I gurgle in expectant pleasure. 'I'm thinking X-rated, I'm thinking X-men, I'm thinking half-naked cowboys in black leather chaps!'

'Ooooh!' is all Emily can manage before Tommy resumes driving duties, taking us on the scenic route via an array of lumberyards and grain towers.

'That's Jimmy Shuman's, Ross Appleton's . . .' He checks off the residents of each house we pass along the way. 'I know everyone here, that's my job.'

'Is it a full-time occupation, being Mayor of Eden?' I ask.

'No, no,' he laughs. 'I also own a storage company but my actual profession is . . .' he eyes us nervously, steels himself then blurts: 'I'm the town mortician!'

We do a full B-movie horror gasp. *Really?*

'This is my office right here,' he says, pulling up outside the Day-Loveless Funeral Home – or Deceased of Eden as I rename it.

'That's a good one!' Tommy chuckles, ready to move on.

'Wait a minute,' Emily grabs his arm. 'Can we go in?'

I must have seen too many episodes of *Six Feet Under* because I too am eager for a tour.

'Well, if you're sure . . .' He switches off the engine.

Once inside the sprawling single-storey building we forgo contemplations on our own mortality in favour of shopping for our dream coffin – I choose the bronze casket with apricot velvet lining (pleasantly warming to a deathly pallor, I feel) whereas Emily selects glossy pine with a baby-blue satin interior. I'm just wondering whether I could get a lid with a built-in DVD player – you know, just in case – when Emily's voice curdles the words: 'The bodies! Where are the bodies?'

Tommy disappoints by announcing that he's actually corpse-free at present but shows us the embalming room as a consolation prize. Considering Emily won't even visit the dentist, I'm stunned by her grizzly fascination with the various probes and gadgets on display, her particular favourite being a staple gun used to stop your jaw from lolling open.

'So this is where you lay out the bodies to work on them?' Emily taps a long metal table.

'That's right,' Tommy nods.

'Why is it tilted into the sink?'

'For, um, drainage purposes,' he smiles apologetically.

I take a deep breath – oh the sweet fragrance of formaldehyde – and prop my queasy form against the cool tile of the wall.

'It's a yukky deal in some respects,' Tommy admits. 'The longer I'm in the funeral business the harder it is for me emotionally – I've been doing it twenty-five years and now everyone I bury is a good friend.'

'That must be awful,' I sympathise.

'Of course, the up-side is that I know what they are all supposed to look like . . .' He opens a cupboard to reveal his very own collection of Max Factor. 'I make them up – men and women – give them a "healthy" glow.'

'What if . . .' Emily's face contorts ghoulishly.

'If they've been in an accident I'll rebuild them,' he says, reading her mind. 'I learned by moulding clay and wax on styrofoam heads.'

'That must be quite a challenge,' I observe, now in desperate need for some fresh air. Where was the front door?

'It's not my biggest problem,' Tommy shakes his head.

'Oh no?' Gore-queen Emily leans in for the juice. 'What would that be?'

'Putting on pantyhose,' he frowns.

Suddenly my nausea is replaced with curiosity. 'Really?'

'Well, even when you're alive you have to wiggle your butt to get into them, imagine what it's like when the body is stiff! Personally I'm a big fan of knee-highs,' he asserts, probably the only man in the country likely to make this claim.

Leaving Tommy and Emily to it, I dip into the anteroom in search of a glass of water. The place is so still and now that I'm alone I am unable to ignore the grief these walls must have absorbed. I press my palm to the wallpaper. All the lamentations of things gone unsaid, undone. Looking at my own life I feel pretty up-to-date in all but one respect: I don't want to pop my clogs not having known a great love, one that made both parties deliriously happy and really meant something. Suddenly I'm even more convinced of the wisdom of taking this journey – years can pass undetected as you busy yourself earning a living; sometimes you have to drop everything and follow your heart. Emily and I joke about finding Mr Right but I can see now this trip has arisen out of a real need. I've got to make it work. And there's no time to waste . . .

'Oh Morticia!' I call through to Emily. 'We really should be going . . .'

'You know something?' she grins as we are reunited with our car. 'That was one of the most fun dates I've ever been on!' (Who needs venison jerky when you've got your own funeral home?)

Looking chuffed, the Mayor of Eden enfolds us in a hug – actually dares to touch us! This isn't right – whatever happened to his initial apprehension and awe? We go one step further and give him a peck on the cheek. Still no blush. Over to Emily . . .

'Bye Tommy!' she husks, switching to auto-flirt and lowering her lashes as she slinks into the driver's seat. 'Or should that be Adam?'

There we go! Deep puce. Our work here is done.

Much to my chagrin, the X-Bar Ranch turns out to be a wholesome family-run business – not a brand-ed buttock in sight. But all is not lost – the thirty-something male heading up the visitor aspect is a definite prospect.

'Stan Meador,' he introduces himself.

'Howdy!' we simper back at him. 'Belinda and Emily.'

Clocking the glint of interest in our eyes, he quickly informs us that the foxy Latino colleague currently preparing our paperwork is also his girlfriend. Ah.

Fortunately jet lag is setting in and we're now too tired to care.

'So, let's get you guys set up at The Round House,' he says, leading the way to our private guest lodgings in his chunky pick-up. We follow behind in our less ditch'n'dirt-friendly rental, stopping intermittently to let inquisitive cattle cross our path. One group of cows have white splurge markings across their faces like the masks from *Scream* – not the kind of thing two hysterical females want to be seeing after dark at a remote spot with no telephones and just a trickle of petrol remaining.

The Round House is just that: a circular stone building with a vast two-storey window for gazing out at the Mesquite trees and seven thousand acres of endless, somewhat barren ranchland. A spiral staircase leads up to two bedrooms – one master, one twin with cute deer-motif duvets – and a bathroom with an intriguing personalised toilet seat inlaid with coins, birds' feet and sentimental trinkets. It's extremely cosy-homely which is just as well seeing as we have no choice but to stay in. We explain our petrol problems to Stan and he tells us he'll return in the morning with a can of fuel and directs us to a giant box of Oreo cookies in the kitchen. It's not quite how we pictured the first night of our Mr Right quest – me and Emily alone with a packet of biscuits – but we're so pooped we're actually quite embracing of the situation.

'Right! Let's crack open a beer and get the telly on!' I cheer, eager to meld into the squishy leather sofa and replace thoughts of dead bodies with sitcom banter.

Unfortunately we can't get the TV to work. We try every button and jiggle all available cables but nothing. The silence is deafening.

'What are we supposed to do now?' Emily humphs.

I'm at a loss, wondering if we should simply drink ourselves to sleep, when suddenly Emily shoots across the room, landing in my lap in a cartoon-like blur.

'What is it?' I wheeze, attempting to soothe her gibbering frame.

'Sc-sc-sc-*scorpion*!' she tremors, pointing back to where a scaly white fella has propelled himself from the rafters, missing Emily by millimetres.

'Oh my God! I've never actually seen a live one before,' I say, peering over at its nipping claws and curly sting. 'Just be thankful it didn't land in your hair – it would have been like untangling a fish hook from lacquered Shredded Wheat!'

'Are you drunk?' Emily reels, gawping at me.

'I think I might be,' I confess.

While Emily scours the house for other ways we might die, I reinforce my laissez faire 'If I get bitten, I get bitten' attitude with another beer.

'I wonder if we should get our cases in from the car,' I slur up to Emily.

'*Now?*' she despairs. 'Can't you manage without?'

41

'I'm just thinking about what Stan said about Mexican squatters and escaped convicts occasionally dropping by looking for somewhere to sleep . . .'

Emily thunders down the stairs. 'Are you kidding me?'

'No, didn't you hear him? Actually I think you were in the loo for that bit,' I breeze. 'Anyway, I don't think he meant to alarm us, it was just a caution.'

Emily slams her hand to her brow in near-hysterical disbelief.

'I'm sure it's fine – I mean, we don't have to worry about them stealing anything, unless they're transvestite bandits—' I titter.

'Let's just get it over with!' she snaps.

As we flounder into the eerie darkness a sudden movement in the undergrowth gives us a full deer-caught-in-the-headlights fright, which is ironic because there, in the headlights, is a deer. Or a doe to be precise and a beautifully timid but tame one too. Suddenly we feel like Snow White with the woodland creatures coming to say hello.

But the Disney-phase doesn't last. No sooner are we back in the house than Emily returns to Exterminator mode, patrolling the master bedroom and barking at me to tuck up the valance so the creepy crawlies can't climb up to us in bed. (We've decided to share to ease the heebie-jeebies.) I suggest she might want to tie up her long golden hair in case they use that as a Rapunzel-style rope ladder, then lazily reach over the side of the bed and start blindly shoving the valance under the mattress. I'm stretching for the far corner when Emily shrieks like a kettle: there beneath my halted hand is yet another evil scorpion.

'Right! That's it! I can't stay here!' shrills Emily as I bolt for the door.

We panic, we pace, but with no petrol and even less sense of direction we have to somehow make it through the night. I choose denial and the guest bedroom, dreaming of a land where the only surprise Texan guests in your bed go by the name of Matthew McConnaughey. Emily opts to create a scene from *Arachnophobia* meets *The Beverly Hillbillies,* sitting in a wooden rocking chair in combat trousers, booted feet hitched up on a small table, determined to stay on Critter Watch all night. All she needs is a big ole shotgun to complete the picture.

By 4.30 a.m. she feels like a lost soul condemned to roam the earth forever more, never finding peace.

At 5.30 a.m. she wonders if she might fit in the fridge.

As the sun comes up at 6.30 a.m., she can bear it no longer and decides it's safe to go and sleep in the car in the daylight. But as she creaks open the front door she hears a strange maraca-shaking sound and looks down to see a small Mexican man in a frilly shirt. Just kidding. What she actually sees is a huge rattlesnake whipping across the rocks. Forget the traditional cockerel alarm-clock technique – this morn the whole of Texas awakes to the sound of Emily's yodelling tonsils.

Hurtling down the stairs, I expect to find her running betwixt the spiky shrubbery and deer droppings quoting King Lear but instead her speech goes something like this:

43

'Convicts! Morticians!' Her eyes widen with each expulsion. 'Scorpions! Rattlesnakes!' she shrieks, then turns on me: *'Is this your idea of a good time?'*

My mouth is still gaping in search of a response when up trundles Stan the Man and his Petrol Can.

'Sleep well?' is his unfortunate opening gambit.

For a minute I think Emily's going to savage him but instead she gives him a playful punch and winks 'Like a baby!', adding 'Up all night screaming and wailing' for my ears only.

'Let me get the petrol cap!' I swiftly divert him, babbling unlimited thank yous as he restores our vehicle to getaway status.

'So, do you girls have plans for tonight?' he asks as he lobs the empty can into the back of his pick-up.

I hesitate. Knowing Emily will want to get as far away from Concho County as possible, I was going to suggest we relocate to Dallas and bag ourselves a couple of billionaire oil barons, but I've yet to run this itinerary change by Emily so I simply shrug, 'Nothing concrete.'

'Well, if you're free, my family would love to come over and cook you ladies an authentic Texan dinner.'

'Really?' I grin, enchanted. 'That's so kind!'

A sound that can only be described as a warning growl comes from Emily's direction.

'But, um,' I fluster. 'I think we'll probably be moving on.'

'Oh, that's a shame,' Stan frowns. 'My brother Chris wanted to meet you girls.'

'You've got a brother?' Emily perks up, scurrying over to join us. 'Is he single?'

Stan smirks at her forthrightness. 'Very. And, er,' he pauses to smile to himself, 'he was going to bring along a friend.'

'Oh?' My eyebrows raise but before I get too hopeful I look to Emily – it's her call.

The poor woman is torn. Who knew there'd be such a high price to pay for an audience with our lonesome cowboys?

'I suppose we could stay one more night,' she finally concedes.

I'm in awe. After all she's been through – whatta woman!

'I can't believe you!' I squeal, pulling her into a hug when Stan's gone.

'Are you sure you can endure another night?'

Emily puffs a bolstering breath. 'Well the way I figure it is this: if things go well our beds will be too full of cowboy for a scorpion to sneak in, and if things go prickly pear-shaped at least we'll have had a nice dinner and then we can go check into the nearest Motel 6.'

'Inspired!' I cheer, giving her another hug.

We divide our day between a rodeo (too much horn-skewering and championship moustache action for either of our tastes) and jail. Apparently we were doing seventy in a thirty-five mph zone and, this being Texas, we were promptly arrested and taken before the local judge who threatened us with a night in the cells. Fortunately Emily's *Get Out Of Jail Free Cleavage* triumphed again, giving new meaning to the term being 'Wanted by the Law'. He even let us off the $240 fine, though the prolonged flirt involved in wangling that result has made us horribly late for dinner – we end up arriving back at The Round House an hour after the appointed time of 7 p.m.

The barbecue coals glow angrily and Stan gives us a mildly stern look before admitting that his brother Chris and ranch-hand buddy Casey are also delayed.

'They'll be over just as soon as they've finished marking the calves.'

'Is that like branding them?' enquires Emily, trying to get back in favour with a little cow talk.

'No,' says Stan matter-of-factly, 'marking is when they get castrated.' Emily looks aghast, but it gets worse. 'Chris said they won't have time to wash or change before they come over so they may have some blood on them.'

'How much blood?' I feel a little unsteady.

'Just a light smattering,' Stan assures me.

'Jeez – whatever happened to a splash of Old Spice?' mutters Emily as we head inside.

As an interesting take on room service, a cluster of the Meador clan have set up shop in our kitchen and are busying themselves with pots and pans of ranch-style beans, potato salad, corn, ribs and relishes. Too grimy to make a good first impression, we attempt to dash past them and dive straight into the shower, only to collide with recently widowed grandfather Ed and Aunt Rose.

'Oh hello! Good evening! So sorry we're late!' I brisk. 'Won't be a minute – just going to have a quick wash and brush-up!' I've morphed into John Cleese. 'Apologies!' I yelp, hurrying up the stairs after Emily.

46

'Oh no,' she whimpers, coming to a standstill on the top step.

I follow her gaze . . . Due to the open-plan layout of the Round House, everyone who has popped up to use the bathroom will have witnessed the disarray in our bedroom – all our sheet-yanking and pulling the bed away from the wall to escape the lair of the scorpion looks reminiscent of honeymoon action. Then we catch a glimpse of ourselves in the mirror – me in denim dungarees, Emily in a short floral dress. Fortunately our dinner companions are too polite to start making knowing comments about *Ms* Right and instead we talk of the musical Stan's father is staging that weekend and mom's tour of cathedral cities in the UK. They really are delightful, God-fearing folk. The kind that make us wish we'd brought along a peach pie instead of a twelve-pack of Budweisers.

'Here they are – just in time,' Aunt Rose welcomes latecomers Chris and Casey.

We're relieved to see them home in on the beer but less thrilled that they've kept their word about being smattered in blood and mud.

'Howdy!' they nod in our vague direction before lapsing into a self-conscious silence, focusing all their attention on the barbecued ribs. On the up-side, this gives us plenty of opportunity to stare at them – Emily likes her men 'all-man' and Chris's Desperate Dan-style stubble and ferociously furry chest meet with her approval. Meanwhile I've always been a sucker for a pretty face and Casey – with his ice blue eyes and sheeny caramel skin – could easily out-handsome a whole herd of male models. Ordinarily this would be our dream scenario – two men perfectly tailored to our needs plus a table full of food – but we're finding the excess of relatives a tad distracting. (To think we complained about having one chaperone earlier – now we've got *five!*)

Suspecting her usual approach – flirtatious wit combined with a dangerous cleavage – may not be the way to go to win over her future mother-in-law, Emily sits uncharacteristically buttoned-up of lip and blouse. Parents are more my thing but these people are so *good* they make me want to draw on extra freckles. I quickly review some former 'meet the folks' encounters, hoping for inspiration. All I can think of is the bottle-blonde mum with a fag forever wavering on her bottom lip. I remember watching in awe as she neatly tapped ash into her bare hand in lieu of an ashtray and then, when she was done, simply shook her hand clear over the carpet. I had few etiquette concerns that day. Here the main problem is that I feel like we're auditioning for two clashing roles – mechanical bull-riding sex kittens for the men, Little Bo Peep for the family – all on the same stage.

Reaching for the salt, I dart a look at Chris and Casey, who have yet to join the conversation. I'd ask them a question but their heads are still buried in their troughs. Fortunately ma and pa are on hand to inform us of their son's recent graduation from Texas Tech, where he's been studying agriculture as a back-up for his planned future: continuing the family tradition as a rancher. Thanks to their starter for ten, he's off:

'At college the cowboys and agriculture students have this hillbilly reputation – we're seen as these dumb guys who can't talk proper English,' complains Chris, perfectly eloquently. 'But these days agriculture is a business like anything else.' He extends a paw for the butter. 'The big joke is that you're never going to make any money at it. Well, you're not going to get filthy rich like you used to be able to in the cattle business but you can do all right.' He takes a chomp out of his corn on the cob then adds, 'Of course, if some girl asks me if I'm going to make a lot of money I'm like, "Oh yeah!"'

We chuckle encouragingly and ask him if he has aspirations of solid silver spurs.

'As long as I can live comfortable, take a few vacations and do what I want to do, I don't care about making millions,' he replies.

Very good, first contestant.

Now we turn our attention to twenty-four-year-old Casey Willis. He grew up with the Meadors and is helping Chris on the ranch for the summer. We want to know if he presses his Wranglers and sports snake-skin boots?

'No way – those city slickers look like jackasses!' he hoots with derision. 'If you walked round the rocks here in boots with heels like that you'd snap your ankles!'

'What about when you go out dancing – is there at least one spangly cowboy shirt in your wardrobe?'

He shakes his head. 'When we go out in San Angelo we just wear baseball caps and T-shirts like regular folk.'

Another cliché bites the dust.

'You know, you just reminded me of something,'

49

Chris leans in, looking amused. 'I had Casey's mom for my teacher in eighth grade and we were penpals with some school kids in New York and they wrote asking us all these silly questions like, "Do you ride a horse to school?", but they were serious! So one day we did a picture album for them – we brought our horses to town and staged a showdown!'

'That's right!' Casey chuckles: 'And then we wrote captions underneath the pictures saying, "In New York y'all have to deal with uzis, we just have old-fashioned gunfights!"'

Emily and I smile happily. They may have had us at 'Howdy!' but it's good to know they can chat too. Suddenly the whole ambience feels a lot more relaxed. Over the course of the evening, everyone's had a chance to join in and make a conversational contribution. We've even shared a few laughs. Better yet, the food just keeps on coming . . .

Chris pulls a face at the bowl of fruit salad placed before him, clearly no fan of lean cuisine. His mum sighs and hands him some cookies to force it down with.

'This has been such a lovely meal,' Emily and I form a gratitude chorus as we polish off our desserts.

'You're more than welcome!' our hosts smile.

'You're more than discreet!' we want to smile back – for no sooner has the last pip and crumb been cleaned away, the clan disappear off down the track in a trail of leftovers and Tupperware. All that remains is Chris and Casey.

Emily and I hum 'I think we're alone now', hand out the Buds and step into the balmy night air. Moonlight and cowboys, what could be more romantic?

As we gather our chairs around the low glow of the fire I realise that this is more than we could have ever realistically hoped for: day two of our trip and we've found a couple of genuine prospects. I feel nervous and excited as I prepare to sneak a look at Casey, wondering if I can take sitting this close to such beauty, but – what the hell? – I turn to find his face grossly distended and bulgy like a bullfrog's.

'Chewing tobacco,' Chris explains, catching my reaction. 'You roll it round your mouth and spit it out.'

Right on cue Casey spurts a gob of squelched muck into the undergrowth. 'Eeewww!' Emily and I squeal in disgust.

He does it again.

'Eewwwwww! Caseeeey!'

His blue eyes twinkle all the more.

Chris tells us that there's fibreglass mixed in with the tobacco to cut into the lining of your mouth so the nicotine can enter your bloodstream.

'You're kidding!' I gasp, scandalised that Casey would want to inflict such damage upon himself. 'You know, I think the sight of you pressing that stuff around your mouth is the ugliest thing I've ever seen!'

Casey looks chuffed and makes me a present of his now-empty Copenhagen baccy tin. I'm absurdly touched. My crush is intact.

'So, Chris,' I sense Emily moving in for an early kill. 'If Casey has these great tongue-twisting skills, what do you have to offer a girl?'

Jeepers! There's no flies on her.

Chris gives the question some serious consideration

then says, 'I guess I'm funny. Well, everyone's always laughing at me . . . !' he frowns.

We giggle on cue.

'And if I found the right girl I think I could be loving. I just don't have anyone to give love to right now,' he sighs, adding, ''cept the cows and I'm pretty mean to them, doing surgery on them all the time. I don't think they like me too much!'

Oh he's adorable! For once I get Emily's taste.

'So how long have you been single?' she asks him.

'A year. Before that I went out with a girl for five years but she didn't know if she wanted the ranching life for the rest of her life – sometimes we had plans and I couldn't go along because the livestock needed tending. I told her she best make sure. We broke up but we're still friends.'

'Would you ever give up ranching for a woman?' Emily cuts to the chase.

'No, because I feel real lucky to have the opportunity to do this. I wouldn't change it for the world.'

Hmmm. That's some serious lifestyle adjustment to consider, one we'd overlooked in our cowboy fantasy. I know Emily's first concern would be de-bugging the neighbourhood. As for me, I've always thought I'd like nothing better than to immerse myself in an alien environment all in the name of love but to arrange my life around the needs of cows could be something of a culture shock. Then again, looking at Casey now, it would seem easily worth it. I'd get up before daylight and lug bags of feed for the chance to scrub his back in a tin bath.

'So what's the longest you've been out with a girl?'

Emily asks Casey, getting the conversation back on track.

'Probably about a month and a half!' he says with an apologetic grunt.

'Hey! Teach me all you know!' I semi-joke.

'Girls act like they're interested, but next thing I know they're going out with someone else!' he sighs, somewhat forlorn. 'Although I really haven't had a broken heart yet.'

Bless him he sounds like he actually wants one! I could certainly give it a try! Oh how I wish the poppers would fly off his check shirt, I bet he has the smoothest chest. I'd happily believe he could be my Mr Right, if only I could be sure he liked me back . . .

'Another Bud?' Emily distributes the beer then shifts her chair a little closer to Chris and asks who his fantasy cowgirl would be. (It's a theory of ours that if you get single men talking about objects of their desire and you're sat there looking available and appealing they'll redirect those feelings to you.)

'Shania Twain,' Chris announces. A good choice but there's room for improvement, seeing as Emily is more of a trainee Dolly Parton. 'What I really want is a good-hearted woman,' he elaborates. 'One who'll always be there for me.' He pauses for a minute and then concludes, 'One that won't leave!'

I put the same question to Casey. He says he likes Elizabeth Shue because of her natural look. I think that's admirable, even if I am more Elizabeth Hurley in terms of never being seen without a full face of 'slap'. Then he goes and spoils it all by revealing his fantasy is to date a stripper.

'Why?' I can't help but ask.

'Because they take their clothes off!' Chris answers for him.

Gee, if that's all it takes . . .

Suddenly a hush descends. 'Did you hear that rustling?'

We have a quick forage hoping for another audience with our lovely doe but she's not forthcoming so instead we tell the guys about the deer safari we went on with the Mayor and how he said that Texan men like to do the asking when it comes to women.

'That's bull!' they cry, united with outrage.

'I really have a problem with going up to people, especially if I don't know them,' Chris admits. 'I never know what to say or do so I go stand in a corner! I have my group that I like hanging out with and that's it.' He pauses for a moment. 'That's probably why I haven't had a girlfriend in a year because I won't talk to someone unless they talk to me first. I *like* women to come up and talk to me!'

Casey nods in emphatic agreement. It seems ludicrous that someone as stunning as him doesn't have the nerve to approach a girl, but he too claims he doesn't know what to say. As if he'd need to even speak, for goodness' sake! I think if he mastered the Fonzie finger-click he could waltz out of the bar with a gal on each arm, no problem. In the meantime, I try to ram home to them that it's not what you say but how you say it.

'If a girl likes you, the nonsense you're spouting is pretty irrelevant,' I insist.

Casey looks encouraged by our warped wisdom and

grins, 'Y'all should move into The Round House and set up a dating school to train the local men!'

'We could call it Rancho D'Amour!' Emily and I enthuse, wishing we could start a little night school right now.

It's ironic that with all this talk of being a little more bold and acting on your feelings, there is no way I can tell Casey that I like him. I just wouldn't know how. In my mind I'm already being way too obvious but maybe I'm wrong. I remember a camera guy I once did a three-day documentary shoot with – I went home every night cursing myself for throwing myself at him in such a shameless way, all to no avail. Then a couple of months later I bumped into him, we went for a drink and I apologised for being so brazen. Turns out he had no clue that I liked him. I was stunned – I thought I'd done everything but write my phone number up his forearm in lipstick.

It's just so hard to judge with someone you don't know well. These guys have clearly stated they like women to come up to them but does that mean it's down to us to make the next move? Short of giving them a lap dance I'm not sure what that move would be. Besides, I can't tell whether they like us *in that way*. Maybe they do but they're not acting on it because we're from a foreign land and therefore how could there be a future? All I know for sure is that I'm paralysed by a fear of overstepping the mark. What I really want is to be lying under a tree with Casey, watching him chew on a piece of grass and listening to his croaky Texan drawl. I'd love to see his shyness gradually ease away so that he'd finally lean over and ruffle my hair and gaze at me through those long black eyelashes and then—

My reverie is disturbed by the backward scraping of chairs. They're leaving! Oh no – where's a lasso when you need one?

'Do you really have to go?' we whine.

The evening *can't* be over!

'It's 1 a.m., we have a 6 a.m. start,' Chris explains his plight. 'Ranching is not the kind of job you can call in sick to.'

He's got a point but we're disappointed all the same – I guess we're not going to see their raw hide after all.

'Let us at least walk you to your truck,' we offer.

I expect it to smell like a butcher's shop – all sawdust and raw meat – but in fact it's yummily sweet like pear drops. I could have sniffed all night but the key is already in the ignition.

'One last thing,' I lean in the window, desperate for one more exchange.

'Yes?'

In the pressure of the moment I opt for the question Emily and I decided we'd put to men in each state we visit.

'How would you say guys from Texas differ from the average American male?'

Chris gives me a naughty look and revs the engine. 'You've heard the expression – *Everything's bigger in Texas . . .*'

And with that, they're off. Emily and I linger awhile tongues a-lolling then stumble to bed, heads so full of the Magnificent Two that we don't spare a thought for our scorpion bedfellows.

*

They are still with us when we wake. For me that's a giveaway sign that I really like someone – if I can physically feel their presence the morning after, I know there's a good chance I could develop some pretty mushy feelings for that person. If I wake up feeling like my normal self, unaffected, then generally they don't have the power to really get to me. Or at least I feel less compelled to pursue them to the point of stalkerdom.

'If only we'd met them on our first night,' Emily curses. 'Do we really have to move on today?'

Unfortunately we do – we have an afternoon flight booked to Los Angeles, and seeing as this is such a whistle-stop tour we have to hit the road as soon as we land. (Our intention is to kip en route to Nice, then spend three nights finding our Californian Mr Rights.)

'It seems a bit disloyal to be thinking of other men when we've just met two wonderful diamonds in the rough,' I sigh, not having anticipated this problem. 'But I suppose the way to look at it is this: we already know we like Chris and Casey so, depending on what happens in Nice, we could always return to Eden when we come back to do the rest of the places on our list.'

'Really?' Emily brightens.

'I don't see why not. New Mexico borders Texas so we could pop by after Truth or Consequences.'

'I like your style,' Emily approves, concluding: 'This is a little taster and next time we come back for a big ole steak!'

'Exactly,' I confirm.

Emily jumps out of bed with renewed vigour and

starts to pack. Midway through rolling her dress she stops.

'All the same, I wouldn't mind seeing them one more time before we go.'

'Oh me too!' I gush. 'We have to say goodbye!'

'The only snag is, they'll be working.'

'It'll be fine,' I assure her, though in reality it's anything but – there seems to be an awful lot of blood shed and squealing involved in castrating cattle. Funny that.

We end up clinging to a metal gate feeling rather queasy. But then the boys redeem themselves by herding the livestock – such an erotic sight I'm surprised the concept hasn't been used in more male strip-show routines.

'Do you hear "So Macho" playing in the background?' Emily giggles as we watch them 'Yarrrr!' and scuff up the dusty earth.

'It just looks so cool and masterful,' I sigh. Although, that said, Casey has already fallen off once today.

'Do any damage?' I ask, channelling Florence Nightingale.

'Nah, I landed on my butt!' he grins.

Oh I just love this man! He's so natural and blissfully unaware of his good looks. My only concern is that last time I dated someone this unspoiled, I over-complimented him to the point of creating a monster. He became so cocky he convinced himself he was too good for me and took to putting me down at every opportunity. I can't see Casey doing that but I would always fear that he'd realise what a catch he was and then run off with someone younger and prettier.

Suddenly twigging that I'm getting way ahead of myself, I tune back into the conversation – Chris is telling Emily about the 'wreck' he once got into at a recent rodeo:

'I was bull-dogging (jumping from the horse onto the cow) and just as I was bringing him to the ground he got free and riled the horse and they both ran over my head!'

Emily and I reel back imagining the battering to his skull but he just laughs and shrugs, 'That was the end of my bull-dogging days!'

We can't believe how casual he is about this!

'When a cow runs over you everyone stops to make sure you're all right and if you are, then it's funny,' Casey helps to explain.

'Riiiight!' we laugh uneasily. Ranching really is another world. We wish we could stay and listen to their stories all day but Stan has just arrived, presumably wanting to check that we are actually leaving the ranch, as opposed to setting up a squat with some Mexican bandits.

'He's looking at us like we're women of ill repute!' I hiss at Emily. 'All we want is a hug!'

That's so not gonna happen – the guys are too shy to make a move and we're inhibited by Stan's surveillance.

Emily tries to prolong the farewell by inspecting a tear in Chris's shirt. 'What did you do to get this?' she asks.

'I don't know,' he says, twisting his sleeve. 'Do you want to fix it?' he adds with a twinkle.

Emily leans in close and confides, 'I'm not really the darning type.'

'So!' Stan steps up, clearly on a mission to chivvy us on our way.

I look at the ground then take a breath – it's now or never.

'Here, this is for you!' I feel positively pre-teen as I hand Casey a pink chocolate mouth on a stick. (I wanted to give him something in return for the Copenhagen snuff tin and it's all I could muster!)

He accepts it, too nonplussed to speak.

Meanwhile Chris can't stop beaming at Emily. 'I'm getting e-mail soon so we can keep in touch,' he tells her.

'Don't lose our number!' she calls back as Stan marches us on our way.

'It's right here!' says Chris pulling it out of his breast pocket. He's wearing a different shirt to the night before so that bodes well!

At the gate we stop the car and turn back for one last look. Even though we'd literally be Calamity Janes out here we can't help but get a little misty as we watch Chris and Casey trot into the horizon.

If you listen closely you can hear us whisper, '*Take us with you!*'

NICE, CALIFORNIA

Men with more tattoos than teeth. Third World poverty. Roadkill. Hardly the Californian Dream and yet this is how the town of Nice has been described to us. And that's by the natives.

'Have you ever been to the Clear Lake area before, dear?' asks one wary tourist-board official. 'Do you know what you are letting yourself in for?' seems to be her underlying message.

I think she's especially concerned because we're coming from LA, home of the Hollywood smile and Platinum Card excess where the dead animals are accessorised with high heels and diamonds. But the worse they paint it, the more defiant we get: we will find a 'nice' man in Nice!

With a five-hundred-mile drive ahead of us we decide to eat our way through rush hour and then set off on the clear night-time roads. Leaving LA under cover of darkness gives us fugitive goosebumps but we manage to get through the 275 miles to Santa Nella with only one brush with the law (a speeding ticket that Emily cleavages her way out of) and one near-death experience (my night vision failed to detect Emily's clear plastic straw bobbing within the water bottle, and as I tipped it upright to drink the last thirst-quenching drops I practically gave myself a tracheotomy from the inside out).

At 3 a.m. we check into a Motel 6 and stumble into bed for a travel-fatigued sleep. What seems like minutes later we're awoken by a ringing phone.

'Hello?' I husk into the receiver.

'Hi! This is Mr Smith calling from the National Lottery – you've just won ten million dollars!'

My eyes spring open.

'Just kidding! It's time to get up – this is your wake-up call!'

Pretty darn droll for an economy motel chain, I think you'll agree.

Another hundred miles and we're entering San Francisco. It seems odd to watch the psychedelia blur by without being tempted to travel the trams, escape from Alcatraz or, at the very least, waft an incense stick. But we do get to ride the magnificent mile of red metal that is the Golden Gate Bridge. Lifted into a true blue sky I marvel at the panorama while Emily makes the interesting safety choice of accelerating with her eyes closed – not a big fan of heights, our Em.

Soon the hectic freeways give way to English-style countryside where we're the only car for miles. We know we're entering Wine Country when we're surrounded by an endless lattice of vines, held in place with perfectly symmetrical sticks and twine. From a distance the landscape looks like the grid on the *Hellraiser* head but our thoughts quickly switch from horror to *Little House on the Prairie* when we spot The Cherry Country Store. Bounding in with all the pigtailed enthusiasm of Laura Ingalls Wilder, we inhale the smell of nutmeg and fresh-baked bread and inspect the shelves of prettily packaged preserves, marinades and a rather curious array of tack: Grapes of Bath soap, mugs announcing *Real Hunters Like Big Racks* and a CD from local Polka legend Frank Yankovic including three of his 'classics': *I've Got a Wife at Home, I Stopped for a Beer* and *Strip Polka*!

A beaming granny fixes us bulging sandwiches and cups of hot syrupy cherry juice and we sit outside on a bench in the sun, revelling in the glorious sense of freedom and adventure as we once again head into the unknown. As Emily toasts the baby-blue sky, a new confidence bubbles within me – suddenly I am utterly convinced that this quest is going to work: we *are* each going to find a man and the sensation that we're missing out on something that so plagues us back home will finally be vanquished. Already I'm experiencing a rare mix of relaxation and in-the-moment content-ment, as if I'm on a childhood picnic where tomorrow and deadlines and obligations don't exist.

I close my eyes to wallow in the feeling, then, taking a deep breath, fill my lungs with exhaust fumes as an almighty truck thunders up, leaving his engine chugging fumes as he runs into the store. I'd love to obliterate him Thelma and Louise style but today is all about being 'nice' so we move on.

Ironically, considering how wild she can be, the majority of Emily's boyfriends have been the epitome of nice – reliable, faithful, do anything for ya – but I wouldn't say any of mine fitted that bill. I used to think nice meant boring or wet. I wanted unpredictable men of mystery, not a lap dog, but I paid for my choices with big blubbery tears brought on by my various boy-friends' flaky lack of consideration. I've had an excess of that and yet I still don't know if I'm ready for nice. Having said that, this environment couldn't be more conducive to a civilised, grown-up relationship. Napa reminds us of Tuscany with its Italianate villas and golden undulating fields and we long to stop off for a month or two and take strolls at sunset with the rich and fragrant. (Oh to be a Chardonnay heiress.) This is definitely a moneyed area – St Helena in particular has a snooty elegance with its wine bars, bookshops and boutiques, including a redbrick Donna Karan Country Store. It is indeed as if a designer 'designed' the whole town. And yet a few miles on we see a most incongruous sight – a British pub.

'The Lord Derby at Middletown,' Emily reads the authentically creaky sign.

We get quizzical then double-take as another – The Stone House Tavern – displays my ancestral flag, the Welsh dragon.

'What next?' Emily hoots. 'A cockney geezer selling jellied eels?'

'Can we really be just fifty miles from Third World poverty?' I furrow my brow.

Emily can no longer manage a reply – we've begun ascending a particularly treacherous, barrier-free

66

mountain path and her hands have turned to slime on the steering wheel. While she concentrates on inching upward, I stick my head out of the window and gawp at the dangerous beauty below. How bad can Nice be? This is stunning.

As the road levels out we see our first sign for Clear Lake, aka 'Northern California's Most Affordable Vacation Secret', as announced by the roadside billboards.

'I think that's basically a polite way of letting people know how poor this area is,' I note as we pass a series of low-rent lakeside towns.

Still, nature knows no budget constraints and the view across the silvery waters is magnificent. A big sign tells me that this is the biggest natural lake in America. And it's also a great place to breathe – according to another boastful billboard Lake County is one of the only smog-free environments in California. I take in a lungful of freshness then push it out with a howl, demanding Emily instantly pull over. She mounts the grassy kerb and gives me a 'This better be good!' look. Across the road is a big earthquake crack in a field. Such things are known as 'faults'. This one has a sign next to it saying, 'Guy's Fault'. I had to get a picture.

'You don't think it's warning us that the local guys are nothing but troublemakers and wrongdoers?' Emily frets.

'Oh don't say that!' I complain. 'I know the tourism lady raised a few concerns but I'm sure, even though they're not going to be wealthy, they're going to be lovely – all apple-cheeked and sun-kissed and smiley with open, honest hearts.' I get more carried away

67

with every breath. 'They're going to help us with our suitcases and offer us a glass of freshly made lemonade and restore our faith in mankind and make us better people just from knowing them!'

'Gosh! That's quite a lot to hope for,' Emily notes.

'Well if you can't find a nice man in Nice . . .' I trail off as we roll into the town itself.

We've slowed out of caution, not because there are any hairpin bends or livestock ambling in our path but because the whole vibe of the place is making us suddenly uneasy. There's not a soul around and yet we're feeling watched, as if by one of those paintings with the shifting eyes. I can't help but wonder, if we were blindfolded could we sense the difference between St Helena and Nice, or does what you see dominate how you perceive things? I've been to run-down places before but never experienced this under-lying threat. Just look at the city limit sign: whereas Eden encouraged us to 'Keep Texas Beautiful', Nice has a sign saying 'Call 911 Emergency'!

'I think we should get straight to our B & B,' Emily urges, as though it's some kind of safe house.

In reality The Featherbed Railroad Company is more of a lovebirds' retreat – I thought it might be a nice theme for the trip, staying in the kind of places you'd come to if you'd already found Mr Right. With nine rust-red vintage train cabooses converted into unique suites, this sounded particularly appealing but now I'm here I can't imagine the town's tangible menace encouraging any loving feelings. Unless it's in a 'Shag now for tomorrow we die!' kinda way.

'I hate to say this but we're going to have to ask for

directions,' I apologise to Emily, realising I only have the name of the place, not the street address. (As Nice only has a population of two thousand or so, I thought it would be immediately apparent. But it's not.) 'It looks like there's some people over in that park . . .'

'You mean the fenced-off patch of grass,' Emily corrects me.

I nod. 'Let's ask them.'

We pull up beside a gaggle of mullets sporting lightly grimed cap-sleeved T-shirts. I'm just about to wind down the window and try to get their attention when survival instinct kicks in and I find myself locking the doors and insisting Emily vroom away – something tells me they've got self-inked tattoos, and that's just the women.

'This is so not nice!' Emily shivers. 'I can't believe people actually come here on holiday.'

'I know. What does that say about where they actually live?' I wonder.

I recall our accommodation claiming a lake view so we trundle water-ward, sliding by a series of those space-age silver capsule trailers much beloved of fashion magazines – you've seen the pictures: a bed-ruffled blonde with smudged eyes and an off-the-shoulder dress sat on the stoop with a plastic grenadine-stained cocktail glass while in the background her troublemaker hubby goofs around with their mongrel dog in a stained wife-beater vest. At least that's the Samantha Morton/Jared Leto kooky young couple version of Trailer Park Trash. The reality is rather more disturbing. It's hard to imagine that Nice ever lived up to its chic French Riviera namesake but in the late 1800s it really was a magnet for the rich and famous thanks to the lavish five-thousand-room Bartlett Springs Resort – an infamous pleasure palace with a casino, mineral spa, concert hall and elegant ballroom. Tragically, back in 1934, the resort – and any trace of sophistication – was destroyed by fire. The closest imitator today is the Konocti Harbour Resort over in Kelseyville but the truth is for sumptuous originality you choose The Featherbed Railroad Company. As soon as we spy those unmissable train cabooses (set on a lakeside lawn interspersed with oak, bay and redwood trees) the dirge of Nice becomes a sweet symphony.

'Oh thank God!' I breathe. 'It's beautiful.'

We pull onto the gravel driveway feeling like we're crossing into a protected haven. The atmosphere couldn't be more different and the proprietors who come to greet us – Len and Lorraine – really *are* nice, but with a healthy helping of sass. (Well, you'd have to have some gumption to survive the neighbourhood.) Clearly a pair of foxes in their prime, Lorraine looks like a Sixties Cleopatra with a jet-black beehive and sultry kohled eyes, whereas Len's sweep of white hair puts me in mind of the grandfather in *Chitty Chitty Bang Bang*. Even though he's pushing seventy, I'm rather taken with him. (Funny, I don't ever fancy men old enough to be my father but grandfather is a whole different thing.) As he shows us around the hulks of rusting iron that make up the individual suites, Len explains that he personally hauled the cabooses all the way from Sante Fe, New Mexico.

'Once I'd got them installed I just wanted to go to

Wal-Mart and buy nine sets of the cheapest bed covers, lamps and tables,' he confesses, 'but Lorraine wouldn't let me!'

Thank God. It turns out the woman has a gift.

As we're the only guests (should we worry?), we get to see inside every uniquely decorated carriage. First up is The Casablanca:

'No way!' I gasp as we step inside – in the alcove by the door is an actual piano with sheet music for 'You Must Remember This'. A red neon sign glows the words *Rick's Café Americain* and in the far corner there's a coat stand draped with Bogie's trademark raincoat and trilby! I'm just contemplating the bed, wondering how many 'beautiful friendships' have been consummated in it when Emily yanks me into the bathroom – there above the sink is a mirror displaying the classic line, 'Here's looking at you, kid'.

'Brilliant!' I whoop, utterly in awe of Lorraine's eye for detail. She's even managed to acquire some black and white film stills of Ingrid Bergman and co. 'It's like a cross between a film set and a liveable work of art,' I decide, feeling extremely happy. I've always been partial to a themed hotel room on account of the kitsch factor but this shows a whole new level of panache. I can't wait to see the next one.

'Wild Wild West,' Emily reads the plaque as she opens the door into what feels more like a wagon rather than a train carriage.

'Imagine if Chris and Casey were waiting here as a surprise!' Emily grins, running her hand along the wood-panelled wall. She stops at Lorraine's wonderfully characterful portrait of a leather-skinned cowboy sucking on the tail-end of a roll-up. 'Reminds me of a cigarette ad I once saw: "Finally a butt worth kissing!"' she giggles.

We then careen between the freshly floral Mint Julep; cosy, rustic Wine Country Lovers' frills and lace and the old-fashioned chintz of Rosebud, quickly exhausting the phrase, 'Oh my God – look at this!' on account of all the darling touches. These rooms are so exquisitely pretty I'm convinced Lorraine is offering a valuable service to the community – pure escapism from only $120 a night.

'Now *this* is my favourite!' Emily decides as we discover the Harley heaven of Easy Rider.

Personally I prefer the Art Deco elegance of The Orient Express but there's still one to go before we make our final decision – La Loose Caboose.

We cross the grass, clatter up the metal steps and pause to read the old Police Department sign on the door: BEWARE PICKPOCKETS & LOOSE WOMEN.

'I think we've found our home for the night,' I smile, venturing inside.

The interior is plum and dusty rose with a flirty pink neon sign inviting us to indulge at 'La Playpen'! There's a shaggy rug beside the raised Jacuzzi, a nude portrait of a woman painted on strokeable velvet and a padded black leather trim to the bed, which comes accessorised with peacock feathers and a mirrored ceiling.

'Don't be surprised if I wake up screaming in the middle of the night,' I say, peering up at my reflection. 'You know how confused I get – I'll probably think someone's skydiving down onto me.'

'Don't worry, I'm sure they've put extra sound-proofing on this room,' Emily notes, jutting her head up into the driver's look-out. 'My only concern is what Len and Lorraine will make of our choice!'

'Perhaps we should mention our hopes of meeting some local men?'

'Good idea,' Emily confirms.

So we do. And then we watch the colour drain from their faces.

Without even exchanging a glance they chorus: 'Forget it!'

'Really, are they that bad?' we query.

They purse their lips in grim affirmation. I get the feeling they don't want to slag off their neighbours but even when we ask for a recommendation for dinner they suggest we get out of town. Not in an offensive way, there just aren't too many fine dining options in Nice.

'What are we going to do?' Emily frets as we traipse back to watch the sun slip into the mercurial waters of the lake from our dinky patio. 'Even the people who live here say we should steer clear of the menfolk.'

'Lakeport looked safe enough, didn't it?' I chew my lip, considering our options. 'We could go back there for dinner, it's only a fifteen-minute drive.'

Emily looks unconvinced.

'It's either that or scrounging leftovers at the Trailer Park.'

'Let's go!' she jumps to her feet.

In a novel twist to getting dolled-up for a night out, we dress down in our grungiest combats, kink and fluff our hair and use a mix of purple and brown eyeshadow to fake the odd bruise and faded lovebite.

'You look rough!' Emily tells me.

'Thanks, you too.'

'This is so wrong!' I sigh as we head toward Lakeport. 'We're actually going out praying we won't attract any attention.'

'It's at times like this I wish I knew karate,' Emily whimpers.

'Oh don't say that!' I fret. 'I'm nervous enough as it is.'

Half of me thinks we're overreacting, the other half worries that we're crazy to even stay overnight. If it wasn't for the amazing accommodation (and this questionable Mr Right quest) we'd have scratched Nice by now and be on our way back to the luscious, elite Napa Valley.

Things are looking rather low-rise everytown as we enter Lakeport, but then we spot an appealingly quirky row of Victorian buildings housing a crystals shop, vegetarian restaurant and mauve-fronted coffee house adding a dash of San Franciscan hippiness to an otherwise plain but pleasant town. Considering pizza to be the safest bet we boldly stride into the Round Table restaurant and try to control the shakes as we inspect the menu.

'It's OK,' I assure Emily, doing a quick recce of our fellow diners. 'There's even a few families here.'

The pizza turns out to be the best I've ever tasted, and as I devour the last artichoke and pesto-laden slice we get talking to our cute blonde waitress, Jessica. She's twenty, studying marine biology and used to date a guy from Nice.

'Tell us more!' we clamour, desperate to learn all

about the natives, (without actually having to come into contact with any of them).

She thinks for a moment then rattles off this disturbing description of a typical Nice man: 'Late twenties to early thirties, skinny, ratty, junkie-looking with scabs on his arms – really gross.' She pauses for a smirk. 'They say the men round here have more tattoos than teeth.'

We blink back at her. It's worse than we thought. And she's not even done yet.

'He's always walking or hitching somewhere. He might go to the park or the laundromat but mostly he'll stay holed up in his house, hibernating and taking drugs.'

In short, the antithesis of nice. Oh dear.

'Are there a lot of drugs round here?' Emily gulps, voicing her most immediate concern.

'Nice is supposedly the methadone amphetamine capital of California,' Jessica informs us.

For a moment I wonder if I should be impressed. It's certainly one claim to fame those boastful bill-boards overlooked.

'Speed is real easy to get round here,' Jessica elaborates. 'In the Lake County hills it's everywhere – people build meth labs in their kitchen and nobody bothers them. We call them crankers or tweakers,' she explains, expanding our vocabulary as she clears our plates. 'I'm frightened of them all!'

Emily and I sit in an anxious stupor until she returns.

'My ex-boyfriend was a crank but I didn't know,' she confides, joining us in our booth. 'We were into the whole Goth scene – I had this black dreaded hair and he wore make-up like The Cure – we were the freaks of Lake County!' she laughs, then gets wistful. 'When I first met him he was really handsome and such a special person. I still miss him.'

'How long were you together?' Emily asks.

'Five years. I actually lived with him in Nice for a while.'

I want to scream, *'Are you crazy?'* but manage to keep it in.

'The trouble was he was too friendly and didn't stand up for himself – crazy people were always coming round and taking our stuff.'

This is a revelation to me – I didn't realise people in Nice had stuff.

'I was always scared when I was in the house alone but I didn't appreciate how miserable I was until I moved back to Lakeport,' Jessica says, downcast at the memory. 'I didn't tell him I was going – I just packed and left.'

'Wow. What did he say when he found out?' I ask.

'He was really sore but I had to go – in the end he was too much of a flake and spent all his time getting high.'

'It sounds horrendous,' Emily is aghast. She's always had the sense to steer well clear of men who favour the grimy underbelly lifestyle.

To me it sounds depressingly familiar. I had a boyfriend who was an angel at heart but morphed into this useless arrogant article whenever he snacked on his secret smorgasbord of illegal substances. The one good thing was that he was super-protective of me – he wouldn't let anyone offer me a puff, toke or sniff of anything for fear that I'd become addicted and he'd be to blame. Fortunately I was never even tempted – I just had to look at him to know how debilitating and character-skewing it was. For months I turned a blind eye – he was so adorable in between-times – and then one day he took me to meet his new best friend and as I walked into this guy's lounge I crunched on a syringe. I went white and couldn't speak, though ultimately I did manage to squeeze out one word: Goodbye.

'What about the *women* of Nice?' Emily asks, suddenly curious about how the other half live.

'Their world revolves around dating and drinking,' Jessica shakes her head then leans urgently forward. 'I want something more – I want to study and travel. The young people in Lakeport are more ambitious but there's not much social life for us, other than the Sports Bowl on a Friday and Saturday night.'

We perk up. Sounds promising . . .

'Yeah, they have karaoke and all the guys hang down there and drink forty-ounce bottles of beer. You might want to check it out.'

'Maybe you could come with us?' Emily suggests.

Would you believe it – now we're the ones wanting a chaperone!

Jessica pulls a face. 'I'm not interested in those guys – I'm actually dating the manager here. He's a really nice guy.'

We wonder if he's nice enough to let us spend the night in the pizza oven – the thought of returning to Nice is giving us the heebie-jeebies.

'Do we have to go back?' Emily asks as we settle the

bill. 'Our stuff is probably already in some speed-freak's basement.'

Jessica gives us a sympathetic look and sighs, 'California – land of sunshine and cheese! If only they knew . . .'

'First Mexican bandits, now thieving junkies – you sure know how to pick a man-hunting destination,' Emily grizzles as we step out into the car park.

'I'm sorry,' I say, fully copping to the blunder.

'I mean, those Nice guys don't appear to have one redeeming quality.'

'Other than their ability to act as removal men at a moment's notice,' I venture.

Emily rolls her eyes and breathes in the cool night air. 'There's definitely a different vibe here in Lakeport, isn't there?'

'It's almost normal,' I confirm.

Perhaps that's why neither of us seem in any hurry to get back in the car. It's as though we're trying to store up this sense of comfort and calm to ward off the approaching evil. Nice try, but it doesn't work. No sooner are we back on the road, we're swamped by dark, fearful thoughts.

'Isn't there anywhere nearby we could divert to?' Emily bleats. 'Texas seemed to be littered with alternatives to Eden.'

I switch on the reading light and squint at the map. We did pass an idyllic spot called Harmony a few hours outside LA but that only had a population of eighteen (I like a challenge but hey . . .)

'There is a Paradise a few hours east of here,' I suggest.

78

Emily brightens momentarily then barks, 'No, not falling for it – if Nice is this nasty then Paradise is probably a living hell.'

'Let's just get through tonight,' I recommend. 'Tomorrow morning when we're sane and rested and the sun is shining we'll decide what to do.'

'Is this us?' Emily peers into the shadows.

'Yes, go right here.' I direct Emily down past the trailers, not even daring to glance in their direction.

Eyes forward we focus on our caboose, chilled to see that the picturesque oaks and redwoods have now morphed into sinister spiky-limbed figures with every twig a syringe. My heart pounds in my ears.

'OK, as soon as I switch off the engine we make a run for it!' Emily instructs as we pull up onto the gravel. *'Go!'*

We scramble out of the car, up the stairs and then lose valuable seconds grappling with the lock, terrified a scabby arm will reach for us any moment.

'Get in! Get in!' Emily shrieks, bundling me inside.

We trip over our suitcases as we enter – amazingly our stuff is just as we left it. Clinging to each other with relief, we do a little dance of joy, then Emily squeezes out one more concern.

'Do you think the car will be safe out there overnight?'

I throw up my hands. 'Not much we can do short of dismantling it and bringing it in here one auto part at a time.'

This really is no way to live. I look at my watch. 9.30 p.m., still early. Luckily we've borrowed *It's A Wonderful Life* from the Featherbed Railroad Company video library (though judging from what Jessica has told us, *Trainspotting* would be a more appropriate choice).

'Let's watch it sitting in the Jacuzzi!' we decide, changing into our swimming cossies and eagerly filling the tub. Ten minutes later we're peering at the opening credits through rising steam, then giggling at the exchange between young Violet and Mary as they eye up George Bailey at the soda fountain:

Violet: *I like him!*

Mary: *You like every boy!*

Violet: *(indignant) What's wrong with that?*

A ten-year-old after our own hearts.

Two hours later we dredge our crimson wrinkled bodies from the water, switch off the fizzing La Playpen sign and settle into our feather bed. Now that our heads are filled with images of guardian angels, loving families and close-knit communities we have no fear. As I close my eyes, I smile: it is indeed a wonderful life.

We awake to sloshing rain and a reality check. Nicc is no Bedford Falls. Much as we love the Featherbed Railroad Company, our fear of getting murdered in our Playpen has well and truly got the better of us. We decide to relocate to tried-and-tested Lakeport, ever closer to those 40-ounce beer-guzzlers (and that heavenly pizza). Miraculously, just as we reach Nice's city-limit sign, the sun breaks through with a dazzling vigour.

'Just in time for our photo opportunity!' Emily cheers, pulling over.

We're mid *ta-daaaaa!* pose when a whirring-creaking noise alerts us to a rangy David Ginola lookalike cycling by. He doesn't appear to have the remotest curiosity in what we are doing (I guess if he's a local he's probably hallucinated a lot worse) but he does definitely make serious eye contact with me and smiles naughtily, and as a result I can barely resist the temptation to leap aboard his handlebars. I've always wanted to recreate that dreamy scene in *Butch Cassidy and The Sundance Kid* where Paul Newman and Katherine Ross fool around in the barnyard to the melody of 'Raindrops Keep Falling on My Head'. Has my moment finally come?

Emily shoots me a look that simply says, 'No!'

'But he looks so romantic,' I pout, staring after him.

'I've never figured out why dirty hair and frayed pockets are such aphrodisiacs to you,' she tuts. 'Why can't your head be turned by a silver Mercedes like normal girls?'

I give a hapless shrug. 'Maybe I watched *Oliver* at too impressionable a young age?' I suggest, followed with a pleading, 'Can't we catch up with him in the car?'

'He's heading into Nice – do you really want to go back there?' Emily shudders.

'He might be the one nice guy in town!' I reason, daylight giving me more confidence than I had last night. 'It's got to be worth a shot.'

'Have you forgotten everything Jessica told us?' Emily rolls her eyes but plays along anyhow.

'There he is!' I pip, directing her to the gas station. I can see him inside by the till.

We pull over and loiter by the air pump until he emerges, bearing a can of 7-UP and a Butterfinger chocolate bar.

'The Breakfast of Champions!' he pronounces, holding them aloft, and I seize this chance to speak to him.

'Errmm!' I step into his path, now just a few feet away from him.

As he smiles, I discover he's seriously short on teeth. But whereas this causes Emily to retreat in disgust, I convince myself that his gappy – OK, *missing* – molars are more Viggo Mortensen than Fagin.

'Sorry to bother you,' I attempt my most engaging smile, 'but we're just passing through and we were looking for a Nice native – would that be you?'

'Yes and no,' he smiles with an enigmatic tilt of his head. 'I do live here but I'm originally from New York.'

'Gosh, you're a long way from home!' I coo. 'What brought you to Nice?'

Unfazed by my nosiness he confides, 'Everything is accepted here – you can get away with *anything*!'

A few dozen warning bells sound but they can't distract me from his mesmerising green eyes or my mission to discover the truth about the men of Nice – namely, are they nice?

'Yes they are, and I am one of them!' he insists, adding, 'Of course "nice" is sometimes seen as a weakness, and people can take advantage of your kindness so some of us have to put up a front.'

That's one way to explain away the dodgy reputation dogging the locals. Maybe they're not as bad as some would say?

'A lot of the people here are eccentric, that's all. They're not afraid to be themselves.'

I love a guy with a theory as opposed to a '*dunno*' shrug. While he's on a roll, I can't resist asking if he has any thoughts on why women go for bad boys?

'Real women like real men. Bad women like bad men,' he concludes with a naughty grin.

I chuckle in response. It's amazing the conversations you can have leaning on a petrol pump with an imperfect stranger. Never mind how erotic it can be to watch that imperfect stranger rolling seductively back and forth in his bike saddle. I have a sudden flash of myself licking the traces of peanut butter fondant from his lips but I don't even know his name . . .

'Gino Bonfiglia,' he introduces himself with full Italian flair.

My knees weaken. I'm telling you, if he leaned over to kiss me now I'd kiss him back with a vengeance.

'Are you married?' I ask, suspecting that nothing can faze him.

'Divorced,' he replies. 'My ex-wife runs The Stone House Tavern—'

'Oh yes!' I recall the name. 'We passed it on the way here.'

'She married an English guy after me. He used to own the Lord Derby but now his ex-wife runs that. She's Spanish.'

'Riiight!' I frown, only just keeping up. Who knew Clear Lake was so cosmopolitan!

Turns out Gino's in the drinks trade too – except that rather than running a pub, he collects discarded cans and bottles and claims the return fee. I'm not quite sure what my face does in response to this revelation (and believe me, I'm not judging him – for all I know this could make him the Donald Trump of Nice) but he quickly adds, 'I'm self-employed, my own boss!', attempting to put a positive spin on his occupation.

His cheeky grin makes me smile but I can't see that washing with my dad. Strangely I find the simplicity of his lifestyle almost sexy; it wouldn't bother me at all having a trash-grubbing bottle-collector for a husband, but maybe it should. Is that part of my problem?

While I ponder this, Gino gets introspective about his life choices. Married at nineteen and a dad by the age of twenty-two, he says he lost his youth and is now 'in the process of finding out what I want to be and *who* I want to be.'

'We've got good blood in our family,' he boasts, revealing proudly that his mum is a famous artist, his sister is a renowned chef and his grandfather once owned the *Denver Post*. Now I'm even more curious about how he ended up going so far astray. (Though from his earlier comment – 'you can get away with anything here' – I think I can probably guess.)

'I miss doing the family thing,' he concludes, 'but for now I'm just enjoying my independence.'

So I suppose a relationship is out of the question? Probably just as well. I could never live in a trailer – I'm just too messy, after a while it would be like living in an upturned bin. Speaking of which, Gino has to get back to work.

'Bye!' I call, waving him off.

'I'm surprised he has to work at all,' Emily muses,

now by my side. 'Think of all the money the Tooth Fairy must have left him.'

I give her a withering look. 'Funny.'

'So, did you get his number?' she asks as we settle back into the car.

'I doubt he even has a phone,' I admit.

'Well, if it came to it, you could always leave a trail of ring-pulls to your door . . .'

I give her a playful swipe.

'What I really want to know is: has Cowboy Casey been usurped in your affections?' Emily asks.

I think for a minute: there was something so free-spirited and chilled about Gino, and Casey seems so naive by comparison. However, I've done the penniless hippy type before and after everything Jessica said last night there is no way on earth I could live in Nice. So Casey wins, jeans down.

'That's a shame,' Emily sighs.

'Why do you say that?' I frown.

'I just thought of the perfect song to play at the Jones/Bonfiglia wedding.'

'What's that?' I ask, warily.

'The Can-Can!' she hoots.

I'm never going to hear the end of this.

With the best part of the day still ahead of us, we had intended to visit every hotel/motel in Lakeport to compare prices, facilities and security systems but we get no further than The Anchorage Inn on account of the twinkly eyed Leslie Nielsen clone behind reception. (Grey hair + sharp wit = So Very Emily.)

When we tell him we're fleeing from Nice he rolls

his eyes and says, 'Did you see the sign calling it 'Little Switzerland?'

We shake our heads.

'Christ! The Swiss are neutral, but if they see that sign they're going to invade!' he hoots. 'It's such an *ugly* place . . .' he rants on as we hand over the $44 for the room and start filling out the registration form, only to get stuck describing the colour of our car.

I'd say it's a shimmery peach but Emily has been referring to it as our 'mango mobile' so we're torn. Leslie looks at us, clearly tempted to knock our heads together, then pulls the form towards him and scribes 'Icky'. Such details are irrelevant anyway, as the fact that we are driving a car at all sets us apart from the rest of the guests – every other vehicle in the parking lot is a pick-up truck. Turns out that Clear Lake is the 'Bass Capital of the West' and we have inadvertently chosen to stay at a fisherman's retreat. And these are no *A River Runs Through It* types, let me tell you.

'What have we done?' I fret as we heave our luggage past gawping, beer-swilling chunks of manhood, too bemused at the sight of us to heckle.

We're half-tempted to stay hidden in our room and order in pizza but the word on the street – not that there's really anyone around to ask – is that the Mexican restaurant on the lake is where it's at. We decide to make a run for it but Leslie sidelines us, saying he wants to introduce us to hotel owner John Tanti aka 'King Fish'. He tells us he's in town to oversee some storm-damage repair work but judging from his workman's hands and soiled clothes he's getting pretty stuck in himself.

'He's a remarkable person,' Leslie tells us while he's tinkering out of earshot. 'He came here from Malta when he was nine years old not speaking a lick of English and not a penny in his pocket; now he's fifty-eight and a millionaire.'

Wow! That's not a word we expected to hear around these parts.

'His other property is The Wharf Master at Point Arena about fifty miles north of here. It's got a view of the lighthouse used in the Mel Gibson film *Forever Young*,' Leslie informs us, handing us a brochure for the 'romantic hideaway'.

It's at this point we confide that we've come to Lakeport looking for love. Mr Tanti catches this line and can't quite believe his ears.

'You want to meet a man who lives *here*?'

We nod.

A strange look passes over his face then he hurries out the door, presumably to reserve a couple of beds for us at the local loony bin.

'Any potential Mr Rights among the hotel residents?' Emily nudges Leslie. 'That way we can fulfil our vocation as fishwives!'

'Bunch of useless goobers!' Leslie dismisses them.

We'll take that as a no.

'What about the local bars – anywhere you'd recommend?'

He gives us a wry look and says, 'You know the bar scene from *Star Wars* . . . ?'

Surely they can't be that freakishly grotesque? We're not in Nice any more.

'They are the offspring of neither man nor beast,' he sneers.

87

This really doesn't bode well. However, I'd say Emily need look no further for her Mr Right.

'Do you have a special lady in your life?' I ask him on her behalf, wondering why I've chosen such a strangely old-fashioned turn of phrase.

He tells us that there is one local woman he has a crush on, but she's married. He then adds that fifty per cent of marriages in California end in divorce, as if he simply has to bide his time.

'Ah, you old romantic!' Emily teases.

'I'll tell you the most romantic thing I ever did,' Leslie's face lights up, knowing how much he's about to tickle us: 'Deliver flowers in Nice on Valentine's Day!'

We hoot at the concept. 'Tell us all!'

'It was a favour to the local florist,' he begins. 'I had so much fun because there were these poor trailer wives who had never gotten a flower before in their life and some goof-up husband finally decides to do the deed, so – just to give a charge to the deal – I said, "These are from your boyfriend!"'

We chortle, delighted. If Emily lived here she'd be dating Leslie for sure. But in many ways this would be no different to me pursuing Gino – we'd both be retracing old paths. This trip is supposed to be about venturing into new territory, so we reluctantly continue on our way, trying to convince ourselves that a pair of fresh prospects are just around the corner.

The Mexican restaurant is indeed buzzing, and with normal-looking people. There's even a strapping hunk at one table. But he's with an equally strapping girlfriend. We celebrate anyway with a pair of frozen margaritas.

'So where do you want to go tonight?' Emily asks, hitching her feet up on the patio decking. 'Sports Bowl or Sports Bowl?'

'I'm just checking the calendar of events to see if there's any alternatives,' I announce from behind the pages of the *Lake County Record Bee*.

'Just keep me informed.'

I continue my perusal then sigh heavily, 'You're not going to believe this – we've just missed the Annual International Worm Races.'

'Noooo,' she crows. 'Would we have been eligible?'

'It says here, "Visitors are welcome to enter – worms will be provided".'

'How considerate.'

Woozy from booze we decide to have a small siesta before our strenuous night of skittle obliteration. I'm just dreaming of gutterballs and squeaky plastic shoes when the phone rings and a mystery voice introduces himself as Mr Right. At least I think that's what he says. I'm trying to give the impression that I'm with it but the reality is that I'm too muzzy-headed to collate all the information he's throwing at me – like why is he talking about racing cars?

'Could you hold on a minute?' I request, hoping to give my brain time to catch up. No dice. I reach over and shake a bleary Emily. 'Who's Mark? Do we know a Mark?'

She looks blank.

'I'm sure he said Mark Tanti, sounds kind of familiar.' I rub my forehead.

'Tanti?' Emily croaks. 'That's the King Fisher's surname.'

'You're right!' I mumble, then frown. 'But it's not him.'

Emily shrugs and falls back to sleep. Great.

'Er, sorry about that.' I return to the call. 'I didn't quite catch what you said before, could you repeat . . .?'

'My name is Mark Tanti – I'm John's son, you met him at the hotel this morning? He said you beautiful ladies were looking for Mr Right. Well, you need look no further!' he cheers with the vocal equivalent of a swagger. 'I'm racing tonight at Lakeport Speedway with my buddy Bobby and we'd like to invite you along to watch. We'll have chilled beers waiting, just come find us on the track after the race.'

'OK,' seems the easiest response. I put down the phone and try to figure out what just happened.

'Do you think this is going to be one of those blind dates where you actually wish you were blind?' Emily asks as we attempt to locate the entrance to the Speedway.

'*Au contraire*,' I reply. 'Leslie gave his blessing so I'm thinking they must be pretty exceptional. Try the next left.'

'Are you sure about this?' Emily scrumples her brow.

The terrain is getting progressively more uneven – I suspect we may have strayed into a neighbouring cow field. We're just trying to identify the source of a wild grinding noise when Emily is forced to karate-kick the brakes.

'Oh my God!' we screech in unison, bracing ourselves against the dashboard – two more tyre rotations

90

and we'd be being shunted around the track by a drove of bashed-up rally cars.

'Jeez! You'd think they'd have some kind of barrier!' I quake, my life still flashing before my eyes.

Emily puts us into a speedy reverse, parks and then we face our next setback – the fact that in the half hour since we stepped out of the motel the temperature appears to have dropped twenty degrees. There we were picturing ourselves in halternecks made from knotted chequered flags spraying victory champagne, and now we're fantasising about Del Boy sheepskin coats and styrofoam cups of tea – it's *freezing*!

'It's like this whole trip has been jinxed,' Emily shivers as we shuffle along the metal stadium seating. 'It's just as well we're going home tomorrow – I think we need to re-adjust our biorhythms or see an exorcist or something before we visit any more locations.'

I feel a little dismayed. Despite the dramas and disappointments and impending hypothermia, I'm having the time of my life.

'Here?' Emily suggests, inadvertently plonking herself down next to John Tanti (our landlord, match-maker and potential father-in-law), his wife and armfuls of grandchildren – two of whom happen to be Mark's kids. (Did I mention that he's a divorcé and a father? I'm not sure he did either but now we know.)

We say hello and take a closer look; if Janea and Julian are anything to go by, Dad should be a dead ringer for Antonio Banderas. They really are out-standingly beautiful with big chocolate-drop eyes and dark mirror-sheen hair. Janea climbs aboard her grandpa's lap chatting knowledgeably about the race and her dad's driving skills, looking as bright-eyed and beguiling as a young Winona Ryder, whereas Bobby's daughter Cecilia is pale and blonde like a prettier version of Gwyneth Paltrow. It remains to be seen if we've found our two Mr Rights but it certainly looks like we've got ourselves a good pair of genes. (Unless, of course, the good looks are all on the ex-wives' side.)

John tells us that we've just missed Mark's first race and though he will be getting back behind the wheel, this won't be for at least half an hour. With no one to cheer for but a very real need to clap and stamp our feet (it'll keep the frostbite at bay) we randomly pick cars to support purely based on their colour. During this time I discover that playing with our potential step-children's four-year-old cousin Mitchell is an excellent way to generate some heat, because of course once you've dropped a small child between your knees and rocked him by his elbows he wants you to do it again and again. And again. The only conversation I get out of him is an impression of the Chihuahua dog from the Taco Bell ad:

'Yo Quiero Taco Bell!' he yelps, grinning up at me.

I grin back and drop him between my knees and rock him by his elbows again and again and again. I'm now steaming.

Still the races rage. Still no sign of Mark or Bobby.

Finally it's their turn and after much bumper-mangling and exhaust-billowing they hurtle into second place, no doubt helped by our near-hysterical whooping.

Once the event is over, Grandpa Tanti and clan up-sticks and bid us follow them down onto the tracks.

Emily and I find ourselves waddling like ducks as we cross the churned-up mud in our inappropriately open-toed shoes, feeling both foolish and timid – it's the moment of truth. We've met everyone in the family apart from the man himself. If we had *Bewitched* noses I think we'd wiggle them and vanish. But we don't, so we give each other's hand a quick 'here goes' squeeze as the racer removes his crash helmet.

Mark Tanti is indeed tall, dark and handsome. At thirty-six he looks like a younger version of spoon-bender Uri Geller crossed with French crooner Sacha Distel. Even covered in car grease he's definitely the sophisticate whereas his co-pilot Bobby Fulton – aged about forty with bush baby eyes and a Village People moustache – has more of a blue-collar appeal. We take to him instantly despite the fact that he hands us a pair of ice-cold beers – just what we need in these Alaskan conditions.

While the family chatter busily, Emily and I do our best not to look like bewildered Russian mail-order brides. Mark and Bobby are unlike any men either of us have ever dated so we don't have a clue what the protocol is. Frankly I'm too cold to know if I even fancy either one – the only thought dominating my head is 'Get me somewhere warm!'

We stand there, shivering smalltalk until Mark cuts to the chase: 'Do you want to come back to my place?'

We gasp and shoot him a disapproving 'not in front of the children' look but then realise he's just being hospitable – it's now 11 p.m. and Lakeport isn't exactly rife with late-night venues. No legal ones, anyway.

Should we accept his offer? I can tell that Emily is

less than keen but I'm seconds away from becoming an ice sculpture and from what he's said, his place is a lot closer than The Anchorage Inn.

'We can't stay long,' I give him an apologetic smile.

'Half an hour max,' Emily stresses.

'No worries – let's get going.'

One stride towards the car park and mini Winnie and Gwynnie tell their dads they want to travel to the house with us. We're so chuffed to have their approval that we blast out music and sing along Girls Aloud-style to show them what great step-moms we'd be. They humour us with the occasional smile, already far more mature than we can ever hope to be. The only downside to them being with us is that we miss out on the opportunity of discussing their fathers as potential sex objects.

As soon as we pull into Mark's driveway we realise why he was so keen to invite us back to his house – we'd show off too if we lived in a big white *Dynasty* mansion. After the abundance of trailers in Nice (not to mention the *goobers* of Lakeport) this comes as quite a shock.

'Now here's a man who's returned a lot of bottles,' I mutter under my breath as we approach the front door.

No doubt property here isn't as pricey as Beverly Hills but a chandelier is a chandelier and that's a mighty big one in the entrance hallway. We step forward and sink knee-deep into plush carpet, then wade through luxurious-yet-tasteful room after luxurious-yet-tasteful room. The place is huge – the lounge is the size of a furniture showroom with sofas that could easily accommodate ten people lying head to toe, the games room has a drinks bar on a par with the Queen Vic and one capacious room has nothing but a tent pitched in it – now that's the kind of camping I could cope with.

Emily tells Mark we intend to move in immediately but he shouldn't worry about us cramping his style: 'You probably wouldn't bump into us for a week!'

He then escorts us upstairs, showing us bedrooms bigger than our entire flats and the kind of pristine marble bathrooms usually found in five-star hotels.

'Now show us the east wing!' we tease.

Mark laps up our incredulous cooing as he sweeps us through his master bedroom towards the *pièce de résistance*: a vast balcony overlooking Clear Lake. Oh, no, my mistake – that's his swimming pool.

We even get to see his garage where a sparkling new Harley Davidson sits alongside a sleek black Thunderbird. It's impressive stuff.

'My wife used to complain that I was a workaholic but she liked all the nice things me being a workaholic bought us!' he observes.

No doubt.

Knowing the children are safely ensconced in their rooms, Mark gets a playful look and asks, 'What do a woman and a hurricane have in common?'

We shrug, clueless.

'They both start off with a slow sucking noise and then they take your house!'

We look perplexed.

'It works really good on divorced men,' he explains, exchanging a knowing look with Bobby.

95

How Mark has stayed single is a mystery. Perhaps he comes off too flash? Or maybe he's a little anal – this house is impeccably neat for someone with kids. As we return to the ivory fantasy that is the lounge, Emily and I don our detective badges and set about grilling Mark on his relationship etiquette, hoping for a few insights.

'So,' we begin. 'Where do you typically take a gal on a first date?'

'Well, if I was on business in San Francisco it would be dinner, a play and then a boat ride at Fisherman's Wharf.'

Perfectly civilised with a dash of romance. I see no problem with that.

'And if you were in Lakeport?' Emily chips in.

'I'd probably take her up to my family's coastal property on the Harley – separate rooms of course – or if the relationship was sufficiently intimate, we might go to the Featherbed Railroad Company.'

'That's where we stayed!' we pip, cutting in.

'Loose Caboose?' He cocks an eyebrow.

'Yes!' we cheer.

'I was there just a few months ago.'

We go to cheer again but instead fall silent as it dawns on us that last night we slept in a bed where – just a few months ago – Mark was having sex with another woman. I'm just wondering whether they dry-clean the peacock feathers when Emily decides to move the conversation on by asking Bobby where he'd take his date?

'Titty bar!' he deadpans.

We fall about laughing.

'No, as if! It would be a nice romantic dinner *then* on to the titty bar!'

Bobby is definitely the cheekier of the pair. His grin is nigh on irresistible and yet, seeing as Mark's the host with the most, we find our attention reverting back to The Catch of Clear Lake.

'So what's your idea of Ms Right?' I ask, mentally licking a pencil and jotting down his response.

He looks at me intently and says, 'Someone who laughs and smiles a lot. Someone like you . . .'

I freeze mid-grin.

'You do have a great smile,' he adds, softly.

My toes scrunch in embarrassment. 'Thank you very much, it's the only facial expression I have. I don't do much except smile. If someone is mean to me I have to get Emily to glare at them because I can only look cheerful . . .' I burble on and on until I have utterly killed the compliment.

'Californian women don't smile too much,' observes Bobby with a slightly glazed look. 'A lot of them are awful snooty!'

'Really? What about Californian men?' I ask, eager to get in our official trip question. 'How would you say they differ to men from other states?'

'I think on the whole we're probably more tanned, more outgoing and more recreational than your average American. We're definitely more romantic – because of the high standard of the women, we have to be. It's competitive out there!'

Realising we've gone off at a tangent without getting a full answer from Mr Enigma, Emily picks up the inquisition baton. 'So, Mark, you were saying

– you want a woman with a great smile; what else?'

'Beautiful blue eyes. Blonde hair. Soft skin. Drives at ninety-miles per hour!'

Cranberry juice spurts from Emily's mouth as she realises she's now become the focus of his flattery.

'Dribbles her drink!' she mutters, adding both a new criteria to his list and a new stain to his sofa.

Thrown by our uncouthness, Mark loses his train of thought and sets off on the mile-long trek to the stereo.

'Your turn Bobby,' I tap his shin with my foot.

'She would have to be madly and totally in love with me,' he states, serious for once. 'I want someone who will honour me and trust me – trust is a big thing.'

'Do you deserve a woman's trust?' We narrow our eyes at him.

'Absolutely! We're both honourable guys!' he insists. 'In fact we have a code of honour we live by.' To my astonishment, it turns out he means this literally, pulling a card from his pocket and reading: 'Keep your word. Commitment before ego. Defend humanity.' And, most intriguingly of all, 'Be a three-dimensional man.'

We're stunned. Not only are Mark and Bobby different to the men we usually date, they are different to men in general. How many guys do you know who are actively striving to be better human beings? I think it's stupendously admirable. Even if I don't exactly understand the wording of their code. I'm just about to ask Bobby to explain when he asks us.

'Do you think most men are jerks?'

'No!' Emily answers swiftly.

I tell him I do.

Emily thinks for a bit then adds, 'Actually, I do. I was more thinking about whether I like men or not.'

'That's OK, you're right. I think it's in our blood. A man can be a jerk but as long as he takes care of that special person in his life, then it's OK. We really can't deny our jerkhood. We have to own our jerkhood!'

I laugh, loving his take on this. 'Where does all this wisdom come from?'

'I take it you haven't met any "Sterling Men" before?' Bobby asks.

No, but we're beginning to get the picture: Mark and Bobby have been on one of those life-enhancing courses so popular in America and so mocked by us Brits. I went on one myself during an extended stay in LA and though it was as inspiring as it was challenging, part of my brain (and all of my friends and family) kept squealing 'cult' so I didn't pursue it. All the same, it seems to have done these guys the power of good; I wonder if lost-soul Gino could benefit?

'I can't reveal the details of the course,' Bobby continues, 'but I can say that I respect the strong focus on family. The rule I relate to the most is "Be a good example to children".'

This is particularly pertinent as Bobby now has full custody of his daughter Cecilia. As a consequence, he doesn't even drink. Emily decides to keep him company playing Sister Sobriety with her cranberry juice, while Mark and I start on the vodka. And let me just restate that *Bobby and Emily are sober*, because what happens next is the kind of behaviour normally attributed to the demon drink. One minute we're talking about the value of taking time out to find out who you are and who you want to be, and then Emily (who's only interested in discussing the meaning of life if it stars Monty Python) begins lightly critiquing Bobby's broom-brush moustache.

'It's just so bushy – does it have a name?'

Bobby rolls his eyes and smiles, too happy to have her attention to take offence.

'Seriously, were you a big fan of Magnum PI?'

On and on she goes – 'Can you dance like that guy in Frankie Goes to Hollywood?' – but whatever she dishes out, Bobby takes it on the chin. (Or, rather, the upper lip.) So she switches to flattery.

'Do you have any idea how sexy you'd look without it? My God!' She falls into a swoon.

I feel like grabbing Bobby by the collar and crying, 'You don't know what you're up against! Just give in now!'

Meanwhile Emily goes for back-up. 'Don't you think he'd look better without it, Mark?'

'Well, maybe . . .' he concedes.

'What about you, Belinda?'

I feel bad about the bullying factor but give an approving nod.

'Oh go on Bobby! You'd look amazing! Shave it off!' Emily rallies.

Bobby rubs his face with a mixture of sentiment and contemplation. 'I've had this thing ten years.'

'Well then you're way overdue for a new look!' Emily trills.

'I don't know . . .'

'I mean seriously, you either need to shave it off or

get yourself some leather trousers and a pierced nipple and hit the gay biker scene in San Francisco.'

Oh God. For a minute I think she's gone too far but to my relief Bobby grins.

'Mark – do you have a razor I could borrow?'

My jaw drops. Surely not? Surely he wouldn't zap his style statement of a decade for a woman he's known a matter of hours? But there he goes, hotfooting it off to one of the multitude of bathrooms.

'I hope the beastie doesn't clog your sink,' Emily frets.

'It's OK,' Mark assures us. 'He's a plumber.'

We wait in trepidation. It's quite some task he's been set. I imagine all the alternate moustaches he could be experimenting with as he sheds his handlebar – from Dr Phil to David Niven. And ten minutes later he emerges, a new, super-smooth, far-more-handsome and modern man.

I gawp in utter, utter disbelief. 'Why Bobby-Sue, you're beautiful!'

He looks dazed but happy as Mark shakes his hand.

Finally, Emily, the transformer, gives him a proud congratulatory hug, sneaking me a look over his shoulder that says, 'Now we're talking . . .'

'And now we've got that out the way,' Emily links her arm through Bobby's, giving him a saucy look. 'Let's play pool!'

Seeing as Mark and Bobby are now officially Sterling Men, they probably don't spend nearly as much time doing trick shots on bar-room pool tables as they used to. Consequently we beat them 3–1 and are not gracious about our victory. I say *our* but really it's Emily

'Pool Shark' O'Neill who triumphs. She's like Steve Davis with boobs. I'm just grateful I haven't torn up the baize – the vodka has gone straight to my head and I keep tripping on Mark's son's Scalextric and getting berated for plonking my drink on surfaces unshielded by coasters. I'm positively dangerous with the cue.

'So what do you girls like to do for fun?' Mark asks, dodging yet another close call as I wave it around.

'This!' we chorus – Emily with a modest flourish towards the pool table, me with an inadvertent thwack of the overhead light.

'How about snow skiing? Water skiing? Fishing?' he prompts.

'We're from England!' I remind him. 'We watch a lot of TV.'

Somehow the time has snuck to 4 a.m. and our stomachs mark the hour with a synchronised growl.

'Lay down your weapons,' Mark advises. 'We're going to feed you.'

Within seconds the Sterling Men are busying themselves in the open-plan kitchen – Mark whipping up eggs and potatoes while Bobby squidges a quad of hamburgers and sets the frying pan a-sizzle. Emily and I take a seat at a breakfast bar the size of Brighton Pier and watch them like a cookery show. For some reason I get emotional seeing people putting a lot of care and attention into food preparation – possibly because I have no skills or patience in that area myself – and the combination of the vodka and these two lovely men demonstrating further virtues is tipping me over the edge. Emily spots my eyes welling up and groans, 'Tell me we just need to put on the extractor fan!'

It's too late; mascara dribbles down my cheeks as I'm overwhelmed with drunken admiration for the masterchefs.

'Tunisia?' Emily smiles, handing me a ream of kitchen towel.

I nod. That was indeed the last time I was hit this hard.

Every night of our holiday we'd go to this exquisitely bejewelled café run by a dwarf in a fez and watch him climb up onto little raised platforms to reach the tea leaves, pots and boiling water and then sink into silent concentration as he prepared the sweet mint tea. Every night my heart – closely followed by my eyes – would overflow. (Emily has less fond memories because we got our picture taken with him and I used to pass him off as her holiday romance.) Anyway, on the last day, I got him back – I'd noticed that his tariff was the one amateurish aspect to his operation, the writing was all scrappy and wonky, so while Emily sunbathed and warded-off the pesky beach salesmen I crafted him a new swirly scripture one. When I presented it to him that night his eyes brimmed with tears and he immediately threw his short little arms around me. I was so touched that he was touched that his left shoulder is probably still damp today. Now that memory is making my current situation worse. I excuse myself and dash to the bathroom to get a grip.

As I lean against the gilded tiles I feel my heart brimming over with bonhomie and hope for all mankind. We did it! We came to Nice and though the prospects were grim, we stuck it out and found two of the nicest men in existence – albeit a few miles down the road!

When I return, now a little calmer, the conversation has moved on to the subject of Mark's work and, following our feast, he shows us photos of the new dredger his company recently purchased. His zeal is electric as he spouts details of power output, weight and cost yet while Emily manages to milk even this topic for maximum humour (she really is the best man-wooing asset a gal could hope for) I find myself slipping into a sneaky kip. Half an hour later I awake to screaming – turns out Mark's birthday is the same as Emily's: May 15th. Amid the jubilation and plans for a joint party, my eye strays to the Big Ben-sized clock on the Marble Arch-size mantel – 6 a.m.! Yikes! We've got a 5 p.m. flight to make and it's an eight or nine hour drive back to LA. We really have to skedaddle.

As I stumble to my feet, Mark and Bobby plead with us to extend our stay, and it's certainly tempting – you don't often find men like them, we feel like goddesses in their presence. But go we must.

At the door we joke with Mark about how he should really be checking our bags and pockets for the family silver and his laugh is such a delightful gurgle my heart flip-flops. So far I've thought of him as the grown-up of the group but the looser he gets the more appealing he is. Then, just when I think I can't love Bobby any more, he grabs our car keys and swings the mango mobile round in the driveway, leaving the engine running so we don't have to go to all the trouble of turning on the ignition. Could he be any more considerate? Yes, actually – he even removes some of the more invasive rubbish from the car and throws it in the bin. Emily is speechless. I'm beaming inside and out but as I let out a heavy sigh of contentment they all swing round and gasp, 'You're not going to cry again, are you?'

I shake my head and blink away any incriminating moisture.

Having not had any previous sense of who liked who best, it now becomes clear: Bobby opens the driver's door for Emily, Mark gets the passenger side for me. He stands there looking all manly and handsome and appealing in the morning light. I take a step forward, then, true to form, bottle it and blow any magic moment by getting excessively chatty. His eyes dart around trying to make sense of what I'm saying then before he even gets the chance to respond I give him a chaste peck on the cheek and duck into the safety of the car. Why? What am I afraid of? Why can't I leave a tender moment alone, as Billy Joel would say? It's the strangest thing – I would probably have kissed Gino the Can Man a second after meeting him but it seems a far bigger deal with someone of Grade-A quality like Mark. I think I've always found it easier to get it on with people I have a simple physical connection with – I know where I am with them and there's no other distractions. But when there's a mental appeal too it confuses me – I really need to learn to do both things at once!

Not a problem for Emily – I look over to what I can see of her from the waist down and see that Bobby is still stood by her. Close by her. They're not talking. I fiddle with my seatbelt and then roll down the window to give Mark a 'sorry you're not getting any of that' look but in the same moment Emily plonks into her seat, squealing under her breath.

One last frantic wave and we're gone.

'Well?' I demand details.

'Oh my God! He just said, "Can I kiss you?"'

'And?'

'He did.'

'*And?*'

'Ooooh! I don't know!' she squirms. 'I'm just glad he shaved off his moustache!'

'But do you fancy him?' I wheedle.

She thinks for a moment and then frowns. 'Not really. Do you fancy Mark?'

'Not in a way I'm familiar with,' I decide. 'But I love them both. Perhaps they could be growers? I mean, on first impression we thought they were so wrong for us but in fact we've had a far better time with them than we do with the kind of men we call our ideal.'

'You're right,' Emily concedes. 'That's a lesson learned.'

As we transfer onto the main road I ask, 'Do you want to try to see them again?'

Emily flicks off the indicator. 'I don't think so.'

'Me neither,' I say, brow furrowing. 'It doesn't make sense – we have one of the best nights of our lives and we don't want to do it again?'

'That's because it'll never be the same again,' Emily deduces, gathering speed. 'Tonight was great because it was the four of us flirting and having fun. Next time I would be with Bobby and you would be with Mark and the whole dynamic would change.

106

It wouldn't be as free. It just couldn't work.'

We sit in contemplative silence and then I sigh: 'Well, we got exactly what we always wished for – two best friends for us to double date – but only for one night.'

Emily smiles as she bears down on the accelerator. 'Yeah, but it was one perfect night . . .'

'Can you go left onto Caledonian Road and then right on Offord . . .' I direct the cabbie through the streets of London N7, passing Londis, the local chippy and Pentonville prison. I smile, remembering our first sight of Eden Detention Center – even those elements that didn't quite fit with our vision of the American Dream were wonderful to me – I can't wait to get back out there!

'Just here by the bus stop,' I tell the cabbie, stepping out into a road heaped with rubbish bags and reverberating with the sound of teenagers exchanging their favourite swearwords.

I rattle my key in the lock, eager to get inside. No sooner am I through the door than I set about raising the funds for our next expedition. Not that magazine journalism is the best-suited career for making a quick buck – it can take several weeks before you even hear back from the commissioning editor about whether or not they like your idea and then, if they do, you have to set up interviews, research your subject, do the deed, transcribe tapes, write the darn thing and then submit your invoice which can then take between six weeks and seven years (or so it seems) to get paid. During the lulls I look up everything I can on our remaining locations and try to find the sexiest love shacks for us to stay in en route.

As for our beaus . . . Bobby called Emily as soon as she got back to the UK, and it was his first overseas phone call! They had a nice chat but she was mortified when he said, 'I think you know I felt the touch of love when we kissed goodbye!' She hates herself for it but has avoided him since. And as for Mark, he actually came to London on business and kindly invited me to dinner but I made an excuse, afraid he'd pounce. Why oh why don't I fancy him?

And our cowboys? Well, several weeks on, Emily is feeling rather miffed that she's yet to receive an opening gambit e-mail from Chris – 'It's never the ones you want who get in touch, is it?' she sighs before encouraging me to try my luck with a call to Casey. I'm glad of the dare but things go awry when Chris answers, noticeably uneasy in his conversation, and I never do hear back from the man himself. Rather disappointing – we parted on such promising terms; what went wrong? – but more than anything it makes me to want to get back out there and find the real Mr Right.

Then, finally, the day comes when I am sufficiently flush to book the flights – oh joy! This is what makes it real for me: a terminal, a flight number and a departure time. I dial Emily with feverish fingers, eager to share the good news. But instead of the shriek of delight I was counting on, she says, in a low, small voice, 'I can't go.'

'What?' My world comes skidding to a halt. 'What's wrong?'

'I've met someone.'

Thwang! Right between the eyes.

'But. . .' is the only word I can manage. I'm stunned. How did this happen? *When* did this happen?

'I would have told you sooner but I wasn't sure how it was going to pan out.' Emily takes a breath.

I *don't*. My chest has entirely seized up.

Then she says, 'I think he might be The One.'

Noooo! I want to cry. This isn't how it was supposed to be – she's meant to meet someone in Weddington, North Carolina not Carpenters Park, Watford!

'I can't believe it.' I fall back onto the sofa. If only we'd had the money to make the trip all in one go, this would never have happened.

Suddenly I get a random paranoia. 'This isn't because of the scorpions and the junkies, is it?'

'No,' she laughs. 'He's real.'

'And you *love* him?'

'I do.'

This is terrible. I know I should be feeling delighted for her, but I'm not. The timing couldn't be worse. 'Couldn't you come anyway – you know how *de rigueur* chaperones are this season.' Of course she can still come. She doesn't have to misbehave, I'll do that bit – she'll just be an extra pair of eyes on the search!

'Actually, we're going on holiday that week.'

110

I don't know which part of the sentence to freak out at first – the 'we' or the 'holiday'.

'Where are you going?' I feel sick. Please don't let it be America.

'Caribbean somewhere – he booked it. I'll be gone two weeks.'

I feel like crying. Scratch that, I am crying. Before I progress from leaky eyes to wobbly-throated sobbing I decide to get off the phone. 'I'm going to have to call you back later,' I gulp, talking as if to a stranger.

I set the phone back in its dock. I feel so betrayed, so let-down. How could she do this? And yet, she's only gone and done what we set out to do. Just in a different location. And without me.

Two hours later, James gets home from work and finds me sitting in the same spot, now in darkness.

'What are you doing, you mad woman?' he tuts, bustling around me switching on various lamps before setting down his briefcase and shopping bags and then tending to the cat.

'She's blown me out,' I say in a daze. 'Emily.'

'I didn't realise you were seeing her tonight.'

'I'm not. I wasn't.' I heave a sigh. 'But I was planning to travel across America with her.'

James stops mid-can-open, much to Cabbage's dismay. 'What's going on?'

Over the cat's incessant mewing, I bring James up-to-speed.

'Well, you'll just have to find someone else to travel with,' he shrugs.

'I can't!' I screech.

'Why not?'

'She's my muse! There is nobody like Emily. There's no trip without her.'

James studies me for a moment. 'So that's it?'

I shrug. 'I can't go with anyone else.'

'What about Sarah?'

'She's got a boyfriend,' I grumble.

'Lara?'

'She's married – we went to her wedding, remember?'

'Oh yes,' he nods. 'What about Nina, she'd be a laugh!'

'Job.'

'Can't she take a holiday?' James demands.

'Not a three-month one.'

'Oh.'

James continues to reel names off at me but I find fault with every one.

'I know,' he says, looking triumphant. 'Kerry.'

'Who?'

'That girl you met on your press trip to Singapore. The Scottish one.'

I shake my head dismissively. 'I've spent a total of five days with her out of my whole life.'

'But you liked her, didn't you?' James badgers me.

'Yes.'

'And you said she was really funny when she was drunk?'

'Yes,' I concede.

'And isn't her current job coming to an end?'

'Yes, but not for a while. I can't remember when exactly . . .'

James looks at me. I look at him. It's a thought.

'Oh I don't know – she's not really slutty enough,' I decide.

'What kind of a reason is that?' James splutters.

'I need my sidekick to act as bait. Kerry's too pure. She's only twenty-two, brought up on Orkney, one major boyfriend that I know of. I don't know how she'd cope with some redneck from Mississippi lunging at her. I don't want to be responsible for corrupting her.'

James pulls a face. 'Maybe she'd like it. Why don't you leave that decision up to her?'

As James wanders off to placate Cabbage, my mind races. On the one hand it is unthinkable to conceive of travelling with anyone other than Emily – we know each other inside out, we never argue, she drives like a demon, flirts like a temptress and makes me laugh 24/7. On the other hand, it is equally unthinkable that I let this project go. I can't tell you how much I want to visit all the places on my list. Maybe I can make it work with another girl?

I call Kerry at her home in Edinburgh. She's more than up for it and I find her fizzing enthusiasm a major plus – it reminds me of Emily when we first met and her no-questions-asked, it'll-be-fun-no-matter-what attitude. There is just the snag of the timing. I've already booked and paid for half the accommodation in Cazenovia and Intercourse for the week after next and she's not properly free till February – three months from now. She can't even take any holiday because she's used it all up. If only there was someone I could take as a filler. Someone who wouldn't mind being cast aside after two locations. Someone who understands my heart's desires.

'I got your favourite for dinner,' James calls over, setting the wok a-sizzle. 'And I meant to tell you, there's a Gregory Peck profile on Living tonight.'

I tilt my head.

'What?' he frowns, noticing me staring.

'Do you want to come to New York with me? And Pennsylvania,' I add, under my breath, knowing it's not such an easy sell.

'What – to find Mr Right?'

I nod.

'I hate to break it to you, but I'm not a girl.'

'You're a raving homosexual,' I remind him. 'Which is close enough.'

James gingerly sets aside the soy sauce. 'What would I have to do?'

'Just come along for the ride,' I tell him, sitting up on my haunches. 'Vet the guys for me, maybe find one of your own?'

'I don't know.' He looks dubious.

'Oh go on, you've always been very discerning when it comes to my men.'

'One of us has to be,' James snips.

I chuckle. He really thinks I have the worst taste. Shame he's right.

'Oh come on, you haven't had a holiday in years,' I coax.

'That's because you're the only person I'd want to go away with but when we do go anywhere we fight constantly.'

Ah. There is that. James may well be the best friend a girl could ask for – after all, this is the man who offered me rent-free accommodation on the sole condition that I followed my dream of writing a novel, and we live in perfect harmony in these absurdly close quarters – but when we venture into the big wide world we're a disaster – we both want to be in control, both think we know best, and this invariably leads to both of us shouting, (shortly followed by me crying).

'What if we made a pact to be on our best behaviour?' I volunteer.

'How long's that going to last?' James gives me a wary look.

'Could you manage a week? I'd throw in a shopping trip to New York.'

'Barneys?' James's eyes light up.

'Anywhere you want.'

'OK – deal!'

Before James can change his mind – which gives me a window of approximately ten minutes – I hurtle downstairs to the computer and bag us a pair of flights on Expedia.

When I tell him what I've done, all the colour drains from his face, Flash Bronzer and all.

'But . . . but . . .' he stammers, looking like he's going to faint.

'Number-one concern?' I bark, ready to zap it.

He looks pained. *'What am I going to wear?'*

CAZENOVIA,
NEW YORK

In his autobiography, the notorious Venetian lover-man Giacomo Casanova shocked his peers by giving lurid accounts of the sex he'd had with 122 women. Not so faint-inducing by today's kiss-and-tell standards, but it does make me all the more aware that I've got a fair bit of catching-up to do: this will be my third state visit and I've done little more than flirt. Oh well, if it takes a sleazy old womaniser to take me to the next level, so be it.

Cazenovia lies some three hundred aisles northwest of the Big Apple and a couple of hundred miles east of Niagara Falls (still touting itself as the Honeymoon Capital of the World long after its heyday).

As we make our approach, my friendly doomsayer James announces: 'I've got some bad news.'

I knew it was too good to be true. So far he's been more than chipper, insisting on renting a scarlet convertible and wearing a suit, tie and driving gloves, even in the passenger seat, but now it looks like the negativity is about to kick in.

'What is it?' I ask, darting a panicky glance at the petrol gauge.

'Cazenovia was not named after Casanova,' he grimaces.

'Oh no!' I cry. It's Eden all over again. 'Who, then?'

'Some Swiss banking agent called Theophilus de Cazenove.' James puckers his brow. 'Sounds like that furry-chested Lenny Henry creation.'

'Theophilus P Wildebeest,' I mutter, disheartened but trying to keep my spirits up. Surely there's got to be one thrusting groin among the 2600 residents?

Not a chance. In the picture-perfect village of Cazenovia, 'concerned citizens fight the undesirable'. So dedicated are they to the preservation of chaste good taste, one café's 'vulgar' flashing coffeepot sign was torn down following a community outcry. (I'm guessing these folks don't holiday in Las Vegas.) In lieu of fast-food stands, plastic facades and drive-thrus, visitors are presented with a wide, serene lake, grand Colonial houses (set infuriatingly far back from the road so no peeping in at their furnishings without trespassing) and an elegant white wooden church that puts us in mind of *The Witches of Eastwick*, (though we're certain that projectile vomiting of cherry stones is kept to a minimum here).

As we mooch around gift shops with names like Sally's Cellar and Lavender Blue, James becomes disturbed by the sedated state of the residents, convincing himself that everyone here is numb from boredom and longing to escape the eerie peace.

'They're not exactly friendly, are they?' he whispers as we sniff our way through a batch of scented candles. 'They don't even seem curious about our accents.' He's got a point. Not one person has greeted us with a gleeful 'Say, are you guys English?' It's making us feel rather monochrome and ordinary. Basically we're not getting nearly enough attention.

'So where are we staying – The Curly Maple B & B? The Beehive Studio? The Country Bumpkin?' James frowns his way through the names of the available lodgings as we continue down Albany Street.

'No,' I say, rolling my eyes at his disdain. 'Right here – Lincklaen House.' I come to a halt outside a handsome three-storey redbrick building trimmed with black shutters and white paintwork.

James peeks through the window and exhibits a trace of approval at the unfussy monochrome décor. 'This isn't so bad,' he concedes, sufficiently motivated to stride through the pillared portico, only to collide with a trunk-sized crystal vase stacked with gaudy, thick-stemmed blooms.

Fortunately the vase is being carried by a hysterically enthusiastic receptionist and, with James's help, she manages to steady herself and make it to her table target without any shattering or spillage.

Without taking a breath she then sets about checking us in with startling pep, and for once it's our turn to think, 'You're not from round here, are you?'

While James does a little more work on his hernia, dragging our suitcases up to our room (no lift, no bell-boys, but a nice line in claw-foot bath-tubs), I casually ask Miss Zing-a-ling if she knows any eligible local men.

She pauses for a second in contemplation then, wide-eyed with zeal, squeals, 'The hotel owner! He's single!'

'Tell me more!' I encourage her.

'His name is Dan Kuper, he's thirty-four, really successful, really nice! Do you want to meet him?' she gawps at me. Finding her excitement contagious I nod vigorously. Talk about convenient – he practically qualifies as room service. She picks up the phone and summons him on the pretext of a guest (i.e. me) needing some information on the local attractions (i.e. him). While we wait, I look around the hotel with new 'lady of the manor' eyes – I could certainly make a grand entrance or two down that twisting staircase and the high-ceilinged lobby is perfect for a champagne reception, plus he's obviously not one to skimp on flowers – every corner is bursting with colour. I'm just picturing a dashing Conran figure in a sharp blazer and Italian shoes when in walks the reality – a pair of grey shorts sporting trainers worn with socks. Beige socks. Dear Dan is the definition of mousy.

He timidly shows me into the empty dining room, presents me with a fan of leaflets on Madison County (not the one famous for its bridges – that's in Iowa) and talks to me like I'm a seventy-year-old historian. I'm just trying to segue on to more personal topics when a wasp begins viciously tormenting us. Dan reaches for a fly swat – not the sexiest of accessories – and flounders around, weakly swiping at the air until the hyperactive receptionist comes to our aid. Beastie thwarted, she brings Dan out in a crushed-raspberry blush by relating the time a fortune-telling guest read his palm:

'She took one look at his love line and said, "You're a great lover!"' she chuckles. 'Isn't that funny – a real Casanova in Cazenovia!'

I smile. Bless her! And bless Dan – he really is a sweetie but my presence alone is making him so uncomfortable it's cruel to continue. Much to the dismay of the receptionist, I let him go.

'I think there may be a flaw in this plan of yours,' James observes later that night as we sup ale in the hotel's olde-worlde basement bar, its only customers.

I knew this was coming.

'These places are really just starting points,' I explain – since Emily and I reaped such a surprisingly positive reward just a few miles down the road from Nice, I have decided to be less pernickety about the geography of this quest. 'If there's no nibble we widen the net.'

'Could we widen it to take in Niagara Falls?' he wheedles. 'I've always wanted to go and it is a famous honeymoon resort so it fits with your love theme.'

'Absolutely,' I agree. I've been thinking the same thing myself.

I tell him we'll leave first thing in the morning but overnight I become convinced that we're giving up too soon – we should at least make one last concerted effort to find a Mr Right contender before relocating to a place overrun with smoochy couples. I'm liking the idea of the hoity-toity-sounding Cazenovia Country Club, picturing golfers with solid gold irons and impressive hip-swivels, but James is championing the local mall.

'At least the men at the mall will be closer to our

age,' he reasons. 'And you don't need to be a member to get through the door.'

He's got a point.

'And I really want a pair of Nike Airs . . .'

The truth will out.

As malls go, the Carousel Center offers an upbeat shopping experience. However, after trying on enough trainers to shoe a marathon of runners, James still hasn't had that Cinderella/glass slipper moment and it's more than I can bear to watch another parade of boxes so I leave James to his shoe-horn shunting and escape to Bath & Body Works. It was my intention to pep up my make-up before making a final sweep for eligible shopaholics, but as I confront my reflection I fear it is too late for salvation – my face is weary, my nail varnish chipped and the tissue I'd wrapped around my blistered toes is unravelling to full leper effect. Not my best pulling look.

Admitting defeat, I leave behind the pots of iridescent goop and focus on amassing some sweeties for the car journey. There must be one of those tubular jellybean dispensers around here somewhere . . . I scan the neighbouring stores and that's when I see Him. I really only glimpse a silky black ponytail and purposeful stride but it's enough. My brain is saying, 'Leave it!', my heart is screaming, 'Follow him!', but my feet are quickest of all – they're already scurrying after him despite the fact that my long, narrow dress gives the impression that I'm running in ankle manacles. I don't want to scare him with my Geisha dash so I fall into the 'lane' parallel to him so I can build up enough speed to head him off at the pass. Keeping my eye on the prize, I draw level, skid in an ungainly manner over to his aisle and pounce!

'Are you in a hurry?' I blurt, obstructing his path. 'Can you spare a couple of minutes to talk to me?'

'Er,' he falters, looking understandably bewildered by my lack of either clipboard or apparent sanity. 'I guess . . .' he concedes.

I realise it's my turn to speak but I'm too thrown by the multitude of piercings glinting at me from around his face.

'Fourteen in total, twelve you can see,' he winks, clocking my eyes playing dot-to-dot from nostril to ear to eyebrow.

'Gosh!' I flush, instantly bombarding him with all sorts of stupid questions about the pain quota and whether fluids would dribble out of the hole in his bottom lip if he removed the stud. In return he indulges me with detailed, wince-inducing answers, all the while bewitching me with his rich brown eyes.

Even though he's highly perforated he's not at all scuzzy: his hair has a shampoo-ad sheen, his skin is a flawless honey, his trousers (a buttery moleskin) look off-the-peg new and I suspect he's even been at his white T-shirt with an iron. As he talks, something about his twisted smile and the playful arch of his left eyebrow triggers a hardcore flashback to the love of my life, Christian. When I learn that he too is a Pisces I get *déjà vù* chills. He seems so familiar and appealing and chats to me like he's just been introduced at a friend's party, rather than shanghaied at a mall. In a matter of minutes I discover that he's a psychology student in his twenties (too young, I know!), he lives in Syracuse (twenty-two miles from Cazenovia), says 'Right on!' a lot and goes by the name of Paul Ghirardelli – great surname (especially auspicious since it's Italian, just like Casanova) but 'Paul' seems far too pedestrian for such a dreamily exotic creature.

All the while we're talking, his eyes are locked onto mine with an alluring mix of amusement and flirtation. I really don't know how I'm managing to hold a conversation and fancy someone this much. I'd do anything to be able to freeze-frame him so I could have a good old gawp and then top up on some oxygen before attempting to resume normal service. But the clock is ticking – I have just seconds before James has security scouring the mall for me. My rational side gets psyched up to tear myself away but the greater part of me wants to drop to my knees and implore him to 'Love me!' Mind you, I think my dilated pupils are doing a pretty good job of conveying the inner message. I know I look teenage-besotted but I can't help it. I'm goo.

'Do you want to get a drink?' he asks, dilating right back at me.

I'm stunned. He can't possibly like me too! It can't possibly be this easy! I'm about to emit a whoop of joy when I remember that I have to turn him down. The first time in years I've been asked out for a drink and I've got a prior engagement with a homosexual in Niagara Falls.

'Couldn't you ask your friend to stay a bit longer?' Paul asks when I explain my predicament.

I don't hold out much hope – James is such a

stickler for schedules – but I tell him that if he can hang on for just five minutes I'll be back with a verdict.

'OK, I just need to go and get some batteries, we'll meet right back here,' he grins. Then we both hesitate, as if we're afraid to leave for fear of never seeing each other again. It seems so precarious. I take a deep breath and scuttle off, shamelessly hitching up my dress when I'm out of sight and cantering back to the sports shop. James is emerging triumphant, keen to show me his spiffy pair of Nikes, but I'm too manic, babbling about how I've just met this amazing man *and, and . . .*'

'Calm down. He won't be there when we get back.' James is dismissive.

'But what if he is? Can we stay for a drink?' I raise up on my tippy-toes, hands clasped like a child imploring her dad.

'We said we'd leave for Niagara at 6 p.m.'

'I know, I know, but it's HIM, it really is. I think I'm in love!'

James rolls his eyes.

'Pleeeeaaaase!' I whine.

He looks stern. I don't want to make him angry. (You wouldn't like him when he's angry.)

'At least come and meet him,' I attempt a compromise. 'OK but five minutes and we have to go, it's a long drive and we're already running late.'

I bounce ahead then get queasily nervous as we approach the bench.

'He's not here!' James announces, somewhat smugly.

My heart sinks. Perhaps I inhaled too many insoles and hallucinated him.

'Let's go.' James is about to escort me from the building when a dark head pops up from the decorative foliage. Hoorah! He did come back! I hurriedly introduce the two men then mediate silly smalltalk while my body temperature raises by twenty degrees at the sheer awkwardness of the situation. Surprisingly James saves the day by teasing Paul about his accent, I add my twopenn'orth and in return Paul is amused to find himself ganged up on in his own country.

Then he looks at me and says, 'I find the way you talk horny!' That's it. I'm on the floor. A complete mess. The minute someone uses the 'h' word I'm done for. I can never say it myself and part of me cringes hearing it but the bigger part of me just writhes with lust. As a consequence, my brain short-circuits and I find myself telling the world, 'I've kissed two boys with pierced tongues.'

Paul laughs at my ridiculous brag and shows me that he has in fact *two* piercings in his tongue – twice the pleasure, apparently. Blimey.

Understandably, James is keen to change the subject and asks Mr Metallica for directions to the freeway.

Paul looks dismayed. 'Do you really have to go?'

I can't form the word 'yes' confronted with such an infectiously saucy gaze so James is obliged to answer for me. ''Fraid so – yes. Onward and upward.'

Paul sighs, takes my hand and says, 'So, what's your name?'

I can't believe how ludicrous this question sounds, bearing in mind how long we've been standing here talking.

'Belinda,' I tell him, scrabbling for my card so he can have all my numbers and e-mail address as well.

He takes the card and returns the favour. Two little pieces of paper that could change our love lives. I want to hug him goodbye but daren't. Fortunately James initiates some basic physical contact by shaking his hand. I extend mine and he takes it and kisses it like an Arabian prince. Only he could carry this off without coming over all George Hamilton.

With a final intense 'I want you so bad' stare I turn and stagger tingling to the car park.

No sooner is my seatbelt clicked into place than I'm desperate to relive and analyse every second of the encounter – wasn't James aware of the electric attraction between us? Didn't he think Paul seemed like a risk-taker, an adventurer?

The most James will say is, 'He's very much your type.' Hmmm, cryptic yet cutting.

Left to my own internal musings, I start fretting that Paul would probably make a terrible boyfriend because he's so overtly sexual, and then I torture myself with visions of him being magnetically drawn to a similarly stapled chick. I slump for a moment then decide I was having far more fun on my besotted high so swiftly return to it.

This is amazing – I can't stop smiling. As my hormones continue to go off like party-poppers I realise this is exactly how I was hoping my life would be enlivened by this trip. I can't believe it's happened so soon – I mean, how often do you get this kind of physical rush for someone and have it reciprocated? Mark and Bobby were wonderful but they didn't stir my loins. And yes, I fancied cowboy Casey like crazy but seeing as he didn't feel the same way I ultimately felt a bit of an old letch. But this is something else. I feel I could burst with lust and curse being confined to a car seat when what I want to be doing is dancing and flinging my arms around and hollering '*Yes!*' at the top of my lungs.

My joy is soon aborted when we miss a vital turning and I find myself involved in a ferocious row with James over directions. As we rant and rally I feel my ecstatic bliss slipping away – *no! Don't go!* I wanted to prolong that feeling for as long as possible! This is so wrong – I feel like I'm being cheated out of the best bit of meeting someone new, the fantasy of what might be, and this makes me all the more huffy. If I was with one of my female friends we'd be busily plotting how I could take Paul up on his offer of a drink and indulging in girlie squeaking, but even when James and I emerge from our sulky silence to make a few tentative, non-combative exchanges I can sense he's not exactly receptive to discussing Paul. Frankly I dare not speak his name. For the rest of the trip he will be my secret pleasure.

I had hoped we'd be spending the night in a candy-coloured honeymoon motel but there's a surprising dearth of love-themed accommodation in Niagara Falls. Despite some false hope with Bit O' Paris and All Tucked Inn, we can't find one vibrating heart-shaped bed. In the end we settle on the retro-look Moonlite Motel on account of its pink neon and prime position – across the street from Denny's.

'Starving!' we cry as we're handed sticky menus, blithely ignoring the overall ketchup massacre and the fact that our table is stacked with egg-smeared plates and half-chewed burgers. What pushes us over the edge is the fact that they've stopped serving alcohol. With barely a word exchanged, James and I order, gorge and grimace. I look at James. 'Can you imagine how catastrophically disappointing this would be if we were on our honeymoon?'

He shudders. 'You come all this way and you can't even get a beer!'

In the spirit of romance we decide to drive to the Falls for a midnight stroll, and as we cruise closer, the cheap motel strip morphs into sleepy suburbia. Closer still and the roads become dominated by big chain hotels (Best Western, Ramada etc.) but we can't seem to find the Falls themselves, despite spotting the checkpoint for the Canadian border.

'Wind down the windows!' suggests James.

We cock an ear and listen for rushing water. Nothing. We must be minutes from one of the natural wonders of the world and yet we can't even find it. This is such a let-down. I remember someone once comparing Niagara to Blackpool – if only! At least Blackpool is luridly vibrant and lousy with chip shops. This place seems so drab and forgotten. My one consolation is that Paul isn't here. I so wanted to bundle him in the car and whisk him away with us but now I'm glad I didn't venture an invitation, as this lacklustre environment would have been such a passion-killer. Nevertheless I spend the night with him – in my dreams . . .

131

*

The next morning James and I convince ourselves that we should visit Niagara's tax-free outlet mall ahead of the Falls themselves as we don't want to be shopping with wet hair. I'm all for this as I know James will be so preoccupied with designer bargains I'll be able to sneak off and phone Paul, and I've had an idea: after Intercourse I have a few nights free before I fly back to London. Once James leaves I was planning to stay on with some British friends on assignment in New York, but what if I went back to Syracuse to see him instead? We could go for that drink he offered.

Leaving James in his element at Tommy Hilfiger I take out Paul's card and dial his number but before it can ring through I cancel the call. Suddenly I'm nervous about the risk of dissolving the illusion. Can he possibly live up to the memory of the fantasy man I'm getting such a big kick out of? There's only one way to find out.

I take a deep breath and press redial – I've never been one for 'who knows what might have been?' I have to take everything as far as it will go, until it ends in tears or humiliation. Better to regret the things you've done than the things you haven't, as Sophia Loren once said. My heart judders in my chest as his phone starts to ring.

'Hello?'

It's him! Oh my God!

I quickly introduce myself as the hysterical British girl who accosted him in the mall and in response he cheers his greeting and we proceed to babble for twenty minutes, powered by nervous energy and peppering our conversation with gentle but obvious compliments and flirtations. I really couldn't say what on earth we talked about – my heart was hammering too loudly to hear – but the gist of it seemed to be that we're both utterly delighted to have met each other and utterly convinced we should meet again. I tell him I'll work on the practicalities.

As soon as we say goodbye I want to speak to him again. I hope he'll call me back but he doesn't. So I draw a veil over my smitten expression, return to James and complain loudly that he's made so many amazing purchases while I simply couldn't find anything in my size.

'I suppose we ought to see the sights now,' he decides, linking arms as we head to the car. For a moment I feel sneaky 'phoning behind his back but I know it's for the best – now I know I'm seeing Paul again, James can have my full attention.

The lead-up to what's supposed to be one of the most stunning sights on earth could be any old park. We stroll over the not-particularly-lush grass (can Niagara Falls really need a sprinkler system?), peek over the barrier and . . . finally! The world's most famous waterfall!

'I thought it would be bigger,' James frowns.

'Maybe it doesn't look so impressive because we're looking down on it,' I suggest.

We stare at it some more.

'Actually it is amazing,' James concedes.

'Yeah,' I agree. Then I look around me. For a place that supposedly attracts ten million visitors a year it's surprisingly uncrowded; our fellow tourists are mostly families and oldies. So much for the Honeymoon Capital of the World – right now James and I are the closest thing they've got to newlyweds. Now that's a frightening thought.

We put a quarter in a viewer. All we see is rushing white froth.

'Now what?' James sighs.

I guess this is where you're at an advantage if you're on honeymoon.

But of course you can't come to Niagara Falls and not take a ride on the Maid of the Mist boat, and as we step onto the jetty we excitedly accept a pair of disposable blue plastic ponchos – essentially a bin bag with a hood. Desperate to remain dry, James pulls his hood drawstring so tight only his nose is peeking through. But as we set sail the wind whips up and inflates his body section so now only his shoulders are covered. This clearly won't do so he yanks it back down and knots the poncho at his groin but that's no good either because the sticky-out bit looks obscene. Meanwhile we glide by the natural beauty of the Horseshoe Falls and all James will remember is blue plastic.

I, on the other hand, choose spray abandon, eager to shower in Niagara Falls water. I spot a rainbow in the dazzling light and lurch and lunge trying to locate my camera and get James in position before it vanishes. He tells me that rainbows don't show up in photographs. Where do people get these ideas from? I remember someone telling me cats can't see through glass once. And I believed them.

The boat stops just short of where the water pounds into the lake. It's like being in a giant glass of Andrews Liver Salts. I gasp with delight as the white fizz mists up my view and revel in the revitalising power of being so dangerously close to a liquid avalanche. To think we put the mall as a priority over this effervescent wake-up call. As I flick the drips of moisture from my eyelashes I get a flash of myself from the outside in – my mum tells me I was the bath-time demonstration baby at the hospital because I loved the water so much and now look at me – being spritzed by Niagara Falls! It's then I have a mini epiphany.

'We can do anything we want!' I whoop at James.

'What do you mean?' He fights the winds to turn to me.

'We're adults with salaries and if we want to take ourselves off to see a wonder of the world, we can!'

I watch James's confusion merge into a grin as he gets my drift – as a child you wait to get taken places, as a teenager you wish you could escape your parents and go to Ibiza with your mates, in your twenties you dream of romantic encounters on paradise beaches, but right now I'm getting a massive thrill at the thought of waking up one morning and saying 'I want to see the pyramids!' or 'I want to dance a waltz in Vienna!' and then just doing it! Who'd have thought passive, tacky Niagara would make me feel like the whole world has suddenly opened up? There's power in them there waters, I'm telling you!

As the boat begins swirling around and heading back to the jetty I wonder if Paul is contributing to my exhilaration? After all, that's one of the best side-effects of falling for someone – you feel so optimistic and invincible, so much more willing to take a risk. I get a sudden internal rush – I can't believe I'm going to see him again in a matter of days! Wouldn't it be funny if I found my true love so early on in the quest? Maybe I should let go of my attachment to visiting all the places on the list. Two was enough for Emily. Maybe three is enough for me!

As we disembark we pass a bin labelled RECYCLABLE PONCHOS ONLY – not a sign you see every day – and then descend on the gift shop. While I flick through a book about Marilyn Monroe's experiences filming the rather depressing thriller *Niagara*, James stocks up on miniature bottles of waterfall water. Then we lose interest altogether. In spite of our shared ambition to walk behind the Falls we forget to do this. Just like that. We're standing staring at the cascading majesty and we think, 'Better head back to the car now.'

'So, what do you reckon?' I turn to James as I settle behind the steering wheel. 'How far do you want to go?'

James studies the map and then confidently announces, 'All the way.'

I turn to him and gasp: 'You mean . . . ?'

He nods. 'Tonight. You and me. Intercourse!'

Ooh James, I thought you'd never ask.

INTERCOURSE, PENNSYLVANIA

Two figures tiptoe around the redbrick building trying not to wake the occupants. One runs his hands along the ledges and windowsills while the other grubs through the borders.

'Find anything?'

'Not yet. Try the porch again.'

These amateur intruders go by the name of James Breeds and Belinda Jones. We rang ahead to let the B & B know that we wouldn't be arriving until after midnight, so the receptionist kindly said she would leave the key to our apartment in a secret hiding place. And when she said secret, she meant it.

'Ow!' James squawks as he retrieves his arm from a particularly prickly hedge. 'This is ridiculous! They could at least have left us a torch.'

'I think most people prefer Intercourse in the dark,' I attempt a joke.

'Not funny,' James grumps. 'I'm knackered – I just want to get to bed.'

I feel bad for him but find this late-night treasure hunt preferable to the alternative daytime scenario – as it was James who made the reservation it would have meant us checking in as Mr and Mrs Breeds. Now Breeds is an ironic enough surname for a gay man at the best of times, but at the Intercourse Village B & B this would have been one step beyond. (And if you're wondering about the Mrs aspect, James always refers to me as his wife when we travel. Mostly because he knows it drives me bonkers.)

'Got it!' I hiss a cheer, replacing a loose brick. 'Let's go.'

With no streetlamps to guide us, we have to feel our way along the fencing to our personal gate one splinter at a time. It's only fitting – our entire journey through Pennsylvania has been a fumble in the dark.

Four hours earlier we decided to stop for dinner and blundered off the 81 freeway into a town called Scranton. (Can you imagine a more horrible name – it's like a cross between 'scrotum' and 'skanky', but quite suitable as it turns out.) The high street was bleak to the point of Dickensian – a sad shamble of closed-down businesses and pedestrians hunched against bad weather even though it was a temperate evening. It actually managed to out-nasty Nice so we decided to seek sustenance elsewhere. That was the plan, at least, but we just couldn't seem to re-locate the freeway. Having driven down the same street for the fifth time, and getting a little anxious that we might have to spend the rest of our lives there, James suggested I try the one unexplored off-shoot, and suddenly our vista was transformed from grime to sublime – even in the dark I could tell this was a picturesque weave up to the top of a hill. A grand building loomed ahead and we set about tidying ourselves in preparation for decanters and fine silverware. However, our mood switched swiftly from High Society to Hitchcock when we spied the plaque marked SCRANTON MENTAL INSTITUTION.

'Oh my God! Oh my God!' I screamed, utterly freaked, wrenching the car into reverse and driving at such a pace we could have burst through barriers and haylofts if necessary. I was so convinced I was going to get dragooned into Electric Shock Therapy I created a whole new route to the freeway right there and then.

It is thus a particular relief to discover that our place of rest for the next two nights is so homey and pristine. The overall décor is farm-animal chic – cow, pig and sheep motifs on everything from the wallpaper borders to the toilet-roll holder – and by the time I've finished assigning oinks and moos to all the fixtures and fittings James is asleep.

Not quite ready for bed myself, I pop on the kettle in our kitchenette and shake out a sachet of hot chocolate. While I'm waiting for the water to boil I find myself eyeing the phone. I wonder if it's too late to ring Paul? I've already spoken to him once today but that was in a different state so I'd say it's legit . . .

'I've been dying to call you but I didn't want to look too keen!' he blurts on hearing my voice, then laughs: 'But I suppose I've ruined the ploy by telling you that!'

'I'm glad you told me!' I assure him, charmed by his candour.

'I've told my friends about you and they're all jealous!' he continues.

'I've told my mum about you!' I confess.

'I've told mine!' he laughs.

'This is so crazy!' I giggle.

'I know.'

There's a short lapse where we just simper down the phone and then we discuss the practicalities of me visiting – possibly in just two days' time! I can't believe we're both so committed to seeing each other again. It reminds me of how I felt when I first met Christian – there were no questions or doubts, we just followed our hearts. I grin as I lie back on the sofa, still clasping him to my ear – I've always loved the idea of a whirlwind courtship – you meet, you know, you marry within a week. Time and again I hear of real couples who did that and are still together thirty years on.

'I'm just so excited that I met you,' he tells me, sounding sincere.

'Oh me too. This whole thing is just blowing my mind,' I confess. 'I only wish I could have stayed for that drink.'

'Don't worry, we'll make up for it when you come back. We'll go to Armory Square and have a tequila in every bar.'

'Fantastic!'

'We'll get really drunk!'

'Yay!'

Once again there's a brief silence but it doesn't worry me – we'll have plenty of things to talk about when we're actually face-to-face.

'I can't wait!' I tell him.

'Me neither.' Paul heaves a dreamy sigh and then apologises for being so 'gay', meaning soppy, mushy, doting. *I hope.*

When we finally bid each other good night I go to sleep dreaming of piglets with pierced ears.

The next morning I peer out of the bedroom window for my first glimpse of Pennsylvania by daylight.

'What can you see?' James asks, still working on his outfit.

'From here – just flat farmland and the occasional grain tower.'

'No one having sex?'

'Nope.'

'How disappointing.'

It really must take some getting used to – having your home town named after a sexual act. I expect everyone we pass to be sniggering into their collars but instead the party of eight awaiting us at the breakfast table are the epitome of twee, clearly keen advocates of both Christianity and wedlock. When they mistakenly presume that we too are a couple we decide to keep schtum about the fact that we're touring America trying to pick up men. I even find myself tucking my left hand under the table so no one will notice the absence of a wedding ring. (James and I bicker like a married couple anyway so we put on a pretty convincing show.)

'So what are y'all planning to do with your day?' asks Bert, the middle-aged Southern gent tinkering with his grapefruit parfait.

'Well, you know women – she's going to want to shop,' James gives a conspiratorial roll of his eyes.

Bert chortles in a knowing fashion. 'Oh I know, yesterday Rose got a lovely patchwork throw that folds inside itself to create a pillow when you're not using it.'

'How ingenious!' I chomp down hard on my slice of toast.

'You'll have to take the little lady across to the Kitchen Kettle Village, she'll love it.'

'I was actually hoping to go for a drive—' I begin, about to explain how little we've seen of the area.

'You have been warned,' James cuts in. 'If you see her behind the wheel – *watch out!*'

'You may not see James,' I smile sweetly. 'I've just had a new ejector seat fitted!'

'Oh you two!' Bert chuckles.

'What are you playing at?' I belt James when we eventually escape onto the front porch. 'Do you always have to be so sexist when you're pretending to be my husband?'

He doesn't reply, he's too transfixed by the sight of a grey-bearded elder in a dark suit, braces and broad-brimmed straw boater, clopping by in his black horse-drawn buggy.

'Oh my God, they really are just like the characters in *Witness*!' He stumbles out onto the pavement and stares after him down the street. 'And look, the lady version . . .' he points ahead to two Amish women, both in full-skirted blue dresses with pinnies, one with a white bonnet (or prayer covering), the other wearing black.

'White shows you're married, black is single,' I decode the look for James, while at the same time trying to rationalise why I feel like I've just seen a unicorn – next to the fast cars and jeans and trainers that surround us, these people look storybook surreal.

'What about the men?' James asks, curiosity growing. 'How can you tell who's single there?'

'If he's got a beard he's married,' I tell him. 'They start growing it on their wedding day and never shave again.'

'They look like joke stick-on jobs,' James titters discreetly as a particularly bushy Brillo-pad passes by. 'How come they don't have hair on their upper lip?'

'Because moustaches have a long history of being associated with the military and are therefore forbidden,' I inform him. 'Amish are pacifists.'

'You seem to know a lot about this,' James narrows his eyes at me.

'Well, in case Mr Right turned out to be Amish, I thought I ought to do my homework.' I blink back at him.

'Surely you can't marry into their faith?'

'Well, it's very rare but not impossible. The trickier aspect would be the no make-up, no hair-straighteners, no hair*cuts* for that matter—'

'With your split-ends?' James is aghast.

'I know! Mind you, the idea is you wear it in a bun for all eternity.' I shrug. 'Plus I'd have to learn the Pennsylvania Dutch dialect which is basically a variation on German and I was hopeless at that at school.'

'And don't the women have to do all the cooking?'

'Yes.'

James gives me a serious look.

'I know. Major obstacle,' I grimace. 'And they have

to get up really early in the morning because they're farmers.'

'And there's no TV or movies or *heat* magazine.'

'But there are all the pleasures of a simple life,' I sigh wistfully. 'The farmyard animals, the fresh air, the quilting by candlelight!'

'All right Paris Hilton!' James giggles, leading me across to the Kitchen Kettle Village. 'I think you need to go shopping . . .'

We have a half-hour mooch around the arts and crafts boutiques selling all manner of lovingly stitched chintz including little squares that you put your pot of hot tea on, thus prompting a waft of lavender or cinnamon or whatever spice is stashed within. There's also every type of jam and relish on offer but one fruit is having a very special day today – it's the Annual Intercourse Rhubarb Festival and if we hurry we can catch the coronation of the Rhubarb King and Queen! Taking a seat on some plastic garden furniture, James and I cheer alongside the fifteen or so coach-loads of middle-aged tourists as a Mennonite (similar faith to Amish but a little less strict) girl is crowned queen and a spotty waiter from the café is named king.

'Oh dear, if he's the best in the land . . .' James looks fretful.

'Come on.' I lead him back to the B & B to collect the car. I fancy venturing a little further afield for a more authentic experience.

Just minutes outside Intercourse we stray into purely Amish territory, the only car for miles. It really does feel a privilege to see these devoted, hard-working people in their natural habitat. James says they must hate being gawped at by tourists but they seem oblivious, so focused on the job in hand – be it pegging out the washing on the line or tilling the fields with a giant plough and even bigger shire horse – that any undue attention glances off them. You can't help but feel a certain reverence in their presence. They are so quiet and dignified you naturally want to be respectful.

I slow to a crawl as I approach a buggy on the road ahead, keeping a non-invasive distance.

'Overtake! Overtake!' James urges.

I'm in no hurry. I actually feel calm by association and am happy to go at their pace, taking the time to admire the buggy's reflective triangle and watch the horse's hooves do their sprightly dance.

'What are you doing?' James hisses, irritation mounting. 'The road is clear – *go, go!*'

'I don't want to go!'

'Look! He's pulling over to let you pass.'

'I don't want to pass.'

'Are you crazy?' James fumes, clearly desperate to seize control of the car.

It's only when I see the buggy is practically doing a wheelie into the hedgerow to make more room for me that I finally accelerate beyond.

Two minutes later James explodes, raging at me to stop the car.

'What?'

'Stop! Right here! *Now!*' he demands. 'It'd be quicker to bloody walk!' he says, scrambling from the car and viciously slamming the car door.

I suppose this country life isn't for everyone.

As I watch him work out his frustrations on the loose

stones of the sidepath I wonder how long I'd last here without e-mail and my fleecy dressing gown and M&S microwave meals. Now that would make a good reality show – instead of jungle life, Amish life. I know one American production company is actually working on a show tentatively named *Amish in the City,* following five teenagers on their 'rumspringa' – that's their rite of passage when they get to experience the modern world – drive cars, get drunk, listen to Eminem – so they can make an informed decision about whether they want that lifestyle or to truly commit to the Amish faith and become baptised. Talk about culture shock – it would be like seeing the world through an alien's eyes – imagine discovering portable telephones that can take pictures, and women that shake their booty like Beyoncé!

Other than the fact you'd surely blow a fuse, you'd think they wouldn't be able to get enough of all the freedom and entertainment options and yet the majority do return. And do you know the most common reason? Loneliness. They are used to having this huge extended family surrounding them and suddenly it's just them and the big, bad world.

I wind down the window and call to James. 'Do you want to go and get some dinner?'

He gives me a dubious look.

'You can drive,' I add.

Over a typical Amish spread of chicken, sliced ham, mashed potatoes, gravy, macaroni cheese, fried sweet potatoes, creamed celery and coleslaw we discuss the merits of Amish courtship as opposed to our own flawed system.

'I think they've got things pretty well organised,' I opine. 'Every Sunday there's these evening "singings" and if a boy likes a girl he gives her a lift home in his buggy.'

'Aka his Ford Fiesta?' James chips in.

'If you like, but there's no funny business in the back seat. Mostly because there is no back seat,' I frown. 'Anyway, I think it's sweet – instead of some beery-breathed oik yelling at you over the music in a crowded disco, you're alone in this intimate setting, fully sober so you can really be aware of every word and emotion.'

'Then what happens?' James takes a swig of lemonade.

'If they like each other he's allowed to visit her at her house every other Saturday night.'

'One date a fortnight?' he gasps. 'So you can't really rush into anything?'

'No. In fact you can only get married in November or December (when the harvest has been completed and before the severe winter weather has arrived) so if you bottle your proposal, you have to wait another whole year.'

'Seriously?'

'Yup. And you can only marry on a Tuesday or a Thursday.'

'Why's that?'

'Same reason – those are the least busy days on the farm. Everything has to fit in around that schedule,' I say matter-of-factly. 'And do you know that when a man proposes, instead of giving the girl a diamond he gives her china or a clock!'

149

'And you wonder why Kelly McGillis got it on with Harrison Ford,' James chuckles.

'You can mock all you like, it obviously works,' I pout, finishing up my last mouthful of shoofly pie and hand-churned ice-cream. 'You know that half the time when I go out on the pull with my friends we don't even talk to any boys, we just end up having a girlie gossip in the corner. At least this way you get introduced and you know they're going to be in the same place every weekend so you can build up a friendship or an attraction. I just hate that now-or-never feeling when you go to a club. It's too much pressure.'

James reaches over and wipes my mouth with his napkin.

'What was it – ice-cream?' I ask him, checking my chin for drips.

'Nope. If you're going to stay here and pull an Amos or a Samuel we're going to have to get that muck off your face.'

'What!' I hoot.

'Come here!' he says, making a swipe at my blusher.

'Nooo!' I squeal, ducking out of reach.

'Harlot!' James accuses as I jump up from the restaurant table and dart for the door. 'Painted lady!' he hollers after me.

And so the name-calling continues, all the way back to Intercourse.

Though it seems vaguely illegal to use a laptop in an Amish community, once we're settled in back at the B & B (you didn't really think there was any

150

nightlife here, did you?) I decide to check my e-mails.

Oh wow, there are three from Paul! I click on the first, barely able to contain my excitement as an image of Blue Mountain Lake comes into view with the following caption: *'This lake is very beautiful but it has nothing on you.'*

I've never been compared to a body of water before but I'll take the compliment!

I click on the second, this time golden-leafed Chittenango Gorge and this note: *'We are going to have to go for a drive and have a picnic. I'm going to have a hard time looking at the leaves 'cause I'm not going to want to take my eyes off you.'*

Such romance and devotion! I'm better-looking than a leaf!

The third is just words (but what words . . .): *'When you told me you were returning to Cazenovia it made my entire year. I'm falling for you real hard and it's shocking how fast it has happened. Who cares how or why, all I want is to be with you!'*

Ah. I think that's what we in the business call a premature enunciation.

It's one thing getting giddy and gushy on the telephone but seeing such full-speed-ahead sentiments in print is a little unnerving to me. Is it possible we're both getting a bit carried away here? Skipping whole chunks of the story in a rush to get to the happy ending? If we were Amish we'd be taking this much slower. I'm beginning to suspect that slow is better.

I gulp and sit back in my chair, wondering how on earth to phrase a reply, when the phone rings. Oh no – it's him! I freeze, as if any motion on my part will give the game away that I'm actually here. Heart juddering, I let his call go to voicemail but then feel disgusted at my cowardice. Two seconds later it rings again. This time I steel myself, answer it, and pretend I haven't checked my e-mail yet. Well, what am I supposed to say about the 'I'm falling for you' confession?

I don't know, perhaps I'm overreacting. I mean, I've thought the same 'just wanna be with you' thing myself in secret. Maybe I'm just so unfamiliar – and therefore uncomfortable – with the notion of a man being both nice to me and completely upfront about his feelings that I'm subconsciously sabotaging any possible relationship? I want to believe that but as we talk I find myself getting irritated at the way Paul and I repeatedly revert to joking about how drunk we're going to get when we meet up ('synchronised tequila-induced vomiting – hahaha!'). That's not the kind of conversation you'd have in a buggy, is it? It's probably just because we only have about fifteen minutes of shared memories to relive, but all the same, my feelings are swiftly morphing from yearning to claustrophobia. If I go to see him, will he be mooning over me twenty-four hours a day? I don't know if I can go from three years single to limpet love, I might freak out. Besides, do we really have anything in common except an overactive, over-romantic imagination?

Tonight my dreams are bittersweet.

Day Two of Intercourse and still not a whiff of sex, so James and I decide to relocate to the one place in

Pennsylvania where we know for sure people will be at it: Caesars Poconos Honeymoon Resort aka The Land of Love. As it's a couples-only establishment, for once I don't mind James calling me Mrs Breeds.

'Congratulations!' We're met with a whoop of enthusiasm as we complete our hundred-mile drive from Intercourse.

'Thank you!' I smile back, feeling like the new Formula One champion.

'How was the wedding?' the chirpy receptionist asks.

'Glorious, best day of my life!' James steps in front of me. 'Still trying to shake off that darn confetti!'

My jaw drops and I yank James back. 'Tell me you didn't!'

'I did.'

'James, no!' I hiss. 'It's one thing passing ourselves off as an old married couple, but newlyweds?!'

'I thought we might get extra treats!' he reasons.

As a matter of fact we do – a giant biscuit tin masquerading as a time capsule, matching Caesars Poconos T-shirts, heart-shaped enamel pins to set us apart from the mere daters and the world's largest bottle of bubble bath. Bit excessive, I think to myself, until I see the volume of liquid it will be attempting to froth.

'Holy den of iniquity,' I gasp as we open the door onto our 'Roman Tower' room.

The vast, four-level red and gold suite is dominated by a two-storey-high champagne-glass bath. I cannot believe my eyes – you actually have to ascend a circular flight of stairs before you can access the Babycham-

153

style tub. I set the taps a-running straight away – this could be the closest I ever get to feeling like a maraschino cherry!

'You've got to see this,' James summons me from below.

Estimating the bath will take a good half an hour to fill, I trot back down to the imposing white-columned lounge area complete with romantic log-burning fireplace.

'Where are you?' I call, unable to spot him in the acreage of settee.

'Over here – by the pool!'

'The what?' I follow his voice. '*Noooo!*' I reel back. There is an actual swimming pool in our room. And it's heart-shaped.

'And there's a sauna and a two-person shower.'

'This is incredible!' I stumble around, wanting to dip into everything. After the past two nights' plain living I feel like I'm on my very own rumspringa.

'Happy, darling?' James grins.

'Oh shut up!' I laugh, giving him a playful slap. I can't deny it – I'm ecstatic. There can't be many single girls that get to experience a room like this!

While James splashes around in the pool I return to the upper level and lower myself into the champagne glass feeling like a scene from an old Busby Berkley musical – I expect a whole parade of girls in shower caps and bikinis made entirely of white bubbles to line the staircase.

'My turn!' James is eager to get in on the bubbly.

'Let's do pictures!' I squeal, reaching for the camera. And we mess around happily for an hour, only wishing we were with a real-live boyfriend about once every second.

If we were real newlyweds we'd most likely order room service and hand-feed each other in front of the fire but we're keen to check out the other couples so venture to the main dining room where a dubious Butlins-style buffet awaits. They're not overly geared up for vegetarians so we have to make do with an excess of iceberg.

'Don't worry,' James nods in the direction of the gift shop, 'we can always fill up on edible undies later.'

We pause to assess the free-seating plan. Most of the large circular tables are filled, but we find one with a space next to a couple from New Jersey – we're talking Big Hair folks, and that's just on his chest.

'Honeymooners! Congratulations!' They toast us as we take a seat.

I feel so guilty that I quickly change the subject. 'I hear the golfing here is wonderful . . .'

No one's biting.

'So, tell us, how did you two meet?' They huddle up.

I know James is dying to tell some elaborate fairy story but I decide to keep the lies to a bare minimum, clipping, 'Mutual friend.'

'Ohhh. And did you get married here in the US?'

'New York Plaza hotel,' James coos, mistaking us for Michael Douglas and Catherine Zeta Jones.

I stomp on his foot. This is so the wrong audience for his Armani/Versace detailing. In fact, the New Jersey couple are so lovely and warm and what with the booze and the fact that I'm convinced the wife can

155

tell that James is cruising the barman I decide to come clean, quietly confiding, 'You know, we're not really married!' over coffee.

She gives my hand a precious squeeze and says, 'Doncha worry, lots of young couples live together first these days – it's a modern world!'

I'm not sure she's ready for just how modern we are so I bite my lip.

On occasion the resort has performers like The Temptations, Randy Travis and Frankie Valli and the Four Seasons to entertain guests but there's just a dodgy comedian on tonight so we skip that and head to the games floor.

'I miss our room,' I confess after an exhausting game of ping-pong and an improvised dessert of chocolate body-paint.

'Come on, let's get back to it!' James casts our empty pots aside and sweeps my weary body into his arms, carrying me over the threshold like a good husband should.

But instead of falling asleep in a pair of loving arms I lie awake, staring up at the synthetic stars, psycho-analysing the Paul situation – my number one concern being that since entering this shag palace I haven't once wished I was here with him. Am I backing away because he's stepping forward? Or is that twisty-sick feeling in my stomach warning me off for a valid reason? He certainly seems worryingly full-on considering the lack of substance to our relationship. I wish I could sustain the giddiness I felt when we first met but if I'm honest I am already dreading any further contact with him. I'm horribly fickle like that – one glitch and I switch off.

Right now I don't even want to speak to him again, let alone visit him. It's then I realise I just can't do it. I'm not going to go back to Cazenovia. And the sooner I end this charade the better. I roll over and look at the clock. It's only 11.20 p.m. I'm going to do it now, then it's done and I'll be able to sleep.

I creep across the room to my phone, make the call but get no reply. I can't just leave a message. Can I?

'Come back to bed!' James groans.

I sigh, flick the phone closed and retreat beneath the covers, warming my cold feet on the closest thing to a husband I have ever known.

In the morning I check my e-mails. That's funny. No word from Paul. I wonder if he sensed a change of heart in my tone of voice when we spoke back at the B & B? Or perhaps he's decided to give that 'playing it cool' thing a try? Suits me.

It's not until James and I get to New York City that he calls me, sounding distinctly frazzled:

'Thank God you picked up! All I've been thinking about is hearing your voice!'

'Er, Paul . . .' I begin. I have to stop him before he goes any further.

'Sorry I haven't been able to call you but I've been in prison!'

'WHAT?!' I balk, thrown off course.

'I got pulled over for drunk driving . . .'

'Oh.' Bang goes the sympathy vote.

'It was awful. One of my best friends had an accident and he's in a coma and I was so worried I just drank and drank.'

'Gosh, I'm so sorry,' I gush, sympathy swiftly reinstated.

'All that's keeping me going at the moment is the thought of seeing you tomorrow!'

'Mmmm,' I mumble, stomach sinking into my boots as he carries on enthusing about how excited he is. *Bugger*. I can't dump him now!

Looks like I'm going back to Cazenovia after all.

Wherever possible I like to overnight in an ex-brothel so I've chosen Dickensen House on James Street as the setting for my tryst with Paul.

Of course, there's always a risk when you choose a B & B over an impersonal chain hotel that you'll have to spend valuable getting-ready minutes complimenting the owners on their exquisite taste in globe drinks cabinets, and at Dickensen House that's a very real concern. Décor-wise it has the works: stone frogs with sensors that set off a *gribbit* as you pass by, a NO SMOKING sign with a sense of humour: '*If we catch you, we'll assume you are on fire and take appropriate action!*' and – most appropriate to my quest – bedrooms themed according to romantic poets (mine is Elizabeth Barrett Browning). Better yet, the second-floor kitchen is stocked with 'help yourself' goodies and, at the encouragement of the owners, I grab a mittful of squidgy chocolate brownies and half a bottle of chilled chardonnay and settle into a world of white wicker, lacy trimmings and hand-embroidered samplers cooing *'To love and be loved is the greatest joy on earth.'*

Ordinarily I might find this a little frilly but tonight the cosy romance is just what I need to ease open my heart. I've decided that seeing as I've come all the way back to Cazenovia I'm going to keep an open mind about Paul. It's true that in the past I've found that men who are so wildly full-on in the early stages generally peak too soon and within a week or two have gone all vague and distracted and fail to keep any of their initial flamboyant promises. However, part of the point of this trip is to let the past go and see the future with fresh eyes so I'm going to drop my baggage in favour of an adage. And the one I've chosen for this trip is 'Love as if I've never been hurt'.

While I wait for my nail varnish to dry, I carefully flick through the poetry books on the dresser. As well as the infamous *'How do I love thee? Let me count the ways . . .'* Liz has some great lines I can totally relate to:

Say over again, and yet once again, that thou dost love me.
Though the word repeated should seem a cuckoo song . . .
Say thou dost love me, love me, love me.

She also speaks of how love can transform you, something I haven't felt in a while but chronically crave:

Thy soul hath snatched up mine, all faint and weak
And placed it by thee on a golden throne!

What if I'm nervous about Paul because I can sense the magnitude of love that awaits me? What if my soul is about to be placed on a golden throne? Dare I believe such things are possible? The half-bottle of chardonnay says, 'Yes!' and suddenly I'm a-flutter with pre-date butterflies.

I give my hair an impromptu back-comb in a bid to look tousled-sexy and then, just shy of 9 p.m., I reach for my phone. I feel a little guilty – Paul did tell me to call him as I was leaving New York but I forgot until I'd boarded the flight (a short internal hop) and then I didn't call him directly I arrived in case he wanted to see me straight away. I felt I needed some prep time, keen for his first sight of me to be 100% goddess. Anyway, here I am dialling his number, suddenly feeling exceptionally lucky: my heart goes out to all the girls getting ready for a Friday night on the town, hoping to find love, when all I have to do is say, 'Come get me!'

'Hello?' It's the dad. (Did I mention he still lives with his pop? A bit of a concern I admit, but I'm Miss Positive now so I'm not going to let it worry me.)

'Hi, this is Belinda! Can I speak to Paul please?' I can barely control my excitement.

'He's staying overnight at his mate John's.'

'What?' I feel like I've been smacked in the face.

'He'll be back tomorrow morning. I'll let him know you rang.'

No, no, no! The morning? That's a lifetime away. 'But, but . . .' I stammer, trying to make sense of his absence. 'I was supposed to meet him tonight – did he leave any message for me?'

'No.'

'Well, isn't there some way we could contact him? I know he doesn't have a cell phone but maybe you have a number for John?'

'No, sorry. Good night.'

That's it? I'm left holding the receiver long after the line has clicked dead.

I don't understand it – we had a date, a dream date according to him. What happened to counting the hours till I got here, and being blinded by my beauty? (I was particularly looking forward to that bit.) Why wasn't he sat by the phone awaiting my call?

I stumble back onto the bed, unable to get my head around the prospect of having to wait a minimum of twelve hours before I can even speak to him. None of this makes sense – why would he have gone to stay at his mate's the very night I'm due to arrive? If he'd had a change of plan surely he would have called me and left a message.

Unless he's deliberately avoiding me . . . I get chills. But what could have changed his mind so suddenly? It can't be anything to do with me because the last time we spoke everything was full steam ahead. What *is* going on?

I pace the floor, eyes filled to the brim with impending tears, fighting waves of hysteria and frustration. I'm an impatient person by nature and all these unanswered questions aren't helping. It's typical, isn't it – yesterday I didn't even want to see him but when I come to town for that sole purpose he pulls a vanishing trick and suddenly I'm so consumed by the need to see him I'm like a woman possessed.

Oh why didn't I call earlier? I might have caught him

before he went out. Cursed vanity! I take another slug of chardonnay, now so riled up with rejection and remorse that I decide the only thing to do is head out into the night and track Paul down – I remember him telling me that all the nightlife in Syracuse centres around Armory Square so I'll just bar crawl until I find him.

I look in the mirror, blinking to bring my reflection into focus – I can do this. One last whisk of hairspray and I'm in the cab. The driver takes one look at me and offers me his hairbrush – I kid you not, he actually gets it out of his bag and hands it to me through the partition – I'm guessing I haven't quite mastered the tousled-sexy look yet. I probably should have turned back then but instead I trawl the streets, stopping any likely looking strangers to ask, 'Where do pierced, long-haired people go drinking round here?'

They look blankly back at me. Even a long-haired, pierced person offers only one dead-end suggestion.

1.30 a.m. Disorientated and desperate on a chilly street corner, I call his house again in the vain hope that his dad has got it wrong and Paul is actually there, waiting for me, kicking himself for missing my call. No such luck. His dad answers again, clearly yanked from a deep sleep, and tells me he has no news. Great. Now Pops thinks I'm a stalker and an ill-mannered one at that.

Back at Dickensen House, trying to creep in without waking the other guests, I realise just how tiddly I am. Every floorboard is a creaker and I can't steady myself on any of the surfaces because they're all booby-trapped with fragile mementos. At the top of the stairs I nearly jump out of my skin as I come face to face with

163

an oversized rag doll with a glinting eye. All I want to do is collapse into bed and chug out my tears but I'm haunted by the note in the bathroom requesting that guests remove every trace of mascara before they so much as look at the snow-white towels. I try my best to conduct my ablutions quietly but the soap shoots out of my hand and sloshes into the toilet bowl, my glass bottles topple into each other and even the cotton wool seems noisy.

Once I'm sufficiently cleansed to lean my cheek on the pristine pillowcase the weeping begins in earnest. I have wasted $180 to be taunted by romance and lace. Every other occupant in this bed has been entwined with their loved one, and I am not just alone but cast asunder.

4 a.m. I can bear it no longer and dial my mum in Devon, barely able to speak through my sobbing. Her soothing sympathy just makes me blub more. As I look at the scrumple of tissues that surround me I realise I didn't get all my mascara off after all.

6 a.m. I'm never going to sleep again – I'm destined for a life of strangled heartache. This is a living hell.

11 a.m. My mum calls to check on me. As I come to, realisation dawns that he still hasn't called and the suffocating sadness swoops back in.

As we talk, I'm forced to admit that my reaction is utterly out of proportion in relation to the relationship – after all, I only met Paul once. But really that's not the point. My grief is not about Paul in particular but my love life in general. I so needed to believe that this Mr Right trip could change my love fortune but here I am in an all-too-familiar position.

'This is not what I came on this trip for,' I blub. 'I can get rejected back at home!'

Gradually I calm down and promise my mum that I won't be using the embroidered curtain tie-back as a noose. In return she convinces me there must be a rational explanation for what's happened and encourages me to try Paul's house once more. So I do, repeatedly. And I get the machine again and again and again.

I'd give up and go home early if I didn't suspect this could turn into one of those gnawing neuroses that would keep me awake in the middle of the night for years to come – Did I bow out too soon? If I'd held my nerve could there have been a happy resolution? – so I decide to allow myself a little more time to (hopefully) find out what's going on.

However, if I'm going to stay another night I'm going to have to track down a cheaper hotel. Ah well, I have nothing to do all day but find one so as soon as I'm dressed and my suitcase is stowed under the stairs, I head out onto the bleak empty streets walking head down, scowling, willing someone to try mugging me or at least accidentally jolt me so I can vent some of my frustrations: 'You picked the wrong day to start with me, buddy!'

On closer inspection the people of Syracuse look even more miserable than me. I stop and look around the high street. Syracuse *itself* looks miserable – grey, dejected, past its prime. If I was visiting Paul on some tropical isle or even down the road in New York City I could find my own amusement, but here? There's not even any Saturday-shopper bustle to buoy me up.

Maybe they're all down the road at the Carousel Center.

I sigh a big white breath and step into a deserted coffee house so I can reprise my 'should I stay or should I go?' dilemma while defrosting over an Almond Steamer. It's the not knowing that is driving me crazy. My mum's right – it could be a genuine misunderstanding but my instincts are screaming 'He doesn't want you.' Or is that my paranoia? Either way something's definitely not right. It's been at least an hour since my last phone call to the Ghirardelli household so I leave one last message begging anyone – father, brother, cleaner, burglar – to leave a message for me telling me what on earth is going on, stressing that at this point even bad news is also acceptable.

What more can I do? I have to give in and admit defeat. Or at least have a Plan B. I call the airline and discover there's a 5.30 p.m. to New York where at least I can find a friendly face. Sanity seems within reach – just three hours to kill and then I can put this deranging episode behind me. In the meantime I decide to write him a note and drop it off at his house.

Hailing a taxi I give Paul's address, saying I just want to deliver something and then be dropped at the Carousel Center – back to where it all began. I'm blessed with one of those 'if I was twenty years younger' cabbies who instantly takes me under his wing. Noticing my misty eyes he tuts, 'It can only be a guy!'

I bite my lip and nod, hoping he won't be any more sympathetic as I'm already so close to tears that one jolt on the brake pedal and they'll come spilling out.

'You wanna talk about it?' He oozes concern via the rear view mirror. I blink back at him. What if he can see what I'm missing? I quickly bring him up to speed but it's a mistake; now he's protesting that I'm far too 'beautiful' and 'special' and 'intelligent' for such a louse and my heart is so grateful for the pep-talk I lose all control over the excess of fluid in my eyes. As we pull up outside Paul's house, he quotes me a line from the Bible in an attempt to raise my spirits and whaddayaknow – it works. I step from the cab, emboldened by the fact that I now have a guardian angel at my side.

It's strange to think how different this first sight of his home might have been – him grinning expectantly in the doorway, embracing me with passionate fervour then welcoming me into his humble home.

Only it's not so very humble. Four bedrooms at least, I'd say. Detached. Nice, well-kept estate. I rattle and ding the appropriate appendages but there is no sign of life (both he and his dad are probably lying on the living-room floor, fingers poised to jab 911 if I create a scene) so I simply tuck my note under the front-door knocker and return to the cab.

'To the mall?'

I nod.

'Who knows – maybe you just met Paul so that you'd have a reason to come back here, but in fact Mr Right is someone else entirely,' Cabbie ponders. 'Someone you are about to meet this very afternoon!'

Frankly I don't think I'd be receptive to meeting Jude Law at the moment but I appreciate the thought. The kindness of this stranger has really calmed me down, and I leave him with heartfelt thanks and enter the world of sanitised shopping.

The mall is like Disneyland compared to Syracuse high street and it's wonderfully comforting to be back on familiar ground. It seems unimaginable how ecstatic I was last time I was here. If only there was a way to erase the recent tortuous hours and get back to that feeling. I try summoning Paul, willing him to be around every corner I turn, vividly recalling my former high. But the minutes tick by producing nothing. I have to leave by 4 p.m. at the latest to collect my luggage from Dickensen House and make it to the airport with an hour for check-in. It's now 3.55 p.m. Why am I hanging on till the last second like this? Can I really still be hoping for a happy resolution? I just can't face the thought of leaving here and never knowing what really happened. Out of habit I head for the phone boxes to make one last call.

'Hello?'

I can't believe it! A real-live human has actually answered the phone!

'Oh!' I snap into action. 'I just wanted to leave a message for Paul—'

'Belinda?' A voice I only then recognise as the man himself cuts in. 'Where are you?'

I can't seem to answer. Is he checking to make sure I've already left Syracuse?

'I, um, I . . .' I stall.

'What's going on?' he hustles. 'You tell me!' I snort, suddenly outraged. 'What do you mean?' he says, sounding baffled. I don't know where to begin. 'Haven't you got my seventy-two thousand messages?' I snap.

'I've just walked in the door – I stayed at John's last night.'

'Yes, I know,' I say coldly. I don't know what to think but if I'm going to give him the benefit of the doubt I'm going to have to be quick. The 5.30 p.m. is the last flight of the day.

'I'm at the mall,' I blurt.

'You're *here*?!' he gasps, incredulous.

'Yes,' I reply matter-of-factly. 'If you can get here in the next five minutes I'll stay. If not I'm going to New York!'

'I'll be there!' he cheers. 'Meet me at the bar by the carousel. We'll sort everything out – I can't believe you're here!' He sounds genuinely chuffed.

Suddenly I'm exhilarated – if confused. And extremely peeved that I didn't wash my hair this morning. And that I'm wearing ratty clothes. So much for 100% goddess.

I take a seat at the bar. Five minutes pass, then ten, then twenty. Panic offers itself as an option but then he walks in the door. Gosh he's beautiful. His raven mane is as shiny as glass, his piercings freshly polished and he's dressed head to toe in black. (Who needs Casanova when you've got Zorro?)

As he steps towards me I scrutinise his face – does he look pleased to see me? Before I can reach a verdict he pulls me into a huge, tight, everlasting 'I can only imagine what you've been through' hug and I melt.

We order a drink and I relate every agonising hour I've spent since I arrived in Syracuse. He alternates between looking horrified and remorseful, all the while holding my hand up against his heart, stroking it like he's trying to soothe away my pain. Then he tells me his version.

'When I didn't hear from you yesterday, I thought you weren't coming,' he begins, head hung low.

'But I told you . . . we'd already arranged—' I stumble.

'You never confirmed it,' he whispers.

'I couldn't get any reception on my mobile.' My wretched phone! It's all technology's fault. (Always best to have an inanimate scapegoat when you can.) All the same, if he'd just stayed home none of this would have happened. I have to ask: 'Why did you stay at John's last night?'

He searches my eyes for a second then sighs: 'I couldn't take it. I know it sounds ridiculous but I couldn't bear to be at home alone – I was so disappointed that you weren't coming I went out and drank and drank. And drank,' he sighs, shaking his head.

He looks up and squeezes my hand tight. I feel sorry for us both – what we went through so unnecessarily. But now it's resolved and, though still a little shaken up, I experience a glimmer of excitement. Once again he pulls me into a strong hug. To think I was worried about feeling claustrophobic in his company – now I long to be lying so close that we're breathing as one. We order another round and, reassured that he really does like me, I decide to really, really fancy him. (Well, seeing as I'm here . . .)

Before we get too plastered, Paul sensibly suggests we collect my luggage and get me checked into a new hotel. All the angst seems worth it as we walk hand in hand through the mall. Normally I feel awkward and slightly stupid holding hands with someone – like a three-year-old trailing after their mum – but Paul is so assured and confident that I feel oddly thrilled, as though I'm walking up the red carpet of a film premiere on the arm of its leading man.

Waiting for the cab we wrap ourselves around each other to counter the cold but this throws up a few awkward moments – we're alternating between easy-going intimacy and the jarring realisation that we hardly know each other. I realise a mall taxi-rank is hardly a rose-petal-strewn gazebo but I wish he'd hurry up and kiss me, the anticipation is driving me crazy.

'After you.' He opens the cab door and then slides in beside me, deciding for some misguided reason that I can drive his car so we'll go back to his house to pick it up before we collect my case. My note is still fluttering beneath the doorknocker. A good sign. It's all been a horrible misunderstanding. As he leads me through the garage entrance I get a twisted smile – I never would have believed I'd be back here again so soon. From rejection to affection in a matter of hours!

We go directly to his bedroom. It's mine-shaft dark, filled with trippy curios and a series of spot-lit Magic Eye posters. I fear I may have stared too long because as I turn and watch Paul fall back onto his bed the whole thing appears to wobble and ripple like a Scooby Doo flashback.

'It's a waterbed,' he grins, noticing my cross-eyed concern and beckoning me over.

'Permission to come aboard?' I gingerly edge onto

the mattress beside him but find the sensation too disconcerting to relax. As I do my impression of a large piece of driftwood, I wonder if he's going to undulate in my direction? I brace myself for a tidal-wave of love but apparently there's no motion in his ocean – no sooner have we settled into a gentle ebb and flow than he jumps back on his feet and suggests we continue on our relocation mission.

Damn. Well, he's probably distracted by the practicalities of the evening, I tell myself. I'm sure that as soon as we're alone in my hotel room it'll be passion unleashed.

The hotel I end up in – just a stone's throw from his house – is your basic Holiday Inn business bore on a busy main road, but what do I care? I'm hardly going to be sitting in my room admiring the décor. I leap into the shower while he watches TV and then emerge in a mock leather shirt that strains at the poppers. His eyes light up with lusty approval and when I ask, 'This OK?' he positively growls his 'Yeah!'

Better yet, I hit it off with his mate John (who comes to pick us up) and by the time we reach Armory Square I'm on top form. It couldn't be more of a contrast with my mood only the night before when I trawled the streets with a bleeding heart. It's still freezing but I don't care.

The bar we go to is great – buzzing yet chilled with mismatched sofas and outsized armchairs you can slump and sup in. We have a couple of brews, ever intertwined and smitten of eye, and then hit a disturbingly brightly lit bar. As we enter, Paul flinches

– a certain hard-faced ex-girlfriend of his is perched on one of the high stools – but he seems determined not to let her murderous glances ruin our evening and even buys me not one but two roses from the Ugandan flower-seller doing the rounds and nuzzles my neck. I'm mortified that one rose has a furry wee bear clinging to the stem sporting an 'I Love You' T-shirt but if these are the lengths you have to go to in order to spite ex-girlfriends then so be it.

Following a snack at a diner we head back to the hotel. My ears are alert for clues as to what's next – despite his ardent attentions throughout the evening I'm not even sure Paul will be coming in with me. I used to think I was good at reading people, but with him I haven't got a clue. We pull up outside reception, and Paul gets out to help extricate me from the back seat. The instant I'm liberated John screeches off. So that settles it. But what now?

I faff around the room waiting to see what he does.

He just lolls on the bed.

I put on my pyjamas and dive under the covers, wishing I was more drunk.

He snuggles fully clothed into me.

I'm blissfully comfortable and stroke his silky hair, but we still haven't kissed other than the thank-you peck I gave him for the roses, so I gradually manoeuvre myself into a more accessible position.

Nothing.

I vaguely wonder if something is wrong but having had more than my fair share of experience with younger men I presume he's waiting for me to make the first move. And to think I had him pegged as such a sex-junkie from my first impression at the mall. At least you know where you are with men who wrestle you to the ground with their passion. These gentle, groin-on-ice fellas are so hard to read.

I mutter some cringey line about longing to kiss him as I stare meaningfully at his shoulder. He obliges but only after pausing long enough to make me wish I could bite back my words. Initially I'm preoccupied with the two metal bolts in his tongue but they only make fleeting guest appearances. It's sensual rather than sexy. Plateau kissing rather than the kind that builds into a crescendo of 'take me now!' urgency. I wonder who he's trying to keep a rein on – him or me. He's definitely holding back. Maybe he just doesn't find me that attractive. Maybe he never gets that worked up. Maybe he's being a gentleman. Maybe he's just tired. SCREAM!

I wish I had a decoding machine that could give me a print-out of exactly what he's thinking and feeling right now. It could just be leftover paranoia but instead of our kisses bringing us closer, I feel like I'm losing him again. He sits up and sheds some clothes but merely in preparation for sleep. Now I feel really unsettled. He's here with me but something's still not right. *Oh for goodness' sake,* I scold myself – it's our first night together! I'm expecting too much. Tomorrow will be better.

The alarm wakes him at 8 a.m. but I'm convinced I haven't slept at all. I feel like I've been lying here witnessing the last stages of drunkenness hand over to the early stages of hangover. I know I look twelve times worse than I feel so I refuse to reveal anything apart from the top of my head and kiss him goodbye through the sheet. But morning-afters are supposed to be awkward so I'm not worried – I'll be extra-lovely later to make up for it.

He says he'll call me about 11 a.m. after his court appearance. That must be preying on his mind, poor thing – no wonder he was a little distant last night. I wish him luck and, still swathed in sheet, reach out to give his hand a farewell squeeze. Then, after he's gone, I doze fitfully in between downing gallons of luke-warm tap water before forcing myself to rebuild my fragile form into what passes for a human being. Before I know it, it's lunchtime. I haven't even had breakfast and I desperately need a big sticky bun followed by egg, chips and beans – the only effective hangover cure in my book. He must be held up at the court but I'm going to have to pop out so I call his house. He answers.

'Oh! You're back! How did it go?' I ask.

'Fine!' he says flatly, giving me only the barest details.

There's a pause, which I expect him to fill with the words, 'I'll be over in ten minutes to whisk you off to the golden-leaved gorge!'

Instead he says nothing. Uh oh.

'So, what are you doing?' I eventually ask.

'Nothing much but I've got an essay I'm going to have to start work on.'

Welcome back to that sinking feeling. He's talking to me like a stranger. I don't get it – he really is the King of Mixed Messages – one minute he's buying me roses and sharing my bed, the next minute he's

175

finding excuses to avoid me. What can have changed since last night? I know I was ridiculous this morning, hiding from him, but even though I was speaking from under a sheet I was perfectly pleasant. So much for his parting words to me this morning: 'I'm yours all weekend.'

'So will I see you tonight?' I ask cautiously.

'Well . . . I have to eat, I suppose we could meet about 5 p.m.'

Charming! He sounds like he's doubling up on chores. More to the point, he's basically just let me know he won't be spending the night – just a mealtime. I came all the way back to Syracuse for *this*?

I know I should just pull myself together, drag my dignity out from wherever I've left it and get out of town, but it's the same story as the day before. Much as I feel a bit lukewarm about him when he's being over the top, the moment he loses interest my insecurities go into warp drive. It's my body. It must be. Not that he saw it or touched it, but he must have sensed my dimpled dumpling cellulite. I access my emergency bravado and blurt: 'Why don't you bring your essay with you? I'm a writer, I can help you write! What's it about anyway?'

He fudges a reply, saying he'd rather have a break and not talk about work at all. The essay is clearly bogus. I feel insulted by his lie and hurt that he's avoiding me after only one day together. Ironic considering I predicted claustrophobia on my part – I thought I'd be fighting to get away from him, now I'm practically begging to see him. Perhaps I'm overreacting? I'll find out at 5 p.m.

In the meantime I'm still starving. The hotel restaurant is closed and only bar food is available, so I order mushroom soup and perch on a seat. The barman is an amusingly dry fellow with a moustache. I'm his only customer and within minutes I've unloaded my worries and await his wisdom. (Well, the cab driver was so comforting, it's got to be worth a try.) He decides he needs to consult with someone more Paul's age and summons a young waiter. As he retells my sorry tale a businessman pulls up a stool and hears the whole humiliation. The young waiter tells me that if I'd come all this way he'd want to spend every minute with me. The businessman offers his opinion: 'Forget him and come to the Dinosaur Barbecue with me!'

Sorely tempted, I nevertheless decline. *Really it's fine – why would I go out with a nice, attentive grown-up like you when I can be rejected and disappointed by a problem child like Paul?* I think to myself.

The hours drag to 5 p.m. I mostly fill my time attempting to make myself look so devastatingly attractive he'll be cursing the wasted minutes. The rest of the time is filled with plain, old-fashioned dread.

The hotel shuttle-bus drops me at his house at the appointed hour and I assume driving duties as we head off to a vast car park trimmed with a few nondescript restaurants and video shops. I try my best to banter and make him laugh but I'm as sparkling as week-old Sprite. I've lost my nerve. It's like when you start telling a story and realise your audience is less than captivated so you limp through the anecdote ending with a hurried, '*Anyway!*' and swiftly change the subject. It's so much easier to be lovable when you think someone loves you. It brings out the best in you. Right now I feel censored by insecurity. It's a horrible, vulnerable place to be.

We peruse the menu, making bland chit-chat. There is no spark. It's like we're going through the motions rather than really connecting, although, confusingly, Paul's taken my hand and is holding it across the table. Again the mixed messages. It's really messing with my head. I need some answers but I don't feel the vibe is conducive to being cards-on-the-table direct. Instead I try this tactic:

'You know, earlier today, I was reading this magazine article and it was debating whether you can stimulate someone's interest in you more by sleeping with them or by withholding sex. What do you think?'

'Withholding,' he answers, without hesitation, and elaborates at length. He even mentions the word 'tease' in his explanation, referring to the tantalising 'wondering what it might be like' aspect.

Suddenly I feel a bit better. OK. So it's a conscious decision for him not to shag around or try it on during a first date. He says it's about respect. Something I'm not too familiar with so no wonder it seems strange.

Maybe he wasn't repulsed by me after all. However, something in the way he talks smacks of mind games and the more we talk the more I realise I've misread him. He speaks of a couple of long-term relationships and one terrifying brush with commitment. At times he sounds quite callous – to think I had him pegged as an ever-shagging love puppy. I don't even know that I like him any more but I'd sure prefer his company to an empty hotel room.

He gets the bill. A nice gesture probably motivated by guilt. I sigh to myself. The bottom line is that it's no crime that he doesn't like me any more. I just wish he could admit it to me – when I try and hint that things have gone a bit awry he looks bemused and dismisses my concerns.

Continuing my carefree act as best I can, we drop the car at his house and then his dad gives us a lift to the hotel. He persists with the constant stroking and massaging of my hands even though I'm in the back seat and he's in the front, thus making me feel more foolish than ever – in order to maintain contact I have to sit forward, looking all over-eager like I'm practically piggy-backing him for attention while he just nonchalantly toys with my fingers.

With anyone else I might take this touchy-feelyness as a promising indicator of things to come. But with Paul I'm afraid to say, 'When will I see you again?' as we step into the lobby for fear of sounding needy. I'm also afraid of initiating a kiss because maybe that is what has made him pull away. And I'm afraid to look him in the eye in case I give myself away. Pathetic, I know. But that's what mixed messages will do to you. I just stand there in limbo. I could do casual on home territory but when you're just in town for one more day you can't really leave it at 'See ya!'

He doesn't appear to be in a rush but I'm very aware that his dad is waiting outside.

When he leans in to kiss me, I'm expecting no more than a peck – well, dinner was awkward and the car journey was like an unfunny game of Twister – but instead he lays a soft, tender kiss on me. And then another. And then the kind of kisses I'm not sure are entirely fitting for a brightly lit hotel lobby overlooked by a perm-twiddling receptionist. Pleasure ricochets around my inner organs. It feels like a love kiss – all slow and meaningful. What's going on? What flipped his switch from distant to doting? On and on, it continues to the point that my heart peeks out from under the pillow it's been hiding behind. Well, almost. So much for all that mumbo about being lost in the world where only you two exist – I may be at Heaven Central but I'm still distracted by the squealing wheels of several trolley-suitcases.

I open an eye to see a gang of airport staff laughing heartily. At us? Is the receptionist still staring? Is his dad getting impatient in the car outside?

Paul gives me an intense gaze, but it all seems a bit practised. I have no idea what's real any more. It's a horribly disorientating feeling. He says he'll call after class tomorrow at 12.30 p.m. and hangs on for that last glimpse as the lift doors close on me, acting all 'parting is such sweet sorrow'.

But if that's the case then why is his body leaving the building? *Anyone?*

My big night out is over and it's only 8 p.m. What next? I can't face another solo appearance at the bar so I retire to my loathsome room and flop onto the bed, hating having all this time to think about how I wish I'd done things differently or plan how I'll be the next time we meet. Why can't it just be what it is? When things are going well you don't even question yourself, but when they aren't I for one over-analyse everything and realise just how amazingly irritating I can be.

Then I decide I don't like him anyway. I realise I'm looking for something from Paul he doesn't have. It's never gonna work. Not even for a few days. So what am I staying for? A clamour of voices tell me to try and be reasonable, to resolve that it's for the best, but I am battling with the knowledge that it's over.

Monday. I wake at 10.30 a.m. My first thought: I'll know within two hours which way my day will go. I'm going to ask Paul if he's staying over. If not then I'm gone. It may sound like an ultimatum but it's how I feel. I run across to the garage to get a milkshake and chocolate for breakfast. The day is sunny but bracingly cool. Perfect. I'm still off-balance but feel less of a victim.

12.30 p.m. comes and goes.

1 p.m. I page him. Nothing.

1.30 p.m. I make profound apologies to the front desk, explaining I'm just waiting for a call to find out whether or not I'm checking out.

2 p.m. Right. The lovesucker is fighting back. I'm outta here. Zealous packing.

2.30 p.m. Check out and page him again from the reception payphone. Nothing.

2.45 p.m. I call his house – his dad answers, says Paul's not back from college yet. I tell him I have to go to New York early so I'm going to drop a note around to the house.

I sit and write my guts out: *You're deluding yourself if you think you are respectful. You have not been respectful of my time or my feelings.*

181

Two pages of HOW DARE YOU! basically.

I clip on the mini-teddy with its 'I Love You' T-shirt for maximum irony and bully the shuttle bus driver into giving me a ride to his house. It's 3 p.m.

We pull into the driveway. His dad's in the garden and looks up, his face impossible to read. I breezily announce that I like his son but he doesn't seem to like me so I'm leaving. He just looks mildly bewildered, clearly unused to having paranoid British women next to his lawnmower. I'm just turning to leave when the door connecting to the house opens, and Paul's head emerges with a 'concerned' look in his eyes.

'You're leaving?' he gasps with a 'how could you?' tone to his voice. I mix utter disbelief with a 'You have sooo been caught out!' snort.

He walks up to me, kisses me on the lips and says, 'Have we got time to get something to eat together?'

I'm utterly, utterly foxed. What IS going on? Am I the only one who can see that this looks like a scene from an unfunny farce? He claims he's embarrassed to be seen in his scruffy clothes and runs off to the shower before I even have time to react. His dad suggests I wait in the house.

I'm too restless to sit. I take the liberty of opening the fridge and squeezing myself a glass of chilled mineral water on autopilot. Still shell-shocked, I wait. And wait. Oh my God – he's hiding some girl in the laundry basket! I go to the bottom of the stairs and call his name. Nothing. I wait some more. I call some more. Nothing. He's burrowed out of the house in a tunnel dug with a spoon and a powerful urge to avoid me!

I can't take this! I have never known anyone blow so hot and cold. The boy needs to wear a barometer on his forehead to give people the 'heads up' on his mood. It is making me feel utterly unhinged! I feel like I have been pushed to my limit. I have to put an end to this now.

I'm just making for the door ready to walk the two miles back to the hotel when his handsome younger brother appears.

'Hey! How are you enjoying Syracuse?'

'I'm not!' I scowl.

'Why's that?'

'Your brother!'

He looks awkward. The dad comes in.

'Have you met Dan?'

'Yes,' I say. 'He's my favourite of your sons.' My sarcasm is growing.

Paul reappears. All smiles. I want to punch him but instead tersely request we talk outside. He walks ahead, stretching out his hand behind him for me to take. I just look at it. Is he mad? Does he really think I'd be stoopid enough to take it.'

We sit on the garden bench. He looks puppy-dog-pityingly at me, playing dumb about the pages and the fact he said he'd call at 12.30 p.m. I tell him he should have let me know he wasn't into this yesterday as I could have been with my friends in New York.

'But I don't want you to go. I want you to stay,' he says simply.

I blink back at him. This is the last thing I was expecting to hear. I don't know if I even *want* to hear it any more. So what was I expecting? Well, I knew

183

that confronting him wouldn't prompt a proper exposé of his feelings but I thought he might concede an 'OK, let's just kiss and say good night' adieu. I'm torn. What's left of my sanity is suggesting in no uncertain terms that I put an end to this unsettling encounter and get the hell out of Dodge. But my instant-gratification side is demanding I embrace this last day with him and end on a happy note.

I look into those bewitching brown eyes and cautiously enquire, 'If I stay, will you stay with me tonight?' He holds my gaze and says he'll have to do a couple of hours' work around 8 p.m. but after that, yes.

'Really?'

'Yes,' he confirms, looking deep into my eyes.

There he is! That's the man I met at the mall! I remember how good it felt to be entwined with him but find myself saying, 'I really think it would be better if I leave now.'

He looks heartbroken. Devastated even. Suddenly I suspect there are real feelings in there – I just need to be a little more patient at nurturing them. God, what if all this is partly my fault? He is a bit younger than me – maybe he's just cautious. Maybe he's nervous too, and that's why he's holding back. So I cave. Apparently my brain stops functioning when someone is holding my hand.

Emboldened by his display of emotion, I ask if we can go for a picnic by the lake in Cazenovia. Initially he looks doubtful – I get the impression that it's a little more effort than he had in mind – but then he concedes it'll be idyllic in the sunshine.

As I drive he puts his hand on my leg. This disturbs me intensely (and not for the obvious reasons of shuddering jelly thighs). I've only been driving a year and have never driven a boyfriend-type before. I've sat in the back seat and witnessed it a thousand times with my mum and her boyfriend, and Emily and her fellas, and generally rolled my eyes or felt excluded or a little embarrassed, as if I'm intruding. When I was younger I used to wonder what it would feel like – in a way it represented the true sign of coupledom. It's such an understated, passive affection and yet makes such a statement – 'I'm sitting but a few inches away from you and it's not enough, I have to reach out and touch you even though we should be thinking about traffic lights and directions.'

I laugh out loud. This 'First' alone has made the trip worthwhile.

Suddenly I find myself looking on the bright side and as my old self returns I begin chattering in a chipper manner. Paul also seems to relax, laughing at my silly jokes, and by the time I park the car beside Cazenovia's languid lake, we're smiling for real. This is all just a silly game. I can now see that when he pulls away or blanks me I get hysterical as if he represents every man who has ever rejected me and I have to win him back at all costs. But when he plays along with me and I am no longer blinded by neediness I can step back and see him objectively. And you know what? He's really nothing special. Oddly this realisation pleases me – I like to think it diminishes his power over me. That is, of course, until the next time he blows from hot to ice-cold . . .

We eat our sandwiches and watch a boat glide across the water, then as the sun sets a chill creeps over us and I suggest we go back and Paul does his few hours' work. Instead he directs me to TGI Friday's and suggests a few beers. I'm triumphant! We down Budweiser and talk about the wildly different ways we'd spend a million dollars – me travelling round the world with an entourage of friends and family, him putting it in the bank after buying a modest house where his mates could hang out. As we chat I realise I'll be entirely satisfied to snuggle up to him tonight and then say goodbye forever the next morning. Things will have run their course and we'll part on good terms. It's all working out for the best. Who would have thought it?

Once again his dad drops me off. More kissing in reception and a request that I call him at 10 p.m. Perfect – I'll check back in, watch a sitcom or two and then fall into his arms.

I wave him off and turn to the receptionist – 'I know this sounds crazy but I checked out this morning and now I'd like to check back in. My luggage is in the storeroom.'

She looks pained and informs me they have no vacancies.

'Not one?' I balk.

'Not one,' she tells me.

Get me a four-leaf clover because I'm all out of luck. I must look like a woman on the verge of a nervous breakdown because she pauses for a moment and then adds, 'Hold on, let me ask the manager something.' She comes back and tells me there's a small conference room with a sofa bed. It's got a TV so I take it.

I watch the clock tick past the hour of ten enjoying my newfound laissez faire attitude – I no longer feel like I'm holding the losing hand. And at 10.30 p.m. he calls me. I'm in high spirits but our banter is cut short when his mate John turns up.

'Can I call you back in ten minutes?' he asks.

'Certainly, sir!' I chirrup and run over the road to the garage for some late-night snacks for us.

No messages when I get back but I'm not worried – obviously John will stay longer than ten minutes. At 11 p.m. I decide to give him a bell in case he called and reception bungled the message. His dad answers the phone.

'Oh hello, is Paul there?'

'No, he's gone out with John.'

Some relentlessly optimistic part of me presumes that means he's on his way over here. John must be giving him a lift. I wait and wait. Nothing.

At first I'm strangely calm but then I become incensed that he 'tricked' me into staying another night, wasting yet another eighty dollars. The only possible explanation is that he has shares in Holiday Inn. What other motivation would he have? I was on my way to the airport and he begged me to stay just so he could let me down again. WHY? WHY? WHY?

If this is emotional abuse I could sure show him some physical abuse right now. I *despise* him. Over the last four days my emotions have been put through a liquidiser – I never knew misery had such a range. I haven't known whether to cry or just collapse in a twitching defeated heap. Now I'm just a pulp of raw despair.

My mum always talks about life lessons. What has this experience taught me? Not to take risks? Not to follow my heart? I can only see the negatives, like how desperate I must have been for some love. And that really seems to be the most pertinent issue here – it wasn't for the sex, it was the affection that I craved. Apparently I'm prepared to spend nearly one thousand dollars to have someone hold my hand.

CONVENT,
LOUISIANA

After my harrowing experience with Perforated Paul in Cazenovia, it seems only logical that I should want to join a nunnery. And what better date to commit to a lifetime of celibacy than Valentine's Day?

'Just as well you're not taking this trip with Emily,' James notes as he heaves my suitcase into the taxi. 'She's about as un-nun as they come!'

'You're right!' I acknowledge, sticking my head out the window for a farewell peck. 'And to think I was worried Kerry wouldn't be slutty enough – she couldn't be better suited to Convent!'

As I trundle off to the airport I muse upon just how much Kerry reminds me of Meg Ryan's youngest incarnation in *When Harry Met Sally* – she has the same breezy innocence and ideals, only with short brown hair and the most singsong of Scottish accents. It turns out she's even nicely primed for celibacy, having just endured a painful split from her boyfriend of seven years.

'I'm so sorry!' I tell her at Gatwick airport when she greets me with the news that she's now single. 'I had no idea!' We're such new friends I didn't even know she had a current boyfriend.

'I'm so sorry for you,' she contends, having just learned the full humiliating saga of Paul.

We spend the flight from London to New Orleans (Convent's nearest airport) bonding over our respective rejections, though hers certainly puts mine in perspective. I can't even imagine what it must be like to break up with someone you've spent a third of your life with (Kerry turns twenty-three tomorrow) and from what she tells me of her ex's behaviour, she's in even more need of a voodoo doll and a set of pins than me. It therefore seems appropriate that we plan to linger a night in N'Awlins where an estimated fifteen per cent of the natives practise that ancient African snake-revering religion. And what with Bourbon Street copping a Mardi Gras attitude all year round, this will be the ideal spot for a little last-minute debauchery. (Well, there's no point in choosing a life of chastity and purity if you don't have a few sins under your belt – every churchgoer needs something to ask forgiveness for.)

'So tell me again about this graveyard dating agency . . .' Kerry prompts as we link arms and go in search of St Louis Cemetery No. 2.

'Well, it's not like someone's set up an office in one of the vaults, it's rather more ethereal than that.'

'Go on,' Kerry gulps.

'The idea is you go to the tomb of Marie Laveau –

New Orleans' foxiest voodoo priestess – knock three times to wake the dead . . .' I pause to let Kerry shudder '. . . then etch a cross in red.'

'Then what happens?'

'Marie's spirit grants the wishes of any woman looking for a husband,' I say, trying to sound sufficiently dramatic.

'No forms to fill out, no video monologues?'

I shake my head.

'Sounds cool.'

This isn't right – Kerry's far too chipper. I obviously need to get more ghoulish if we're to approach the tomb with sufficient reverence. 'Do you know why all the dead bodies in New Orleans are buried in above-ground crypts?' I ask, trying to channel Christopher Lee.

'Do I want to know?' Kerry looks wary.

'It's because New Orleans sits below sea-level and early settlers found that if they buried the corpses in the ground they would eventually bob up to the surface. Can you imagine a nose or an arm poking through the earth? It would be just like in the *Thriller* video!' I come to a halt and look both left and right. 'Didn't we just come down this street?'

We stare up at the legacy of lacy balconies. All these French Quarter streets look the same – shuttered windows, arches of wrought-iron filigree, and hanging baskets spilling tickly ferns and blooms of purple velvet. All proudly jutting American flags and concealing shady courtyards with rippling fountains. All absolutely gorgeous. I sigh. It really is too perfect a sunny day to be mincing around mausoleums. If we don't have any luck at the end of this street we'll give up and go in search of some of New Orleans' famously fabulous food. (Besides, I saw on the Internet that you can just download the picture of Marie's grave and use the paint programme to make the crosses.)

'So what kind of husband would you like Marie to conjure for you?' I quiz Kerry as we turn down Rue Royal.

'Someone good-looking, trendy, arty, a bit cocky. Preferably a musician.'

I open my mouth to warn her off every character trait she's just uttered but instead prompt, 'Like . . . ?'

'Roddy from Idlewilde,' she simpers, looking faint with lust.

I wouldn't know him if he jumped out of a lobster bisque and put a hex on me but I nod anyway.

'What about you?'

I'm about to tell her how I want someone who can make me cry with laughter and kiss for three hours straight when Kerry emits a blood-curdling scream – we may not have found the cemetery but we've located the New Orleans Historic Voodoo Museum, complete with alligator-head 'juju' above the front door.

'I don't think I can go in,' Kerry says nervously, peering into the eerie interior.

'Oh come on, how bad can it . . . be,' I falter as an ashen-faced woman exits at speed.

I always thought it would be a lark to stock up on gris-gris and passion-inducers but this place is so freakin' freaky it's not funny. Both the Occult and Altar rooms are crammed with carved African totems, death masks, skulls, skeletons, crucifixes, beads, bongo drums, glass jars containing unidentifiable putrid objects and dusty cases displaying decaying bones, teeth and shedded snakeskins – basically all manner of things to make you go, 'Ugghhh!' When I discover just how many of the assembled concoctions and desiccated animal parts are designed to make someone love you, I realise that a) I am far from alone in my quest – centuries of women have felt my frustration – and b) I'm not as desperate as I thought I was. I just couldn't go this far. Even if I was guaranteed the result I desired, it would ultimately feel like cheating and I'd constantly be living with the fear that 'he' would wake up from the spell and do a runner. Besides, what kind of message are you sending yourself if you think the only way to make a man love you is to drug him? I'd rather wait for the man who volunteers his heart. (Mind you, had I been offered a sure-fire bring-him-back love potion the day husband-material Nick left me for the spin instructor I might have wavered.) Just as well there is no such thing as voodoo Avon ladies making house-calls to the recently broken-hearted.

As I sidestep the wishing stump I decide that for now I'll stick to twentieth-century love voodoo in the form of syrupy lipgloss, push-up bras and pheromone-heavy perfume.

'What are you doing?' I catch Kerry rattling a rickety cupboard door in the corner.

'I just wondered what the "pretty white" thing was inside,' she shrugs, pointing at a plaque marked *Jolie Blanche*.

I'm about to leave her to her amateur break-in when I sense some movement behind the mesh panel of the door.

'Kerry!' I screech, yanking her away just as a giant albino python rears its spitting, yellow-scaled head.

'Oh my God! Oh my God!' Kerry spins around; not knowing which way is out. Fortunately I do and we exit with equal velocity and pallor to the ashen-faced woman.

Just as well we're so close to Bourbon Street – we need a drink.

'Why don't they just label it SNAKE instead of *Jolie Blanche*?' Kerry knocks back her shot with a shaky hand.

'Would you wear a name-badge saying HUMAN instead of Kerry?' I retaliate.

'I suppose not,' she pouts, wincing as the tequila hits home. 'Come on, let's get something to eat.'

We follow our noses to Petunia's – a baby-pink Creole townhouse serving 'the world's largest crepes': bulgy fourteen-inchers oozing with bright orange cheese. We order a pair and then instantly regret it – as with many outsize American platters, one look at the monstrosity before you so daunts your stomach it ends up cowering behind a hip bone whimpering, 'I know I said I was hungry but I've changed my mind!'

We look up at our blond Frankenstein's monster of a waiter as if seeking help.

'Enjoy!' he says with an evil glint.

'Is he good-looking or scary? I can't decide.' I watch him as he manoeuvres his six-foot-five frame around the wonky-legged tables, ducking his large forehead under the gabled doorways.

'There's something about him,' Kerry concedes, though she's not entirely sold on his shaven-sided ponytail.

The third time he stops by to check on us we decide to take the conversation beyond, 'Mmm, lovely, cheese!' and ask him if he's ever been to Convent. He hasn't.

'We were thinking of dressing up as nuns when we go, what do you think?' Kerry gets bold.

He shrugs, unfazed. 'An old girlfriend of mine used to do that – wear a nun outfit and go bar-hopping.'

'Did it work?' I ask.

'What do you mean?'

'Did it help her pick up guys?'

He looks stricken. 'She'd never do that. She was going out with me!'

'Oh, sorry,' I fluster. 'So, why the habit then, was it for you?'

'No,' he growls looking stern. 'She just liked making fun of nuns.'

'I think I may have blown it!' I grimace as he stomps off.

'Don't worry – I think we might be chatting him up for the sake of it. You don't really fancy him, do you?'

'Not a jot,' I confess, realising she's right. 'Shall we get the bill?'

Kerry looks down at our plates – neither of us have ingested more than a spoonful of the cheese-drenched asparagus but already our insides feel coated with glue.

'Let's go,' she nods, respectfully veiling her plate with her napkin.

'Are you ladies familiar with the Southern tradition of communicating your love messages with a fan?' Weird Waiter suddenly reappears at our side, all former grievances seemingly forgotten. (I've known cats like that – you piss them off and they look at you with such utter disdain you'd think they were going to ignore you for the rest of their life, then two minutes later they're all giddy and nuzzly over you.) 'It was very popular in the 1800s among the upper classes,' he begins his tableside lecture. 'You can signal twenty or so terms – a fan placed near the heart means "You have won my love", a closed fan touching the right eye is "When may I be allowed to see you?", putting the fan handle to your lips is "Kiss me!"'

'Wow – what a minefield!' I'm not entirely sure why he's launched into this little bit of history, but I don't want to be rude. 'It must have been like being at an auction – one wrong twitch and you're in real trouble!'

He nods enthusiastically. 'But if you understood the nuances it was an excellent way of communicating with strangers. The guys knew which girls to go up and talk to because they'd already let them know they were interested – as soon as they walked into the ballroom the ladies would take their fan in their left hand and place it in front of their face and that would mean, "I am desirous of your acquaintance."'

'Really?' I raise my eyebrows in fascination – I might start a campaign to bring back the fan – then quickly duck them down under my brow, concerned that he might be trying to convey a little message himself.

'Um, can we get the check please?' I falter, eager to avoid any awkwardness.

He hands us the bill directly.

As I rummage in my brand new handbag for my purse I notice the plastic tag still looped around the shoulder strap.

'Er, excuse me, do you have a pair of scissors I could quickly borrow?'

'Sure, I get off about 6 p.m.,' he replies.

What?

'Um, I just need to cut this off my bag?' I try again, this time holding up the relevant prop and making snippy motions with my fingers.

'Yeah, no problem – I'd be happy to show you round.'

Kerry emits a snuffle of disbelief. He must think we're speaking in code! I daren't say any more for fear of how he might interpret my words. Instead I simply lay the money on the table, get to my feet (motioning for Kerry to do the same) and then back away smiling and nodding until we reach the door.

'What was that?' Kerry splutters as we erupt into the outside world.

'No idea. But I tell you one thing, we'd better find a good hiding place at six o'clock.'

Although I'm mildly disconcerted, it occurs to me that if this sort of reading between the lines is typical of New Orleans it could actually be a real plus – my big obstacle with Cowboy Casey was finding a way to tell him how much I liked him, yet here the guys seem to get the message even when you're not conveying one.

Following a matinee performance of Cirque Du Soleil's *Dralion* (just in case the nunnery doesn't work out we thought we'd have the circus as backup) and a stroll along the muddy milkshake that is the Mississippi, we return to our hotel. And what a hotel! I can't imagine a more perfect place to stay in New

199

Orleans than Soniat House. It is so typically French Quarter in its courtyards and balconies yet the design flair sets it apart. Our room has its own forty-foot wooden corridor suggestive of servants with silver trays, leading to a bedroom with a four-poster painted aqua gloss with a canopy of ruched white silk flaring out from a central knot. The walls are crème caramel and khaki, the rugs vibrant pinks, oranges and greens . . . There's a pair of outsized sliding panelled doors opening onto a drawing room with a scarlet sofa and a Louis XIV chair re-covered in a tweedy combat print. Push aside the heavy floral drapes and you step out onto a veranda that could accommodate a cocktail party of twenty. That's it, I'm done. I want to live here. I work out it would only cost me five thousand pounds a month to rent this room – a snip considering how much it does my heart good just to be experiencing such high-ceilinged splendour.

The icing on the cake is the 'serve yourself' bottle of champers downstairs in the reception room. Having showered and slipped into night attire, we chink glasses then head to Bourbon Street in search of a traditional jazz bar. There's no shortage of options – every other venue has a live musical act, some more accomplished than others – but one song calls to our very souls: Bon Jovi's 'Keep The Faith'.

'I think someone's trying to tell us something!' I chuckle as we forgo puff-cheeked trumpeters and jangly piano men in favour of a bunch of frazzle-haired rockers revamping the 80s.

'Foreigner, Heart, Guns 'n' Roses,' Kerry identifies each medley segment with ease. 'It's just like being back at Matchmakers in Orkney!' she cheers – rather worryingly considering Kerry was only seven when Axl and co were at their peak.

As we lean on the bar and let the music surge through us, I give the band a look-check – I love the electrocuted mane and shredded-tonsil vocals of the wild-man singer but have to acknowledge that his type would probably be more a *Coyote Ugly* gal thrust into jeans and busting out of a tight leather waistcoat, as opposed to me wafting around in one of my floor-skimming skirts. However, the audience appears to comprise about five guns to every rose so there must be someone here for us . . . Aha! I lock onto a semi-attractive suspect jutting his jaw in time to 'Sweet Child o' Mine'. As I reach to alert Kerry, a body blocks my pointing finger and a low voice enquires, 'Can I get you girls a drink?'

For a second Kerry and I are too stunned to speak – the man doing the asking has supernaturally blue eyes, a jet-black quiff and cheekbones like an alpine crevasse. And he's offering to buy us drinks? I'd keep him in Jack and Coke just for the privilege of looking at him.

'Actually we just got one,' we gulp transfixed, holding up our glasses.

'Oh well,' he shrugs and turns to walk away.

'Wait!' I squeak. 'We can still talk to you . . .'

He slays us with a wolfish grin. 'I'll get my friend over.'

'I can't believe he came up to us,' I mutter, still in shock.

'His friend's not even that bad,' Kerry observes as he leads a tawny-haired tag-along through the crowd.

Our attempted salutations are drowned out as the singer puts the deaf in Def Leppard so we step out onto the street where we're only contending with general hubbub and the occasional crackle of plastic drinking cups underfoot. That's one of the excellent bonuses of boozing on Bourbon Street: not only can you take your drinks out onto the street but you can walk them into the next bar, no problem. Or rather, 'No worries, mate' as our suitors might say – both are Australian. For a moment my heart sinks – strictly speaking they don't fit with our American Dream Guy mission. But then the Elvis-alike turns the full force of his Superman-blue eyes on me and the jolt to my heart resets my brain – he's *in* America, isn't he? That's close enough! I think it's about time I knew his name.

'I'm Kane,' he growls.

'I'm yours,' I want to gurgle back. Could there be a sexier name than Kane?

Actually yes – Kane Mason. How stone-sculpted stunning is that? It suits him so well. He tells us that his travels were due to have taken him to New York by now but he ran out of money and is thus having to fund the next leg of his trip with bar work. He's actually a cameraman by trade. Even does a bit of acting, which I suspect he's rather good at.

As we get jostled by a conga-ing bachelorette party, Kane recommends we relocate to his joint.

'It's less hectic and I can get us cheap drinks there.'

I look to Kerry for her approval – for a while it seemed that she was equally entranced with Kane, and who could blame her? He's sassy and challenging as well as a looker – but now she's nowhere to be seen.

'Over here!' she calls from the bar across the street. She's yappering away to a man with a shaved head and Dexy's Midnight Runners dungarees while beckoning us frantically.

'We have to go in!' she insists, grabbing at our cuffs.

'Why?' Kane frowns, unconvinced – from our vantage point it seems the tinpot band is scaring off more punters than it's drawing in.

'Because it's my birthday!' Kerry states, as if that is all the reason we need.

I look at my watch – and she's right. Midnight does indeed make it February 13th.

'Happy Birthday!' I embrace her, finding myself manoeuvred inside while still in her arms.

I'm relieved to see that the boys follow and Kane treats Kerry to some ookie-looking cocktail, watching with glee as she slugs it back.

'What was in that?' I ask him, mildly concerned.

'No idea,' he shrugs. 'I just liked the clash of colours.'

Kerry is like a beguiling child when she's drunk – all wide-eyed and winsome with exaggerated cartoon expressions. It's hard to take your eyes off her. Kane pulls his chair a little closer and asks what it's like having a birthday so close to Valentine's Day. My heart sinks – obviously I want them to get along and I appreciate him paying her special attention on her birthday but don't leave me out in the cold, please!

'What's that lovely smell?' Kane enquires, leaning closer to Kerry.

'Lenor,' she replies.

'Really?' Kane inhales deeply. 'You could sell that on the street – three bucks a sniff!'

She looks chuffed. My stomach gnarls with jealousy. I don't know Kerry well enough to know whether she'd step back on account of me liking someone or whether she would simply seize the opportunity and run with it. Maybe she's just being polite – she can't very well ignore him. Maybe she doesn't even know that I like him. It was so much easier with Emily – she knew instantly when I was keen and would always do everything in her power to help me snare my prey. It didn't matter that the men always fawned over her first because we had such opposing tastes; things always worked themselves out in the end. The trouble is, I don't know what I'm dealing with here and it's making me anxious. I just hope we don't have identical taste. I get a chill at the possibility. Competing for a man's attention leaves me cold – I hadn't even considered this might be a problem because I'm so much older than Kerry (twelve years to be precise) but then again I always seem to go younger and if she favours older then we're going to meet in the middle and—

'Another round?' I grab the passing waitress.

The gang nods their approval, now embroiled in 'worst Valentine's Day' anecdotes. Kane had a corker in his late teens – caught his girlfriend snogging his best mate.

'That's terrible!' I cry. 'Double whammy!'

'They ended up together too,' he sighs.

Oddly I'd have thought that makes it slightly more bearable – at least it wasn't just a meaningless encounter.

'What did you do?' Kerry asks, looking concerned.

'Went off with *his* girlfriend,' he shrugs.

204

Well, it's only logical.

My worst V-Day was spent with a relatively new boyfriend (someone I'd met giving out salsa samples in a health-food store) who I was actually on the verge of dumping (he was a little troubled, it has to be said) but the novelty of having someone to spend Valentine's Day with was incentive enough for me to hang in there for at least one more day. Anyway, we went to this Thai restaurant, got a little tiddly (a lot tiddly) and then went home and slept with each other for the first time. Afterwards he seemed particularly eager to get a detailed critique of his performance. When I asked him why, he said, 'That was my first time.'

I was mortified! Having been cruelly dumped directly after my first time I couldn't conceive of doing the same to him so the relationship limped on for several more weeks. (Though we never again did the deed.)

'Other than that it's just been generic cardless misery,' I conclude.

'It's funny isn't it,' Kane notes. 'Considering February fourteenth is supposed to be a celebration of *amore*, the majority of people never feel more unloved.'

As we continue on to cheerier topics, Kane seems to be flick-flacking between Kerry and myself, as though he is undecided about who to go for – one minute he seems to be giving me a special look and the next his body is fully addressing her. Maybe ten years on women are still inter-changeable commodities to him? (I almost forget that his friend is available for the runner-up – Matt isn't really contributing much in the way of personality or sexual magnetism.) Focusing on squeezing lime into my drink, I tell myself this is not a popularity contest and Kane should be free to find attractive whoever his hormones favours. But do you think if I wish hard enough – *Choose me! Choose me!* – it might have some effect? I really do like him. (For a guy, he seems to possess more than the usual supply of sass.)

In my favour, Kerry's other main trait when drunk is flitting off every few minutes to strike up a conversation with a total stranger. She's like a drive-by flirter, entrancing every passing male then casting him aside. At one point she's gone for a good fifteen minutes and then returns looking like a metal-plated armadillo.

'What the . . . ?' I gawp at her torso of ridged armour.

'It's a rubboard!' she announces grinning from ear to ear. 'I was just on stage playing zydeco – that's a type of Creole music!'

'Why didn't you tell us?' I wail. I can't believe I missed her Bourbon St debut.

'You were great up there,' a girl steps up and drapes an arm around Kerry's shoulder. 'We want you to have these as a souvenir.'

She hands her a pair of bent spoons bound together with silver masking tape.

Kerry wells up with gratitude.

'Er . . . ?' I prompt her, mystified as to their significance.

'This is what you use to play zydeco!' she says, giving us a lively strum on her washboard stomach.

I can't help but marvel at Kerry. She is truly someone who could benefit from becoming an alcoholic – booze gives her twelve times her usual quota of energy and mischief and makes her practically irresistible to all mankind.

'Water?' I say, offering her a large glass.

'I think I'll have another vodka.'

'I don't want you to get too dehydrated!' I say, peddling the diluter.

'Let's go on to my bar,' Kane suggests.

As we step out onto the street, Kane links arms with me. Now that's a new move on me! I've known guys to cradle your elbow in their palm to guide you somewhere or surreptitiously take your hand to show that he cares but this linking arms feels more akin to shopping with the girls. Is this Kane testing the water with me without actually laying it on the line? It could just be pally-casual and yet I'm secretly hoping this means he has indeed chosen me.

'Oh dear God!' I suddenly avert my eyes.

'What is it?' Kerry gasps.

'That woman just flashed those guys!'

Kane gives a nonchalant shrug. 'Welcome to Bourbon St.'

'No, look – *that* woman. The middle-aged, conservatively dressed one with the grey-haired husband.'

'Noooooo!' Kerry can't believe it and instantly darts in her direction.

I watch her march straight up to the woman, tap her on the shoulder and boldly demand, 'You never just flashed those guys, did you?'

The woman responds by lifting up her jumper and giving Kerry a bumper eyeful of pendulous, crepey breast. I snort with shock and mirth, and I swear Kerry's eyes actually leave their sockets.

'D-d-did you see that?' she stammers, returning to us with a look of such horror it could well be etched on her face till next birthday.

'Well, you did ask,' Kane tuts. 'They're probably after a threesome.'

'Och nooo!' says Kerry, sounding more Scottish than ever. 'I need another drink.'

This one she's earned.

Once inside Kane's bar we take a seat at a small table by the window while he does the deal with the barman. When he joins us he immediately pulls the spare chair round to my side of the table and turns it to face me so we're sitting knee-bumping-knee. Kerry is occupied coaxing a conversation out of Matt and thus oblivious to our intimacy. As we chat – mostly about films – he takes my hand and my insides do a trampoline-style *b-doinng*! A smile creeps onto my face and I try to hold his gaze to show I'm not fazed. This develops into a staring contest. Weirdly, I feel like one of his eyes is emitting a warm, sexy glow while the other is more reticent and assessing. It throws me, I blink, he wins.

As Kane loudly congratulates himself on his victory, Kerry looks over – smiley, happy, still full of beans . . . until she clocks our clasped hands. Her face instantly falls.

'I'm really tired, I'm going to go.'

'What?' We're all equally startled. 'But it's your birthday.'

'I need to go to the loo.'

'Go to the loo here,' I say, pointing to the rest rooms.

'No, I'll go when I get back to the hotel.'

'It's quite a hike,' I caution her.

'I'll be fine.' She gets to her feet.

'You can't walk back by yourself,' I reprimand, yanking her back down.

'Yes I can.'

'Do you even know the way?' I may not know Kerry well but one thing is certain: she has the all-time worst sense of direction. She's more likely to end up at Marie Laveau's grave than Soniat House.

I sigh heavily. 'I'll come with you.'

'No, stay. You obviously want to.'

Oh it's like that is it? I feel a flicker of irritation. It's not like I'm doing anything illegal! This is what we came on this trip for – a little bit of love.

'We'll all go.' Kane gets to his feet, saving the day.

Or so I think.

Instead of the four of us strolling back enjoying the last of the magnolia-scented evening, Kerry power-walks ahead, stiletto heels grinding indelible grooves into the paving slabs. I'm torn between enjoying Kane's attention and fretting about Kerry. This passive-aggressive sour-graping is really getting to me. I don't know what to say to bring her round – a couple of times I try and catch her up but she just marches faster. I feel like I've done something wrong but strictly speaking I'm not sure what – she didn't even seem that interested in Kane after the zydeco incident. Maybe it's not him per se, maybe it's just that I appeared to be with someone when she wasn't. Maybe that doesn't usually happen to her. Plus everyone gets a little unhinged on their birthday.

As we quick-march along, Kane continues to chat easily. A couple of times there's a lull that I would normally fill with one of my over-zealous showpieces but instead I take a breath and smile, happy to find that with Kane I don't have to take the conversational lead every time. I even feel comfortable just strolling without talking nineteen-to-the-dozen which is a rarity for me.

'Listen, mate – this hotel is further than I thought.' Matt stops and leans his weary bones against a set of park railings. 'I think I'm going to head back to the bar.'

'OK,' Kane shrugs and goes to walk on.

'Bu-but . . .' Matt halts him. 'I don't want to walk back by myself.'

Great! Now we're being pulled in both directions.

'I'm walking the girls back no matter what. It's your choice,' Kane states simply.

I love him! That was so manly! So direct!

Matt groans then stumbles onward with us. By now Kerry is so far ahead she's actually back at the hotel. The rest of us loiter on the pavement below our balcony and I point up to our room, tell them how fabulous it is then apologise for not being able to invite them up.

'Now she's safely back you have to come for a drink with me,' Kane insists.

'I can't!' I shake my head.

'Why not?' he sighs.

'It's her birthday, I can't leave her on her birth-day . . .'

'But she'll be asleep in five minutes.'

210

He's right. So what's stopping me?

I hear the balcony door creak open and Kerry peeks down at us. I wave up to her – what a wonky Romeo and Juliet scenario this has turned out to be. She disappears back inside without a word.

I sigh. I can't remember when I last felt this disapproved of. It's like she's my mum and I'm the slutty, errant daughter hanging with the wrong crowd. I suppose I should get inside before I'm grounded, and yet I can't bring myself to leave Kane without a kiss. But how is that going to happen with Matt standing by impatiently tapping his fingers?

'Please come with us,' Kane steps closer.

I take a chance and snuggle into his chest for a hug. Matt makes a grumbly gooseberry noise and edges away. Sensing a tiny window of opportunity I tilt my head up towards his so there are no obstacles between his mouth and mine. He continues to try and persuade me to go with them and, despite the fact that he's stroking my hair away from my face, I continue to insist that I can't – this is mine and Kerry's first night away together, I can't risk peeving her so early on in our trip. He sighs, a picture of frustration. I snuggle closer to him and he finally gets the hint. As his lips meet mine I hear a noise on the balcony and a door slams but instead of leaping back guiltily I fall further into him. His kiss is perfection. I find myself smiling inwardly – this is just the tonic I needed after Punctured Paul: someone gorgeous wanting me but taking nothing from me. Neither of us are particularly drunk by this point, just consenting, content. My hand creeps up to rumple his hair but strikes wax even at the base of his neck so my fingers retreat and discreetly wipe themselves on his sweatshirt. Again I smile to myself. This is great – I don't feel nervous or wobbly or too yearning. I'm just enjoying the moment.

'Oh come on!' Matt hisses.

We part.

'Can I see you tomorrow? Or I suppose that's actually later today?' Kane breathes into my ear.

'We're going to Convent,' I explain.

'When are you coming back?'

'Well, it depends how things go there, maybe V— um, the fourteenth. But not until late afternoon.'

'Meet me. *Please*.'

Oh my God – don't look now but I've got a man lined up for Valentine's Day! I grin joyfully.

'Is that a date?' he whispers.

I nod, longing to kiss him some more. His shoulders are so broad and his back feels so strong beneath the fabric. I can just imagine—

'Kane!' Matt snaps.

He rolls his eyes, kisses me tenderly and then disappears into the night.

For a while I just stare after him. I feel so vindicated. With one kiss Kane has vanquished the anguish of Paul, both re-balancing me and giving me a renewed sense of optimism. I should do this more often – pick cashmere over acrylic – it's so much more satisfying to brush up against quality. But then my smile fades. I have to face Kerry.

She's still awake, sitting up in bed watching me closely as I bumble around the room.

'You don't really like him, do you?' she scoffs.

212

'Actually . . .' I begin. 'No, of course not,' I correct myself.

'Are you going to see him again?'

Of course! I want to cheer. But I say, 'Probably not.'

I'm just about to slip between the covers when the phone rings. Who on earth would call at this hour?

'Answer it!' Kerry urges, up on her knees.

It's Kane, wanting to know the number of where we'll be staying when we get back to New Orleans. I tell him I'm not sure yet so he gives me the number for his hostel. He sounds so grinning, so lovely, so sexy. I have to turn away so Kerry can't see the glee on my face.

'Blimey, he's keen!' Kerry snorts when I put down the phone.

'He's just drunk, he'll forget the whole thing by the morning.'

Why do I feel obliged to cover up like this; it's crazy! I'm a grown woman! But I feel like I would be being selfish to pursue this – we've come out looking for love and yet if only one of us finds it, it seems the appropriate course of action is to sacrifice the man in the name of female friendship. It's so messed up. What is the answer to this? Travelling with someone who would actually be happy for you? Wouldn't that be nice! What about someone who already has a man? But then their heart wouldn't be in the game and it could bring up other resentments like, 'It's all right for her, she already has someone . . .' So much of it is how you feel about yourself. And some part of me clearly feels that I'm not allowed to put the guy first – it's not sisterly. I remember excitedly telling one of my closest

213

friends about a brand-new prospect and before I was halfway done she blurted, 'But if you go out with him then I'll be the only one without a boyfriend!'

I close my eyes feeling a little vexed, yet I can't deny the secret swirly happiness I'm feeling – I've got a special something going on in my heart and it feels wonderful.

We greet the new day with *café au lait* and *beignets* (a relative of the donut) on our sunny balcony. My suspicion that this is the most idyllic spot in all New Orleans is confirmed when the hotel's tortoiseshell cat joins us for a sprawl.

'Heaven!' I sigh, burying my toes in his warm fur.

'Come on Sister Belinda!' Kerry issues a chirpy reminder of our pledge to join a nunnery. 'We have to pack.'

I watch as Kerry zips her stiletto heels, Lenor top and zydeco spoons into her bag, confident now that she'll be leaving last night's tension in the room. I'm going to do the same – you can't help but feel renewed when confronted with a sky this magically blue.

Convent lies halfway between New Orleans and Baton Rouge, the state capital. We take Highway 18 which on the map looks like it wiggles alongside the Mississippi all the way, but in reality the mighty muddy river is rarely in view – we're lucky if we get the odd swamp.

'Not the most picturesque drive, is it?' Kerry stares out the window at the flat, balding terrain spiked with shivering trees.

Despite the bleakness of the winter landscape we

still get a kick out of the fact that we're driving in L'weezyanna. All we need now is a little radio zydeco for Kerry to tap her spoons to – I twist and tune the dial, locking onto a classic from local fiddling legend Doug Kershaw aka The Ragin' Cajun! According to the DJ his songs have even been broadcast in space – one of the US astronauts on Apollo 12 was a big fan.

The scenery gets a little more industrial at Lutcher, where vast cylindrical tanks cluster and rusting cranes appear to be elbowing at each other for prime position, and then, finally, a silver water tower with 'CONVENT' spelled in neat black paint guides us to our destination. Our humble expectations are temporarily skewed as we're confronted with a building that could easily be mistaken for The White House. In keeping with its grandeur, nature has supplied a magnificent brotherhood of oaks dripping skeins of wonderful wispy moss. It's only as we pause to admire these eerie grey beards that we notice a menacingly pronged fence perimetering the property.

'Do you think it's to keep people in or out?' Kerry queries, looking a little uneasy.

I can't tell, but after my experience in Scranton I have no interest in finding out. Kerry grips the dashboard as I supercharge our speed until the vista resumes its former trend of basic bungalows and sparse vegetation.

'Have you noticed that we're the only car on the road and we haven't seen a single person – nun or otherwise – for miles?' Kerry frowns. 'Does anyone actually live here?'

'There's an official population of two hundred and

fifty,' I inform her as we approach a church that looks like it could easily hold double that.

'Now this place is pretty snazzy.' Kerry eyes the striking redbrick structure featuring an array of cream arches, arranged at random and inset with foot-high statues.

According to the plaque it was built on the former site of St Michael's convent.

'Ooooh,' Kerry nudges me. 'Does that mean we're off the hook – no more nunnery!'

'Well, it's not like it's been replaced by a go-go bar,' I reply. 'I think we still need to do a little soul-searching.'

'Isn't that where we're staying?' Kerry points a few buildings ahead to the Poche (pronounced Po-shay) Plantation – Convent's only B & B and, yup, our home for the night.

It's a fairly modest set-up by *Gone With The Wind* standards but the classic white pillar and porch design (trimmed with smart ivy-green shutters) is a sprucey delight to our eyes. The entire property is bordered with a mile of white picket fence, prettying up an otherwise unadorned and element-ravaged lawn. I make a mental note to pop back in the summer when I fancy the borders will be blooming with roses.

As we step from the car to identify which of the cute guesthouses out back has been assigned to us, we're overwhelmed by the tranquillity of the place. It's no longer troubling us that there's no one around, instead we revel in the stillness.

'There's a note,' Kerry calls over to me, forging ahead. 'And a key.'

Our quarters far exceed our style expectations – we walk on glossy golden hardwood up to a pair of neat single beds, snug under white cotton counterpanes with canopies of muslin draping over the mahogany headboards. I love the contrast of dark and blond woods and the white is so fresh.

'Full kitchen unit, hi-tech TV, Jacuzzi tub in the bathroom,' Kerry checks off the features. 'And – oh ho ho!' Kerry cheers. 'Granny rockers on the porch!' This really is the perfect place to catalogue your sins and re-evaluate your life. If we weren't so hungry we'd stoke the fire and settle in till spring.

According to the leaflets fanned out on the side table, a joint called Hymel's is the only eatery in Convent. We clock the 3.5 miles as per the instructions and find ourselves drawing level with a sign saying 'TOMATOES FOR SALE'.

'I don't know about you but I fancy something a bit more substantial,' I jest.

Continuing down the road, we're forced to swerve to avoid a dead beagle (a horrible, horrible sight) then Kerry squeals, 'Hymens!'

'It's Hymels,' I correct her, following her gaze to a large prefab shack adjacent to a gas station – always nice to inhale petrol and exhaust fumes while you're eating.

Before we lose our nerve we tumble in, first to the dark bar, then through to the fluoro-lit restaurant. Against all odds it possesses real character, thanks to the team of stocky, sixty-something 'don't-mess-with-me' waitresses. Our old bird glares stoically as we scan the menu. I opt for twelve fried shrimp, which come

with a pale, dusty, spicy coating I haven't before encountered (they look like they've been rolled in a
sandpit) and a chaser of no-name ketchup which gives
off vinegary wafts when you squeeze the bottle. Kerry,
meanwhile, goes native and orders gumbo.

'You are brave,' I say, peering into her bowl of spicy
stew. To me it looks repugnant – like chunks of brain,
trotter and chicken claw bobbing in a dark rice-based
gravy.

'It's actually really nice,' Kerry insists, assuring me
that what I think is a curl of animal ear is just a slice of
sausage. 'Sure you don't want to—' She stops mid-
offering to hiss, 'Handsome hick alert!'

Through my streaming eyes I spy two guys take the
table nearest the jukebox. One of them is a dish, the
other looks a bit disturbed. Kerry agrees but has them
pegged the other way round.

'Your one's got village idiot hair,' she sneers at his
overly gelled-and-pinched Caesar fringe.

'Your one's got psycho eyes,' I shudder, turning
away. 'He looks like he's staring down the barrel of a
gun at us.'

Still, beggars can't be choosers – everyone else in the
place is middle-aged and pre-paired. And I know the
fact that we've exhibited different tastes should be a
huge source of relief to me but truth be told, I have
minimal interest in these guys since the memory of
Kane's kiss lingers so vividly on my lips. Not that Kerry
would be aware of this – we haven't mentioned the K-
word at all today, it still feels taboo and I don't want to
risk ruining the mood. So for now, I'm all for playing
along. Until Kerry suggests putting on a tune.

'Oh I couldn't!' I gasp, paralysed by horror. I'd feel like I was trying to recreate some movie scene – girl strolls up to the jukebox, gives the guy a heavy-lidded look then picks a song. No sooner has the disc clattered into place than he's by her side, so moved by the significance of her choice that he feels compelled to breathe softly on her neck and then ask her to dance . . .

'They've beaten us to it!' Kerry curses, pointing over to where 'my one' is resting a tanned, toned arm atop the box.

My eyes flit to his shorter, pastier buddy who seems to have a more urgent appointment in the Gents. We're on tenterhooks, eager to hear his choice and read some hidden message into the lyric, but the waitress cuts in, tugging at my guy's T-shirt and growling, 'Y'all settin' fire to the table!'

He looks back at the fast-melting melamine beneath his unguarded cigarette and yelps, 'Shoot!'

Why she didn't just stub it out is a mystery. Maybe this is how she teaches the young whippersnappers a lesson.

Just when we think we're going to go un-serenaded, out booms 'Too Legit To Quit'!

'MC Hammer?!' I splutter in disbelief. There's no way that qualifies as a romantic exchange so I turn my attention to the slab of Chocolate Suicide Cake – doubling as Kerry's birthday cake – that has been placed before us.

'Come on, we can do better than that,' Kerry rallies. 'To the jukebox!'

'I can't!' I bleat, despite a rapidly increasing

curiosity about the options lurking beneath the neon tubing.

'Oh don't be such a wuss! We'll be right by them, if we talk loudly enough they'll hear our accents and before you know it we'll be chatting.'

I take one more quick mouthful of cake, then, sucking the brown goo from my teeth, resignedly get to my feet. I feel absurdly self-conscious but it turns out the tortuous trek is worth it for the song titles alone – next time I'm feeling hard-done-by in love I'll know exactly what to pick:

'The Emptiest Arms in the World' by Merle Haggard, 'Mona Lisa Lost her Smile' by David Allan Coe and 'Lonely Too Long' by Patty Loveless. There's even a track called 'Love Voodoo' by Duran Duran which I'd be curious to hear, but in the end Kerry opts for her tried and trusted all-time fave: 'Hotel California' by The Eagles.

As predicted our accents do garner us attention, but it's the one young waitress whose curiosity is piqued. Her name is Heather and she's Britney-Spears-stunning with a bright, worldly quality whereas our boys – chums of hers it transpires – are the epitome of 'local'. Patrick (my one) is a shy-but-sweet builder whereas Kerry's John is a rather more intense army sniper (hence, I suppose, the permanent narrowing of his eyes). He tries to tell us about life on the front line but the deadly combination of his Louisiana twang and local slang means we're forced to rely on Heather to translate. Meanwhile I'm providing subtitles for Kerry – her Orkney accent leaves the trio gawping with a mixture of fascination and confusion. Overall, this doesn't make for the smoothest of conversations so I decide to ask my one key question before communication breaks down altogether: How do Louisiana natives differ from men from other US states, particularly in terms of dating?

'We're all about family,' Patrick states emphatically. 'It's the most important thing to us – a guy wouldn't even consider being with someone that didn't get along with his folks.'

'Are you serious?' Kerry can't believe it.

'Why would you pursue that kind of aggravation?' he shrugs. 'It's going to affect you every day of your life.'

Every day? This couldn't be more removed from my reality – my dad has met just one of my boyfriends (the cinema projectionist) and though my mum has encountered a few more likely lads, she's always reserved her true opinion until after we've broken up. In Louisiana, it seems the parents speak their mind from the word go.

'Oh yeah,' Heather agrees with a wry smile. 'And that goes for *not* having a boyfriend too – round here you're considered an old maid if you're not married by the time you're twenty-five.'

'What?' I splutter, shocked at how far beyond my sell-by date that makes me. I'm about to announce that it's different back in England but then I realise my own father would fit right in here – poor man, his shoulders slump every time I visit and he finds no husband or offspring bringing up the rear. (My stepmother's kids have already notched up four grandchildren and my dad – highly competitive by nature – seems to feel I'm letting the side down.) Lately he's started to imply that I'm being selfish and indulgent choosing a career over family, but honestly I never felt I *had* a choice – my writing has always been good to me but my relationships have always been bad.

I'm pulled out of my musings by the arrival of Patrick's girlfriend, who doesn't seem to like us. At All. So before she has Sniper slip her a weapon, Kerry and I return to the Poche Plantation with a view to perfecting our spinster rock on the porch.

'It's ironic,' I muse, handing Kerry a rug for her knees. 'I live in England's capital city where – statistically at least – I should have infinite mating options, and yet I can't find someone to have a crush on, let alone a relationship with. Meanwhile in Convent – population 250 – everyone is happily hooked up!'

'I know!' Kerry shakes her head. 'You'd think they would have exhausted every possible dating combo by the age of seventeen!'

'Maybe that's why they marry so young,' I surmise. 'There's no one new to play with.'

In the old days these youthful unions might have satisfied them for life, but with the modern day penchant for disposable commitment I'd give 'em ten years until they start eyeing someone else's husband or wife. That's what happened with my parents in the tiny Oxfordshire village where I lived till I was seven – one divorce prompted a whole domino-effect and before I knew it, my mum had switched to the man who lived beyond the cricket pitch and my dad opted for the woman whose cottage I walked past every day on the way to school. Not that these were fickle flings – my mum spent twenty years with the lovely Charles, and my dad is still with his soulmate Suzanne. Maybe these tiny towns are the answer after all.

There's certainly something extremely relaxing about knowing there's nothing to do for miles – you don't have to worry that you're missing out on anything. And after last night's excesses on Bourbon Street, the changing colours of the evening sky are all the entertainment we need. As the sun sets the serene blue-grey wash is slashed with burnished orange creating a glowing backdrop for the bare black branches of the trees to strike their poses like a pageant of multi-handed Thai goddesses.

'If only all hangovers could be whiled away in this manner,' I sigh as the last drip of gold melts into the horizon.

'I wonder how many die-hard romantics are doing what we're doing right now?' I muse out loud the next morning, my words echoing around the heaven-nudging arches of St Michael's Church.

'How do you mean?' Kerry turns to frown at me.

'Well, look at us – walking down an aisle on St Valentine's Day!'

Kerry laughs and links arms with me. 'Don't we make a lovely couple?'

'If this was Vegas they'd be queuing round the block, here it's just you and me.' I sigh. 'Not even a priest to have a *Thornbirds* moment over.'

'You know, I tend to forget there's a saint involved with February fourteenth,' Kerry harks back to the day's celebrations. 'Hallmark, Interflora and Thorntons have somewhat stolen his thunder.'

We take a pew and silently survey our environment. This is no humble place of worship – the interior is lavish with red carpeting, jewel-bright stained glass and a collection of elaborate grottoes and shrines. Ultimately our gaze settles on a petite painted nun statue, representing the Order of the Sacred Heart.

Hearts *should* be sacred, I decide. They should be treated with the greatest reverence, care and compassion. But instead they get pinched and shot at and stomped on. Paul must have known he was hurting me and yet he did it anyway. If I put myself back in the game there's a fair chance it could happen again. Like with Kane: right now the memory is perfect, but if I meet up with him tonight there's a risk it could end in tears. Even if it went well there's a new minefield of emotions to negotiate. Love is a dangerous game – the more you like someone, the more you stand to lose. So many times I've sworn, 'Never again!' but my heart – however crumpled – never truly accepts this, it still believes there is someone out there who it could flourish with. Can I really tell it to stop hoping? I don't think so.

I lean over to Kerry and let her know that our love pilgrimage is back on.

'So we don't have to forgo all male attention and dedicate ourselves to a life of abstinence?' she checks.

'Nope.' I shake my head.

'You don't think God will be disappointed?'

'Nah,' I say as I get to my feet. 'God's a woman, she'll understand.'

*

In a matter of hours we've swapped penance for decadence – checking into a deluxe suite at New Orleans' five star Windsor Court Hotel (recently voted 'Best Hotel in the World' by readers of *Condé Nast Traveller* – well, if ever a single girl needed to lavish herself with TLC in the form of goose-down pillows and chocolate-dipped strawberries it would be on Valentine's Day). I'm feeling rather swanky and optimistic but within a few hours my mood has changed entirely.

First there was a duff tarot reading in which Kerry was told she doesn't need a man at all and I learned that I was destined to marry an accountant. (I don't know which of us has the worse deal.) Then, over afternoon tea, I tried to bring up the subject of Kane, confessing 'I really am rather taken with him!' But Kerry just looked at me like I was mad and changed the subject. Secretly I was hoping for her blessing – I wanted her to say, 'You know what, if you like this guy you should be with him. You have to carpe diem when it comes to love!' That's what I would have done. I know that for a fact, because I've done it time and again for my friends, and as miserable as it is being the gooseberry, there's a certain virtue to knowing it's all in a good cause. Besides, when you're on an official manhunt, surely such gestures should be a given? Not as far as Kerry is concerned, it seems.

As we head off to The Praline Connection for an early dinner (to avoid the candlelit lovebird factor), I find myself getting increasingly antsy. Yesterday I thought I might be able to let this follow-up date go – I liked the idea that I could walk with a new-found

'Judge-me-not-on-who-I-can-get-but-who-I-can-let-go'
swagger, but now I'm back in New Orleans I'm feeling
a keen longing to see Kane again. It doesn't help that
our route takes us past where we met. Every other step
I find myself spasmodically checking my pocket to
make sure I still have his number. Somehow, some
way, I'm going to make that call.

'Oh look – Esoterica!' Kerry points out one of
New Orleans' most notorious voodoo potion/herb
emporiums, a place we had intended to visit on our
first day.

We're just about to creep inside (will we never
learn?) when a religious loony-tune leaps out at us,
ranting and screeching about saving our souls. In a bid
to avoid an evangelical lynching we dart into the cutie
boutique next door and an hour is promptly lost and
multiple purchases made as we get all Magpie-eyed
over the glitzy jewellery and bedazzled T-shirts. Our
rapture is heightened as we watch the *Rouge Beauty*
assistant wrap everything in sheaves of red tissue and
spirals of pink ribbon. Oh the joy of being a girl!

'Now, where were we . . . ?' We stumble dizzily onto
the street, venturing beyond the French Quarter into
a pretty residential neighbourhood with just enough
edge to make us feel that we've strayed from the
tourist trail into real life.

'Hey, this is slick!' I admire the stark monochrome
interior of The Praline Connection – checkerboard
flooring, those black lacquered chairs typically found
in cabaret-style dance sequences and staff sporting
cropped trousers, sharp shirts and tilted trilbies.

'How *Billie Jean*!' Kerry observes as the best-looking

man in the place takes our order then moonwalks to the kitchen. (Not really but I bet he could if he wanted to.)

Both our moods seem vastly improved and, having toasted each other with a glass of wine, Kerry pips, 'Let's have another look at what we just bought!'

We make a big show of clawing through the red tissue and cooing twinkly-eyed over the gifts within. And then I have an out-of-body experience – we're having dinner-à-deux on Valentine's night looking to all intents and purposes like we've just exchanged love tokens! Why does this keep happening to me?

'Kerry!' I hiss.

'What?' she says, still admiring the pink diamanté dove ring she's placed on her wedding finger, of course.

I quickly convey my concern.

'Oh my God – you're right!' she says, quickly snuffling our wares back into the bags.

We look furtively around the restaurant to see who might have clocked our ostentatious display – four women at one table, two at another, six at the long one in the corner. All with distinctive haircuts.

'I don't know what we're worrying about – looks like we'll fit right in here!' Kerry takes a large gulp of wine, then suddenly looks aghast. 'Maybe that's what the tarot lady meant when she said I didn't need a man!'

'Oh come on,' I reach to give her hand a reassuring squeeze. 'There's plenty more pecans in the pie – look at our waiter, he's divine!'

'Ladies . . .' He appears that very instant with our food.

All he needs now is for me to let go of Kerry's hand, then he can set the plates down.

'Happy Valentine's Day!' he says with a wink.

'Oh no! Now he thinks—' Kerry rolls her eyes.

Any remorse is soon sluiced away by saliva. Never was there a more steamy-fresh set of dishes – crawfish étouffée, stuffed crab, baby-back ribs, candied yams and the world's all-time-best macaroni cheese. This is 'down home' soul food at its best.

'You can stick your fourteen-inch crepes and sandpit shrimps, this is it!' I whoop after half-an-hour's contented chomping, now totally happy, not a little woozy and suddenly extremely fond of Kerry. Not in *that* way, I just seem to have lost the resentment I'd been feeling over the Kane issue. As we order another bottle of wine I decide it's silly to bear a grudge – so I lost a little ground with him the other night but I can make it up tonight. Mmmm, I get tingles just thinking about seeing him again. Suddenly love doesn't seem nearly so elusive. After all, all it takes is one person to turn things around. Right now I feel so much closer to the reality of being with someone and it makes me feel both reassured and tickled with anticipation at all the good things that are to come.

Our plan once back at the Windsor Court was a quick dolling up then a night of sophistication in the Warehouse District but the suite is so darn sumptuous we waste valuable time swanning like starlets around the acres of gold carpet and making unreasonable demands on our imaginary entourage. As the wine wears off, I once again hear the voice in my head nagging at me, 'When are you going to call Kane?' My stomach flip-flops as I realise I am running out of time. In order to talk freely I'm going to need an excuse to take me out of the room – what can it be? Maybe a run to the ice-machine? I'm about to try that line when Kerry announces that she's taking her turn in the marble-walled shower. This is my chance – I grab the phone and scoot through to the living area, burrowing deep into the kitchenette for maximum soundproofing. With a quaking hand I dial the number of his hostel. Engaged! *Nooo!* I dial again and again, intermittently darting back to the bedroom to hear if the shower is still powering in the bathroom. Finally, ringing. And a reply.

'H-hello, is Kane Mason there?' I feel all wobbly with urgency and eagerness to hear his voice.

There's a pause while the receptionist checks for him. 'No, sorry, he's gone out.'

I look at my watch. 9.45 p.m. Of course he's not going to be sitting in on a Friday night!

'Can I take a message?' the receptionist asks.

I hear the bathroom door open and Kerry emerge.

'No-no!' I clip, clicking off the phone and making exaggerated clinking noises within the minibar.

Oh why didn't I pay any attention to the name of his bar or the street it was on? I wouldn't have a hope of finding it again. I feel queasy-sick with the knowledge that I've blown it. My one chance to be with him again and he'll think I wasn't even that bothered. I rack my brains for a solution. There's only one thing for it – return to the scene of the crime! I have to persuade Kerry to go back to our hot-rocking Bourbon St bar.

Settling before the make-up mirror I feel somewhat shifty, as though I'm planning something illegal and underhand.

'It's nearly 10 p.m.,' I say, busying myself with shimmery eyeshadow. 'What time shall we aim to leave by? And where do you want to go?'

Kerry ceases the vigorous spritzing of her hair. 'Oh, shall we just go back to Bourbon Street?' she humphs. 'That way we can walk.'

'Really?' I can't believe my luck.

'If you don't mind?' she blinks her blue-blue eyes at me.

'No, no, not at all. I think it's a great idea.'

Bourbon Street was bawdy the first time we visited but now the crush is obscene. One bar, blaring out Eminem, is having an Anti-Valentine's Day party but Kerry suggests we bypass it in favour of a Van Halen voddy. Result! My heart starts to judder as we approach the bar. Oh please let him be there! Please let him be trying to find me in the crowd too. It's agony knowing that he could be just a few revellers away from me. My eyes scan the faces pressing past but not one has his striking features. I try to visualise him, imagining how it would be if our eyes met, how I'd propel myself into his arms and he'd bear-hug me back. I want so badly to feel his arms around me again – it was such a good feeling.

'Oh no!' Kerry wails, stalling at the entrance.

For a minute I think she's spied him but all too soon I share her distress. The rocker geezers have been replaced by a sleazy DJ on a mission to get the boozy girls he's lured on stage to flash flesh – be it booties or boobies – to the assembled mass of slack-jawed males. Kerry and I look on with disgust – you couldn't find an environment less conducive to true love.

'Shall we move on?' Kerry suggests.

I don't want to leave – there's still a trace of Kane in the air – but it feels too degrading to stay. Unfortunately every bar we enter has the same set-up. We're about to slump into despondency when Kerry does a double-take over a six-footer with a cool haircut. Sufficiently tipsy, she bowls straight up and sets about entrancing him with her drunken ingénue routine. It's working like a charm until a pair of fully-exposed 36DDs jiggle into view.

'How am I supposed to compete with *that*?' she reels, returning to my side.

I shrug. Any hope I may have had of bumping into Kane has now gone. I can't muster up any enthusiasm for new quarry so all I seek now is a distraction from my sad, regretful heart. And so, 'I think it's time for a little equal opportunities,' I say, leading Kerry across the street to a male strip revue.

'I've never been to one of these things before,' Kerry gulps, latching onto my arm as we pay the entrance fee and step beyond the rope.

Me, I've been to more strip shows than I care to count but never one like this – the venue is nothing more than a cordoned-off courtyard with a makeshift bar doubling as the stage. (Hence it's unwise to pull up a barstool unless you like your drinks with a twist of underpants.) We sit on a plastic garden chair under a tree at the back and brace ourselves for what has just sprung onto the bar top. At first I dismiss 'Rico' as a

231

skinny kid in bovver boots but seconds later I'd swear he was part-Spiderman as he skitters up the neighbouring brick wall with nothing but dollar bills to propel him on his way. He then gets resourceful with the few props he's got – pole dancing on the drainpipe and doing pull-ups and erotic twists while hanging from the balcony. Back on the bar, his dancing (both vertical and horizontal) exhibits the most ooo-inspiring display of muscle control and buttock-writhing. Kerry can't believe her eyes.

'He's amazing!' she gasps, genuinely impressed.

Next up is a big lumbering lug with no sense of rhythm. He looks so leaden and unsexy after Spiderboy but the group of middle-aged chicks down the front love his farmer-boy looks.

'Yeah! That's right!' To our left a woman is getting a private dance from what looks like a black WWF wrestler.

'Is that some kind of joke?' Kerry gawps at the bulge in his underwear. 'It can't be for real! And yet . . .' she tilts her head in closer inspection.

Meanwhile my eyes drift to the balcony two storeys above where a towering transexual is leading a bespectacled anorak to a room with a red light. Surely not? I did notice that we were next door to a trannie bar – hard to ignore the collection of supermodel-stunning six-footers outside touting for trade – but I thought they were just trying to get people into their club, not into bed. I can't take my eyes off the room with the red light; Kerry can't take her eyes off Mr Coke-Can's pants. Which is why we don't notice the semi-naked guy standing before us offering us a lap dance.

'So you want me to . . . ?' He flips a thigh over our heads.

'What?' we start, caught off guard.

'I could . . .' He makes another lunge.

'No-no!' I bark, halting his progress. 'Really, no need – we're fine, thank you very much.'

He moves on looking miffed.

'Oh now I feel bad,' Kerry sighs after him, looking fretful.

I blink at her in amazement, experiencing a full resurgence of resentment – she's actually more concerned about a stripper's feelings than my own! Boy did I make the wrong choice tonight. I didn't think it was fair for me to have someone on Valentine's Day and Kerry not, so we both went without. Now look at us! We're sitting in a place where you have to pay for affection! And it's all because of my own spinelessness, masked as consideration for others. I should have stood up for my heart. We could at least have come up with a compromise – us girls party till midnight and then I get the last dance with him.

I'm not saying men should take priority over friendship but the only friend worth making these kind of sacrifices for is the one who wouldn't ask it of you.

Well, I've learned my lesson: life isn't fair and feeling a real spark with a man is rare. Next time I get an opportunity like the one I had with Kane, I'm taking it.

KISSIMMEE, FLORIDA

No trip to Orlando's little sister Kissimmee would be complete without a visit to Disney World, or Walt-Mart as I like to call it. Now Disney World may not appear to be the most obvious place to pick up men, but according to a recent study the endorphin rush you get from theme-park rides is akin to the buzz of being in love and thus can perfectly set the mood for an attraction.

However, I suspect that sitting in a slowly rotating pastel teacup on the Mad Hatter's Tea Party ride may not quite qualify. With hindsight we probably would have fared better at the more adult-friendly Epcot but we couldn't resist the Magic Kingdom on account of it being home to Cinderella's castle and therefore Prince Charming.

'Here he comes!' we gurgle, deftly manoeuvring our way through the waist-height crowd to get a better look at his gold epaulettes. He's revolving in a spherical glass carriage and when he does finally wave in our general direction we're disappointed to see he's not all that. But hey, he's Prince Charming not Prince Handsome, we should give his personality a chance! We wait like groupies for him to finish his part in the snazzy cartoon-cast sing-along, then make our move.

'Hey – where'd he go?' We look around, bewildered. Both he and his heavily lacquered hair have disappeared into thin air.

'I bet he's gone off with that Mulan chick,' Kerry narrows her eyes. 'I saw that extra-special eye contact they had going on.'

'Oh who are we fooling, he's probably gay,' I shrug, re-christening him Prince Charmaine.

Personally I'd take a pirate over a prince any day – ever since Adam Ant first smouldered at the camera in a billowing shirt and leather trousers I've loved the idea of being commandeered by a straggle-haired rogue, and Johnny Depp's smoky-eyed turn in *Pirates of the Caribbean* further fuelled that fantasy. At this point in time I don't believe there is a sexier incarnation of manhood than Jack Sparrow – dreadlocks, tattoos, dodgy past: my kinda guy.

'But he sounded like Keith Richards!' Kerry protests.

'I always felt it was more Tommy Cooper,' I frown, undeterred, as I lead Kerry to the ride that inspired the film. For a moment things seem to be looking up – we're assigned a seat alongside two single guys, the first we've spied all day. We have to squeeze hip-to-hip to fit into the boat but instead of taking this opportunity to make a flirtatious 'mind the booty' quip they complain, 'I think you were supposed to take the row behind.'

Charming!

Fortunately the ride effectively suspends reality, taking us into a dark underworld of tattered Jolly Rogers, splashing cannonballs and drunken, heckling animatronic pirates consorting with grubby, buxom prostitutes.

'Bring me the redhead!' one rum-swigger demands, giving me the biggest thrill of the afternoon.

We've just about managed to convince ourselves that Messrs Bloom and Depp are awaiting us around the next corner when a mobile phone rings in the row behind us. The owner proceeds to answer it and then takes a business call without even attempting to explain away the raucous 'Yo-ho-ho-ing' in the background.

'He should be made to walk the plank!' I seethe as we stagger back onto dry land.

The rest of our afternoon is a washout – quite literally on the Splash Mountain log-flume ride – we see only three good-looking guys in the whole park, two sauntering with their girlfriends and the third is too busy with his duties at Snow White's Scary Adventures to engage with us. We've decided to call it a day when Kerry makes a last-minute dash into Tinkerbell's Treasures gift shop. I follow behind, finding myself drawn to a heap of royal-blue satin cushions embroidered with the words '*Looking for Prince Charming . . .*' in silver thread. I'm just fondling one with a view to a purchase when I hear a mum and gran talking behind me . . .

Mum: 'Oh that's cute – shall we get one for Sophie?'

Gran: 'No, you don't want to encourage that kind of thing – Prince Charming doesn't exist.'

I drop the cushion like a hot potato. Disney World is the last place I expected to get a reality check but BAM! there it is: There is no perfect man to sweep me off my feet and carry me to happily ever after. He doesn't exist.

This message is amply reinforced at Downtown Disney's Pleasure Island (eight nightclubs for one cover charge) and later on in the old town's less tourist-infested bars. Despite multiple encounters (the men here are not backward in coming forward) we've yet to find a native Floridian. It is therefore unfair to make sweeping statements about this state's men but at the same time, every man we meet seems to have adopted a horrible kind of presumption when it comes to women – I spoke to you therefore you must shag me – and if you try and turn them down you suddenly find yourself in an absurd negotiation reminiscent of a haggle with a particularly persistent beach vendor in Tunisia.

Having foolishly mentioned where we're staying to the two most ardent suitors, I decide that we should upgrade from our motel (neatly positioned between a $5.99 prime rib buffet and a gift shop in the shape of a giant orange) to Kissimmee's swankiest five-star accommodation: the Gaylord Palms Resort.

'You know how you've carefully chosen place names because of their promising love or romance tie-in?' Kerry says as we pull into the sweeping driveway.

'Yes,' I say, knowing what's coming next.

'Gaylord?' she questions.

I give a cheerful shrug. 'I like a challenge!'

The place is fancy-schmantzy with a dramatic four-acre, glass-domed atrium designed to represent three contrasting themes of the Sunshine State – the historic, old-world cobblestone charm of St Augustine, the tropical island spirit of Key West (complete with steel drums and sunsets) and the mysterious Everglades with faux-fog luring you down rustic walkways to where the alligators glide. It's a bit like the Eden Project – but with boutiques and fish restaurants nestled amid the foliage – and it gives us the urge to venture down the road to Gatorland where the real alligators thrash and gnash.

We enter Kissimmee's oldest attraction (established a good twenty years before Disney World) via a giant set of cement jaws and quickly assess the fold-out brochure. 'If we hurry we can make it to the Jungle Crocs show,' I announce. 'We just need to find the pond with the burned-out plane fuselage.'

After hacking through bamboo, wobbling across rickety wooden bridges and shuffling down sandy paths, we find it. There's already quite a crowd assembled and we have to weave amid the sweaty torsos to find a decent vantage point. As we wait for the show to begin, I spy something moving in the bushes to my left and slot on a pair of imaginary binoculars – hmmm, if I'm not mistaken . . . *yes!* There it is again! I'm getting the briefest of flashes but there's no mistaking its beauty.

'Kerry, I've seen one!' I grab her arm, excitement mounting.

'There's thousands of them here,' she responds with a what's-the-big-deal shrug.

'Not an alligator, *a man*,' I whisper. 'Look!'

I point to the khaki-clad vision approaching the fenced off area. He has black bush-baby eyes, exotic stubble and the most exquisitely shaped mouth. If George Clooney and Kristen Davis had a late-twenty-something son, this would be him.

'Oh my God – he's gorgeous!' Kerry palpitates as he introduces himself as Tony and the crocs as Starsky and Hutch. He then demonstrates some pretty nimble moves, avoiding a severed limb for the third time in as many seconds. 'I'm in love!' she swoons, pinning herself to the wire meshing. 'Do you think a guy like that would ever go for a girl like me?'

Hello? Did I miss something here? I wasn't donating him, merely pointing him out. How did he become the object of *her* affection? And who does that leave me with? I eye his colleague. He's certainly quick-witted but more the love child of Jason Statham and Sarah Jessica Parker. As Kerry presses herself ever closer, I skulk back, more than a little peeved. I didn't want to continue feeling aggravated by The Kane Situation so I decided to adopt a 'New State, New Start' policy when we got to Florida, but the first guy I express an interest in, she's instantly claimed for herself. This doesn't bode well.

'What's the next show?' Kerry demands the second Tony wraps up the presentation.

'Gator Wrestlin' at 3.30 p.m.,' I tell her.

'Come on!' she hurries ahead, through the breeding marsh and bird rookery, to a huge sandpit encircled by a moat housing several submerged gators.

Clattering up the stadium seating we realise we're behaving like boyband fans and try, in vain, to compose ourselves.

'Any minute now . . .' Kerry leans forward eagerly.

'Are you ready to see me wrestle one of these guys?' The wrangler steps from the sidelines, rousing the crowd.

Kerry heaves a disappointed sigh. 'It's your one.'

'He's not my one!' I protest, outraged. 'I don't fancy him at all.'

Mind you, he's certainly a good showman – luring an eight-footer up into the sandpit with him, sitting astride it, tilting its jaw upward and resting his own on the tip. Insane! And then I learn something essential should I ever find myself dating Tarzan – alligators fall asleep if you stroke their belly. Just like that – a quick tickle on the tum and they are out for the count. (Of course you have to flip them over first but details, details . . .) It really is one of the weirdest sights I've ever seen and I applaud rapturously.

'He's got to be at the next show,' Kerry prays as we continue on to the Up Close Encounters venue – a low wooden stage loaded with crates of various sizes and labels ranging from FRAGILE to VENOMOUS. 'Expect the Unexpected,' she reads, suddenly hesitant. 'I don't know if I like the sound of this.'

'Do you want to see Tony or not?' I snap.

Quashing her anxiety Kerry boldly takes a seat in the front row. I sit beside her and almost instantly find my knee clamped in a vice-like grip. It's OK, it's Kerry – Tony is indeed running this show, this time

243

with a quirky-cool sidekick by the name of Nicholas. He's long and lanky with curious Rockabilly sideburns and an amused twist to his mouth. That's more like it – the offspring of John Travolta and Jennifer Connelly.

The guys kick off by drawing a line in the sand dividing them from us and issue a strict warning against crossing that line unless specifically invited. They then each pick up a crate and stagger alarming close to the audience. Everyone shrinks back. Tony pauses, then drops his crate directly at our feet causing Kerry to scarper five rows back. I can't bring myself to retreat – apparently I'm prepared to risk being bitten, mauled or stung, all for the sake of lust.

'Let's have a look in here . . .' Tony pries open the crate and hoiks out a scorpion, dangling it right before my whirring video camera.

'You want a close-up?' he teases, clicking its clippers against the lens.

I'd gasp but I don't want to leave my mouth open.

I turn back to check on Kerry and find she's now shot a further five rows back.

Tony gives an amusing and informative commentary as he works his way through the rest of the mid-size boxes then muses, 'Which one shall we open next?'

'The big one!' the crowd chorus.

'All right, but we're going to need some volunteers.' Tony strides over to me and asks, 'Where'd your friend go?'

Not the words I was hoping to hear. I point ten, make that twenty, rows back.

'Come on,' he beckons her down.

'No, I can't!' she bleats from afar.

'Yes you can,' he asserts, hypnotising her with his dark shiny eyes.

Unable to resist his come-hithering, she clops down and takes her place at the end of a line of six people. I feel a mix of jealousy and relief that it's not me up there.

'Heads or tails?' he asks her.

'Heads,' she says confidently, until realisation dawns – he's not talking about a coin. Her eyes widen in terror.

'Keep facing forwards,' he insists.

'As long as it's not a snake,' I hear her mutter.

I watch tremulously as they slide off the lid of the box and reach deep inside. Uh oh. This isn't good – not only is it a snake but it's an albino python, identical to the one that reared up on Kerry in the Voodoo Museum. She is going to FREAK! I try desperately to get her attention but her eyes are fixed resolutely forward. And then she sees it. To her credit she neither faints nor flees. For that alone she deserves first dibs on Tony.

Once the show is over, we linger to watch the guys repackaging the reptiles then sidle up and ask a few innocent questions. Turns out Tony has been coming to Gatorland since he was two and a half and always dreamed of being a wrangler, whereas this is a sideline for Nicholas who is currently studying to be a Harley Davidson mechanic – he's certainly got the *Greased Lightnin'* look down!

Putting fifteen years of journalistic expertise to use,

I then subtly segue into an enquiry after their romantic availability. That's when tragedy strikes – we learn that Tony has a girlfriend. Kerry pales as if she's just ingested a deadly poison. The girlfriend's name is Zora, and I know later we'll refer to her as Zorba but it won't help. Kerry's utterly crushed – 'Tony and what-might-have-been' is all she can talk about for the rest of the night.

Nicholas, on the other hand, is young, free and single – with the emphasis on young, as he's just twenty. He actually invited us to his house for beer but Kerry was too bereft to go so I decided to try and lift her spirits with a visit to the hotel's 'Jammin' Piano Bar'. I thought the duelling pianos would be a lively distraction but we ended up drinking way too many Key Lime Martinis on account of some fool repeatedly requesting Elton John's 'Crocodile Rock' . . .

'So what do you want to do with our last few hours in Florida?' I ask the next day, studying the guide to Kissimmee attractions as we sip orange juice on the terrace of the hotel's Villa de Flora café. 'We could take an airboat ride on Boggy Creek or play miniature golf or meander through A World of Orchids . . .'

Kerry makes an attempt at a 'don't mind' shrug. She's barely got the strength to lift her forkful of pancake to her mouth.

'Or we could go to Rite Aid and get the pictures of the Gatorland guys developed in an hour.'

'Yes-*yes*-YES!' she squeals orgasmically. She may not be able to have the man himself but the chance to see his beautiful face again will tide her over till she finds a Tony of her very own.

I'm equally delighted when I realise that Rite Aid is directly opposite a Ross Dress for Less store (think TK Maxx). I can't tell you how much I love bargain-hunting there. In LA it's considered rather a lowly pursuit as the clientele there are primarily Russian immigrants and poor Mexicans, but I'm quite happy rifling the rails alongside them. And my Spanish is coming along nicely.

'OK, I'll meet you at the till in forty minutes,' I say, eager to get rummaging.

I could do with a couple of new pairs of knickers and oooh, is that a BCBG top at a third of the original price . . . !

With just five minutes' shopping time remaining, me and my cluster of hangers rattle into the photo album and notebook aisle. I'm just inspecting a pink pad with a 'Kiss Me!' logo when my peripheral vision registers a striking dreadlocked dude in the main aisle. He strides past, giving me a millisecond's eye contact which immediately arouses my hunting instinct. Should I give chase? He looked like a prime cut of man. I take a moment to consider – no, I'm too knackered and hungover. I don't have the energy to act alluring. Besides, we're leaving for Colorado in an hour, is there any point? Oh my God – he's coming down my aisle! I bend over and quickly scrabble through the notebooks to look occupied. In a bar situation I may be bold but if I find myself in close quarters with an attractive stranger in a brightly lit shop I just keep my head down and dart off at the earliest opportunity.

But not this time – his presence is too powerful to

ignore. There's something so dramatic, so knowing, so *ready* about him, I feel compelled to speak.

'Am I in your way?' I ask, bum still jutting out, inadvertently coming over all Benny Hill sketch.

'No I'm fine stood right here,' he says in the deepest, most luxuriant voice, holding my gaze in the most masterful way.

There's a rushing in my ears as I stand upright and take in his forty-something Marley-esque face, strong dancer's stance and elaborately tattooed forearms. Suddenly Casey, Paul and even Kane seem like mere wannabes. This, my friends, is a man.

'I'm Troy,' he says with positively regal delivery, reaching to shake my hand.

Unfortunately I've got myself in a tangle trying to shield my undies with the BCBG top and don't have a hand free to match his.

'Here, let me take that for you,' he offers, noticing my struggle.

'Oh no! I'm fine,' I fluster, trying to un-entwine the hangers and regain the blood flow to my fingers.

'Really, let me help you.' He makes a grab for my things.

'It's underwear,' I whinny, jumping back.

'All the more reason,' he purrs.

'Not that kind of underwear,' I grimace.

'Oooh,' he nods, understanding. 'Functional?'

'Yes,' I blush. 'I actually came in for a T-shirt . . .' Like he needed to know that. Why am I so uncool in these situations?

'My colleague is doing the same thing.' He motions over to the till, mercifully re-directing the attention to his friend. 'See the guy in the blue . . .'

'What, the model?' I want to cry as I clock the Smith-from-*Sex-and-the-City* doppelgänger. Give him a guitar and an outsized ego and he'd be perfect for Kerry! The downside is that his name is Quentin and he couldn't look less interested in interacting.

'So you two work together?' I turn back to Troy, trying to calm my raging hormones. 'What do you do?' I'm guessing something showbiz-related.

'We're truckers!' he announces.

'No way!' I gasp, disproportionately delighted. Could he be any more macho?

'Got my eighteen-wheeler outside . . .' he winks.

'Ooh, Pink has a song with a lyric about being run over by an eighteen-wheeler truck,' I babble, forgetting to censor my inner voice.

'You like her?' He raises an eyebrow.

'Love her,' I confirm.

He smiles approvingly then growls, 'So, do you want to see it?', his every word loaded with innuendo.

Do I want to see his big truck? You betcha!

'I've just got to find my friend,' I say, getting up on my tiptoes to scour the store for Kerry. 'Over here!' I wave her over from the shoe department in the far corner. As she makes her way across the store, I ask about his melange of tattoos and rather deftly establish that most vital of factors – his star sign.

'So where are you staying?' he asks, looking at me with eyes that manage to project respect as well as lust.

'Right here – Kissimmee,' I reply.

'Don't tempt me,' he rumbles, a wry smile twisting his lovely mouth. 'I'd love to!'

My inner organs spasm. Lordy, he's a hottie!

'You know I once wrote a poem about kissing, he quotes a few lines and I can't help but swoon – it's like having Barry White as your literary professor!

'Well, hello!' Kerry eyes Troy then gives me a saucy look. 'I see you've been busy.'

'She picked me up!' he announces, looking very pleased with himself.

'I didn't!' I protest.

'You did!' he calmly insists.

'Actually, I did, didn't I?' I realise, feeling chuffed and revelling in the warm look he's giving me.

'Are you going to introduce us?' Kerry prompts me.

'Oh yes, sorry! Troy, this is Kerry.'

'Hey I dig your creamy complexion,' he tells her as he shakes her hand. 'You look like you haven't seen the sun in your whole life!'

Oh here we go. My stomach twists anxiously – please don't let him fancy her more.

'And look at those pretty toes,' he says as his gaze drops down to admire her scarlet nail polish.

I roll my eyes – he better just be charming my friend to get on my good side otherwise I'm going to have to take the rest of this road trip with Kerry locked in the trunk – she's just too much competition out in the open.

'That's Troy's friend,' I say, bodily directing Kerry to the Calvin Klein ad babe heading our way.

Unfortunately he walks straight past us and out the door without so much as a nod.

'I guess I should be going,' Troy shrugs resignedly. 'He's not one for hanging around chit-chatting.'

'We'll walk you to your truck,' I quickly volunteer, not ready to say goodbye just yet.

'You've got a truck?' Kerry gapes.

'Eighteen-wheeler,' I boast. 'He's driving to Ohio but he lives right here in Florida.'

'So what's your take on Florida men?' Kerry asks as we walk.

Without pause he decrees: 'They're very opportunistic, they think every women is there as a potential person for them to hit on.'

We can't believe how spot-on he is.

'Most of them just want to screw like porn stars,' he tuts disapprovingly. 'I like it slow and easy.'

Oh. Er. *Help!* I don't think I ever met an individual who projected such assured sexuality.

'Would you say you're a good lover?' Kerry has a moment of extreme boldness.

'I know I am.'

I chortle at his arrogance. 'How can you know for sure?'

'I used to be a male escort,' he says matter-of-factly.

Kerry and I screech to a halt, gawping at each other as we try to get our heads round this revelation. I can't believe it! We just popped out to get some pics developed and we've inadvertently exposed an ex-male escort! Better yet, he's now a trucker poet! Too much. Too fabulous!

Continuing on to the car park, he tells us how back in his twenties, when he was a beach bum and male stripper (it just keeps getting better!), he met a rich woman on her honeymoon and they began an affair that led to a seven-year marriage. When she tired of

251

him she recommended him to her rich friends and pleasing them was how he earned his living.

We're still stunned at how candid he's being when he sighs, 'I wish I could stay and take you to dinner. It would be such a pleasure to have some intelligent company.'

I don't know what gives him the impression we're intelligent but I too wish we could extend this conversation – I just know we would venture into new and stimulating territory. Already he's made me sit up and pay attention – no mean feat considering how groggy I was feeling. I do love an opinionated man and the fact that he's also got a sense of humour and is a little bit naughty is so very appealing. Not to mention the fact that he's clearly had an intriguing and eventful life. I long to know more.

'Here's the truck,' he steps off the kerb and gives the metal monster a flourish.

'OVERSIZE LOAD,' Kerry reads the banner on the bumper. 'We've got to get a picture.'

Still ignoring us, Quentin hauls his neatly packaged cookies up into the driving seat and starts the engine. Oh no! Why does he have to go so soon?

'Give me your address, we can be pen pals,' Troy suggests, pleasing me greatly.

We exchange a quick scribble and a meaningful glance and then he's up in the truck cab behind a slammed door. I didn't even get to touch him. Probably just as well, I may have spontaneously combusted.

'How funny, we couldn't be more opposite to Thelma and Louise,' I muse as we watch them roar out of the parking lot. 'Look at us – we're actually trying to pick up the truckers!'

As we stroll over to Rite Aid to collect the pictures I once again bless Ross Dress for Less – you really do get the best stuff there.

'Did you see the bats tattooed on his right arm?' I ask Kerry as she moons over the photos of Tony.

She shakes her head.

'He says he likes things that fly.'

'Are you thinking of taking it up?' Kerry chuckles, still engrossed.

'Maybe. You know he's a Pisces?'

'Uh oh.'

'I know.'

Piscean men have been both our most significant romantic downfalls.

'It's his birthday in a couple of days. He's going to be on the road but I think I might call from Colorado and leave a message on his home phone.'

Kerry looks up from the photos. 'He really was amazing, wasn't he?'

'Tony?'

'No, Troy. I was impressed.'

'Really?' I light up.

'Yeah, he's so wise and articulate and *interesting*.'

'Oh I know!' I crow. 'He just seems to have so much more substance than the average whippersnapper I normally entangle myself with.'

'Maybe you've found him.'

'Maybe I have,' I pip.

'Oh my God!' Kerry suddenly throws down the pictures and turns to me.

'What?'

'Remember when you got here you said your ideal guy was Johnny Depp in *Pirates of the Caribbean*?'

'Yes,' I say, failing to make the connection.

A huge smile creeps across her face, 'You wanted dreadlocks, tattoos and a dodgy past – *you've got it*!'

'Wow!' I gasp, realising how spot-on she is. He's got everything bar the Tommy Cooper accent – this could be big!

CLIMAX,
COLORADO

Any moment now we'll get to Climax.

'Keep going, that's it, nearly there,' I gasp, feeling dizzy and short of breath.

You would too at ten thousand feet above sea level. Apparently the excessive elevation here in the Rockies can also cause insomnia, light-headedness and mental confusion – finally Kerry and I have an excuse for being so unhinged.

'We should be there by now,' I frown as the mileometer clicks on another notch. 'Where is it?'

Slowing to a crawl, we peer at the pine-lined hard shoulder – no signs nestled amid the perky, pointy branches; no sneaky side-roads weaving between the telegraph-pole trunks. We continue on, squinting for several miles, feeling like we're trying to locate a secret portal into another world. Nothing. It's hard to imagine that back in 1960s the mine at Climax supplied half the world's molybdenum – not quite as glam as gold, it's a product that is used to harden steel. (Those innuendos just keep on coming, don't they?) Today's Climax is essentially only of interest to skiers but, even so, they'd have to mark the spot, surely?

We know we've gone too far when we arrive in the old boomtown of Leadville. Also known as Cloud City, Leadville is officially America's Highest City at 10,152 feet. Though we're tempted by the bar billing itself as a 'THIRST AID CENTER', we venture instead into the historic Delaware Hotel on account of it being a former haunt of Butch Cassidy. The lady on reception has a world-weary air and doesn't seem overly concerned that a pair of non-skiing Brits are desperately seeking Climax. She directs us ten miles back down the road we just came in on, then returns to her filing.

'I don't know how we missed the sign,' I mumble as we turn to leave.

'Oh, that got knocked down by a snow plough last winter,' she calls after us. 'And then someone stole it.'

My mouth falls open. No sign? Oh God! Is that a sign in itself? Before I overwhelm myself with dread foreboding, Kerry reminds me that we have a fairly decent Plan B in the form of a visit to a dude ranch a few hours north of here in swinging Steamboat Springs. It's been a fantasy of Kerry's ever since she saw *City Slickers* but for me it will be more of a personal pilgrimage – the brother of my only quality beau (art student Don) used to be a ski instructor there (I remember this clearly because I still have a Steamboat Springs enamel pin Don once gave me as a present) and I'm hoping against hope that I'll be able to trace him through the local ski community. It's years since

Don and I lost contact in London and yet I've never been able to kick the feeling that a little part of me is missing. I couldn't come to Colorado without at least giving it a try . . .

'You know, if we skipped our overnight here we could spend two nights in Steamboat,' Kerry wheedles.

It's certainly tempting – though Leadville once had enough prospectors to keep 106 bars in business, today there's just the hinge-creakingly deserted Silver Dollar Saloon. Frankly the liveliest venue in town appears to be the 7-Eleven. All the same, I'm reluctant to leave without pictorial proof of our anti-Climax.

'I suppose we could make our own sign and stand where it ought to be?' I try to rouse myself from my 'crestfallen on the counter' pose.

'Good idea,' Kerry enthuses, eager to leave the dusty Victoriana behind. 'But what with?'

The receptionist kindly donates a sheet of A4 and a stocky stinky-marker pen and I immediately set to work.

'There!' I try and sound encouraged at the sight of my flimsy imitation. 'I guess it won't be the first time a gal has faked it!'

We jump back in the car and retrace our route, carefully clocking the miles, only to find ourselves at an unfamiliar fork.

'I don't remember this – left or right?' I frown.

We opt for left, which is wrong, but as we turn back in confusion we're greeted by a sign bearing both the words *Leadville* (with an arrow to the right) and *Climax* (with an arrow to the left).

'That's good enough!' I whoop, throwing our mock sign onto the back-seat.

*

In our eagerness to get on our way to Steamboat Springs we mistakenly take the 24 south instead of north and unexpectedly find ourselves in Granite – talk about being stuck between a rock and a hard place. Up until now we've totally bought into the idea of Colorado being 'the Switzerland of America' – snow-dazzled peaks, sky-scraping pines and every plant and flower vibrantly in its prime – but here the landscape is grittily harsh with chalky roads escalating through what looks like a giant, perilous rockery.

Up and up we climb, giving us further and further to drop.

'Would it kill them to put up the odd barrier along here?' I complain, hunched over the steering wheel as we grind along another hairy hairpin bend at five mph. I'm starting to feel out of my depth, like I no longer have the power to swim to safety. Not a moment too soon we begin our descent into a green and sheltered valley with – oh joy – a two-lane highway. Finally I can breathe again. We build up some pace and before we know it we're in Glenwood Springs – most famous as Doc Holliday's burial place. As we look out for somewhere to stop for tea, we spot a sign for a white-water rafting experience.

'Oh, I've always wanted to try that!' Kerry turns to me. 'What do you think?'

My hand automatically creeps to my painstakingly ghd'd hair. 'Ummm . . .'

'They're bound to be young action men hosting the trips,' Kerry reasons. 'With lovely bulgy biceps from all that frantic paddling!'

Suddenly I want to slap myself – I'm in Colorado for goodness' sake! I need to get with the carefree, outdoorsy, Abercrombie & Fitch vibe of the locals. Besides, now the sun has taken a stronghold in the sky, it's actually really hot – clearly an ice-cold sluicing while astride a bright yellow inflatable is the best way to cool down.

At least we're right on that score but, as for the pulling potential, we're wildly off-course having been assigned a raft with a female hostess and a family of four from Georgia. However, within seconds of battling and thrashing at the rushing river we're enjoying ourselves too much to care. There's as much squealing as paddling to be done and we decide this is a far superior rush to any ride at Disney World. With the worst rapids behind us we now enjoy the luxury of a dreamlike drift, gazing up at the pink-ridged cliffs that cut a jagged path for our flow. It's easy to picture outlaws hiding out in the nooks and as we scour the scenery for stubbly individuals with cross-your-heart bullet belts Kerry notices a rather handsome fisher-man on the bank to our left. As we carefully shuffle around to get a better look he sets his rod aside, drops his trousers and moons us.

'Ohh!' we gasp, laughing.

'I heard they favour the *au naturel* look here!' Kerry chuckles.

And then the heavens open and drench us with raindrops the size of water-bombs.

We emerge from our trip squelching but exhilarated. It's actually quite liberating to let all concern for the ironed-straightness of your hair go. As I shake out my sopping kinked locks – looking like a dog doing an impression of a car-wash brush – I feel as though all pretensions are out the window. It's then I make a decision: I'm going to call Trucker. I've been um-ing and ah-ing all day about whether to leave him a Happy Birthday message, wondering what I might be starting, worrying about a Paul-like sequel, but suddenly it's no big deal – if I can survive the raging rapids I can survive a man. I dial his number and leave a simple, cheery message. There, nothing to it!

In the past such a move would have left me fretful and on edge – oh I do hope he responds, oh what will he think of me? – but this time I just do it and then get on with the drive, feeling a new affinity with the minty-fresh streams slashing along beside the tarmac.

While Kerry paints her toenails on the dashboard and I follow the signs to Steamboat Springs, my mind naturally drifts to Don. I was a nineteen-year-old pop-obsessed journalism student when we met. He was an art student and intriguing sophisticate, very much his own unique creation. Initially I was intimidated by how articulate and well-read he was but gradually I began to see me through his eyes – to him I was this quirky, creative, sexy (believe it or not) individual who was utterly unconcerned with convention or looking cool – he never could get over the shameless way I'd state my allegiance to bands like King or Then Jericho. Anyway, end of college meant end of us (his instigation) but he handled it so graciously that we remained friends, enjoying the occasional fling until he married a French goddess and became a papa. (One of the worst moments in my life was holding his newborn baby for the first time and getting the distinct feeling that the roles had been wrongly assigned – I should have been the mum!)

In many ways, losing contact with him was like losing a reflection of my best self. He appreciated things about me that no other (straight) man ever seems to notice. I remember taking my mother to a restaurant he was working in to finance his art and afterwards she couldn't get over the admiration and affection in his eyes when he looked at me – everyone commented on it. I suppose that's one of the things I'm trying to regain: a vision of myself as I truly want to be seen.

It's 6 p.m. by the time we arrive at Steamboat Springs, a picturesque ski town with a fun, upbeat vibe and a nice line in retro signage. I'm particularly taken with the pink and white neon directing us to the Rabbit Ears Motel – if we weren't already booked in at Vista Verde I'd be more than happy to make that my warren for the night.

'So, are you ready to sleuth?' I challenge Kerry.

She nods, fully primed.

We start at the top end of the main high street taking one side of the street each and dip into every ski shop, boutique and internet café en route with the same question: 'Y'all ever hear of a guy named Doug Short?' We draw a blank every time, but then again the majority of staff we encounter are in their early twenties and it's actually fourteen years since I knew for a fact that brother Doug lived here. Reconvening at the bottom end of town, we turn to the local phone book – several names match but when we call we discover their Doug is either fifteen or fifty-five, not the thirty-something I'm looking for.

'I guess he's moved on,' I sigh, defeated.

'Maybe you should too?' Kerry raises an eyebrow.

'I'm not clinging on for love,' I explain. 'I just liked having someone that opinionated and original in my life.'

'Maybe we can find you a replacement at the ranch?'

I look at my watch. 'I suppose we should get going if we want to make it there for dinner.'

'Too right – I'm starving,' Kerry rumbles. 'What do you think they'll be serving?'

'Stew and beans on a tin plate, I imagine.'

I couldn't be more wrong – the reality is sautéed soft-shell crab with a green bean salad tossed with chive flowers and tomatoes and drizzled with a Dijon aioli, followed by grilled wild boar served with chipotle yams, haricot verts and apple chips.

Turns out Vista Verde is a dude ranch for the discerning – and, let's face it, *rich* – Wild West wannabe. No slops from a chuck wagon here, the dining room tables are cloaked in white linen and the food is accompanied by the chef's recommendation of New World wines.

The other surprise is how much of a family experience this is. Yes, Vista Verde has been known to entertain the odd stag party but by and large the male guests are married and dangling toddlers. We join a couple from New York (their offspring ate earlier, wolfing down hot dogs and other kiddy treats on the porch). She works for VH1 and recently produced the *Divas Las Vegas* concert starring Shania, Anastacia, Lisa

264

Marie Presley et al, and her husband works for Random House publishers. They have an apartment on the Upper West Side with a balcony overlooking Central Park. Are you getting the picture?

By now we should have wised up to the fact that we wouldn't be kipping in a sleeping bag in a hayloft but, nevertheless, ranch manager Sarah stuns us further when she guides us across the 540-acre sweep of land to our cabin, set in a woodland dell beside a trickling stream.

'This is Big Agnes,' she says, introducing us to our home for the next two nights.

Our eyes roam every which way, trying to take it all in. 'All this, for us?'

She nods.

We can't quite believe it – I mean, what does the word 'cabin' mean to you? A cosy one-room shack with a pair of red long-johns drying in front of a wood-burning stove? A blanket-wrapped bed and a sprig of flowers in a milk jug? Here at Vista Verde we're talking a massive two-storey lodgepole house with a spacious bedroom, bathroom and lounge both upstairs *and* down, a neat little kitchen with a gourmet food basket and a Jacuzzi on the broad front deck.

'No way!' we gasp, tearing around inspecting the chunky pine furniture, tartan curtains and throw pillows with fly-fishing hook motifs. It's country-club quality with no dodgy membership policy. Suddenly I don't need shops, I'll be more than happy to play rustic housewife.

But first there's some do-si-do-ing to be done at the evening's barn dance. Every member of staff will be

265

there (so far the only employees we've clocked are a couple of sparky waitresses) and Kerry is convinced we're going to be spoiled for choice with innumerable Brad-esque 'dudes'. Personally I think it's much more likely the ranchers will be weather-beaten Jack Palance types, narrowing their eyes at us while chewing a cheroot, but there's only one way to find out.

Feeling more than a little nervous, I don a popper-studded check shirt, Kerry ties on a pink neckerchief and we stroll across the grassland to the barn. The good news is that there are indeed twenty or so cowboys awaiting us and they're all fine-looking fellas under thirty. The bad news is that we're the last to arrive and everyone has already mastered the synchronised steppings of the *Tush Push*.

'Oh God!' I cringe, watching them strut-slide-twizzle, then neatly switch direction. 'That's the worst thing about line-dancing – there's no hiding at the back.' Sooner or later everyone becomes the front row.

'Shall we just run away?' Kerry asks.

'We'll be fine after a few drinks,' I assure her, secretly relieved that I'm wearing a skirt so long that no one will actually be able to see what my feet are doing. But then disaster strikes.

'There's no alcohol!' Kerry gasps.

I come to an abrupt halt. 'What?'

'It's just coffee and water and choc-dipped straw-berries,' Kerry studies the trestle table.

'Are they kidding?' I spin around hoping to spy a stray crate of moonshine but instead get swept into a *Boot Scootin' Boogie*. Kerry isn't far behind. She finds her stride almost straight away but my espadrille-soled flip-flops seem incompatible with the floorboards and repeatedly bend back causing me to trip, or instead fly off altogether during the step-kick movements. As I break from the pack to chase my shoe across the barn I decide to aim for the hay bales where the kittens and old folk are nestled. My aim is to get to bale-level four (out of reach of any line-dancers on a recruitment drive) but before I can even scale one, Kerry is at my side.

'Come on, you've got to join in!' she insists, pulling me back.

'I will in a minute,' I tell her, digging in my bare heels.

'No, now!' she urges.

'I'm not ready,' I reason.

'Oh come on!'

'No,' I growl, sensing that people are beginning to stare.

I want to announce, 'This isn't me – I always join in!' but I know how it looks, I know what *I* think when other people bale (pardon the pun) on such lively activities – they don't want to make a fool of themselves. But honestly that's not my concern. I just need a moment to collect myself.

Kerry isn't buying this and persists with her pleading. 'Come and dance!'

Oh great. Now there's a big cowboy at her side. 'I'm Jeff,' he says. 'You're dancing.'

I get the feeling that short of clunking him on the head with a horseshoe, I have to obey.

This time the steps prove to be the least of my worries – it's the puff required for all the high-kneed skipping between the potentially dislocating underarm turns that slays me. Within thirty seconds I'm wheezing like a pair of cracked and cronky bellows.

'I'm going to have a heart attack!' I grip my chest as the skips come around quicker and quicker and I fall into a series of men's arms, grateful that for the most part they are strong enough to keep me upright and deft enough to guide me in the right direction. If everything wasn't such a blotchy-blur this would be a great way of eyeing up the talent. All I know is that there's one guy in a black shirt whose arms I'm particularly happy to be in and a five-year-old who's got moves that could out-swivel Ricky Martin. But finally, mercifully, it's all over. And I thought it was the horse-riding that was going to kill my thighs.

I collapse onto a hay bale only to be nutted by a basketball. (Ricky Jnr has decided to practise shooting hoops. Note to him: stick to the dancing.) I had presumed this would be the beginning of the more relaxed sector of the evening, maybe with a little freestyle dancing to 'Sweet Home Alabama', but almost instantly the coffee is cleared away (good riddance!) and the families and staff members swiftly return to their cabins. Now there's just Jeff and a pretty, chatty Dubliner called Eve-Marie who introduces herself as a kid wrangler.

'So when do you get to be a grown-up wrangler?' I ask.

'No,' she tsks, 'I work with the kids, hence kid wrangler.'

'Oooh, sorry!' I fluster.

Kerry joins us.

'This is Eve-Marie,' I tell her. 'She's a kid wrangler.'

'A kitten wrangler? Oh how cute.'

Amazingly Eve-Marie stays to chat with us for the next hour, along with Cowboy Jeff. Or should I say Wrangler Jeff?

'Cowboy is a term used to describe another, not yourself,' he explains earnestly. 'That would be presumptuous and instantly reveals you as a wannabe.'

Jeff is originally from Missouri but he looks the part and seems to know the ropes. Speaking of which . . .

'Can you teach me how to lasso?' Kerry sidles up to him.

'Why, yes ma'am!' he grins, instantly setting her up with a surprisingly stiff rope and a makeshift wooden calf to practise on. 'This is where you want to aim for,' he says, tapping the horns.

'OK,' she says, gingerly working the rope into a rhythmic whirring action according to Jeff's instructions. Then, with her chin ducked down on her breastbone to avoid an impromptu hanging, she makes her move.

'Oh no – I lassoed myself!' she wails as the hoop of rope drops in a neat circle around her ankles. 'How did that happen?'

'Here, I'm not so good at explaining – I never had to teach anyone before. Let me show you . . .' Jeff resets Kerry's rope, removing the kinks and then spoons up behind her so he can help her get her hand motion just right. It's all in the wrist, apparently. Kerry smiles contentedly – from this vantage point Jeff could indeed be Brad Pitt.

'You're doing great!' he encourages, stepping back to let Kerry fly solo.

As her Annie Oakley alter-ego emerges she begins whipping the rope round so frantically it creates a buzzing whine and I half-expect her to raise off the ground like a human helicopter.

'You don't need to go so fast . . .' Jeff soothes her.

Kerry slows from a tornado to gentle breeze.

'OK, *now*!' Jeff directs.

Kerry releases the rope, setting it neatly around the horns of the wooden calf. She's ecstatic. 'Take a picture! Take a picture!'

'It might not really do the moment justice,' I warn as I snap Kerry grinning like a fool at the end of what is essentially a large piece of string.

'You're a natural.' Jeff is genuinely impressed and sets about teaching her a professional trick where you enlarge the loop as you're spinning.

'Do you get many cowgirls?' Kerry asks as she works on her new moves.

'You mean do I pick up many?' Jeff looks slightly taken aback.

'Noooo!' Kerry chuckles at his misunderstanding. 'I mean, are there many cowgirls in existence?'

'Oh sure. They're not the rarity people might think.'

As for the other interpretation of the question, I'd guess he doesn't do badly. He's no Brad or even Casey (the blue-eyed beauty from Texas) but earlier I saw him working his wholesome Midwest shtick on a blonde cowgirl who by rights should have been way out of his league and she blushed responsively. Then there's his frequent tussles with Eve-Marie who says she doesn't fancy him but seems to get a kick out of being lassoed by him. (One of his party tricks is to get a girl to walk ahead of him, kicking up her heels as she goes; he then lassoes her by the ankle and yanks her to the ground.) Not a bad pulling technique and it's certainly working on Kerry.

'That's brilliant, do it again!' she whoops with 'Chase-me! Chase-me!' enthusiasm.

Ordinarily I'd interpret this kind of behaviour as flirtation but seeing as *I* don't fancy Jeff I feel the only way to find out for sure is to ask Kerry outright.

'So, could he be your Mr Right?' I ask as soon as we're safely back at Big Agnes.

'Noooo!' she tuts, slipping on a pair of fluffy bed socks. 'Well . . . No. Well . . . Maybe. I mean, he is very masterful and he did call me ma'am.' She looks wistful.

'So you fancy him?'

'A bit, I suppose. Not really. Oh I'm not sure. Do I?'

Seven hours later I have all the proof I need that a potential frisson is in the air. While I had my nose pressed against my bedroom window watching a deer tiptoe through the long grass, Kerry was getting busy in the gift shop. She is now sporting an immaculate white cowboy hat, a pair of buttery-soft leather gloves and the sheriff's badge she snapped up in Leadville.

'Do you think Jeff will like it?' she asks, giving me a twirl.

'Let's find out.' I lead her to an alfresco patio breakfast with a real-live chef rustling up customised omelettes on his sunkissed stove.

'Kerry, look at this!' I cry repeatedly as I remove a series of heavy silver lids from ever-more-tempting dishes. But I cannot get her attention for bacon nor hash browns. She only has eyes for Jeff. He seems pretty pleased to see her too, admiring her new look and boasting to every passer-by about her lassoing skills.

'Uh-oh, I see you're wearing a Sheriff's badge,' he nods to her lapel accessory. 'I'm going to have to watch myself in front of you.'

'It's a Leadville badge – I have no jurisdiction here,' Kerry sighs.

I could be mistaken but I swear Jeff looks faintly disappointed.

'Where do you want to sit?' I ask Kerry, surveying the set of wooden tables dressed in fetching red- and white-check cloths. I feel like I'm on a stage set for *Oklahoma!*

'Wherever,' she shrugs, without turning round.

'Do you want me to wait for you?' I ask, noting that her eggs are nearly done.

'No, you go on. So Jeff . . .'

Oh I see! I forgo Kane to be her attentive companion but when she's working on a beau I'm dismissed in a second! Suddenly I feel like I'm back at school, abandoned by my only friend and left to fend for myself. I take my plate and glass of juice and nervously approach a table of mixed-sex wranglers.

'Um, er, do you mind if I join you?'

'Help yourself,' they say.

I settle into my seat aware that I've killed their previous conversation dead.

'Sooo,' I smile, anxiously crumbling my muffin. 'Where are you all from?'

Ten minutes later we're all chuckling away,

listening to Jenn recount how she became the first Prom Queen at her school to wear jeans instead of froufrou.

'Where did you go to school?' I ask.

'Syracuse, New York,' she tells me.

I try not to twitch too violently at the memory of Paul and focus on my breakfast.

'So, are you doing the full-day ride today?' they ask.

'No. I've ridden before, I know the pain,' I tell them. 'We're just doing a couple of hours this morning.'

'Actually, Jeff thinks I should do the full day.' Kerry appears by my side.

'But you've never even been on a horse before,' I remind her.

'He thinks I can handle it,' she rallies. 'Besides, I grew up on a farm.'

'Oh, well then,' I shrug. I grew up in Oxford so I guess that means I have a degree.

Kerry beckons manager Sarah over and informs her of her change of plan.

'I think it might be wiser if you try it out first before committing to seven hours in the saddle,' she cautions. 'We can always take you out again after lunch if you like it.'

Kerry's face falls. 'What do you think, Jeff?' She looks imploringly at him.

'More juice anyone?' I decide to leave them to it.

Ultimately, Sarah's more sensible advice wins out, leaving Kerry with a jutting bottom lip. 'But I want to be with Jeff,' she pouts as we head back to the cabin to while away the hour until our ride.

'Well, why don't we go over to the stables now – at least we can watch him saddle up the horses?' I suggest, by way of consolation.

Kerry's feet immediately switch direction. As she lolls over the gate ogling Jeff, I take a look at the pen holding the four-legged creatures – sixty or so elegantly gleaming horses and one fuzzy sheep. Curious.

'He thinks he's a horse,' Sarah shrugs, by way of explanation. 'Hangs out with them all day. By the way, help yourself to boots . . .' She nods over to a multi-hued selection on the veranda.

Conker brown, dusty donkey, honey beige, even baby pink. I run my hand along the worn leather and fancy stitching, eventually opting for a once-white pair. The strangely angular heel has me walking like I've had my ankles replaced with Slinkies and I have to clutch onto the rail as I descend the stairs to rejoin Kerry.

'Here he comes!' she pips as her hero leads a kiddie convoy out of the stable yard.

Now you might think a tot on a Shetland pony is cute – and it is – but wait till you see a wee mite atop a great big brute of a horse! Suddenly you've got cute *and* brave. My heart tugs inside me – I want one!

'Ladies . . .' Jeff taps the brim of his Stetson as he clops past us.

Kerry emits a whinny of pleasure. 'Just look at him!' she squeaks, stumbling forward.

'You *do* fancy him, then?'

'YES!' she nods, looking fit to burst.

Part of me is jealous that she has someone to fancy and I don't, part of me feels cast aside because she's so

274

preoccupied with him, but the greatest part of me is rejoicing in the knowledge that, for once, we're not fancying the same man! I must admit I was having serious doubts about making it through the rest of the trip with her but if Kane and Tony were flukes we could be in the clear.

'Ready girls?' Sarah announces that it's our turn to saddle up.

I'm not entirely sure it's wise to put Kerry on a horse when she's still within cantering distance of Jeff – I half expect her to yell, 'Yarrrr!', jump the barn gate and rip across the fields to him – but instead she sits obediently as Sarah adjusts her stirrups.

'How does that feel now?' she asks, slotting Kerry's feet back into place.

'Much better,' she confirms.

'And you?' Sarah checks on me.

I say I'm fine but actually I'm never physically comfortable on a horse – I get this kind of shin-splint sensation in my knees as though they're being skewed against their will. I put this down to the fact that I had troublesome knees as a child and once a month had to go to a doctor and have them manipulated. They really only give me grief now when I'm on a horse. Which does somewhat beg the question: Why am I going riding? Well, it's hard to match that special connection you have with nature when you're traversing glorious scenery astride one of God's more magnificent beasts (especially one called Red who's having an exceptionally Good Mane Day).

We climb grassy hills embroidered with purple larkspur and white daisies, plough through fields bursting with paint-like spatterings of mega-yellow dandelions and try to snatch at the wispy cottonwood seeds that air-surf around us. Everywhere we look is a more vibrant shade of green. The only thing more abundant than the greenery is the forever blue of the sky.

All the while we're escorted by Sarah's dog Slim who divides his time between weaving perilously close to the horses' hooves, darting ahead to forge the way, then running back to let his master know it's all clear.

'Slim was a rescue dog,' Sarah tells us. 'We got him from a shelter in Minnesota so he went from being cooped up in a pen to ruling this kingdom.'

I can't think of a happier ending for a dog and find my eyes glossing with tears. As I turn back to give Kerry a wobbly 'isn't life wonderful?' smile, I discover that she's riding virtually at a forty-five degree angle to the horse. Though she seems utterly unconcerned by this, Sarah feels duty-bound to dismount and yank Kerry and her saddle back to mid-point. But after just a few minutes of a slow walk, she's back to slanting off to her left again, giving a whole new meaning to the term 'riding side-saddle'. Sarah contemplates her for a moment and then seems to decide that it's only really a problem if she ends up at 180 degrees, her Stetson grazing the ground.

When we reach a quaint brick building in a clearing, Sarah stops.

'This is the Homestead cabin where we come for breakfast on our early morning rides,' she explains, adding, 'You've met Stephanie, right?'

We nod. She's the marketing girl and a dead ringer

for Sandra Bullock in looks and manner.

'This is where she got married.'

'Really?' Kerry coos, no doubt picturing herself and Jeff exchanging platinum spurs at sunrise.

'She had no intention of staying in Colorado but she met Todd while volunteering at a ski event in Steamboat Springs in '97 and she never left. Same for me – only I met my husband right here at Vista Verde.'

'So it's quite the romantic hothouse?' Kerry draws level with Sarah's mule.

Sarah smiles. 'I suppose it's only natural that the staff should get along – if you choose to come and work here you're going to have certain things in common: most likely you'll be outgoing, outdoorsy, adventurous . . . so things cook up,' she shrugs. 'Having said that, we always suggest they think long and hard before getting involved – three months is a long time to be around someone if you make a mistake in the first week.'

Worse still, what if you end up the one lonesome cowgirl while everyone else pairs up around you? It's not like you get much contact with the outside world to broaden your options. Mind you, I suppose there's always the chance of *guest relations* . . .

'Oh no, that's completely forbidden,' Sarah assures us.

Kerry and I exchange a concerned look, shortly followed by a sly smile. We'll see about that.

I spend the afternoon lolling on the daybed on the upper level of our cabin. I love the way the floor-to-ceiling windows peak to a triangle and look out over the branches of the aspen trees, it makes me feel like I'm in a tree-house. I sip Celestial Seasonings tea – which actually originated in Colorado – and shroud myself in moss-green fleeces. I haven't felt this relaxed in ages. I keep meaning to do something constructive or explorative but instead default to staring contentedly into space. It's only when I drag my handbag over to rummage for a Gummi Bear that I realise my phone battery has died. I reluctantly haul myself upright to plug in the charger and a second later I'm alerted to a new voicemail message. Oh my God! It's Troy the Trucker! His vocals are so chocolatey-rich my knees tremble and I find myself thudding against the wall.

'I was touched to receive your message,' he says. *'It put a smile on my face and in my heart.'*

What a lovely sentiment! I smile as I listen to how the poor guy spent his birthday in a dodgy bar in Tennessee where Quentin got into a fight then threw up on himself. Now he's looking for a new job where he drives alone. He concludes his mini-monologue by saying that he felt 'a nice attraction' between us, by which time I'm on the floor. I've never met a man who managed to sound both majestic and sweet at the same time. As soon as the line clicks clear I do a euphoric pogo around the den and then grab the main phone and dial my mother in Devon (11 p.m. her time) so I can play his message to her.

'Listen to this!' I squeak, omitting any kind of explanation or greeting.

'Well?' I ask her when he's done.

She responds with a breathy: 'He's hot!'

Hot?! Well, yes he is, but my mum's from Wales and *never* says things like that! Oh my God! This is serious.

'When are you going to call him back?' she demands.

'I don't know if I'm ready for an actual conversation!' I confess, still beside myself.

'Call him now,' she instructs.

So I do and subsequently we're on the phone for an hour talking about *everything* with limitless vigour, like you do when you're hoping this person will be The One and thus worth all the energy you're putting in. We both seem equally intrigued by each other and, in contrast to the cringingly repetitive exchanges with Paul, Troy has so much to say and it all comes out in perfectly structured, considered, expressive sentences. I'm impressed, especially since I'm such a messy orator, forever whizzing off at tangents. Most people periodically lose track of what I'm saying but Troy has no problem keeping up and it's such a relief not to have to backtrack or re-explain myself – I really feel like he 'gets' me. He also seems eager to delve deeper, asking me all sorts of probing questions like: Are you closer to your mother or your father? What has been your biggest achievement in life? Have you ever been in love? I'm on my toes but I can't dance fast enough. He even talks politics, as though I'm his intellectual equal! I'm not used to this. Normally with my younger guys I take the lead and provide the majority of the audio-entertainment but Troy is just as yak-happy as me, though – I must confess – his opinions are way more informed. Like Don! Suddenly I get a further surge of attraction – maybe I *have* found a replacement!

279

As we run through our respective employment CVs I learn all sorts of surprising things about him – he was in the Navy for nine years, then became a surf bum in San Diego, and later, during a brief flirtation with acting, he appeared in the same episode of *Miami Vice* as Phil Collins! I tell him that with his Barry White rumble he should really be doing voice-overs. Naturally the mere mention of Barry segues us onto the topic of sex, at which point he proclaims, 'I can't do it if it doesn't mean something. I'm not that kind of person.'

'And yet you were a male escort,' I feel compelled to observe.

'That was the Eighties and there were drugs that made that kind of thing "doable",' he says, sounding regretful.

It fascinates me that he's had this whole other existence. I must say I find it hugely appealing that he's such a complex and at times contradictory human being. One day I'll probe further but for now I decide to move the conversation on, asking him if he's currently seeing anyone.

'Not really,' he says, sounding atypically uninspired. 'Recently I've been on a few dates with a few different women but nothing that's made my monkey fly.'

I laugh at his choice of expression then tease, 'You do like things that fly, don't you, Troy?'

'Yes, Belinda, I do.'

My heart does a little skip hearing him say my name with *that* voice. And when he adds, 'You know, meeting you was the highlight of my trip' I feel the start of something. It's so different to my overwhelming, mind-addling 100mph swoon over Paul – with him I was caught up in the excitement of a crush, blind to the details. With Troy it feels like there is far more substance, far more potential for things to develop from a stronger friendship basis. I like how honest and direct he is and I appreciate that he's not just telling me what I want to hear. Yet I'm still on my guard. His insalubrious past makes me a little nervous – I don't want to be played. I must proceed with caution.

'I really should go,' I tell him as I spy a now bow-legged Kerry making her way home after her afternoon ride (turns out she could have managed a full day in the saddle after all).

'Really?' he sounds disappointed.

''Fraid so.' I heave a sigh, equally reluctant to prise myself away. 'It's been divine speaking with you, though,' I tell him, meaning it.

'Times twelve for me,' he smiles into the receiver. 'I'll call you in a couple of days.'

'OK. Bye then.'

After I put down the phone I sit for a moment in stunned reverie, not a little exhausted from all the mental activity. That was fun! Moreover I actually feel like I've made some kind of personal progress – I was so caught up in listening to what Troy was saying, I forgot to forage for hidden meanings and, come the farewell speech, I didn't feel all needy or unsure about what was going to come next – there was a lovely forgone conclusion to our speaking again. He said he's a man who likes to take his time and that could be exactly what an impatient, impetuous, hurry-head like me needs.

The other thing that struck me was when he made a single man's lament that he misses having a special someone to go to gigs with . . . A few weeks ago I would have felt the same hard-done-by hankering but apparently a shift has taken place within me whereby 'Poor me – I haven't got a boyfriend!' is no longer my overriding *cri de coeur*. I still have wants in that area, but they are no longer driving me.

Suddenly I feel all the more confident about my motivation to keep in touch with Troy – I'm going to follow through because I like him, not because I'm desperate to fill a gap. Having said that, I'm not going to get so hung up on him that I don't give the men in the remaining states a chance. There's no rush, after all. What I will do is put my feelings for him in a safe place. He could be a keeper . . .

Dinner is another culinary triumph (pan-seared Muscovy duck breast with a hash of Yukon Gold potatoes and Portobello mushrooms splashed with a Pinot Noir reduction followed by a dessert of crème brulee garnished with a whisper-thin shortbread spoon!) and the smart, informed, debating conversation of our fellow diners seems to be very much in Don and Troy's honour! I love that I can't predict what will be said next.

Kerry and I are the last to leave the dining room – having lingered over herb tea with the woman from VH1 – and when we step outside to enjoy the sunset I have to stop for a moment just to take in the scene before me: the reed-trimmed pond has a second circumference of young girls daintily practising their fly-fishing techniques, the dads who were previously discussing the merits of Harvard over dinner are now engaged in a vigorous game of Frisbee with their doting, yelping kids, and over by the campfire, tiny charcoaled fingers are pushing powdery pink cushions on the ends of long, skinny sticks.

It's an idyllic scene but I find myself flinching as I flash back to my marshmallow-toasting debut: I must have been nine or ten and enjoying my first weekend stay away from home at my friend Caroline's. On Sunday afternoon her (American) parents lit us a little campfire in the garden and kitted us out with the appropriate props. We were having great fun singeing our eyebrows until Caroline's marshmallow ignited and in a desperate bid to extinguish it (by waving her stick wildly in the air) she thwacked the flaming goo onto my brown corduroy trousers which promptly went up in flames.

When my mum came to pick me up my first words were: 'They set me on fire!'

I never did stay with Caroline again.

I'm sensing similar dangers around Kerry who has chosen the longest stick (all the better to poke your eye out with) and is currently incinerating her marsh-mallow in the hottest part of the fire. I decide to shift out of her reach to a spot where I don't feel like a smoked ham, but wherever I go the wind seems intent on gently lifting the ashes from the fire and dusting me with them. I take a few more paces back, leaving gravel for grass, and find a sanctuary midway between the soft woodiness of the fire and the freshness of the night air. Again I stop and look around. As the daylight bids its final retreat and exhausted, floppy kids are carried off to bed, there comes such a stillness to this place. I feel uncharacteristically still myself. My breathing has quietened to barely discernible inhalations – I'd say I was in a trance but for the fact that I feel entirely present. It's a feeling I will treasure. I may not have discovered my calling as a cowgirl like Kerry, but just spending time in this verdant haven has done my heart good.

But what of our chances of romance? It seems almost greedy to expect more from Vista Verde – it has already given so much. Besides, I'm still thriving on my earlier conversation with Troy. Suddenly a small warning flare goes off in my mind – I don't want to fall into the trap of missing out on what is on offer now just because I'm mooning over something that might never come to be, however tempting it feels right now. I take a step closer to the fire and assess the situation: last night Eve-Marie suggested rousing a rabble to go into town but this appears to have been forgotten and Jeff has vanished altogether, leaving Kerry more than a little miffed. Now the only folk remaining are us two girls and three men in Stetsons. Hey, I'm liking the odds. Then again . . . we've already chatted to John from Maine who seems a little too worthy and (forgive me, Lord) religious. There's Dan, who bizarrely used to sing opera in Italy and is lovely but again worryingly un-letchy. Which leaves Kyle.

My heart sinks as Kerry and I simultaneously make a bid to cosy up on his tree stump – three times is beyond coincidence! Could this be a serious sidekick switching issue? We come eye to eye but before either

284

of us can back down – and neither of us looked like we were going to – he responds with a swift good night. We're starting to think 'hot chocolate back at Big Agnes' when a new silhouette scuffs his way from the shadows. With just low-glowing embers and distant stars to see by we can't properly make out his features but he sets himself apart by sporting a baseball cap instead of the traditional Stetson and a large diamanté stud in his left lobe. (We promptly christen him the Rhinestone Cowboy.) From the pace and flirtiness of his banter he's clearly demonstrating more streetwise sass than them-there country boy wranglers and within seconds he has both Kerry and I corralled.

'So you girls ready to party?' he asks, firing off a round of pheromones.

We pant a yes and he suggests a local bar called the Elk River Tavern promising a glimpse of 'real Colorado men' and the opportunity to sup Fat Tyre – the curiously-named local beer.

'We can take our car!' Kerry volunteers, adding (to my dismay), 'Belinda can drive us there!'

Just the one Fat Tyre for me then.

Bed and bible hold more appeal for John from Maine but opera-singing Dan is game and takes the front passenger seat alongside me. Meanwhile the Rhinestone Cowboy (or RC for short) has found something of interest on the back seat.

'What's this?' he hoots, holding up our discarded CLIMAX sign.

Oh no! 'We can explain!' we clamour, scrambling for the slip of paper.

He snatches it out of our reach.

'Do you girls hold this up at an appropriate moment during sex?!' his eyes widen with mirth.

Aghh! We're forced to explain our mission.

Looking to gauge his reaction in the rear-view mirror, I get to study his face for the first time: his looks certainly live up to his sexy presence, if you like olive-skinned boy-band members. And I do. *Did! Did!* I'm over that! Hmmm. I wonder how old he is? I'd ask but he's currently engaged in low-volume conversation with Kerry. Thanks to Dan's dignified silence I can eavesdrop . . .

'Your accent is just the sexiest thing,' I hear him murmur, audibly aroused.

Kerry giggles appreciatively.

I feel mildly nauseous. This is getting to feel like a real problem, not something that might go away of its own accord. I can't blame Kerry for having the same taste as me but if this pattern continues I can see myself ending up a bitter onlooker. I miss Emily.

'If I was five years older I'd beg you to run away with me,' RC continues his wooing.

'Why five years?' Kerry frowns. 'How old are you now?'

'Nineteen,' he shrugs.

Ah. That'll make him officially too young to drink and me old enough to be his mother. Methinks it best I turn my attentions to those 'real Colorado men'.

'Here we are.' Dan shudders visibly as we pull into the car park fronting a simple, shack-like building.

We push open the door, alert with expectation, but instead of a bar lurching with saddle-sore cowboys and whiskery eccentrics we find just one occupied table –

286

and they're all staff from Vista Verde. Still there's always the barman with his dark hide-like skin. I bet he's rustled a few cattle in his time.

'ID,' he makes his gruff request as we hoick ourselves onto the bar stools.

'Ahh, British passports!' he notes. 'I used to live in High Wycombe.'

Foiled again.

We order our drinks (RC courtesy of that great American institution – the fake ID) and I tell the barman that I coincidentally spent many a childhood weekend in High Wycombe, playing table tennis at the Handycross sports centre.

What I don't tell him is that particular venue was the setting for one of my all-time most embarrassing teen moments – I spilled scalding hot chocolate in my lap and had to exit the sports centre with my pudgy white legs exposed in front of the very teenage boys I'd been trying to impress with my slicing serve.

'You OK there?' RC lures me out of my reverie.

I blink at his golden eyes. He really is a cutie.

'You are beautiful.' I hear the words but what surprises me is that it is RC saying them – to me.

I splutter, unable to respond. Teenage again.

'You are,' he assures me.

'You too,' is all I manage in return.

I definitely get the sense that RC is a gal-magnet but he tells me he's never been in love.

'How do you think you'll know when you are?' I ask him.

'I'll want to be with her every day. She'll feel like my best friend. You know, I'll just love her!'

My heart acquiesces. I'd say he's pretty much got it on the nose. He's not proposing any unrealistic notions about love transporting you to a higher plane; he just seems to be focusing on the companionship factor. I feel a genuine pang. Every time I think I'm done, something reminds me of how good it can be to love someone, and I get back in touch with the want within.

'My parents have got the most amazing relationship so I know it's possible, but I get scared that I'm not going to find that special one or they're going to find someone else before I get to them,' RC confesses.

I'd say the odds are stacked in his favour but sympathise all the same. I know too many loveable people that love has overlooked.

While I've been chatting to RC, Kerry has managed to get herself exceptionally tiddly, though I'm not sure how because just now I caught her sucking up nothing but air – it's at times like this you need a friend to remind you that you get more liquid relief if the straw is actually in the glass rather than merely alongside it.

'Oh my God!' Kerry reels at her faux pas, quickly ordering another round to make up for lost time.

True to form she then gets her karaoke head on, which for Kerry means just one thing – 'Hotel California', over and over again.

She's bellowing, foolishly releasing her grip on the bar top.

I leap to my feet and manage to convince her that there are superior acoustics in the car. RC and Dan go along with the plan.

Once ensconced in the back seat, Kerry starts hollering, 'You're the one that I want!', garnering enthusiastic 'Oo-oo-oooohs' from RC who really comes into his own for 'Greased Lightnin''.

I cast a glance at Dan, the one professional singer in the group, and find his lips firmly closed.

'Why don't *you* sing something?' I encourage him.

'What do you want me to sing?' he looks anxious.

'I don't care, *anything*! What about the piece you performed that got you the gig in Italy?'

'I can't remember it.'

Kerry's howling reaches a nerve-jangling crescendo.

'Dan, please!' I beg.

His eyes roam around in the dark, a man in search of a tune.

'Look, there's no need to feel self-conscious, you've heard how bad we are, anything will impress us.'

Kerry is now in melancholy Edith Piaf mode but despite my badgering Dan, Dan the Opera Man to bust a lung he remains miserably silent for the rest of the journey and by the time we de-car he looks positively suicidal.

'Sorry I picked on you,' I apologise as we head for the cabins.

'Sorry I couldn't sing,' he shakes his head, a broken man. 'I mean I stood up in front of thirty thousand people in a stadium in Italy but I couldn't sing in the car.'

'Don't beat yourself up,' I lay a sympathetic hand on his check shirt. 'I had all these disco-dancing lessons when I was twelve and I was fine during competitions but when my cousin asked me to dance at his sister's wedding I just stood there paralysed – should I do the Bus Stop or the Bump? I just couldn't move.'

'Mmmm,' Dan nods, yet remains inconsolable.

He's such a good chap, I feel awful for making him so uncomfortable.

'Anyway. Good night,' I smile, desperate to put him out of his misery.

'Good night,' he sighs.

For several minutes I stand alone in the ink-black night feeling the chill air weave through my clothing and penetrate my bones. I shiver and shuffle the grit beneath my feet. What's keeping Kerry and RC? If I go on ahead will they be able to find their way in the dark? I wave the torch up into the night sky, playing dot-to-dot with the stars, then try to signal to them by boring the light into the bushes where we parted company. No response.

'Kerry!' I call softly.

'What!' She snaps back.

'Oh pardon me,' I strop. 'I'm just standing here in the freezing cold waiting to light your path back to the cabin.'

'No need!' she trills, still hidden from view.

I tramp on in a foul temper and start hurling my clothes into my suitcase ready for the morning's departure. Or maybe I'll go tonight! Maybe I'll just leave her here and see how she likes that! All my frustration at the Kane situation comes flooding back – it's interesting to note that she doesn't give me a second thought when the shoe's on the other foot. Consequently, when she eventually appears, all pink of cheek and gleaming of eye in my doorway, I find myself snapping, 'Thanks for biting my head off back there!'

'What? No! I didn't!' she protests.

'Yes you did.' I stand firm.

'I didn't mean to,' she insists, earnestly. 'We were just . . . watching the car.'

'Watching the car?' I repeat, eyebrows raised. Does she take me for a fool?

'You left the interior light on.'

'No I didn't.'

'Yes you did. We were watching it for at least five minutes, that's why we were stood there. It didn't go off.'

This is ridiculous.

'Why didn't you say something at the time,' I grump. 'Like when I was down there with the keys?'

'Do you want me to go back?' Kerry offers.

'No,' I sigh heavily, pushing past her. 'I'll do it.'

I go clumping out onto the porch only to spy the Rhinestone Cowboy hiding behind a tree.

'What are you doing there?' I bark.

'Nothing!' he whimpers, cowering away from me.

'Just get inside,' I scowl, feeling like a disgruntled headmistress as I stomp onwards to the car park.

Unsurprisingly, there's no light on, either inside or outside the vehicle. I'm growling irritation to myself when Kerry appears by my side, puffing wildly.

'What now?' I roll my eyes at her.

'I didn't want you to go by yourself!' she pants, wielding a second torch.

'The car's fine,' I tell her. 'See?'

'Honestly, the light was on,' she frets.

'Yes, yes,' I huff, crunching back to the cabin yet again, this time with a Bambi-legged Kerry following behind.

RC is now sat awkwardly in the downstairs sitting room, which is officially my quarters – oh no you don't! As Kerry opens a bottle of wine I tempt him upstairs to her parlour with, 'Have you seen the view from up here?'

When I retreat back to the kitchen to get my tea, Kerry hisses, 'What are you doing? Now I'll have to get off with him!'

'Oh poor you,' I say sourly, dunking my pepper-mint teabag as she sloshes out two large glasses of wine.

Back in my room I realise I can hear every word they slur so I stuff my ears with cotton-wool, pull the duvet over my head and settle down for yet another troubled night's sleep.

'Morning!' I sing at 8 a.m., relieved that last night's grizzliness has evaporated along with my dreams of Alpen boxes featuring cut-out coupons to send off and win a real-live Troy. I realise now I was just being a sore loser. I wanted to get the guy but there wasn't an appropriate guy for me to get. It's only right that the Rhinestone Cowboy chose Kerry and I should be pleased for her that she had a night of passion. However, though I know I'm going to be fine with her today, the long-term picture is less rosy. This love rivalry between us is a serious concern and I've come to the conclusion that I've got two options: 1) I do the British thing and grin and bear it, possibly risking screwing up both my dream trip and my friendship with Kerry, or 2) I tell her the truth in the most tactful way I can, then recruit a new sidekick. My fourth of the trip. Oh dear, is it me?

'Kerry? Are you awake?' I stick my head up into her quarters like an inquisitive gopher.

'We didn't do anything!' Kerry blurts, sitting bolt upright in a bed that tells a very different story and a T-shirt that's both back-to-front and inside-out.

Acknowledging that she doesn't want to talk about it, I hand her a mug of tea then dip back downstairs and concentrate on loading up the car, settling the bill and saying my goodbyes.

Cut to half an hour later in the car: we've just emerged from a dirt-track diversion and seen a lone white horse trotting bareback down a main road when Kerry idly murmurs, 'I can't believe how different circumcised penises are.'

I turn to raise an enquiring eyebrow at her. She blinks back at me, seeming slightly startled to discover that she said that last sentence out loud. I wait for her to say more but she doesn't.

Then something occurs to me: 'Remember in the bar how both you and RC said you'd never had a one-night stand before?'

'Yes,' Kerry nods.

'You just did.'

A strange expression transforms Kerry's face, as though she is looking at herself from the outside and barely recognising the person she sees. Then she hurriedly composes herself and reasons, 'But it's not really a one-night stand because we didn't . . .'

'No?'

'No,' she confirms.

'But near enough,' I suggest, perhaps insensitively.

293

I'm just not used to my female friends being so delicate in these matters.

Finally, over pancakes at Winona's café-bakery in Steamboat Springs, Kerry tentatively opens up and we chat about the unexpected intimacies that can occur when you are tiddly and in 'enthusiastic' company. It's my belief that it's all too easy to inadvertently progress things further than you intend – you might, for example, find yourself unbuckling a fella's belt just to pass the time and bring a little variety to proceedings, not really thinking through the consequences of such an action. Then, before you know it . . . Well. It's a bit like trying to get the lid back down on a springy jack-in-a-box toy.

We have a good laugh and then I dare to test out the 'honesty is the best policy' theory by announcing, 'Kerry, you're too young and pretty to be my friend.'

She chuckles merrily as she squidges her last forkful of pancake into a puddle of syrup.

'I'm serious,' I say, setting down my hot cider. 'Well, you can be my friend but I don't think we're a good man-hunting match.'

'What do you mean?' she looks concerned.

Tentatively, I try to explain. 'This isn't a criticism of you, I think it's just a chemical thing – when it comes to men I feel like there's this underlying competition between us, and if we continue going for the same guys we're going to end up falling out with each other.'

'Oh no!' she cries.

'I'm not imagining it, am I?' I tilt my head at her.

'I didn't realise you liked RC,' she says, eyes wide.

'Yes you did,' I tell her plainly.

She looks down at the table. 'Maybe I did. But I really fancied Kane!'

'You see my point?' I smile.

She sighs and nods, pushing her plate away. 'So, is this it?'

Oh God! I feel like I'm breaking up with her. To counter my waver I force myself to think of her obstructive strop over Kane and the way she swooped in on Tony, RC and Kyle, not to mention the fact that she practically disowned me in favour of wooing Jeff.

'I think it's for the best, don't you?' I say lamely. 'I mean, if this were just a normal holiday . . .'

'But it's not,' Kerry states, suddenly getting it. 'You're on a mission. I understand – a girl's got to do what a girl's got to do.'

'Really? Are you sure you're OK with this?'

She nods bravely, silent for a few minutes before whispering, 'I've had a really good time.'

'Oh me too,' I insist, sliding down the bench to give her a big hug. 'I'll never forget the sight of you parading around Bourbon Street wearing that zydeco rubboard! Or holding that dirty great python in Gatorland!'

'Oh no!' Kerry laughs, hands up to her face.

'And you learned to lasso!'

'Yes I did!' she says proudly. 'So it's not all bad?'

'Of course not. We've both got some great memories but it's time to go our separate ways. For now.'

She's a good kid but I have to be ruthless.

'Who are you going to get instead of me?' Kerry asks as we return to the car and clunk our seat-belts into place.

295

'I really have no idea,' I answer truthfully as I turn the wheel in the direction of Denver airport. 'But it'll have to be someone with terrible taste in men!'

A name, a name, just give me a name . . .

NINA! My eyes spring open. Why didn't I think of her before? Oh, I remember, she has work commitments. Work-work-work – she rarely even gets around to taking her allotted annual holidays. But surely now that I just need a couple of weeks to complete the trip, she could wangle the time off?

I scrabble out of bed eager to call her and then realise it's still dark. 4 a.m. Darn this jet lag! What am I supposed to do for the next four or five hours? I schlep up the stairs to the kitchen (James and I live in an upside down house) and pop a couple of slices of bread in the toaster. It's only as I'm staring into space that I realise I haven't opened my post since arriving back in London.

I thumb through various bills and subscriptions until I come to a package with USA stamps and a Kissimmee postmark – Troy! Oh my God! He must have sent this while I was still in Colorado. I rip open the envelope and pull out a cute teddy card heavily doused in aftershave and a selection of photos. Oh goodie – I only got one hazy one of him, I hope he's sent a good 'un. I start flicking through – trucks at sunrise, trucks at sunset, a series of trucks photographed in a wing mirror of another truck and some voyeuristic shots of bare feet up on the dashboards of passing cars – fetish alert!

I read the accompanying note: *'If these don't do anything for you, send them back.'* Oh God – what exactly are they supposed to *do*?

I study them more closely. Hmm, that big black shiny truck with the Rolls Royce grille is kind of sexy – *what am I saying?* He's clearly a complete freak! My stomach churns uneasily. I've done it again – picked another nut. I quickly shove the pictures back in the envelope. Let's just forget he was ever a contender.

As I return my attention to my now cold toast, I get a pang of regret as if I'm losing a friend. Our conversation in Colorado was so wonderful, I really thought there might be something there. We just seemed to get along in that special way that really makes you feel good about yourself – I felt really happy and engaged talking to him. It seems a shame to let that go . . . *No! No! No! Do not succumb!* What does Iyanla Vanzant say? *'If you see crazy coming, cross the street'.* The sooner I hook up with a nice sane Arizonian the better . . .

And by 11 a.m. I've got Nina on board. She's just had the most stressful week of her life, working till midnight every night to get a last-minute magazine supplement designed and her boss is in no position to turn down her request for a well-earned break. Besides, once I'd mentioned Graceland was part of the itinerary I knew it would only be a matter of minutes before her Elvis pyjamas hit the suitcase.

Tennessee is actually the last stop on our trip but I have a good feeling about Nina enduring as a cruising partner – we've known each other twelve years, worked together for three, holidayed together, never argued, never ever gone for the same guy (major bonus!) and she's just about the most entertaining person I know – drunk or sober, I could just sit back and watch her like a sitcom.

She also has a tremendously loving heart that is currently going to waste. I stop and reconsider my last thought – is a loving heart really wasted if it's not loved back by a man? That's how I felt at the beginning of this trip but now I'm not so sure.

All I know is that I wish her love – preferably with a surfer or a military guy (that's her two strangely contrary predilections) – if that's what she truly wants. Since emerging from her last heavy relationship Nina's priority has been having fun so I'd say we're pretty much on the same page as far as men go – one day we're craving love so badly it's paralysing, the next we're embracing our freedom, wondering if the reason we're single is because we secretly like it that way. It'll be interesting to see if we feel the same way four states from now . . .

VALENTINE,
ARIZONA

There's not a single heart – real or paper or candy – in Valentine, Arizona. (So-called because Arizona achieved its statehood on Valentine's Day.) All that remains is a stack of bricks in the shape of a schoolhouse, some rusting railroad tracks and a couple of bungalows with nobody home.

What Valentine does have going for it, however, is its location – it stands astride historic Route 66, just 170 miles from the Grand Canyon.

Or the Goddamn Grand Canyon as Louise referred to it.

'So do you want to be Geena Davis or Susan Sarandon?' Nina asks, knotting her denim shirt at her enviably trim midriff.

Her clear green eyes seem to have acquired an extra sparkle since we touched down on US soil – I get the sense she's intending to make the most of every moment on this trip, so thrilled is she to be away from the pressures of work. For my part, I feel a lot more relaxed – it feels good to be with someone delightfully familiar who I can really trust.

'As long as we both get a Brad, I really don't mind,' I grin back at her, slotting on my shades.

Now this is truly thrilling! *Thelma & Louise* has got to be my all-time favourite movie so getting to recreate even a small part of their journey is a turbo-charged trip! I was living in Brighton the year the film was released and Thelma's hard drinking so inspired me that I bought my first whiskey miniature directly after the credits rolled and then sat drinking it on the beach, staring out to sea wondering when my adventure might come along. I couldn't think of anything more exciting than going on the run in America – shacking up in roadside motels, watching diner waitresses in tennis shoes pouring endless coffee and revealing the occasional hitchhiker hickey to a squealing pal. Back then I couldn't even drive, but look at me now – cruising along Route 66 with a brown paper bag of authentic Wild Turkey miniatures in my lap about to gawp over the edge of a mile-deep chasm. This feels great! Viva Arizona!

We reach the Grand Canyon at sunset. It may be one of the most visited natural wonders of the world but the real beauty is that it's so vast (a 215 mile drive from the North to South Rim) that you can easily find your own craggy cliff-edge to perch upon and marvel at the sky turning from blue to burnished gold without being jostled by backpackers. We sit side by side, experiencing a mix of sentimentality, optimism and peace.

Then Nina remembers the true purpose of our visit.

'Coo-eee! Brad!' Nina calls along one of the raggedy pathways weaving around the rocks. 'Are you down there?'

The trek to the bottom of the canyon takes a couple of days and – judging from the 'gifts' they've left behind – a good many people travel by mule. We decide to edge down one path to get to a more prominent ledge populated with angular-calved hikers but as we shuffle along a dust storm blows up in our faces and we're forced to cling to the bare rock for dear life.

'Ugh! Mule!' Nina spits, pronouncing the word 'mewwwl' for added emphasis as she sputters stray straw from her mouth.

The instant the rigorous tousling subsides we scurry back to safety. It's one thing propelling yourself off the edge in defiance, quite another to be toppled to your death by accident.

'Thelma and Louise never had this problem did they?' Nina rubs her sore, gritty eyes as we trek back to the car.

'No, we've got it much worse than them!' I confirm as we stroll into the Bright Angel Lodge for dinner.

I'm not sure if an avocado sandwich quite projects the 'wild woman' image I'm aiming for but curiously it's this prop that prompts our first male attention of the day – no sooner is my platter placed before me than the guy at the next table leans back on his chair and slavers, 'That looks delicious!'

Being a daring young thing, I reply, 'Want some?' and push my alfalfa explosion towards him.

'Is that rye bread?' he frowns.

I nod.

'I can't eat caraway seeds – I'll puke if I do!' he shrugs, returning to his beer.

Not a great response but it's good to know that if he gave us any trouble we wouldn't need a gun to defend ourselves, just a bag of Trail Mix from the local health store.

Once we're done eating I leave Nina to tot up the bill while I trot through to reception to book us a room. Bad news – every last motel/hotel room in the Grand Canyon is booked. While I have a small heart attack, Nina's having a small lust-attack as our strapping blond waiter (John Mitchell, 6'4", originally from Hawaii) offers us his floor to kip on. His shift is over, he's on his way home – do we want to go with him? We're on the verge of accepting when the receptionist calls me back and proudly announces she's found us a room in a motel eight miles down the road. Shame on us but the promise of a fully sprung mattress wins out.

'Thelma would have gone with him,' Nina grumbles as we drive into the black night. 'Where's our devil-may-care attitude?'

'Maybe we're delirious from jet lag,' I reason – my eyes are bloodshot and my skin is misbehaving, all the signs are there.

'Maybe,' Nina concedes. Then she gets cross all over again. 'Really, what are we playing at? It's what we've come on this trip for: to have some fun, to have a fling, and when it's handed to us on a plate, we turn it down!'

'I think we're lost.'

'Lost causes or lost as in we don't know where we are?' she checks.

'Lost as in it's midnight and we should have been at the hotel forty minutes ago. I can't even find us on the map. We could be anywhere.'

We pull over and once again curse ourselves for not taking advantage of the waiter. In every sense of the word.

'Wait here,' I tell Nina, heaving myself out of the car. 'There's a lodge across the street, I'm going to find out if they've got a room.'

'Try not to frighten the staff,' Nina warns.

She's got a point – I'm exhausted, tetchy and, let's face it, not looking so very gorgeous.

Once inside, I ding the reception bell and then it happens – the Brad-moment we've been waiting for. In fact it's a Brad/Jimmy combo – remember the black-quiffed Michael Madsen from the movie? This guy has all his sex appeal and none of the OTT squinting up through a furrowed brow.

'I don't normally look this rough,' is how I greet him.

'Is that an English accent you got there?' he asks with a shiver-inducing Tennessee drawl.

'Mm-hmm,' I simper.

'Wow, that's great. I love England. How can I help you?'

'Er, well, we were looking for the Grand Motel but if you've got a room we'll happily spend the night with you. Er, *here*,' I fluster.

He does indeed have a room – hoorah! – and while he sets that up I discover his name is Ken (you can't have everything), he's thirty-two and originally trained as a civil engineer but is doing late-night (11 p.m.–7 a.m.) accounting at the lodge until the park starts work on its monorail.

'So what part of Tennessee are you from?' I ask, desperate to keep him talking. (Listening to him is my new favourite thing.)

Twenty minutes later a mightily peeved Nina stomps into the lobby.

'What's taking you so—' she stalls as she clocks Ken. 'Oh! Oh! We don't normally look this bad,' she jabbers, trying to hide behind her hair.

'That's exactly what I said,' I mutter under my breath, reaching to squeeze her hand.

She squeezes it back, letting me know she fully endorses my captivation. I'm just flirting with a paranoia that he may be the first guy we ever fight over when he casually mentions he has a brother called Jake.

'And is he living locally too?' Nina smiles beguilingly.

'As a matter of fact he is.'

Having been utterly knackered we're now shimmering with excitement. We chat a little more, totally on-form, delighted that he's laughing in all the right places, then skip off to our room even though we're now way too hyper to sleep.

'He's sooooooo sexy,' we squeak repeatedly, bouncing from bed to bed. (With Nina there's no competition, just a shared glee.)

'Those eyes! That voice!' She spins around elated. 'And I just love that plaited rope thing around his neck.'

'And doesn't he seem really genuine?' I moon along. 'Kind too, I bet. And romantic . . .'

'I think he's the best I've ever seen,' Nina admits.

'Oh definitely,' I concur.

Nina hugs her pillow to her chest. 'Imagine if his brother is as good. We could have a double wedding – Vegas is only five hours from here!'

'And then we could honeymoon in Mexico – remember how Thelma and Louise were headed there to start a new life?'

'We'll be drinking margaritas by the sea, mamacita!' Nina sighs as we finally succumb to sleep.

The next day starts unnaturally early as we make a bid to catch Ken before he clocks off. We make it just in time and manage to lure him on a short stroll in the woods. He looks even better in the tree-dappled sunlight (though pleasingly unaware of his charms) and for once I can imagine being in harmony with someone – walking and talking and smiling all at the same time! It feels good. Then, over a breakfast of oatmeal and brown sugar, he tells us the worst thing we've ever heard: he's got a girlfriend. And so has his brother Jake. Suddenly, throwing ourselves off the edge of the Grand Canyon seems like the only way to go.

There's no disguising our disappointment so we make our excuses and leave – being in the presence of something that pretty but that off limits is a killer.

'I can't believe our luck,' Nina sobs, bereft.

'I know.' It's just like the Rhinestone Cowboy feared – you meet The One and it's too late, they've already hooked up with someone else.

The only way we can think to lift our spirits is in the

literal sense – flying over the Grand Canyon in a helicopter.

It's $100 per person for a half-hour trip and worth every cent, especially when our pilot says, 'Have you seen the movie *Thelma & Louise*?' just as we plunge over the edge! He then does some stomach-lurching, knuckle-whitening promontory dips and pinnacle swoops while hooting, 'I feel I've got a knack for this shit!'

A man after our own heart, Martin confesses that he and his Kenai pilot pals watch *Thelma & Louise* a couple of times a month.

'It's such a cool film!' he grins.

This experience has almost made us feel better but there's no dodging the deed that must be done. The time has come for us to shuffle to the very edge of the precipice and make that leap.

'You're a good friend,' Nina looks into my eyes for the last time.

I blink back the tears. 'You too, sweetie. The best.'

And then we clasp each other's hands and take a leap into oblivion . . .

Well, actually it's more of a little hop on the spot.

'I don't want to die never having experienced true love, do you?' I ask Nina.

'What do you think that was back there with Ken?'

I laugh. 'We've got to believe that there are more like him out there.'

'I guess we'll find out when we get to Tennessee!' she says as we turn back to the car. 'Maybe they're all like him there.'

'We can dream.'

After a couple of hours' drive we stop at the Galaxy diner in Flagstaff for a malt shake and a grilled cheese sandwich. I have to admit our prospects don't look good – there's clearly no point in going back to Valentine so we need to come up with a new address. While Nina puts a quarter in the jukebox for a tune called 'Willie and the Hand Jive' (I kid you not) I study the guidebook and consider our options: to the west we have the gunslinging ghost town of Oatman where Clark Gable and Carole Lombard spent their wedding night. To the east lies Holbrook, less picturesque but home to the legendary Wigwam Motel with its unique cement teepee rooms. I'm mentally ricocheting between the two when Nina returns to the booth and sends me off at a tangent by demanding a totty tot-up.

'I need you to bring me up-to-speed on all the love action you've encountered so far,' she says matter-of-factly, daubing ketchup on her plate.

I reach across and dunk a French fry as I review the previous seven states.

'Well, in Eden there was definite Brad-potential with Casey the Cowboy – he was gorgeous, would have been the perfect one-night fling – but nothing happened.'

'Why not?' Nina frowns.

'Lack of opportunity more than anything,' I decide.

'Nice?' Nina prompts as she reaches for an extra napkin – our toastie is deliciously greasy.

'That's where I met Mark, my first grown-up!' I smile. 'There was definite chemistry but . . .' I falter.

'. . . not the kind that made you want to kiss him?' Nina accurately completes my sentence.

311

'Exactly!' I confirm. 'And then there was Cazenovia – but we don't talk about that.'

'OK,' she concedes. 'Although full marks to you for giving it a shot.'

'You don't think I was a fool to go back for Paul?'

'Of course not!' she insists. 'How else would you know if he was The One?'

Marvellous! I'm not stupid, just thorough!

'Intercourse was a big let-down,' I continue checking off the list.

'Isn't it always?' Nina quips.

'Mind you, I did get to share a mirrored boudoir with a tall, dark, handsome man.'

'You mean James?'

'Yup,' I nod, defeated. Nina knows me too well.

I watch as she pushes her plate aside before starting on her chocolate shake. 'Go on – Convent,' she urges.

'Ah, the lovely Kane,' I sigh, reaching my straw across for a taster. 'Now he was boyfriend material.'

'Did you try and contact him again after you'd left New Orleans?'

'Yep, I called the hostel a few days later but he'd already checked out. No forwarding address. He's probably somewhere in New York by now. Or maybe even back in Australia.'

'A little too long-distance,' Nina confirms. 'So on we go to Climax.'

'Kerry fared better than me there. It's kind of disappointing – if I had to pick anywhere to relocate to in America, Colorado would be right up there with California. Anyway, you missed one.'

'I did?' She thinks for a moment and then ventures, 'Kissimmee?'

I nod, experiencing mixed emotions as I say the name 'Troy!'

'A-ha!' Nina grins. 'Now I know you found *him* sufficiently attractive.'

'I thought he was one of the sexiest men on the whole trip!' I confess.

'And he wasn't even a pasty teenage hippy – imagine that?!' Nina teases.

'Quite the opposite, in fact!' I acknowledge. 'And he was just so great to talk to. After our big ole chat in Colorado I really thought there might be something there. But those truck photos . . .'

'Well you always said you wanted someone who enjoyed their work.'

'Not that much!' I hoot, then sigh. 'But I don't want to dismiss him unfairly. Do you think I'm writing him off too soon?'

'Well, I think you could at least chat with him again – now you know he has cuckoo-potential you'll know the signs to watch for.'

'Yeah, maybe, but for now I think I'll just set him to one side.'

Nina shrugs then clasps her hands together and adopts a formidable tone. 'So, in conclusion, despite a few promising forays, there has been no actual sex?'

'No,' I reply, feeling a little scolded. 'But that's partly intentional – after what happened with Punctured Paul I thought I should wait and review all my options before I get physically intimate with any of these guys. Less chance of getting mangled that way.'

313

Nina rolls her eyes. 'Do you know what I think?'

I shake my head, half-dreading what's coming next.

'We should go to Phoenix.'

'Oh!' Not what I was expecting. 'Any particular reason? I mean, I know it's the capital of Arizona but I don't think there's much there other than resort hotels.'

'Well, you know how Valentine has a population of ten?'

I nod.

'And Oatman has one hundred and fifty and Holbrook five thousand.'

'Yes.' I can't argue with these facts.

'There's a million people in Phoenix.'

Oh I get it – the numbers game!

'Plus! Ken has got me thinking – maybe the Moqui Lodge isn't the only place in Arizona with delicious male reception staff. I propose we cruise around all the swanky hotels and check out the staff before we check in.' Nina gives me a purposeful wink.

'OK,' I agree, wondering what the odds are of finding someone as gorgeous as Ken who also happens to be available and interested.

Astonishingly, we find him the first place we walk into – a zen retreat on Camelback Mountain called Sanctuary. He's wearing a black silk Nehru-collared jacket and a name badge that says Ricky Hart. What a great name! And what great hair – a jutting ledge of jet emphasising his Gareth Gates meets Will Young looks. I take a closer look at his face: he is indeed The Chosen One, with gel-blue eyes, flawless sun-blushed skin and sensual wide lips.

'Ken who?' Nina nudges me.

As he talks us through the property's award-winning assets – the largest infinity pool in Arizona, an Asian-inspired spa, the opportunity to fine-dine alfresco with fire bowls to keep you toasty – I feel anticipation mingle with an instinctive optimism, as though I know something will happen here. And yet there is nothing in his behaviour to indicate this. Despite Nina and I amping our personalities to the max, his beautiful eyes remain downcast during our interaction and his only non-business comment is 'Aren't you hot in that?', directed at Nina, who for some reason is modelling a poncho and an ABBA-knit crocheted skullcap despite the ninety degree heat.

'It was cold at the Grand Canyon,' she cringes, suddenly self-conscious and thus uncontrollably giggly.

'As I was saying,' Ricky chooses to ignore her convulsions, 'if you ladies were to stay with us for two nights I can upgrade you to one of our one thousand square-foot mountainside casitas overlooking Paradise Valley.'

We're sold – after our Grand Canyon motel trauma we feel we deserve it!

'Is there anything else I can do for you?' Ricky asks as he hands us our room key.

A co-worker has now joined him behind the desk so we'll have to keep it clean.

'Actually we were looking for a native Phoenician,' Nina offers. 'Someone who could tell us a bit more about the area . . .'

'Jack's lived here sixty years, we could put you in touch with him,' the co-worker chips in.

Our faces fall.

'I'm third-generation Phoenix,' Ricky trumps him. (Thank goodness.)

'Oh really? Maybe we could have a little chat with you later.'

'Sure, I'm here till 10 p.m.'

Hmm, we're rather more interested in an after-hours conversation but it's a start.

As our accommodation sits halfway up a steep incline, we're invited to step aboard a golf buggy manned by an eager-to-please youth sporting a light veil of sweat. He chugs us past boxy buildings bordered with twisty trees, bright red flowers and the occasional Flintstone-esque boulder, then graciously leaps ahead to open our door. Ooeee! Could our casita be any chicer? For starters there's an expansive living area with copper and tan sofas, a real fireplace set into the whitewashed breeze-block wall, a gleaming six-seater dining table and a black granite kitchenette complete with tequila and jelly beans. The bedroom is dominated, as it should be, by a big ol' bed (not so much king as King Kong) with bright white bedding and smooshy chocolate-brown cushions. The bathroom causes even more whoops with its walk-in/walk-about/take-a-seat shower, parade of tea lights and chunky block of black soap.

'How weird – you go into the shower to get clean and come out looking like a coal miner,' I note, experiencing the dirty grey suds first hand.

'That stuff's designer – we're talking at least eight pounds a bar,' Nina calls to me from the bedroom as she racks back the white slatted shutters to reveal an enormous terracotta-tiled patio.

'I feel like a rock star!' she laughs, striking a pose on one of the mesh sunloungers.

'Isn't it amazing how a hotel room can actually *thrill* you?' I breathe in a lungful of sunshine and lean out over the balcony rail to take in the vista: it basically comprises rubble and shrubs, sandy earth and scratchy greenery set against low, donkey-brown mountains. Doesn't sound too inspiring and yet throw in the occasional elongated palm and a sky of such a vivid, sheer blue it plays as a forever of periwinkle silk, and you've created an oasis fantasy. My heart doesn't just leap with gratitude, it stays suspended.

Within seconds Nina is splayed out in her bikini, gearing up for a marathon tan-athon. But I can't settle. I pace the room, restless from the urge to see Ricky Hart again.

'Darn! I'm all out of cigarettes.' Nina throws her empty carton on the table.

'I'll get you some!' I quickly volunteer.

'Where from? We're in the middle of the desert.'

'They must have some shop or kiosk or something here,' I bluster, eager to get going.

'You like him, don't you?' Nina peeks over her sunglasses at me.

'Who wouldn't!' I shrug. 'I mean, do you?' It suddenly occurs to me that Nina might also have a hankering and I don't want to step on her toes – I got first dibs on Ken after all. (For what it was worth.)

'I like him but I don't fancy him. He's all yours!' she grins her approval.

'I wish!' I huff. 'Oh Nina, what do you think? He's barely even looked our way.'

'I don't know,' Nina pulls a face. 'I've got a feeling about you two.'

'Oh me too!' I confess, animated once again. 'I know I'm probably setting myself up for another fall, and I know my 'feeling' is basically lust, but . . .'

'There's only one way to find out,' Nina smiles, tickling my palm with a $5 bill.

'Hi. Um. Cigarettes?' My heart is pounding so loudly I can barely hear my own voice.

He directs me to the spa. I have more to say – I've even come armed with a prop – but I'm shaking too much to carry it off. This is ridiculous. I always was a sucker for a pretty face, but wasn't I supposed to be looking beyond that? I trot down the steps past the mesmerising infinity pool and into the spa shop. It seems something of a contradiction that amid all the oxygen masks and cuticle potions I'm purchasing cancer sticks for nicotine nails. I pick up a treatment leaflet to at least show willing. Inner Harmony for $150 – bargain!

By the time I've scaled the two flights of stairs back to reception I'm too out of breath to be nervous so I bowl on up and lean casually on the reception counter. Ricky looks expectantly at me as I try to control my wheezing.

'OK,' I puff. 'I thought I'd give you some forewarning of the kind of things we wanted to know, so . . .' This is where the props come in – yellow Post-It notes, each with a different question (grooviest bar, most romantic restaurant in town, etc.). I slap them in an abstract pattern before him then add, 'I'll give you

318

a while to think about the answers if you like.'

He gives me his first grin. 'OK – I don't want to sound stupid.'

'What – the retard on reception?' I quip, instantly regretting such un-PC alliteration. 'Anyway, we'll be coming down for dinner later, so I guess we'll see you then.'

I go to scuttle out, intent on burying myself under the nearest heap of sand when I hear him say, 'Sounds good.'

Now I don't need a golf cart to scale the mountain – I've got bionic legs.

At 5 p.m. Nina and I swim in the mountainside pool adjacent to our casita. We have it all to ourselves, which is heaven – such a rarity not to feel self-conscious in a swimsuit. For the first time on this quest I feel like I'm on holiday.

At 6.30 p.m. we start getting ready for dinner, which in our world involves a pair of lime-green towel turbans and me chasing Nina's Martini glass around the room with the cocktail shaker.

At 8 p.m. we stroll down to the 'elements' terrace restaurant. The surrounding terrain is sprinkled with golden lights, there's a feisty fire bowl set on the low wall beside us and slender candles lend our table a welcoming glow, yet the blackness of the desert night is so pervasive our waiter actually presents us with a pair of dainty torches to illuminate our menus! Nina is so radiant she hardly requires hers – it has always been one of her keenest ambitions to be taken for a romantic dinner-à-deux, but in eighteen years of dating this simple event has somehow eluded her.

Most people know her as the comical, lairy, fall-down-drunk girl but if they could see her now! Aside from her French-tipped nails and immaculate posture, she is displaying one of the most enviable and elusive attributes – natural grace.

This feels like a very special occasion and I tell her so, chinking her glass with the words: 'To your inner Audrey!'

'Oh don't say the Hepburn word – I'll cry!' she smiles mistily at me, then pauses to take in the exquisite food, wine, setting, even our gentle waiter loitering to pounce on any whim we may have. 'This is just so perfect!' She quells a tear. 'I always wanted a man to take me to dinner but now I'm here with you I wouldn't change a thing!'

I congratulate her on what I consider to be one of the keys to happiness – being flexible with your dreams. Not to mention being grateful for all the unexpected pleasures that happen along the way. In the twelve years we've been friends, Nina and I have never once fine-dined on a balmy night – we had no idea how lovely it could be!

'What a gift this is!' I sigh, spinning with satisfaction.

After a dessert of caramel cheesecake we step through to the 'jade bar' for cocktails which instantly make us silly. Seeing as it's nearly 10 p.m. we decide to sneak round to reception to see if we can tempt Ricky through to the bar after his shift. Unfortunately reception is positioned around a corner and we realise too late that it's not him stood behind the desk but a stern-looking middle-aged woman. Under her suspicious gaze we feel like naughty schoolgirls and feign a sudden fascination with the minimal artwork to cover the purpose of our visit.

And then it dawns on me – he's already gone for the night. We've missed him.

'Maybe he's finishing up behind the scenes,' Nina suggests as we skulk back to the bar.

'I suppose he could just have popped to the loo.' I try to maintain hope as we take a seat in the restaurant lounge where we can keep a close eye on all comings and goings. I feel totally on edge and can't seem to quell the sick feeling in my stomach.

'There he is!' Nina yelps. His sharp silhouette gives him away.

I experience a rush of relief mixed with a whisk of euphoria. We give him a few minutes to get back into position and then trot round the corner after him. He's right there, behind the desk. Next to the stern lady.

'Oh!' I blurt. 'Hello again.'

She looks unimpressed. He looks shifty.

'Um . . .' There's nothing for it but to take the bull by the horns. I introduce myself to the woman who is evidently his boss and tell her that Ricky is kindly giving us a bit of local history.

She raises an eyebrow. Oh God I feel such a groupie. He must get girls fawning over him all the time.

'I can't answer your questions right now,' he squirms. 'I'm kinda shy if I have to speak in front of more than two people.'

'Shy?' Stern Lady scoffs, then beckons me closer. 'What do you think of his hair?'

'His hair?' I repeat, stalling for time – I don't want to lose her support or alienate him. 'It's how all the young people are wearing it today.' Great, now I sound fifty.

She just tuts and shakes her head.

I sigh, frustrated. What I really want to say is, 'It's perfect. He's perfect.'

'Well, let us know when you're done.' I give him a little wave and dart back to the bar to down another drink.

'I can't walk straight,' Nina notes as we relocate to a window seat. 'My legs have gone all funny.'

Unfortunately my nerves are keeping me sober. I can't believe he's just around the corner and any moment he will appear. Like right about now!

'Hi!' he says, approaching our table.

I instantly get all jittery and overly chatty, trying to buy him a drink, offer him a seat, ask him how he is and apologise for embarrassing him in front of his boss – all in one go.

He hesitates before he responds, looking awkward. I've overdone it. He's going to make an excuse and leave, I just know it.

'Actually I can't stay,' he whispers.

'Oh. OK. Well another time, perhaps.' I try to sound unfazed.

'I just mean I'm not allowed to drink in this bar.'

'What did you do?' Nina gasps.

'Nothing,' he laughs. 'None of the staff are allowed to drink in the bar or eat in the restaurant, it's hotel policy.'

Oh no. Where else can we go? I mean we've got a huge suite with a minibar and a cocktail shaker but I couldn't suggest that, it's too forward and no doubt against hotel policy.

'Do you want to come to our room?' I say it anyway.

'Yes.'

'I mean, I realise—' He said yes. I didn't even have to get persuasive. 'Oh. Great. Should we, er . . . go up separately?'

'It's probably best.'

'OK. Well, we'll um . . .' I down my drink in one and Nina follows suit. 'See you there shortly. Casita Five.'

'I know, I checked you in.'

'Right!'

We scurry back up the hill, whinnying excitement under our breath and tearing around the suite checking nothing untoward is dangling over the back of a chair. Then we wait. And wait.

Finally there's a knock at the door.

'Sorry – I got lost!' he apologises.

Nina takes herself onto the balcony for a cigarette, leaving us with a fantastically subtle yet effective, 'I'll just leave you two cats to it.'

From the moment we hit the sofa we're babbling nineteen to the dozen. He's definitely younger than me but he's also ten times more entertaining than your average stunner and when he confesses he lost his virginity at fourteen to a thirty-five-year-old woman I want to whoop with joy – if he can handle a twenty-one-year age gap, he can handle me!

'You realise that was totally illegal?' I feel compelled to observe.

'We were in Greece,' he shrugs. 'My dad had a bar there.'

'Was she a native?'

'No, she was from California. Actually she was going out with one of my Dad's friends but she left him for me!'

'Ouch!' I exclaim.

'She was my teacher. She taught me how to treat a lady and it's definitely worked to my benefit,' he gives a sly smile.

'Did you love her?' I ask, trying not to fall to the floor and kiss his feet. He definitely seems like someone built for *amore* – the ultimate toy boy.

'Oh no, I knew the difference even then. Sure, I'll always remember her – she was my first – but I've only been in love once in my life and she left me.'

'Oh no. When was that?' This is great – I can't believe I'm getting all the vital info upfront.

'About two years ago – we moved in together a little too early. Every day I woke up and I'd say, "You're so beautiful, I love you so much", and when we split up she told me I said it too much and it got old and didn't mean anything.'

'Ungrateful wretch!' Nina observes as she saunters past us to the kitchen.

'What's her situation now?' I ask.

'She's married,' he says quietly. 'She was engaged three months after we broke up.'

'That's happened with two of my ex-boyfriends,' Nina empathises. 'We split up and they get married almost straight away.'

'I've had four that are now gay,' I volunteer.

'Are you serious?' Ricky hoots.

'I don't take it personally,' I shrug.

'Perhaps you should,' he teases. 'I think four is a little more than a coincidence!'

'It's a habit I'm trying to break,' I tell him.

'Apparently you've got to have your heart broken five times before you meet your true love,' Nina tells us.

'Mine must have been and gone then,' I mutter as Nina heads to the bedroom to retire. (Gotta love that girl – there's no slamming of doors or huffing from her. She's that rare breed of friend who is genuinely happy for you to be happy.)

Ricky goes on to tell me that his dad has been married six times but he's only met two of his father's brides, one of whom was his real mom. I've got a few family corkers of my own and it's fun to talk about such things with someone who's had worse but still thinks it's funny, as opposed to sinking into a mire of self-pity. I like his spirit! The only downside to the evening is that Ricky's mobile phone rings repeatedly. He doesn't answer but looks ever more vexed with each disturbance. I fear it's a girlfriend trying to track him down but I don't ask because I don't want to know. I've never made a move on someone I knew had a girlfriend and I'm not going to now. Of course if he made a move on me, that's a whole different story.

Finally the ringing gets so relentless he apologises and says he has to leave. Damn! But when he's halfway out the door he turns back and asks about our plans for tomorrow. I tell him we have none. (Yes we should be exploring Phoenix's botanical gardens and Old West art but we're so in love with our casita we can't bear to leave.)

'How about I take you girls for ice-cream in the Old Town?'

'That would be lovely!' I beam.

'Pick you up around 3 p.m.?'

'Perfect!'

He likes you! Nina grabs me as soon as he's out of earshot.

'I thought you were asleep!' I laugh, surprised by her pyjama-clad pogoing.

'I told you I had a feeling about this one!' she crows as I shoo her back to the bedroom. 'I've brought you luck!'

'He's just being nice!' I fervently deny his interest but inside I'm doing arabesques.

After yesterday's disappointment with Ken this is just the boost I needed. I am so on the brink of being smitten. I try to settle my breathing into sleep but I can't; I'm grinning too much and my toes are jiggling with joy. I just pray he doesn't have any weird fetishes – if he turns up tomorrow with an assortment of reception-desk photos I'll just die.

The Ricky Hart that meets us the next day is in possession of a very different persona to the confident, worldly creature he was last night. He's smiling and genteel but apparently his prior claim to shyness is for real, by day at least. Fortunately we're blessed with plenty of things to 'oooo' over and point at in charming Old Town Scottsdale. The only snag is the heat – even in the shade of the Old West shopping arcades it's ninety degrees.

'About that ice-cream . . .' I nudge him.

Ricky smiles and guides us into The Sugar Bowl – a retro ice-cream parlour with pink leather booths, chrome trimmings and a giant gobstopper dispenser. I love it so much I buy a commemorative mug along with my cherry swirl ice-cream.

As we chat, we mention to Ricky that we were in Valentine the day before yesterday and ask for his take on the festivities that go along with February 14th.

'I've always thought of Valentine's Day as the girl's holiday,' he smiles thoughtfully. 'Last year I took my girlfriend to dinner at Cowboy Chows ($100 a head), booked fourth row seats for the opening night of *Rent* and while we were out I got a friend to put candles and flowers all around our apartment. It took me months to save up but it was worth it because she said it was her all-time favourite night.'

'You freak of nature,' I gasp. 'I've never had anyone do anything like that for me.'

'Me neither,' Nina confirms.

'I like to spoil. I love making girls happy. I used to stop off on my way home from work to buy her a flower – $3 to bring a smile to her face, how can that not be worth it? I don't understand how something like that would be hard for people. It's pretty basic.'

Basic, yes. Common, no. If only more men twigged a) how easy it is and b) the great rewards they will reap from a few simple acts of affection. That's one of my main gripes with the modern male – they can never be bothered to go to any trouble to demonstrate their feelings but are happy to suck up any treats or surprises you throw their way with barely a murmur of gratitude. Whatever happened to reciprocity?

'Have you had girls do sweet things for you?' Nina asks, reading my mind.

Ricky nods. 'On that same Valentine's Day, my girlfriend hid thirty cards around the apartment, in the fridge, on the TV . . . and when I went to work she gave me a gift bag with eight more – one for every hour I was gone. And the last one said, "Hurry home . . ."'

I shake my head. 'The kind of guys I've been out with, if I did anything like that they'd move to a different country.'

Nina agrees. 'I've never even considered it because I know they wouldn't appreciate it. They'd just wonder what the hell was going on.'

'Well, I've never been out with a girl that put so much effort in. I was impressed.'

It's official: Ricky is The Perfect Boyfriend – not only is he sexy-funny-gallant, he's not afraid of commitment, has a degree in romance and says *I Love You,* even when he's sober!

He's clearly a rarity. But what of the average Arizonian? I have to ask, how does he think the locals differ from guys from the other states.

'They're definitely more wild, they like to party,' he gives a naughty grin.

'Big drinkers?'

'Oh yeah, which is just as well because there's basically nothing here but bars and restaurants.'

We ask if there are any particularly sexy dining establishments he would recommend and he tells us about a fabulous fondue place called The Melting Pot which has cloaked-off booths for couples. I am instantly ga-ga – I used to play with my mother's fondue forks as a child (while listening to her Demis Roussos LPs) but I've yet to experience the real thing.

'Shall we go tonight?' I grab Nina's hand.

'You can't really go there without a date,' Ricky frowns. 'I'm working till 11 p.m. but I can find you a couple of guys if you like.'

I don't quite know what to say. 'Oh. That's very kind of you,' is the best I can muster. This isn't quite what I had in mind – him setting us up with his friends.

'I'm sure they'd be happy to take you – a couple of hot British chicks . . .'

Ooh Mr Hart, you flatter us!

'Imagine if they walk in and they're absolutely gorgeous!' Nina pips, now back in her natural prone state on our casita patio.

'I don't want to be a pessimist but I think we need to prepare ourselves for the exact opposite.' I remind her that there's generally just one looker in a group of guys and I'm guessing Ricky's it. 'Just pray they've got a sense of humour – that's what will get us through the night.'

It's at this point that Ricky calls up from reception to tell us that fondue is off the menu – his friends, Jason and Nathan, want to stick to liquor. That's fine but it does mean we'll need some snacks to tide us over so I go cruising in search of a couple of party platters so we can play Seventies hostesses should the need arise.

At lunch Ricky mentioned that Scottsdale is rife with high-maintenance silicone blondes on a mission to

329

hook a millionaire husband, and at the swanky local supermarket I find a selection of women who have clearly succeeded – you've never seen such a profusion of designer labels at a deli counter. It's like a cross between Harrods Food Hall and *Valley of the Dolls*. I swear these women must get manicured on the hour. As I scuff around feeling like the hired help, I wonder what it would be like to live like they do – to have the mansion, the Mercedes, the businessman husband with his own walk-in wardrobe. It's so far removed from my reality I can't even imagine the kind of conversation you might have with a man like that. Would you talk about shares? Golf? Chilean wine? Despite the undeniable appeal of upscale desert living – and if Sanctuary is anything to go by, it *is* magnificent – there would be too many dinner parties and handbag dogs for my liking. Besides, I don't have any of the necessary attributes to become a trophy wife. Hey ho, I'll just have to make my own millions.

On the way back to Sanctuary I wind down the car window and let the warm breeze filter through my fingers like a cashmere caress. All my senses feel magically heightened here, so much so that I can't help but wonder if we're on a ley line or something. As I take in the luxuriant blue of the sky I feel like I'm gliding on an other-worldly plane – my chest lifts, my eyes widen and my heart brims over with love for everything and everyone. If only I could feel this open and optimistic every day.

As I re-park the car, I can't resist the urge to stop by reception to see Ricky, hoping that this feeling of abundant love might prove contagious.

'I'm so happy!' I tell him, glossy-eyed and beaming. 'I just wanted you to know!'

'Thank you for sharing!' he winks back.

'You will be joining us later, won't you?' I try not to beg.

'Well, I don't finish till 11 p.m. but if you want me there . . .'

'I definitely want you there,' I state, keenly in touch with my desires. (This is no time for pussyfooting around – we fly to New Mexico tomorrow so tonight is my last chance to be with him.)

'OK, I'll see what I can do.' He gives me a neat salute.

On the hike up to the casita I can't stop smiling. I love it here! I love feeling like this!

'I'm having a bit of a moment,' I call ahead to warn Nina as I hurry to join her on the patio.

'What is it?' she gasps.

'I feel so full of bonhomie I could fly!' I announce, arms flung wide.

'Oh me too!' she says, scrambling to her feet, her face transformed with misty-eyed emotion. 'My stomach keeps going around and around and just now when I was staring out across the desert, it was so beautiful I nearly cried!'

I grip on to her, excited to be sharing this happy delirium with someone so special.

'It's amazing!' Nina quavers. 'I've never felt like this in my whole life!'

As we hug, giddy with gratitude at our good fortune, I realise I've been lucky enough to have had several moments of transcendental contentment since beginning this quest – there was the picnic bench outside The Cherry Country Store in Northern California, the balcony at the Soniat House Hotel in New Orleans, marshmallow night at Vista Verde in Colorado, indeed last night's terrace dinner was a strong contender, but this is Number One. I sigh to myself – it's such a beautiful thing: going in search of bliss and actually finding it.

It's only when we're back inside getting ready for our date that I realise none of the pinnacle moments I've cited have involved a man. Certain guys – Casey, Troy, Ricky, even Paul before I got to know him – have stirred up major desires and given me a delicious thrill, but with them it was all about the buzz of attraction and anticipation, about wanting more, whereas today's bliss was about being entirely happy in the moment – happy for everything to be exactly as it is. The closest I've come to that feeling with a man was when I was kissing Kane because, for once, my mind wasn't racing to future possibilities. I was just enjoying having my wish granted.

It's funny – people say love will come along when you stop looking for it and yet, for me, life has come along while I'm looking for love.

And it's so much more than I could have hoped for. For starters, who knew there were so many amazing emotions to be had outside of Boyfriend Land? In my mind I thought all the most soul-soaring emotions were only accessible by being in love. Now I can see that's not true – there are infinite ways to have your heart fill up and spill over, the range is as varied as a colour chart in a paint shop. I used to think it was as simple as red = love but I had completely underestimated how powerful life can be when you expose yourself to new experiences.

Of course, this doesn't mean it'll always be a breeze – on the way down to the bar to meet Ricky's boys, I get a spectacular attack of nerves. I don't think I've ever been on a blind date before. (Yes I've dabbled with Internet dating but at least with that there's been some correspondence and a photograph, however misleading.) While I try to coax the startled look from my face, Nina falls foul to nervous giggling. By the time the guys arrive she's doubled up, not a good look considering one of them (Jason) is miniature and I'm fairly certain he thinks she's laughing at him.

'Don't mind her!' I trill, trying to block her convulsed, tear-stained face from view. 'Can we get you a drink?' I address Nathan, a normal-size chap with a Fifties vibe to his shirt and hair.

'Actually we should probably go – we've left a friend in the car,' he explains.

'Why? What's wrong with him?' Nina composes herself sufficiently to ask.

'Nothing,' Nathan looks bemused. 'He just wanted to wait outside.'

Whatever the reason, I'm delighted to hear we're not a neat little quad and gleefully trot out to the car park.

'Oh look at his big hat!' Nina coos as we approach the third man, who is leaning on the side of a Ford Focus.

'It's an afro,' I hiss, wondering how many more blunders Nina can make in one night.

Our first stop is Lucky 7 – a techno-styled sports bar with a maze of metal walkways and the kind of staircases that invite guys to look up a girl's skirt. (Clocking the raging pick-up vibe, Nina renames the joint Get Lucky's.) We claim a table out on the terrace and take full advantage of the phenomenal dollar-a-drink policy. The boys seem to know every other person at the bar and introduce us to a friend of theirs called Jennifer, who Nathan confides every one of them – except Ricky – has slept with. Nina promptly christens her Jenny been-around-the Block and gives her a faux J-Lo serenade every time she walks past. She's on a roll!

We're all getting along great and Ben – he of the afro 'hat' – quickly becomes my favourite on account of his cuddly bear demeanour. Were it not for Ricky's prior claim on my heart I would probably have quite a crush going by now. But then he shows me his grizzly side . . . a tiddly stranger has been drawn over by Nina's accent and mid-conversation draws up a chair next to her. Ben is absolutely outraged and gives him a verbal clouting.

'What was that in aid of?' I gasp, shocked by his hostility.

'That is so incredibly disrespectful,' he rants. 'He didn't even acknowledge us guys before he sat down.'

'What?!' I splutter. 'You want him to ask *your* permission before he talks to Nina?'

'That's not what I'm saying . . .'

We're still in a hearty debate two hours later – so many chips-on-the-shoulder, so little time.

Around 11 p.m. Nathan's cell phone starts to ring

but he doesn't deign to answer it. I can't help but feel panicky – is that Ricky trying to locate us? If so, why didn't he speak to him?

'Another round?' Nathan gets to his feet.

'Sooooo, is Ricky coming along later?' I ask, trying to sound casual.

All three boys roll their eyes.

'What?' I ask, feeling unsettled.

They then take turns to critique and spoof him, and not in the most affectionate way. The whole thing feels a bit teenage-mean and seriously lowers my opinion of the company we're keeping.

'Shall we go somewhere else?' Mini-man Jason mercifully breaks their run of ridicule.

Sugar Daddy's is far more to my taste – hand-painted Frida Kahlo-goes-voodoo artwork and a live Latin band. Despite the fact that we're with three guys, men keep bowling up to ask if we'd like to dance. One older fellow is so annoyingly insistent I'm tempted to set Ben on him, but oddly this behaviour doesn't seem to bother him at all. Apparently he only freaks when chairs and tables are involved.

'In England a guy would never approach a girl if she was with someone else,' I tell him. 'In fact they rarely approach you at all . . .'

'Arizona guys are wild,' Nathan confirms. 'Hey! *Come sta?*' He turns to greet a stray Milanese guy.

Nina listens agog as they yabber together in fluent Italian, emitting a whimper of lust at a level only best friends can hear. Nathan doesn't know it yet, but he just pulled.

We now have quite a group going, including a few

friendly 'I like your shoes!' females. They're a fun crowd, I'll admit, and Nina is having a whale of a time but I'm still a little on edge, *waiting* . . .

Finally Ricky walks in and I try not to buckle at the knees. He's wearing a dark wool pea coat over a white shirt and looks simply stunning. I give him a petite welcome hug but don't want to look too gushing so quickly resume my conversation with Nathan. Ricky falters, sensing that he's out of the mix, and dips to the bar. While I continue chatting to the ensemble, I glance back and spot him downing a quick succession of shots, presumably to catch up with the rest of us.

When he returns, I shyly catch his eye.

'Looks like they've hit if off,' he nods over to where Nina and Ben are now vigorously twirling each other on the dance floor. 'I've never seen him look so happy!' Ricky adds, shaking his head in amazement. 'And he never dances!'

'It's actually Nathan she likes,' I confide.

'Are you sure about that?' he asks, studying Fred and Ginger a little closer.

'That's just her having fun,' I tell him. 'You wait and see.'

Over the next hour or so I notice that no one else is paying Ricky much attention and it's affecting his confidence. That, in turn, makes me feel fretful and self-conscious. Last night we had so much to talk about but now I can't think of anything to say. If only I could get him alone.

My first opportunity comes when the bar closes and it is decreed that the party will continue chez Jason. Ricky's car is parked right next to his yet everyone automatically resumes the original seating plan in Jason's car. I delay my squeeze into the back seat, hoping Ricky will invite me to ride with him, but he doesn't. What *is* going on? Why the segregation? I don't get it!

By the time we get to Jason's apartment the plan has changed – the party will take place at our casita, but with Jason's liquor. Everyone hurtles inside to grab a bottle – except Ricky, who remains alone and sullen in his car. I walk over to him and do my best prostitute lean-in.

'You OK?' I ask.

'Sure,' he shrugs, looking anything but.

I can't tell if he wants to be left alone or he's just not interested in my company but I decide to take a chance and ask, 'Can I sit with you for a bit?'

He avoids eye contact but motions for me to help myself to the passenger seat. Once inside the car I put on my best counsellor voice and ask him what is troubling him. He's a tough nut to crack but I badger him until he finally blurts, 'It's just that on the way here there were five of you in one car and just me in mine.'

'You didn't offer anyone a ride!' I protest, rather too emphatically. (Trust me, I would have noticed!)

'You're right, I didn't,' he concedes.

Silence.

'I just feel like I'm interrupting.'

'Don't be silly,' I place a reassuring hand on his knee.

He takes a breath then asks, 'Have they been bad-mouthing me?'

I pause for a moment and then say, 'Yes.' I think he should know the truth; he seems to suspect it anyway.

'God! I hate it when they do this! I introduce them to girls to be nice and because they never meet anyone on their own, and then suddenly there's this weird vibe and the girls don't want to know me any more.'

'Yeah, they did a great job on me.'

He looks up.

'I'm here, aren't I?' I smile. 'Mind you, it's a good tactic. They make a girl feel such a sucker for liking you – it is, after all, the ultimate cliché to go for the good-looking one!' I wink. 'So they put doubts in her mind and consequently the girl feels like she'd be a fool to fall for your charms. She wants to laugh along with the gang, so the easiest thing is to ignore you. And tonight, with you acting so standoffish, it was very nearly a *fait accompli*.'

Ricky now looks more miserable than ever. Perhaps I should have just said, 'Nooo! They were singing your praises.'

'You have to know it makes them look bad,' I assure him. 'Deliberately undermining you – what kind of mates do that?'

'I've known those guys for years, they're good friends really,' he defends them. 'It's just this one thing we have an issue over.'

I almost feel sorry for his friends – it must be galling when every girl automatically goes ga-ga over Ricky. He's spoiled for choice and they're left picking up scraps. It's got to make it worse that they can't dismiss him as 'just a pretty face' – they must surely envy his unmistakeable charm and cosmopolitan vibe. If only

338

they realised they'd do better to learn from the master rather than try and vanquish him.

'Have you ever told them how you feel about this?' I ask.

Before he can respond, the gang comes piling out. When they see I'm consorting with the enemy, their faces fall.

'That's right!' I want to taunt, 'Your evil plan didn't work!' They can sneer all they want. I know where my priorities lie – I want to be with Ricky.

'Can I travel with you back to the Sanctuary?' I ask, showing my solidarity.

'I don't know if I'll go,' he sighs.

'Oh come on!' I rally him.

'Do you want me to?' He looks over at me with mournful eyes.

A huge grin spreads across his face when I reply, 'Yes.'

When we get to the hotel we park and make the most of the time alone, chatting about the curious dynamics of friendship and the different people we become in a group situation, depending on the roles we've been assigned. (I can't help feeling this particular posse could do with some time apart.) There's no flirting or sense of an impending kiss, and once again his phone rings incessantly. But this time it's the boys. They want to know what's keeping him. *Where is he?* I'm starting to get annoyed – why can't they just leave him alone? Twenty minutes later Ben gives an emergency holler – he got fed up playing gooseberry to Nina and Nathan (quick told-you-so to Ricky) and so he left the party but now he's broken down and he

339

needs Ricky to rescue him. I can hardly believe the cheek of it!

'I've got to go,' Ricky tells me.

'Of course you have,' I say, stepping out of the car with a surprising degree of resignation.

'I'll try and come back later but—'

'Don't worry,' I tell him. 'You do what you've got to do.'

When I enter our suite I find Nina and Nathan entwined on a starlit sunlounger.

'We're getting married!' Nina trills when she spots me. 'Tell her!' She tweaks Nathan's cheek.

He seems to think it's an excellent idea. As they run through the wedding plans, I can't help but chortle to myself. Nina really is The World's Most Irresistible Drunk, beating even Kerry. There's only ever been one guy she targeted for a snog who actually tried to prise her off and though he looked to me for help I just shrugged and told him the easiest thing was just to go with it. When she gets filled with that level of exuberant energy she's a force of nature. At the moment Nathan can't believe his luck but there's something he doesn't know about a Nina this tiddly – he has just a small window of sexual opportunity before she conks out.

I look at my watch.

Any minute now . . .

Yup, there she goes – head nuzzling into his neck, her arms reaching around him like she's cuddling a big teddy, then a full body slump. Gone!

When he twigs that she is beyond revival, Nathan carries her through to the bedroom, lays her out on the bed, plants a kiss on her forehead and exits. I suppose I should join her but I'm not ready – for me the evening feels incomplete. I curl up on the sofa and watch vintage *Saturday Night Live,* still light years away from sleep. Ordinarily I'd be either crying or having a tantrum at this point but tonight I feel oddly detached and calm. I wanted Ricky so much but I guess it wasn't meant to be.

Drrinnnng! It's the phone.

'Hello?'

'I would have thought you'd be asleep by now.'

It's Ricky!

'I'm just watching TV,' I tell him, trying not to let my smile show in my voice.

'Look, I'm sorry about earlier – my mood, all the distractions—'

'It's fine,' I cut him off in my most soothing voice.

I hear him sigh. 'Do you still want me to come over?'

My heart leaps! Yayyy! I get a second chance!

'Ben said he'd like to come back too,' he adds.

Oh knickers! 'Is he in a good mood now?' I ask.

'No,' Ricky admits.

'Well, then, I think not.' I really couldn't cope with any more aggro.

'What if it was just me?' he says softly.

For once I'm going to be mature. 'Look, you've had a pretty stressful night and I don't want to load on any extra pressure. Just do what makes you happy.'

'It would make me happy to be with you,' he says.

Phew! 'Well then, come on over!' I chime.

The second the phone is replaced, I spring up and chase my tail around the room, fluffing my hair, putting on an angora jumper so I look all snuggly, taking it off again when I discover it itches on bare skin, trying out various sofa poses. Finally the ring of the doorbell halts my mania.

'Hello,' Ricky smiles as he steps inside.

'Hello,' I sigh, wondering just what this late-night visit could mean – it still doesn't feel entirely like a sure thing.

While I fix the drinks, he lights the fire. This is just so cosy. It feels like our very own pad.

Again we settle into the sofa and start to talk. Last night the mood was excitable and all about soul-bearing in a show-off kind of way. Tonight there's a lingering melancholy left over from earlier events and Ricky's former brashness has been replaced by tangible vulnerability. Though some of the fizz has gone, the vibe is now more intimate, more real.

'I think you're one of the nicest people I've ever met,' he tells me at one point, then looks embarrassed and hurries over to the minibar to replenish his drink. By the time he gets back I've launched into some endless saga and as I yapper away, he reaches across to me and gently traces his fingers over my hand. His touch is so light and erotic it's all I can do to keep on track with my story. This is probably the point where I should just shut up and surrender but I'm bitten by nerves and babble even more fervently.

He continues with his caress.

I start to lose concentration and stumble over my words.

I'm still talking though half of me is lost to a giddy free-falling sensation. This has got to be the best bit. Just before . . .

He lifts my hand to his face and dips a finger into his mouth. I can't believe the sensation. I swear my finger actually changes composition – liquefying and then reforming in his mouth. I've never experienced anything like it before. We merge into a kiss and I find myself flashing back to my first vision of him on reception: so alluring and yet so remote. I can't believe that thirty-six hours later I'm in his arms.

As we kiss I feel him morphing from soft and sensual to a ferocious beastie. I take what I can and then scrabble away to catch my breath.

'Wow, you're kind of forceful,' I say, touching my overly ravished lips. Not quite what I was expecting from The Perfect Boyfriend.

'I know, I can't help it,' he says quietly.

Seconds later the wrestling match resumes. He's so full-on I can feel myself getting battered and bruised from all the rolling and tumbling and clawing, not to mention inadvertent jabbing from sofa arms and fireplace cornices. It occurs to me that if we just had sex the whole thing could be over in a matter of minutes but I hesitate for two reasons – 1) I don't want to end up hospitalised (Lord knows how much more frantic he would get if we were actually doing it) and 2) I'd be doing it for the wrong reason. I've been here before – not for a while admittedly but I'm reminded of that awful sense of 'I've started so I'll finish' obligation and the truth is I don't feel inclined. I fancied him to death before we started but now we appear to be such a sexual mismatch there would be no pleasure in following through. For once I'm not going to go along with proceedings because it's the easier option. I'm going to listen to my body. I cock an ear . . . Yup, it's definitely saying, 'No!'

A while later, I sneak a look at the clock – it's now 6 a.m. and all that fruitless tussling has reduced us to a heap of indistinguishable limbs on the sofa. I couldn't be any more uncomfortable. When I realise Ricky is asleep, I try to sneak off into the bedroom.

'You're not leaving me here alone are you?' He catches me, mid-shuffle.

I look at the big white-sheeted bed then back to the narrow itchy sofa.

'Do you want to come through,' I beckon him.

He looks unsure on account of Nina being in the same bed.

'It's fine,' I assure him. 'You could fit ten people in here without anyone even touching. Besides, we'll just be sleeping.'

So we do, and this bit I like – when he's lying dormant he's lovely, all silky skin and interlocked fingers. We get to lie like this for two whole hours and then the upcoming daylight stirs Nina, which in turn stirs Ricky.

'I should really go,' he whispers, looking the definition of sheepish.

Here it is – the dreaded morning after. I've always felt that if I were a natural beauty I could handle things so much better but as it is I can't fight the urge to hide my face behind the sheet and that doesn't make for the most communicative environment. Ricky swings his legs out of bed and heads for the bathroom. I just know he's thinking, 'What the hell have I done?' so I'm more than happy to bundle him on his way as soon as he's showered. I just can't bear it when they try and be sweet and make like they're going to call.

As I escort him to the front door I get that queasy, miss-you-already feeling. He's so beautiful – you've never seen anyone look so good on so little sleep – and I really don't want to say goodbye to him. Shame he doesn't feel the same way about me. I should never have got it on with him, up until that point he seemed so keen.

'So where do you go from here?' he asks me, hanging in the doorway.

'New Mexico,' I tell him, unable to look him in the eye.

'For how long?'

'Three nights.'

'And then?' He tilts his head.

I dare to peek up at him. 'North Carolina.'

'Is that a direct flight?'

'Actually, we have to come back to Phoenix to change . . .' The penny drops as I say it.

His face flashes with mischief. 'So, if you delayed the second half of your flight by a few hours we could go to the fondue place together.'

'Yes we could,' I smile.

Ooo-hoo! Now I'm in trouble!

TRUTH OR
CONSEQUENCES,
NEW MEXICO

We chose Truth or Consequences with a view to pondering the question, 'How important is honesty in relationships?' But when confronted with the city-limit sign we have a more pressing query: who chose such a bizarre name for this town, and why?

The answer, it turns out, is this: back in the 1940s there was a popular light entertainment radio show called Truth or Consequences and, after nearly ten years on the air, host Ralph Edwards one day announced that the show was seeking a US city to change its name to Truth or Consequences, basically as a stunt to celebrate their upcoming anniversary. In return, the show would be broadcast from the city thus guaranteeing a good deal of media attention, which in turn would boost tourism. Several cities put themselves forward but Hot Springs, New Mexico – a quirky little sun-baked town on the banks of the Rio Grande – had the edge. (The show's producer particularly liked the idea that the town's mineral baths had benefited many rheumatism and arthritis sufferers as this fitted with Ralph's humanitarian profile.)

So, on April 1st 1950, Truth or Consequences was officially christened with a lively fiesta attracting ten thousand well-wishers. Quite a turnout when you consider today's population runs a little over seven thousand.

Even though the agreement was just for the first year, show host Ralph Edwards made the trip to the T or C Fiesta every spring for fifty years. He's not here for this year's event, but we are. The sad truth is that we don't even know it.

'What's that noise?' I frown as we bypass an ornamental wagon and pull into the driveway at the Sierra Grande Lodge, our adobe-style accommodation for the next two nights.

Nina cocks an ear. 'It sounds like a band.'

'Hmmm,' I muse, switching off the engine. 'Did you notice there's a fairground in town – that's fun.'

'Oooh look, there's a spa at the hotel – let's get a facial!'

And so, out of undue concern for our pores, we miss the annual Truth or Consequences Fiesta – the one time of year when an otherwise crusty and eccentric backwater has the chance to shine. We're not entirely to blame – when we checked in we did ask the chap on reception what was worth checking out locally and he just made some hazy reference to some street art. So while we were being steamed and squeezed, Miss Fiesta was being crowned, and while we were sitting in our room pondering the best place to survey the local men, they were parading by beneath our window.

It takes us forever to twig – even at dinner we're still not getting it.

'Why is that guy over there wearing all those beads?' Nina whispers to me as we take our seats in the swish hotel restaurant, still wafting aromatic oils an hour after our treatments.

I turn for a discreet look, expecting to find some hippy guru type in a kaftan but instead my eyes meet those of a suave thirty-something in a retro knit top overlaid with the kind of cheap metallic-plastic beads so abundant on Bourbon Street.

'Strange,' I frown, returning to my perusal of the menu. 'Maybe he's come from some party.'

'That band's still going strong,' Nina notes, watching her cutlery tremble in time to the beat.

'Mmmm,' I murmur absently as I turn to the wine list.

Really. We're that dim.

As we chat and sup on merlot, Nina's eyes intermittently flick the way of the beaded one. 'He keeps looking over,' she hisses. 'Do you think he's interested?'

'Are we interested in him?' I try to get our priorities straight.

'I'm not sure,' Nina screws up her face. 'I need a zoom lens.'

'Who's he with?' I ask. I didn't get a proper look earlier.

'A couple of guys, one older man, a girl with long hair. Looks like some kind of family affair.'

Not the easiest party to crash, so we decide to leave

them be and concentrate on our olive crusted salmon.

It's an interesting thing: now I'm getting into my stride with this trip, I don't feel like I have to rush at every potential prospect. Prior to the first outing I was just desperate to meet someone I felt a connection with but now – nine states in – I feel I'm living in a world of infinite possibilities. And that, in turn, is making me more discerning. Or so I like to think.

I cringe, recalling some of the men I've stuck it out with in the past, just because I didn't feel I had any other options – I used to tell myself I should be grateful to have anyone interested in me, that maybe this was the best I could hope for. (That desperation is certainly part of why I hung around for Perforated Paul so embarrassingly long.) But now I see how absurd that attitude is. It's all too easy to excuse myriad incompatibilities because you're lonely or feel the need to prove to yourself (and the world) that you're loveable, or because you're hooked on the physical side of the relationship. That's the beauty of moving on after each initial crush period – rather like the Amish once-a-fortnight dating rule, it gives you the chance to stand back and get some perspective.

Take Ricky, for example: I was so smitten in his presence that, as we were saying goodbye, Lenny Kravitz' yearning ballad 'Again' started to play in my head, fuelling my romantic fantasies. I even convinced myself I was feeling the touch of love, as Nice-boy Bobby might say. Now both my hormones and my imagination have had the chance to calm down (and the geographical shift has certainly accelerated that process) I have to acknowledge that our sexual mismatching is a significant obstacle. I'm also more willing to admit that there may be a touch of 'ladies' man' to his persona. He's definitely got skills in that area (probably inherited from his married-six-times dad) and I suspect it's taken him a lot of practise to get them that honed!

This doesn't mean I don't want to see him again, but next time it will be with open eyes. Maybe every early courtship should have a brief cooling off period before you commit to taking it further? I know so many people who have inadvertently found themselves in a long-term relationship with someone they were never that wild about in the first place, just because they never had sufficient reason or opportunity to break it off.

Of course the other really helpful element to getting a clear perspective is having relevant comparisons. Back in the real world, it's so rare for me to be knocked out by someone that when I am, I run with it until a) I come to my senses or b) the restraining order is made official. But this trip has been a revelation: now I'm fortunate enough to be able to say, 'Well, Cowboy Casey was every cowgirl's dream but now I've conversed with Trucker, I know there's no going back – I have to have someone who can stimulate my mind and my soul.' And perhaps if I'd met Kane before Paul, I would have realised how important it is for me to feel equal to someone, not in charge of a minor like I did with him, but was too blinded by his shiny ponytail to see. Is it possible that I'm cultivating a more balanced vision with which to view potential heart candidates? I do hope so!

After a dessert of Mexican pressed chocolate cake, we decide to wander into town, although that makes it sound a trek when essentially it involves crossing the road. T or C is a curious place, not somewhere I expect to become a link in the Starbucks chain any time soon. But that's a good thing.

The bad thing is the lack of bars. The only one we can find resembles a strip-lit working man's club. As there appears to be some kind of 'Mullet Compulsory' hair code, we continue along the main commercial street, finding ourselves drawn to a rhythmic pounding and grunting coming from one of the larger shops. We creep closer wondering what kind of pagan orgy is taking place within, then the door flashes open and we see a drum circle – ten or so topless men with bongos – and a crowd of writhing, arm-waving, barefoot women in batik.

'Shall we go in?' I venture, hypnotised by the beat.

'Are you crazy?' Nina balks.

'Come on, it'll be fun. It looks like there's a bar at the back, we'll just head for that.'

We're no more than a toe through the doorway when we're slammed by a wall of BO so powerful it sends us reeling back onto the pavement.

'Dear God!' we cry, eyes watering, nostrils tingling.

'That was *pungent*!' Nina shakes herself free of the smell. 'It's like National No Deodorant Day in there.'

'It was bad, wasn't it?' I admit. 'But I'm sure if we hold our breath till we're past the dancers we'll be fine.'

'You want to go back in?' Nina is incredulous.

'This may be the only thing going on in town,' I reason.

'What about the fair?' she suggests. 'Bumper cars are always a testosterone-fest.'

'Five minutes?' I plead.

'Oh God!' Nina rolls her eyes, then takes my hand and together we hurtle through to The Other Side.

'Jesus!' Nina pants, relieved to find that the air in the back area – all murals and low-set purple sofas – is actually breathable.

I open my eyes and come face to face with New Mexico's answer to Orlando Bloom – a skinny, fine-featured, tufty-haired sprite with huge coal-black eyes. He's so elfin he really could have strayed here from the set of *Lord of the Rings*. I feel weak in his presence, possibly high on patchouli oil.

'It's not a proper bar,' Nina complains, having done a quick recce. 'They've just got soft drinks. Let's go.'

'W-wait!' I stumble, still transfixed by my elf who has walked past twice, both times locking eyes with me in such an intense manner that all I can see is him, the rest of the room is a blur. (So much for my new-improved clarity of vision – I've fallen smack-bam off the wagon.)

'What is it?' Nina asks.

'I've just got to talk to him,' I say, lifting a limp finger.

'He's fourteen!'

'He's not. He's beautiful,' I protest, disconnecting from all rationale – these hippy honeys just make me melt.

Sensing I've gone beyond reason, Nina takes a seat beside the kiddy play area muttering something about persuading him to relocate somewhere more fragrant.

I approach him directly, with none of my usual hesitation, just a tremble of anticipation.

'Hello,' I breathe, instantly lost in his eyes, which welcome me as if he too had been waiting years for this moment.

He steps closer and says, 'Do you want to see my crystals?'

A minute later we're shoulder-to-shoulder and thigh-to-thigh on the sofa admiring his case of azurites and zeolites and all the crunchy-sparkly clusters in between. Though he tells me his name is Marco, to me he's now Aladdin.

Somehow, as our hands overlap in the inspection of his wares, I manage to ask if he's got a girlfriend.

'No,' he says simply, 'Relationships don't work.'

'They don't, do they?' I'm oddly gleeful to find someone of a similar mind but need a little elaboration here – at twenty, he's too young to be bitter. 'Remind me why not?' I ask.

'Because it always becomes about possession and that's not love. You should love every one and every thing, not just focus on one person.'

This seems like the wisest insight ever. I am utterly in agreement. It's simple logic – romantic love is an impossibility. I feel a sense of relief – there's a reason I can't find it: it doesn't exist! And yet here I am, in a dreamlike trance with an other-worldly creature looking at me with something approaching desire.

'Do you smoke weed?' he asks.

'No,' I grimace, feeling like a big girl's blouse.

'Only we're going up to Elephant Butte with the

drums and then we're going to camp there for the night. Do you want to join us?'

My mouth falls open but no words come out. I look at Nina. *Not On Your Nelly* might as well be emblazoned on her face.

'I, er . . .' I push out a breath. 'Camping?'

He nods. 'Under the stars.'

Oh God. I wish I could. I wish I had the nerve. I want our leaning to become nuzzling and the nuzzling to become kissing and to get that floaty, spirited-away sensation. I'm sure he wouldn't morph into a beastie, he's far too languorous – reminds me a little of Christian. He was never in any rush, reminded me of a loving pet most of the time.

'Let me just ask my friend,' I stall for time.

'You want to go camping at Elephant Butt?' I can see Nina barely recognises me in this moment.

'You pronounce it bute,' I correct her. 'Like the start of beaut-iful!'

She rolls her eyes. 'Are you seriously considering sleeping on a rock?'

'No,' I say, looking at my shoes, feeling a little caught out by Nina's blunt reality check. Ordinarily I wouldn't be able to resist such an offer and would subsequently lose three months of my life mooning over that one starry, starry night, but halted in this way I'm forced to acknowledge that I'm never going to live in a bivouac or wear tie-dye.

'And I really don't like lentils,' I find myself saying.

'Well then,' Nina gets to her feet. 'Can we go?'

'Just let me say goodbye . . .'

When I return to my little drummer boy he's

357

surrounded by his ratty-haired peers and our connection is lost.

'You're not coming?' he says shyly, reading my expression before I even speak.

'I'd love to but my friend's an alcoholic and we need to find a bar,' I try and make a joke.

'Oh, OK, well . . .'

I want to touch him – get one last fix – but there are too many obstructive bodies.

'Bye, then,' I croak, stomach churning. Turning to leave is a major struggle – desire versus logic. For once logic triumphs – I have to face facts: I am not and never will be anyone's Arwen.

Deciding the hotel bar is probably our safest bet, Nina drags me back there and takes a seat on the patio while I order a couple of glasses of wine inside, all the while trying to come to terms with the uneasy – and unfamiliar – feeling of growing up. Just because there's an attraction doesn't mean you have to act on it. When I return I find Nina has been joined by a woman and two men, one of whom is wearing rather a lot of beads.

'This is Cem,' she introduces me. 'Pronounced Gem like the precious stone. He's from Paris.'

I shake his hand.

'Allo!' he says, offering me a respectful dip of his head.

'The beads are from the Fiesta,' Nina explains, giving a quick run-through of all the fun we missed, including a procession by the local sheriffs and their respective posses – so many truncheons, so little time!

'I'm Alexa,' a husky voice announces, reaching her hand out to mine.

'She's a music video producer from New York,' Nina adds, obviously impressed. 'And finally, Karim of Turkish-French-Puerto Rican descent!' Nina shoots him a look to check she got it right. He nods his approval. 'Karim's also based in New York,' she continues. 'And currently working on a documentary about Truth or Consequences.'

'Really?' I sound intrigued but I'm only half paying attention as he explains his project. I'm still trying to shake off the last traces of coulda-shoulda-wouldas for Marco and besides, Karim is so stylishly presented with his designer-vintage shirt and precision stubble, he looks like he'd expect to find himself with an intellectual supermodel not a girl with bed hair and après-dermabrasion skin. I feel like he can see my every split-end and sense that my top is from Ross Dress For Less. And yet he doesn't have a judgmental air. He is softly and wisely spoken. So calm you feel that even if you spilt red wine on his trousers he wouldn't so much as flinch. Turns out there's a good reason for this understated mastery – Karim's father owns the Sierra Grande Lodge.

'Also Raoul's restaurant in New York,' Cem brags on his friend's behalf. 'You have heard of it?'

'I'm afraid not,' I tell him.

'Oh,' he looks disappointed. 'It is very good.'

I can't tell who – if anyone – Nina fancies at this point. These guys are hardly her usual scruffy surfer type yet she seems happy enough to sit and chat on subjects as random as breastfeeding, tarot and Apache Indians. (The legendary warrior Geronimo died on the very site where this hotel was built.) We also learn of Cem's recent and painful divorce, not that he wants to talk in any detail about that – he'd rather we all go to the Pine Nut.

The bar is crammed to the rafters on account of it being Fiesta night 'n' all but we find a small table near the dance floor and the boys order shots and get ready for a big night. Shamefully Nina and I fade almost instantly. I'm just about to suggest we slink away when the music switches from country to salsa and Cem drags me up onto the dancefloor. He's a nifty little mover and doesn't stop grinning encouragement for a second but I just don't have the energy to match him. Looking over to Nina in the hope she'll step in, I find she's actually nodded off at the table.

'Oh dear, look – I think I'd better get her home.' I take my excuse and run with it.

'Nice guys,' Nina yawns as she kicks off her Mexican blanket and snuggles down into bed.

'Really nice,' I confirm. 'So why don't we fancy them?'

'Maybe we're just too tired and hungover from last night,' she suggests, reaching for the light. 'They said they're up for going out again tomorrow night so perhaps if we get some sleep and then drink a bit more, something might click.'

'They could be growers.' I throw a theory out there.

'I think you could be right,' Nina agrees, snapping us into darkness. 'Night!'

*

By morning the insistent, tugging yearning for Marco has been replaced by a distant ache for what might have been. But, seeing as we're in Truth or Consequences, I feel I should be honest with myself about what exactly 'what might have been' would have entailed. Yes my superficial senses would have been temporarily sated but ultimately our time together would have amounted to nothing more than another brief encounter with a manchild who has never used a nail brush. I can see now it was a completely impractical attraction driven by habit and hormones, whereas Cem and Karim are charming, well-educated, well-mannered adults worthy of further consideration. See – I'm getting the hang of this now!

'You know, the chef's not bad-looking.' Nina nudges me as we work our way through a lush breakfast of exotic fruit salad, creamy yogurt and freshly baked cakes in the hotel's open-plan kitchen-diner.

'Maybe we should engage him in conversation? Compliment him on his buns?' I suggest.

'Actually, I take it back,' Nina suddenly recoils. 'I think there might be something wrong with him.'

I glance back to give him a once-over and find myself jumping – yikes! Could his eyeballs bulge any more?

'So, where y'all from?' he drawls, stepping up to the table to check we've got enough hot water for our tea.

'England,' we answer swiftly and succinctly.

'I'm from Pittsburgh, Kansas,' he tells us.

'Riiight!' we say, making a mental note to never go there.

'What's your name?' I ask. (Always handy to have this information ready for the police.)

'Chef.'

'Your name's Chef and you're a chef?' I can't believe the coincidence.

'No, my name's Bill but they call me Chef.'

'Ah.'

'So what are y'all doing in town?'

With every exchange, his stare bores deeper into Nina. Frankly I don't know why he doesn't just pop his eyes from their sockets and drop them down her cleavage and have done with it.

When he goes to refill the jug of orange juice, Nina looks pleadingly at me. 'Can we go?'

I nod, hoping we can make our escape before he emerges from the fridge but the squeak of our chairs alerts him.

'Gotta go! Sorry!' We scramble out the patio doors, ignoring his expression of abject dismay.

'I feel like he's still looking!' Nina shudders as we quick-march across the driveway to the car.

I turn back. Chef is now out on the patio, gawping after Nina with skin-burrowing vision.

'Don't be silly!' I laugh, bundling her into the car and screeching off in a twister of dust.

Seeing as T or C seems to pride itself on having a population of freaks and geeks, we decide to spend the morning in search of rad snowboarder types at White Sands National Monument, about 150 miles southeast of here. Apparently you can surf three-storey-high dunes on what look like giant Frisbees and if that doesn't attract thrill-seeking dudes by the dozen I don't know what will.

'I can just see them now – wraparound shades, O'Neill T-shirts, sun-bleached hair,' Nina rapturises. 'Do you think they have orange campervans out here like they do in Cornwall? I love a campervan.'

We switch onto Highway 70 at Las Cruces, pass through a blip of a town called Organ and then come upon a sign at the side of an otherwise blank stretch of road.

'White Sands Missile Range,' I read, then frown. What happened to White Sands National Monument? I pull over and consult my guidebook – it informs me that the surrounding roads are often closed due to missile testing. Oh how scenic – every day a different landscape! What's more, you are invited to come take a look at the site of the world's first atomic-bomb explosion, although why anyone would want to get any closer to an area of potentially hazardous activity is beyond me.

'Can we go in?' Nina takes me by surprise.

'Are you serious?'

She nods.

'Why?' I'm dumbfounded.

'I don't know, it sounds exciting.'

How can I say no when she braved the BO for me last night? I take the next exit and follow a dusty track for a mile or two feeling oddly daring. Until, that is, we reach a big red radiation warning sign crammed with phrases like 'don't stray from the path' and 'proceed at your own peril'.

Now I just feel like we're asking for trouble.

'Roll up the windows!' I urge.

'Don't you think you're being over cautious?' Nina's eyes narrow.

'There's contamination all around!' I bleat, trying not to inhale too deeply.

'OK, hold on a minute—' Nina opens her passenger door.

'What are you doing?' I screech.

'I want to take a picture, I'll just be a moment.'

'You're getting out of the car to take a picture of a sign that says "*Please remain in the vehicle at all times*"?'

'Yes. I'll be really quick.'

I can barely look in her direction for fear that she'll tread on something she shouldn't and disappear in a puff of toxic smoke. But she doesn't. She returns safely back to the car. Well, I say safely . . .

'You've just trodden the contamination into the car now, you know that don't you?'

'Just drive.'

Around the next corner we hit a checkpoint but are not allowed to proceed on account of Nina having left her ID back at the hotel. I'm secretly relieved and swiftly return to the dune road. But just a few miles on we reach another military checkpoint.

'ID please.'

'Um . . .' Nina explains her predicament.

'You should carry your ID with you at all times, ma'am.'

'Is it really necessary – we're just here to see the sand,' she reasons.

'You're just seventy miles from Mexico. This is border control.'

'Oh.'

We sit quietly as the cars line up behind us, hoping that simply being female will serve us better than words.

'Well, I guess I'll let you through,' he concedes, falling for our plan. 'Just remember your ID next time.'

'Yes officer, thank you officer.'

It's easy to spot the entrance to the monument – the white sands are seeping out onto the tarmac to greet us.

'Any minute now – surfer dudes!' Nina pips.

We stop off at the Visitor Centre to buy our 'sand boards' which sell for £6 each and resemble a big plastic dustbin lid. The price includes a cube of wax which you rub over the base of the 'board' every other slide to lubricate your descent. As we breeze through the exhibit, eager to get to the dunes, we learn they are home to mysterious wildlife including the 'false blister' beetle, the kangaroo rat and the bleached no-eared lizard! And that many films – from *King Solomon's Mines* to *Tank Girl* – have been shot here. It's easy to see why, it's just about as mesmerising a backdrop as you could imagine.

'It's like a different planet out there,' Nina coos, nose pressed up against the passenger window scanning our ethereal surroundings for the ultimate dune. 'Here?' she points ahead to a pale, powdery peak.

I nod my confirmation. 'Let's boldly go!'

We leap from the car, bound to the base of the dune and then two strides up we're sunk – and you thought walking on the moon looked hard! Every step we take our legs seep knee-deep into the crystals, making any kind of progress a monumental effort. Even climbing to a ten-foot ledge leaves me gasping for air, which isn't a great situation when the air is whisked up with gypsum. But on we persevere to the top, expecting to find a whole wonderland of sand-surfers beyond the ridge. When we get there we realise it's just us. And sand. For miles. We soon find out why – violent winds are gathering, already redistributing the sand like caster sugar being chased across tracing paper. When we first arrived the sky was blue, the sand was white and the road was tawny. Now there is zero contrast between the three. Everything is white. It's like being in heaven. Were it not for the brightly painted hut marking the parking area, I wouldn't know which way was up.

'Are we going to try this before we get buried alive?' I suggest, battling to turn around while my wind-whipped hair slices at my face.

'Let's do it!' Nina cheers.

'OK – here I come!' I yell, placing my bottom in the lid and bracing myself for immediate take-off. Nothing. I shunt forward a little. I go no further than half a metre and stick again. 'Oh God! I think I'm too heavy for it to slide!'

'Don't be silly – try again,' Nina shouts encouragement.

I shuffle and jiggle, ready to whoosh. Nothing. Instead I have to make an ungainly descent hoicking myself forward using my feet and bouncing in the disc, creating little ridges as I chug down.

'Why can't I do it?' I whine as I struggle to my feet.

'Did you wax?' Nina enquires.

'Ahhhh!' I groan, tapping my head reproachfully. Actually I did but I like to think that maybe I wasn't thorough enough.

Wax cube worn to a mere cuticle, I turn back to try again but the wind is against me and I only manage to struggle halfway up the dune using the disc as a shield against the stinging needles of sand. Flumping into position I'm ready to try again. One little jerk and I sail down. Not exactly a blur but the unassisted motion feels good. I'm panting as I get to my feet, a gritty smile on my face. Ordinarily I expect people – kids especially – get hours of exhaustive fun out of this location but after just two goes I feel like I've run a mile in lead boots while being chased by a tornado. Nina is already back in the car. The door nearly blows off its hinges as I attempt to join her and, as I struggle to close it behind me, the dashboard disappears under a layer of white as the sand races to join us on our onbound journey.

'I'm covered in the stuff,' Nina groans as she excavates a cupful of crystalline powder from her cleavage.

I flip down the mirror and part my sand-strewn tangles. 'Oh my God – I look like I've got the worst case of dandruff!' Peering closer, I see that my lipgloss has acted like glue and I now have a white frosted mouth.

'Pwah!' I spit.

'Good though!' Nina grins.

'Brilliant!' I agree.

'Lunch?'

'Starving.'

Having been blinded by the white, I feel like shouting, 'I can see! I can see!' when we get back onto the main road. Suddenly everything appears more beautiful, though that may just be because it is. We're now on winding Highway 82 and it is lifting us skyward – up, up and away from the flat desert to lush pine-packed mountains that remind me of Colorado. This diversion will add a couple of hours to our journey time but we're rather taken with the idea of lunching with the resident ghost at The Lodge at Cloudcroft. Rebecca was a flirtatious redhead who, having been done wrong by a former beau way back in 1900, continues to haunt the corridors in search of a new lover. A woman after our own hearts.

When we get to The Lodge we find it is more refined than we imagined – posh ladies in nice blouses with real jewels sipping Sancerre and nibbling asparagus. Seeing as we look like we've been dragged through a hedge backwards and then electrocuted, I'm not sure we're going to be welcomed with open menus.

'We can't go in looking like this,' I fret.

'Have you got your Wet Wipes and your make-up bag?'

'Always.'

'Well then, we'll just duck into the loo and tidy ourselves up, it'll be fine,' Nina assures me.

We crunch lightly past reception, dart through the gothic lounge and manage to locate the loos without frightening any veterans. As Nina sets to work shaking the small desert from her hair, I empty a knickerful of sand into the toilet bowl.

'Oh my God – no!' I hear Nina howl.

'What is it?' I stick my head out of the cubicle, trousers still at half-mast, fearing she's found a no-eared lizard half-strangled in her mane but she's simply mortified by the ever-increasing enormity of her hair.

'It's 1983 and I'm Keren from *Bananarama*,' she wails at her reflection.

'How did it get like that?' I gasp at what would ordinarily be a two-cans-of-Elnett job.

'I was hanging upside down to get the sand out and now I can't get it to lie back down!' she explains, trying in vain to flatten it.

In the end we settle on winding it into a bun. Me, I look like a backcombed Ginger Spice circa 'Say You'll Be There' and there's nothing that can be done. (Secretly I'm loving my newfound volume even though the texture is pure wire wool.)

With two fresh coats of foundation and all the trimmings, we're as preened as we can be and present ourselves at the sun-streamed dining room.

'Good afternoon, ladies?' The maître d greets us with a question mark.

'Yes, two for lunch, please.'

'Oh I'm so sorry, we stopped serving ten minutes ago.'

Ten minutes? So spending twenty minutes getting ready was probably a mistake? Our bellies flop with dismay.

'Can you recommend somewhere else?' we whimper.

'Of course.'

The restaurant he recommends is certainly better-suited to our ravaged demeanour but frankly I wouldn't recommend the food to a dog. I end up soothing my stomach with a tub of mint-choc-chip from an ice-cream parlour two shops along.

Cloudcroft is a good-looking town with super-fresh air, stunning views and dinky log cabins, but we're strangely homesick for T or C – in just one night the town and all its resident oddballs – did we mention the chap on reception is named Glass? – have got under our skin. It's going to be tough to tear ourselves away tomorrow but I've promised Nina an overnight excursion to Santa Fe, home of the Georgia O'Keeffe gallery featuring the largest collection of the artist's work including her most famous frame-filling blooms. This will be a mini dream-come-true for Nina who has devoted an entire wall of her flat to re-creating O'Keeffe's orange poppy painting.

'Oh no, not again!' Nina points ahead. 'Border control!'

This time they're not so casual. They tell us to pull over, step out of the car and then shut us in a small room with a two-way mirror. I don't blame them – we're missing vital documentation and since we got so roughed up by the sands we actually do look like fugitives freshly emerged from a tunnel.

'I'm so sorry,' Nina apologises. 'I'll never go out without my passport again.'

'Which one's the writer?' a voice barks through from the office.

It's not Nina, it's me they're after – I'm the Code Red. They look me up and down and use the word 'deportment' and they're not admiring my posture. Apparently the problem is that my US visa is so new it's not yet showing up on the system. Not a lot I can do about that except protest my innocence. Then a portly Mexican gentleman is added to the mix. He's told to lift up his shirt and twizzle so they can check he's not harbouring a weapon in his belt. We're tempted to bump bellies like Karen and Jack do during the opening credits of *Will & Grace* but before we know it, he's on his way. After a considerably longer period of incubation, we're released.

By the time we get back to T or C the fairground is being dismantled and we're told we're too late for dinner at the café we had our eye on. We ding the hotel reception bell in the hope that Glass will be about to recommend somewhere half-decent but up pops Cem.

'What are you doing there?' we gasp, bemused.

'I'm filling in for the night. It is windy out there, huh?'

We touch our hair, still a little sensitive about its sand-encrusted bulk and ask if he knows anywhere within a twenty mile radius still serving dinner? Our hero, he does. And it's only a couple of streets away. We listen closely to his directions and start edging towards the stairs, eager to shower away the grit that is currently exfoliating our inner thighs.

'So what time did you leave the Pine Nut last night?' I call back from the third step.

He pulls a 'don't ask' face.

'What?' I probe, leaning over the banister.

'It's Alexa,' he sighs. 'She's in jail.'

'What?!' we screech, tearing back down to reception.

'I got pulled over by the police on the way back, I was driving too slowly . . .' he shakes his head with remorse.

Turns out Cem didn't have his ID on him either, and even when he did locate it, being a terrible combination of French (much derided for not supporting Bush's war on Iraq) and Turkish (a country bordering Iraq) he had to do some dainty and genteel 'yes, officer, no officer' apologising. They then moved on to Karim. He showed his ID and that was fine. Then the cops made the big mistake of waking Alexa. She went into instant banshee mode, hurling abuse, refusing to show her ID, lashing out and eventually getting arrested for assaulting a police officer.

'Oh my God!' We're aghast, but more than anything we're hungry.

'Go! Go!' Cem senses our predicament and sends us on our way. 'Maybe later Karim and I, we join you?'

'Great!' we cheer.

'I think they're going to get there before us,' I grumble as we take yet another wrong turning and trundle down an uneven, unlit street. 'This can't be right.'

'He said opposite the road for the Pine Nut . . . try down here!' Nina suggests.

'That's where we just came from!' I sigh. 'I'm going to go and ask in this motel. What's it called again?'

'Las Vargas.'

'Are you sure?'

'Maybe Varkas.'

'Well, they won't understand the accent anyway,' I shrug. 'Back in a mo.'

I push open the door and step into an overly cluttered reception guarded by an enormous Alsatian. Rather than baring his teeth and bidding me keep a respectful distance, he pads up, tongue lolling, seemingly glad of the company.

'Hello!' I call through the archway that leads to the owner's residence.

The dog and I cock our ears for a response. Nothing. But I'm sure I can hear what sounds like a meal in progress so I call again. Again no response. Oh well. I give the dog a farewell ruffle and step back out onto the street.

'There's someone in there,' a ratchety voice wafts from the darkness.

My eyes dart around trying to locate its source. Then, through a screen of bamboo, I see a flame spring up and then tilt as it is sucked into what I'm guessing is some form of pipe. I'm unbelievably creeped out and can't seem to move.

'You should keep trying.' The figure shifts as he encourages me, but does not reveal himself.

'Er, actually I'm just trying to get directions to a restaurant,' I address the flame – 'Les Varquis?'

'Los Arcos?'

'That's it!'

'Keep going up the street, you'll see it on your left hand side.'

You'd think we'd found the lost treasure of the Incas from our sheer delight as we enter the great-smelling, Sixties-style steakhouse and immediately celebrate with a pair of killer margaritas – so strong I have to order a Sprite to dilute the bite – followed by an excess of home-made coleslaw. For two girls who thought they were going to have to survive on bar snacks we couldn't be happier. Then, as the waiter comes to clear our salad plates, Nina removes her knife and fork planning to reuse them for her main course of baby-back ribs. When he attempts to collect them from her, she snatches them out of his way.

'Er, ma'am? We'll bring you a clean set for the next course.'

'Oh!' she looks embarrassed, finally persuaded to release them into his custody.

'Where I come from we jus' lick 'em clean!' I tease her in my best Trailer Park Trash accent.

At Nina's guffaw, I splutter margarita across the table, which sets her off again and just as we're perfecting our impression of a pair of frothing, cackling mental-hospital escapees, Karim and Cem appear by our side, looking the picture of class and refinement in immaculate un-food-spattered shirts. But hey, the night is young and we're exceptionally messy eaters.

'You found this place OK?' Cem asks, politely ignoring our hysteria.

'Well, no!' we confess, still trying to moderate our sniggering.

Oh why couldn't they have seen us in Sanctuary-mode? We were a far more elegant proposition there.

In the absence of sensible conversation we decide to try on the boys' trendy rectangular glasses to see if that is the secret to their New York cool. Bad move – Nina looks like a boffin from a science lab while I've morphed into Nana Mouskouri – but it does serve to loosen up the chaps and we find ourselves chatting easily, laughing far more than the night before. The chemistry may not be electric like it was with Mark and Bobby in Nice but we're certainly all comfortable in each other's company – anyone would think we've been friends for years.

'So, we're going along to the jail at midnight to see if the bail bondsman can persuade them to release Alexa tonight,' Karim informs us once the bill is settled. 'D'you wanna come?'

As novel date propositions go, this rocks. Karim suggests we drop our car back at the Sierra Grande before continuing on in theirs, and as we still have time to spare back at the lodge, the boys opt to show us their casita with its own private hot spring.

'You want to go in?' Cem gives a persuasive jiggle of his eyebrows.

I know I must be drunk because I'm actually considering grabbing my cossie and having a dunk. The water's steaming hot and, but for the stars, the night is dark. Nina is dubious, more so when a trim sixty-something male with striking white hair and matching beard steps totally naked into the tub. Mercifully I turned away before I got an eyeful but the look on Nina's face says she saw it all. I look to Karim for an explanation but he has backed off into the shadows.

'Is everything OK?' I stage whisper to him.

'Fine,' he grumbles with a look of resigned mortification, adding, 'thanks for killing the vibe, Dad.'

So that's his father! Now that would be

embarrassing. All the same, I can't help but smile – Karim thinks there was a vibe!

I turn back to the tub just in time to see Cem enter the water. Also totally starkers. Gosh, these Mediterranean types – they're so shameless!

'You want to feel?'

'Pardon?'

'The water, it is so warm,' he entices me over.

I lower my hand in – not too deep for fear of what I might accidentally swish – and end up holding hands with Cem.

After ten minutes I pull my hand out. 'Oooo, it's sooo soft!' I gasp, suddenly transfixed by my own palm. 'Look! Feel the difference – baby-soft, normal, baby-soft, normal.' And I happily entertain myself playing 'before' and 'after' until it's time to go to jail.

On the way over I remain utterly preoccupied with my new improved hand and try to get Nina in on the guessing game by putting her jacket over our arms so that Cem will have four hands to select the softest from. Sadly, it's only me that finds this remotely fascinating.

'We're here,' Karim says with gravity as we pull up outside the jail.

Aware that I am behaving like a fool, I suggest I'd better stay in the car. Nina follows suit. Nevertheless we get a clear look at Alexa as she is marched, handcuffed, from her cell to some office. Hardly a picture of contrition, she's still got an aggressive 'want some?' swagger and we shrink down in our seats not wanting to give her any more of an audience to play to. After ten minutes or so Karim settles back behind the driving wheel releasing a string of well-enunciated expletives, mostly in reference to the uselessness of the overweight bail bondsman. Swearing doesn't suit his refined demeanour so we're guessing this is his version of freaking out and sit quietly till he's done.

It's at this point that I discover my baby-soft hand has now become wisened-old-crone hand.

'Look! It's all shrivelled and dry!' I cry, convinced it's going to stay that way for life.

Bless him, Cem is happy to hold it anyway.

We could all do with a brandy but the bar is closed and there seems no option but to call it a night.

'We'll walk you to your room.' Karim leads the way. 'You guys are opposite the suite, right?'

'What suite?' Nina humphs after him. 'Why aren't we in the suite?'

'You will be next time you come here,' Karim takes her arm, 'because we will be married . . .'

'. . . with seven kids,' Nina chuckles, happily playing along.

Hello? Is that a frisson developing between Nina and Karim? If it is, it's going to be a slow-burner – with not even a hint of hanky-panky they bid us good night.

I'm just about to close the door when Nina asks, rather too loudly, 'Why don't you kiss Cem?'

'What?' I hiss, shushing her.

'He's willing!' she eggs me on.

'No, I couldn't!' I shake my head.

'Why not?'

'I don't know, I—'

'Go on!' She attempts to jiggle me out the door, calling after him, 'Cem!'

'Nooo!' I struggle to remain in the room, gripping onto the doorframe, but lose my footing and fall out into the corridor with a thud.

Cem turns back, looking concerned.

'Night!' I call, giving him a casual little wave from the carpet.

'Ciao!' he frowns, giving a little Gallic shrug before continuing on his way.

We get up at the crack of dawn for a quickie in a neighbouring hot spring – one mercifully free of male genitalia – and then, unable to face Chef, head to the Firewater Bakery for breakfast. At first I think I'm groggy on account of last night's margarita but my streaming nose and achy, addled brain suggest flu. Confronted with a wonky muffin and a hot chocolate, I realise the only breakfast I'm interested in is served at the pharmacy counter at Rite Aid. 'I'll have a large bottle of Dayquil with a side of Strepsils and a sachet of Vitamin C to go, thank you.'

Feeling increasingly disorientated, I step from the pavement into the road without looking.

'Woah!' Nina yanks me back, seconds before I stumble under the wheels of a vintage Wacky Races-style convertible.

'What a cool car to get nearly run over by!' I reel.

'Did you see the driver?' Nina gasps, fair winded from his beauty. 'Total male model!'

'No!'

'I'm serious – blond hair, beauteous biceps – quick, they've pulled into the discount store car park!'

We hurry over then hastily hang back as a brassy

378

blonde female gets out and heads straight into the shop. He, meanwhile, turns and walks in our direction.

Our jaws drop simultaneously as he smiles a 'Hi!'

He's such a walking-talking Calvin Klein ad, Nina can't stop herself exclaiming, *'Oh my God, you're so good-looking!'*

'Excuse me?' he looks shell-shocked, sure he must have misheard.

'I mean, what an amazing car,' she squirms.

He gives a lazy smile. 'It's my dad's, he designs them.'

Nina's turn to speak.

'Oh my God, you're so good-looking!' she blurts for the second time, unable to control her rapture. 'I'm sorry,' she apologises, 'but are you a model?'

He gives her a sheesh-no look.

'I mean, it's worse than I thought,' she swoons, taking in his angular features, denim-blue eyes and the butterscotch-smooth skin of his arms.

'Sorry about my friend, I think she spent too long in the hot tub.' I try to make a joke but when his face cracks into a smile I, too, lose it and gawp, 'Can I have my picture taken with you?'

'I was actually just going to get a haircut,' he looks shifty.

'You don't need a haircut, you look more than fine just as you are.' This time it's not me or Nina gushing over him but the brassy-haired woman who turns out to be his stepmother. She looks bemused but not entirely surprised by our ga-ga reaction. I'm sure she's heard it all before, just not with an English accent.

'So how long are you girls in town?' he asks.

'We're actually just about to leave,' Nina laments.

'Oh.' He looks disappointed.

'I know,' Nina sighs, 'we could have gone to the Pine Nut together!'

'He can't go there!' Stepmom chips in.

He gives her a 'cheers, thanksalot' look.

'Are you banned?' I query.

'Not exactly.'

'Yes you are,' Stepmom asserts.

'Not forever,' he reasons.

I raise an eyebrow.

'Just six months. I got into a fight. I went there with my girlfriend and this other guy tried to take her home.'

'But she wasn't going to go with him, surely?' Nina gasps.

'Actually she was.'

We take a moment to consider what manner of manhood could be preferable to the one stood before us then Nina announces: 'You should have hit your girlfriend, not him!'

He looks taken aback.

'Not literally, I just mean to say that she was the one at fault, he just happened to have the same taste in women as you.'

'Did you go to jail?' I ask, trying to spot a trend.

He nods. 'I spent a week there.'

'We were there last night!' Nina says helpfully, thrilled to have something in common.

As we chat on we discover he's originally from California, which explains the looks but makes it all the more mystifying that he's chosen to live in T or C. Turns out he has grandparents here. All the same, I can't help but wonder – was he wanted by the law in Cali too?

'No,' he shakes his head. 'That's all cleared up now.'

Nina and I exchange a look then ask if we can sit in his car. It's really just an excuse to sit next to him and we take a few hundred pictures to make sure the moment is well and truly captured. It's only then we realise we won't know how to caption them – we haven't even asked his name.

'Eugene,' he tells us.

Only in America would a stud like this have the ultimate geek name!

'So what happened with your girlfriend?' Nina asks while inspecting the dashboard. 'Are you back together with her?'

'No, she's still with him,' he looks visibly crestfallen. 'I saw them together last night at the dance.'

There was a dance? How did we miss that?

'You know there's only one cure for getting over someone – you have to get with someone else,' Nina insists, looking ready for duty.

'Yeah – there must be plenty of other women eager to take her place . . .' my eyes stray around the deserted streets '. . . in a town like this,' I falter.

He looks unconvinced. 'You two are probably the best-looking women around here!'

'What do you mean probably?' I joke.

He's too miserable to respond.

It's a crime that we can't stay and console Heartbroken of Truth or Consequences but just in case an opportunity presents itself at a later date, Nina takes Eugene's phone number, turning back twenty or so times for a last look at his amazing bodywork as he walks away.

'I know he's not all there but what a cutie!' she sighs before offering to load up the car while I check out.

What seems like an efficient plan is foiled by Glass's desperate lack of computer skills. For a full twenty-five minutes he eyes the screen like he's solving a *Matrix* encryption. When I do finally step out into the sunshine I too feel like I've just been released from jail.

'Over here!' Nina beckons me over to where she's pulled the car round.

I'm impressed by the size of the throng gathered to wave us off – Cem, Karim, his dad (now clothed), a newly liberated Alexa, Chef, and two elderly gent guests who swiftly introduce themselves as an ex-movie star and a horse-trekker.

'They're coming with us,' Nina announces before I launch into my farewell speech.

'All of them?'

'Just Karim and Alexa, they need to get to Albuquerque airport, it's on our way and it'll save Cem driving them later.'

'Then why is he getting in the car?' I spot him trying to stow away.

'He's coming with us as far as Sonic Burger then walking back to the hotel.'

'I see.' A lot has happened since I went to check out.

As predicted, we feel quite a tug leaving T or C.

'It won't be the same here without you,' Cem sighs as he disembarks at the retro burger joint. 'But we will keep in touch, no?' he asks, looking deep into my eyes as he hands me a piece of paper lovingly inscribed with his contact details. I return the favour. He squeezes me *au revoir* and we're off.

I've never driven at 100mph before but if ever there was a road that lent itself to speeding it's the 25 Freeway. The landscape is entirely flat and open so you can see both miles ahead and behind (crucial in terms of spotting cop cars). I want to bomb the whole way but my headache is tuning into high-frequency pain, not least because we're blasting out a rap station at Alexa's request. (Well, she clearly doesn't want to discuss her jailbreak so it's easier to listen to 50 Cent than make small talk.)

Nina takes over the driving as soon as we've dropped Karim and Alexa at the airport in Albuquerque and insists I lay out on the back seat. For the next hour I shiver and gibber and try not to fly into the footwell every time she stops at a traffic light. I want to cry with frustration. Why now? Why this attack of germ warfare just as I'm getting to the good bit – Santa Fe is consistently voted one of the loveliest towns in all America, with a swanky clientele and residents including Shirley MacLaine and Val Kilmer. And then there's my return visit to Ricky – he's hardly going to want to kiss someone this sickly.

'We're here,' Nina alerts me as we approach Santa Fe, seemingly the adobe capital of the world – every low-ceilinged, round-shouldered building is jutting wooden poles and plastered a uniform pinkish-brown.

'Makes for a pretty cosy look,' Nina notes. 'And I

love the clusters of dried chili peppers strung in every doorway.'

We do a circuit of the historic plaza, passing an imposing building with a veranda that would very much lend itself to a sword-fight and an arcade crammed with Native American crafts-sellers who crouch over heaps of silver and turquoise jewellery. I know I must be ill because I've given up the will to shop.

'Well, if you're going to spend your time here dying on a sickbed, we'd better make it a nice one,' Nina decides as we pull over to assess the hotel situation.

It turns out they're all nice, and evocatively named – Casa Pueblo, Inn of the Anasazi, Dancing Ground of the Sun – but we're swayed by the peaceful cobbled courtyards at Inn of the Five Graces.

Positioned opposite America's oldest church on East DeVargas Street, this ambient hideaway equally conjures the mysteries of Morocco and the Orient, offering many artsy distractions for the delirious patient – carved elephant side tables, hand-painted fish blowing marble bubbles in the bathroom, a latticed skylight above the bed.

'It's beautiful,' I sigh, refusing to be taunted by the Kamasutra headboard. 'I couldn't imagine a more romantic setting for a rendezvous.'

'Another time, eh?' Nina sighs, flumping into a low leather chair.

'Hey, you're still in with a chance,' I cajole her. 'Go to it!'

'Are you sure?' Nina reaches over and gives my clammy hand a squeeze.

'There's no point in us both missing out. Go explore – be my eyes!'

'I'll be back by 7 p.m. Call me if you need anything.'

'I will.'

I'm out for the count before I even kick off my boots but then, back in the waking world, I hear my phone ringing.

'Santa Fe Sickbed,' I croak into the receiver.

'Allo?'

I recognise that accent. 'Cem?'

'This is Belinda?' he checks.

'Yes this is. What's left of her.'

'What do you mean, left?'

'I'm dying, Cem.'

'My God, what happened?'

'No, no. I'm just ill. Some kind of instant flu thing.'

'I must come to you!' he rallies.

'Now's probably not the best time,' I resist.

'I must bring you goat milk!' he exclaims.

'Goat milk?'

'Yes, it will help,' he says, matter-of-factly. 'I am in Socorro, I can be there in two hours,' he says, a man on a mission.

'But—!' I begin a protestation.

'Yes?'

'I'm not looking my best, Cem. And I'm not going to be great company.'

'Doesn't matter. I want to see you. I will make you better.'

I don't have the energy to argue. Besides, if he

comes along then at least Nina will have someone to go out to dinner with tonight.

'OK,' I say as my eyes flicker closed.

What's that knocking? I can hear knocking. Are they building my coffin? By the time I reach the door, Cem's knuckles are raw. And his goat milk has curdled.

'Sorry!' I slur, feeling disorientated. 'Have you been there long?'

He gives a hapless shrug.

'Come in,' I beckon, stumbling thwack back into a Tibetan trunk as I do so.

'Woah, you should be in bed,' Cem saves me from an outright tumble.

'Well, I was before . . .' I trail off, limping back to my pit.

'Wait!' Cem halts me just as I'm about to climb aboard. 'You are still wearing your boots!'

'I don't care.'

'Please, let me help you.' He takes hold of my ankle, unzips and tugs me free of the leather.

'Thank you,' I sigh, collapsing into a pillow.

I wait a couple of minutes for the throbbing in my temples to subside then try and focus on the Frenchman stood to my right.

'May I?' he asks permission to join me on the acreage of bed.

I grant it.

For the next half an hour he lies on his stomach, head propped up by his hands, gazing up at me but not crowding me. I tell him he'll have to do most of the talking so he chats about his life back home in Europe, which up until recently involved opening new branches of Marks & Spencer in France.

'Really?' I frown. He doesn't seem the type.

'Yes, this shirt . . .' he pulls at a sheeny-cream polo top '. . . is M&S.'

'It looks designer on you,' I tell him.

He beams back at me. 'You are a special person, I can sense that.'

'It's the drugs,' I tell him.

Although Cem had previously mentioned he was going through a divorce, it's only now I learn that he has a young child. One he has regretfully spent only a brief amount of time with. It may sound a strange thing to say but he seems too slight to be a father. Too slight, in fact, to be considered boyfriend material for me; I'd crush him in any kind of clinch. Not that he seems in any hurry to get to that level. He really is extraordinarily patient and gentle and kind. And understanding. I don't think I've ever experienced those qualities up close in a man before. I find myself contemplating him as if he's some kind of endangered exhibit at the zoo.

And then I think of my mother. For twenty years a man called Charles looked at her the way that Cem is looking at me now. Like he'd do anything for her – nothing would be too much trouble if it made her happy. Could I live with that kind of devotion? Is it even possible for me to believe that I could inspire such behaviour? Right now, the obstacle seems to be that I don't feel like I've done anything to deserve it. Oddly, though my time with him was much more fleeting, I get why Troy would like me – when we started talking, there was a mental double-take as well as a physical one. With Ricky, I'd say he was flattered by the attention, saw an opportunity and took it. But with Cem, I'm left thinking, 'Why is he looking at me like I'm some kind of dainty goddess? It doesn't make sense!'

Then Nina joins us, brimming over with tales of the amazing unsupported staircase at the Loretto Chapel, the world-famous ice-cream baked potatoes at the Cowgirl Hall of Fame and, of course, her beloved Georgia O'Keeffe paintings.

'There was this great quote from her in the film they show about her life,' Nina enthuses. 'She said, "When I first got to New Mexico I thought it was mine. It fitted me exactly." I know what she means, don't you?'

She doesn't seem remotely fazed to find Cem here.

'Is it OK?' I whisper to her when he steps out to the bathroom.

'Of course, why wouldn't it be?'

I love Nina. She's so *no problemo*!

'So, do you think you're up for having dinner out? The lady at the museum recommended this restaurant called Pasqual's – sounds fab.'

Something about the pinky sunset and mellow company has soothed me, and by 9 p.m. we're toasting each other with 'Rio Grande Outlaw Lager' in a room that's decorated like the aftermath of a fiesta. I thank the Lord my tastebuds are still functioning as we mix and dip into plates of Iroquois corn tamales, red onion enchiladas and roasted acorn squash served with chipotle chile crema, cilantro rice and grilled bananas.

'I don't know why you don't like Cem – he's handsome, he's charming, he adores you . . .' Nina steals a moment with me over dessert.

'I don't know why either,' I admit.

'Maybe he's a little serious at times, but he's intelligent, respectful, polite – you could definitely take him home to meet your mother.'

'Are you inferring my tattooed trucker might be less of a hit?'

Nina pulls a face.

'You don't know my mother!' I tease.

She takes another teaspoon of watermelon granita. 'So, how are you feeling about seeing Ricky tomorrow?'

'Half-nervous, half-numb,' I tell her.

'Numb?'

'I think it's a self-inflicted numbness. I don't want to get stung again. But it's OK, I've got no great expectations.'

And I mean this in the most positive way. Instead of letting my mind race imagining how things might be, I'm just going to wait and see.

'He's back,' Nina smiles as Cem rejoins us.

Though it's a crime to miss out on the bars – Swig and the Pink Adobe look particularly promising – we're all pooped and decide to call it a night. As we wander back to the Five Graces I worry about how I'm going to break it to Cem that he can't stay the night. (Even though he's a perfect gentleman and we have a separate lounge with a sofa, I know I won't be able to relax if he's there.) Ordinarily I'd feel obliged to accommodate him but as with the Ricky sex-tustle, I

389

decide to do what feels right to me as opposed to pleasing a man I hardly know and tell it like it is. He doesn't bat an eyelid, even though this now means he has a four-hour drive ahead of him. I stand there and blink at him. What, no bullying? No emotional blackmail? This guy has class!

'Well, good night then.' I stand awkwardly in the door.

'Bonsoir, mon ange,' he kisses my hand and vanishes into the night.

I wander through to the bedroom feeling like a grown-up – I think I'm getting the hang of this now. Maybe I am a girl who can say no!

Then I notice a dreamcatcher laid on the turned-down sheet of my bed with this auspicious note attached: *This dreamcatcher is decorated with bright beads and feathers in order to promote the finding or sustaining of a romantic love. The hope is that the romantic vision in one's dreams will be caught and then fulfilled in waking life.*

Gosh. Talk about careful what you dream of! I wonder who will visit me in sleep tonight? Cem? Troy? Ricky? If I try really hard could it be Hugh Jackman?

I didn't think it would happen for a second time but the instant we emerge from Phoenix airport, Nina and I re-experience major bliss. There's definitely magic in the air here, or maybe it's just that the local blend of CO_2 happens to be the perfect match for our lungs. For me, there's just one small snag: I'm still congested and disorientated with flu. The flight was the worst – the cabin pressure made me feel like I had needles threading through my brain, and part of me wondered if this was my punishment for going back to a guy when I swore that, after the farrago with Paul, I'd make them come to me. Is someone trying to tell me he's not The One? Really, it's not necessary, I already know that. I just want to have a fling! Besides, I'm not really going out of my way to be with him – he's on the way, honest!

'Where to?' the airport cabbie requests.

Wanting to spare Ricky any undue sneaking

around, we forgo the Sanctuary in favour of a property directly on the other side of Camelback Mountain's hump: The Royal Palms Resort & Spa. I think you can guess from its name that we're not exactly skimping on our accommodation and when we pull into the entrance courtyard of this mock-Mediterranean paradise, Nina decides to go one step further by booking into her own casita.

'Firstly, I don't want your germs,' she explains her decision to me as we stroll past trellises entwined with bright pink bougainvillea and fountains burbling onto hand-painted tiles. 'And secondly, I don't want to have to pretend I'm asleep while you're having sex with Ricky.'

I give her a wry look. 'Trust me, I won't be having sex with him.' Even if he could tame his voracious alter ego I'm way too ill to feel inclined.

'Then why are we here?'

I think for a moment. 'I just like that flirtatious feeling when I'm with him. I like having someone that beautiful looking at me with desire.' I expel an elongated sigh. 'But most of all, I want fondue. Are you sure you won't come with us?'

'I don't think gooseberry goes well with cheese.'

'He could bring Nathan,' I suggest.

'No, no, no.'

'No?'

'No.' Nina gives her head such a firm shake she cricks her neck. 'Just give me a full report in the morning.'

Our rooms have matching wrought-iron four-posters with Jacquard-print furnishings lending a court-jester vibe to an otherwise Spanish-style setting. As we lean over the wall of our respective olive-pitted patios, Nina announces that she's heading straight for the pool. I consult my watch – I have a good hour before I need to start getting ready but I don't want to aggravate my earache by swilling my head underwater so instead I stroll the fragrant gardens, happening upon a hammock strung between two smooching palms. I ease myself onto the knotted string, creating a human quilt effect as the diamonds embed into my clothing, then close my eyes and let the sun warm me to the core. I think I've just discovered the ultimate sick bed. From now on I'm going to have all my ailments at the Royal Palms. The heat is so comforting and intense it somehow dulls my aches and pains. I suppose psychologically I associate lying out in the sun with holidays so for a moment I fool my body that I'm actually having a lovely time.

Ordinarily all my thoughts would be fast-forwarding to tonight – what is it going to be like to see Ricky again, what will I wear, what will he be thinking when he first sees me . . . but I find myself languishing in the present instead. That has got to be one of the greatest gifts of this trip – I feel like I've been reminded that I have a whole set of feelings aside from those pertaining to men. What I mean is, I can have feelings about a man (good and bad) without them overwhelming how I feel in myself. Maybe because of Paul I'm learning to centre myself before I step into the fray. And that makes me feel stronger, even a little invincible. One of my biggest fears is letting the influence of a man swamp my life and now I feel I have a choice over whether I would allow that to happen.

This calls for a celebration! I tip myself out of my string cocoon and wander in a sunny stupor until I find the hotel bar. The room is already filling with early diners enjoying a cocktail from deep within the fireside armchairs so I pull up a bar stool, happy to people-watch. One elegant fifty-something captures my attention as he moves among the guests like a bewhiskered Cary Grant, meeting, greeting, flattering, teasing, smiling, charming, bowing.

'Who is that?' I ask the barman, my curiosity further piqued by the mystery man's exotic accent.

'That's Paul Xanthopoulos,' he replies. 'He's our Director of Romance.'

I blink in disbelief. 'That's his actual job title?'

'Yes ma'am,' the barman confirms with a nod. 'He's also the restaurant maître d.'

'So what exactly does he do, romantically?'

'Well, he might make the arrangements for a proposal over dinner – you know, having the ring dropped into a champagne flute or snuck into dessert.'

I gulp disapprovingly – way too risky for my tastes, both from a dentistry and digestion p.o.v.

'Or, as the couple are seated for dinner, he will glide up and say, "As this is your first time dining with us, it is customary for me to give you a brief tour of our enchanting property before dessert. Will you allow me?" They of course accept his gracious offer, he returns after their main course, shows them a few beauty spots in the grounds then leads them to a nook pre-prepared with rose petals, candles, champagne and dessert for two. At which point he disappears!' the barman laughs, adding,

'They say he's a direct descendant of Eros.'

I smile, happy to believe him – if I was a relative of the God of Love this is precisely where I would shack up.

'Let me introduce you.' The barman beckons the maestro who promptly kisses my hand, lowering his head like he is in the presence of a deity. Apparently this is how four years ago he went from being 'the little guy with the beard who looks at women a certain way' to Director of Romance!

'You are a very, very beautiful lady,' he says, studying me intently. 'I can see the passion in your eyes, also reflected in your mouth . . .'

I'm instantly, self-consciously a-twitter. Worse still, the combination of my flu and the over-zealous air-conditioning is making my eyes stream.

'I love to make a woman's eyes water,' he rumbles suggestively.

I think he means well-up. I *hope* he means well-up.

'Are you looking for love?' he leans closer, mesmerising me further.

I nod, feeling strangely vulnerable, as if he's some all-knowing guru who can see straight through to my heart. 'You don't happen to do matchmaking on the side, do you?' I joke.

He smiles. 'People are always asking me to do that and I have made matches that resulted in marriage but others have been terrible fiascos!' he confesses with a shudder. 'I believe there are many people who are suitable for a person but you have to cultivate and explore the people you meet – bring out the best they have, don't dismiss them after the first sentence.' He gives me a stern look. 'You have to go deeper than the surface.'

It's almost as if he knows I've got a date with a pretty boy tonight.

'So, you're not actually an advocate of love at first sight?' I venture.

'I don't believe in rushing into things,' he affirms. 'I have men coming to me who are planning to propose after two months but that is so shallow, so thoughtless. They are risking the well-being of the other person.'

Gosh. I always thought it would be wonderful to have a whirlwind romance and be so sure so soon but he's right – maybe people act that fast because they don't want a chance to see someone's shortcomings or face their own doubts.

'Ah, welcome Mr and Mrs Martinez – it must be two and a half years since your last visit! Wonderful to have you back.'

I know he's busy but before he departs I beg the love guru for a word of wisdom in terms of my finding Mr Right.

'Choose someone who gives more than they are willing to take,' he says sagely, before guiding an anniversary couple through to their table.

I run a quick check of my previous boyfriends – they were all takers bar Don. A rather depressing thought until I realise that Troy, Cem and Ricky are all definitely givers. Wow. I must be getting better! I think that calls for another celebratory drink!

Now, two vodkas down, my laissez faire attitude towards my date with Ricky has revved up to a tap-dance of anticipation. I find myself hurrying back to the room where adrenalin overrides illness and I shower and dry my hair with vigour. Half an hour later I'm done, though I do leave the make-up on my nose to the very last minute so I can snuffle and blow right up until the doorbell rings.

7 p.m. comes and goes. I twiddle the foundation bottle distractedly.

7.15 p.m. I'm starting to feel mildly anxious.

7.30 p.m. I start pacing and panicking. Have I set myself up for another burn?

7.40 p.m. I feel sick. It would seem I attract flakes. Or maybe I choose them – Cem wouldn't do this to me.

7.50 p.m. I crack and phone Ricky. He answers all breezy as if there's no problem. And in fact it turns out there isn't – I'd forgotten that Arizona is an hour behind New Mexico time and it is in fact 6.50 p.m. Arghhh! I peaked too soon! All that stressing for nothing – I'm my own worst enemy, it's official.

Dead on the real 7 p.m. the doorbell rings. Ricky looks wonderful in a pale blue short-sleeved shirt, pimp shades and a rather large accessory in the form of Nathan.

'Where's Nina?' he asks, looking eagerly around the room.

'Um!' I wasn't expecting this. 'She's got my flu. Only worse. We've had to put her in quarantine in a separate room.'

'She's worse than you?' Ricky frowns into my bloodshot eyes.

'Much worse,' I confirm. 'She's dosed up with pills and potions, just trying to get as much sleep as possible before our flight tomorrow.'

Oh please don't let her come skipping by in her bikini! I make a silent prayer.

'Oh well, I suppose I'll just go home.' Nathan looks crestfallen.

'Nooo! Don't be silly!' I protest. 'At least come eat with us.'

'I don't know,' Nathan looks hesitant.

'Really, it's fine.' I mean this. I'm feeling surprisingly nervous around Ricky and, not having had a romantic dinner-a-deux for a while, am relieved to have a third party along to make things easier.

It's not until we're seated in the restaurant booth that I finally make eye contact with Ricky. He too seems a little on edge and I'm hugely relieved when he sneaks his hand under the table to take mine. I was beginning to think he was regretting suggesting this rendezvous, but now I can relax and enjoy myself, starting with the ceremonial dunking of fancy bread and apple chunks into a pot of stretchy Gruyère sauce seasoned with white wine, garlic, nutmeg and fresh lemon – mmm, tastebud heaven!

With each course, Ricky's behaviour becomes more adorably boyfriendy – following the salad break he sets my cube of pork tenderloin a-sizzle in oil, carefully assessing the cooking time on my behalf, then prepares a perfect little platter for me, all in the most caring, attentive way. I look on in wonder, lost for words, grateful that with any lull in the conversation you can play 'identify the meat cut'. This really is a great date place.

Meanwhile, Nathan copes with any self-conscious third wheel moments by making origami napkin ducks

398

and offering such conversational gambits as, 'It's not that I don't like fake boobs, I just don't want to have to pay for them.' (Apparently a lot of local girls presume elective surgery should be financed by their suitors.) He also claims to be supremely romantic but I don't believe him for a minute – I'm still convinced Ricky is the only likely successor to Mr Xanthopoulos's petal-strewn throne.

After drowning morsels of banana, pineapple and brownie in a chocolate fondue swirled with Baileys, any normal person would happily expire for the night. But not us. At the boys' insistence we trawl a series of half-empty bars creating instant despondency on my behalf. By midnight even Nathan appears to have given up the will to live, yet he shows no sign of going home. I'm tiring of trying to include him in the conversation when all I really want is pillow talk with Ricky (who incidentally keeps disappearing for suspiciously long toilet breaks, and by that I'm suggesting illicit flirtations as opposed to drugs). When he suggests yet another venue I find myself throwing up my hands and crying out that I can't take any more – I have to keel!

Seconds later Ricky is whisking me back to the hotel in his car, apologising for keeping my sickly frame out after hours. We're just at the final set of lights when a girl draws level with us and hollers a delighted, 'Ricky Hart!', leaning across the passenger seat to give him an ultra-flirtatious 'Hey baby!' look. 'Whatcha doing?' she husks.

'Driving a lady-friend home, what does it look like?' I feel like cussing.

'Nothing much,' he shrugs, looking awkward.

'You going on somewhere?' She looks expectant.

'No, this is it for us.'

'OK,' she shrugs in a 'your loss' kind of way before vrooming off.

I so know that I'm going back to my casita with the No. 1 ladies'-man-about-town but I don't care. Despite his auspicious surname, Ricky has no hold over my heart (mostly because I've realised I don't trust him), all I want is his company. There'll definitely be no hanky-panky – I'm groggy with a whole new set of symptoms and I don't want to pass them on, and we've even agreed there will be no kissing. I give my teeth a vigorous clean all the same, then scoot into my pyjama bottoms and my most expensive T-shirt on account of it being the most flattering cut. (I may be too sick to sin but I still want him to want to!)

'Come here you,' he says, pulling me beneath the covers and into his chest.

I snuggle deep into him. This is nice. No pressure. No mauling. Just togetherness. I'm just drifting off when KER-ZAM! He springs into action like Kato launching himself on Inspector Clouseau! Ye gads, it's horizontal martial arts all over again. I'm just re-awakening my defence reflexes when I hear a starchy ripping sound and look down at my chest to see bare flesh where material used to be.

NO!

'That was my best T-shirt!' I gape at the slash reaching from breastbone to navel.

'Sorry, but you should be flattered I felt so passionate,' he growls, eager to resume proceedings.

I'm too stunned to reciprocate. *He just ripped my best T-shirt!* is all I can think as I bat him off me. I do wonder about men sometimes, he knows I found him too full-on during our first encounter at Sanctuary so instead of taking it down a notch he goes the other way and morphs into the Incredible Hulk, only it's *my* clothes that ended up ripped. I shake my head – I'm sure he has a vast sexual repertoire, he just needs to work on matching the appropriate move to the appropriate girl/situation.

Ardour finally subsiding, he asks, 'Am I just your boy in Arizona?'

'Yes,' I tell him matter-of-factly.

'But I love you,' he protests.

'No you don't,' I tut. That's just ridiculous.

'I do,' he insists.

'Ricky, it's sweet of you to say but you don't.'

He looks confused. This isn't how it normally goes, I'm sure. I'm a little dazed myself but somehow in my muzzy-headed, mauled state I've found a moment of clarity.

'Well, when am I going to see you again?' he pouts.

'I don't know,' I tell him, sounding more carefree by the minute.

I don't really know why he's asking. Habit I suppose. Saying things he knows girls want to hear. I like him, I really do, but I know there's no future for us – we're both just messing around, biding time until The Big One.

'Night then,' he sighs, finally accepting the impasse.

'Night,' I smile, happily returning to my own side of the bed.

The next morning, with Ricky long gone, I check my e-mails for the first time in a week, and my heart does a little star jump at the sight of one from Trucker Troy entitled 'I dig you!' I can't help but smile – only he could carry off that phrase and make it sound indescribably sexy.

I quickly click it open – a nice chunky paragraph in which he confesses to having saved my Happy Birthday phone message and replayed it over and over just so he can listen to my 'kick-ass accent'. Love that! He also says, 'I can't believe you don't have a significant other – you seem like Miss Personality.' Flattery will get you everywhere, Mr T. Maybe he's a freak in a good way – I've always secretly thought that the perfect match for me would be something of an oddity. And I like the idea that we're two oddballs who only make sense to each other. Let's face it – I'm not the sanest, most rational person on the planet. So he likes trucks! I'd rather he was eyeing fenders than other females.

I look at my watch. He's three hours ahead in Florida. Nina has just gone for a farewell swim so I definitely have time to call him now. But dare I? What will I say if he brings up the truck pictures? I'm still wretched with flu and can barely construct a sentence, let alone a quick-thinking retort, but I decide to go for it anyway.

'Troy?' I make a tentative enquiry.

He laughs heartily in recognition of my voice. 'It's you!' he cheers, sounding absurdly pleased to hear from me. 'Hello!'

'Hello,' I smile, surprised at just how happy I am to speak to him again. 'I'm a bit croaky, you'll have to forgive me . . .' I give him a quick run-down of my symptoms expecting the usual 'Poor baby!' brush-off but his sympathy is both abundant and heartfelt.

'I hate that I'm not there to take care of you,' he laments. 'I'd feel so much better if I knew that someone was bringing you chicken soup.'

Caring is a new vibe for me in the boyfriend realm. First Cem, then Ricky at the restaurant and now Troy. I like it! Especially as Troy's 'someone to watch over you' stance doesn't extend into prying about what I've got up to in Arizona or New Mexico. He knows what my trip is all about and I expect a snide remark here and there but he's nothing but respectful. Things certainly don't feel precarious with him like they tend to in the early days of most of my romantic encounters. Maybe it's the age difference – with twenty years' life experience on Ricky, Troy's really taking things to the next level!

There's a rap on the window.

'Twenty minutes!' Nina mouths to me.

'I really have to go – I haven't finished packing,' I tell Troy.

'So, Miss Jones, what are the chances of you dropping down to Florida when you come back over to the East Coast?'

I get a charge of excitement – he wants to meet up!

'I suppose I could stay on for a few days after Tennessee?' I volunteer casually.

'Belinda, I would love that,' he breathes.

Just hearing him say my name makes me shiver.

'I could take you out in my truck . . .'

Oh, here we go! 'Er, thanks for the pictures by the way!' I cut in with a grimace.

'Did you like them?'

'Mmmm.' What am I supposed to say?

'I've got hundreds more, I can show you when you get here. But what I really want to do is . . .'

'Troy!' I gasp, as he descends into sultry innuendo. 'Stop! I've got to go!'

I put down the phone feeling all churned up – both anxious and elated. I really don't know what I'm dealing with here but I'm definitely feeling a magnetic pull. I jump up and run into Nina, eager to tell her that Trucker wants me to visit him in Kissimmee.

She swings me around, equally ecstatic, then suddenly halts. 'Hold on, I thought you said the next one has to come to you?'

I chew my lip. 'I did, didn't I?'

'I realise Ricky doesn't count because he was—'

'On the way,' I complete the sentence. Besides, I knew Ricky could do me no harm. But Troy? He's a far riskier prospect. There is no way I want to put myself through another Paul/Cazenovia scenario.

'You're right,' I tell Nina. 'I'm going to ring him back right now.'

'Fifteen minutes!' She calls after me.

'I'll be ready!' I call back.

I have to do this now or it'll get all messy and awkward. I'm going to tell him that I want to see him but I've realised it's not practical at the point we discussed – I'll need a bit of time to recover from all the travelling. However, I will be spending a month or two at a friend's in Los Angeles at the end of this journey so perhaps, if he wanted to, he could visit me there? I feel extremely fretful as I once again dial his number. If he's anything like the men I normally go for, he's going to get all shirty about the rejection factor . . .

'I totally understand. I don't want to put you under any unnecessary pressure,' he says calmly. 'Just let me know when is good for you. I'll wait.'

'Th-thank you . . .' I put down the phone feeling a little woozy. He's so patient. Anyone would think he actually cares about what is best for me. My hand creeps up to my chest. Wow. There he is – I can feel him in my heart.

WEDDINGTON,
NORTH CAROLINA

When it came to scheduling our trip to Weddington, North Carolina, the choice was between Nina and I rubbing up against thirty thousand testosterone-crazed racing fans at the Nascar Coca Cola 600 or accepting an invitation to 'Swivel like Swayze and Boogie like Baby' at a *Dirty Dancing* revue overlooking the lake where the movie was shot back in the Eighties. There was no contest. We had to go Dirty Dancing!

I believe in Frances Houseman and Johnny Castle – they're such an endearing, enduring couple; that flick is nearly twenty years old and tell me if their arched-back sway to 'Cry To Me' isn't just the sexiest movie scene *ever*. You can keep your sweaty, torrid yelping! Watching Jennifer Grey's tiny hand lightly traverse Patrick's tanned, muscular back just slays me.

'Imagine getting to re-create that moment in the very location it was filmed but with a hot new torso!' Nina pips. 'Not that I wouldn't want to do it with

Patrick Swayze but I don't suppose he's in town right now.'

I love that Nina is equally psyched about this – the girl has always loved to dance! Being in Kellermans country is something of a dream for both of us.

But first we have a date with a real-life love story.

'So let me get this straight,' Nina twists around in the car seat as we make the fifteen-mile dash from Charlotte airport to Weddington. 'We're going to meet a husband and wife team who co-write novels in which real-life couples are the heroes and the heroines?'

'Exactly. They publish them to order: you fill out a form with your name and the name of your beloved – you and George Clooney if you wanted – then give them your eye and hair colour, pet names for each other, your career, home town, favourite perfume/ aftershave, favourite band etc. and they take those details and weave them into a personalised romance.'

'What a lark!'

'I know – and they do mild and wild versions, depending on how racy a read you're after!' I chuckle.

'And are all the stories set here in North Carolina?'

'Just two, others are set in Austria, Alaska, the Caribbean . . . so I'm guessing they know a fair bit about romance in exotic locations. I thought they might be able to give us a few pointers for our man hunt here.'

An excellent decision as there is frankly nothing else to do in Weddington – essentially an upscale, characterless suburb of Charlotte. Except perhaps go shopping for million-dollar homes . . . so with a little time to spare before meeting the love scribes we venture onto a brand new estate of show homes. The sales team know that ninety per cent of people are lookie-loos and are cashing in on this by actually charging people twenty dollars a head to gawp at the lavish mansions with their black walnut flooring, cream granite kitchen countertops, playrooms with rock-climbing walls, master bathrooms with heated flooring, not to mention exterior pools, spas, cabanas, koi ponds, basketball courts and in one case, a waterfall.

'It's all very nouveau riche, isn't it?' Nina observes. 'I mean, you've got English Tudor next to "Nantucket" next to Georgian. And as luxurious and perfect as these homes are, you can't imagine anyone with any class purchasing a property that everyone within a thirty-mile radius has tramped through.'

It's certainly quite a contrast to the environment we found ourselves in half an hour earlier – we took the wrong turning directly as we left the airport terminal and ended up in a rather dodgy, shanty-shack neighbourhood. I decided to ask for directions at a gas station, and fill up the tank while I was at it, but I couldn't get the pump to work so went skipping in to ask for help. Everyone turned and gawped as I entered, probably because I was the only white person and everyone else seemed to have some weeping sore or bandaged limb and the cashier was heavily clanked and padlocked into a protective cage.

'Um, terribly sorry to bother you chaps,' I announced, sounding exactly like Joyce Grenfell, 'Can't seem to get the darn pump to work.'

One homeless vagabond limped over offering to

assist me. I know the deal – if they fill the tank for you, you slip them a few bucks by way of thanking them for not mugging you. So I stood by, slightly tense, watching him do his business, money at the ready. But when I offered it to him he hesitated and said, 'Are you sure?'

'What?' I stumbled.

'You don't have to,' he gave me a shy look.

'No, of course, I want to,' I insisted, pressing the cash into his hand, utterly beguiled by his sweet demeanour. In my experience pump-loiterers generally look down at the scumpled notes and give a derisive 'Is that all?' snort. This fella even gave us excellent directions on how to get back onto the 74 South. Part of me wanted to take him away with us.

It was a very green drive. Everything in North Carolina seems to be green – nothing but rain-drenched trees and grass for miles. After the dusty deserts of Arizona and New Mexico everything seems refreshingly lush. And though Weddington is a little bland, I'm liking the overall vibe of North Carolina.

'Back in a mo!' Nina tells me she'll catch me up in the coffee shop where we're meeting the yournovel.com couple – she can't resist the opportunity to wander the aisles of the whopping supermarket next door. 'I just love looking at biscuits and yogurts in different countries,' she says as she excuses herself.

Kathy and Fletcher are already latte'd up when I walk in. I take an instant shine to Kathy, she's like an exuberant auntie you could talk to about anything – so warm and enthusiastic and fun and empathetic, and a vision in apple green! Fletcher is more of a quiet, all-knowing tufty-haired owl. They are both super-smart and articulate and explain to me how in the beginning Kathy was writing more of the romantic love scenes and then when Fletcher saw the fun she was having he was like, 'Wait! I want to get in on that!' so now they share that, giving both the male and female viewpoints.

It's a neat little set-up – she's good at the descriptions, he favours the technical research; he nudges her when she's having a lazy moment, she edits his dashed-off words. Together they've turned an original idea into a career that supports them both – at $50 a pop, they earned $300,000 last year, thanks in part to coverage in magazines like *People* and *InStyle*.

'It's the best job description in the world,' raves Kathy. 'We write about love with the one we love and our job is promoting love! It doesn't get any better!'

'Love is the only thing that really matters,' Fletcher adds, sounding like he really means it.

'I think I'm having a very different life experience to you people!' I confess.

'You just haven't met the right man yet,' Kathy winks. 'Look, I grew up with the old black-and-white movies and I totally believed in "My prince will come!" but in the real world you have to be a grown-up and take care of yourself and these days women don't wait to have men support them – nor should they – so you go on and develop yourself. Keep in mind that I married Fletcher when I was thirty-nine years old. And truth be told, if he had come into my life five years sooner we probably would have passed in the night.'

'How so?'

'When I was younger I was very independent, very into my career – I was doing my own thing. I had family, I had friends, but as I got older I realised what I was missing, and that was a life-mate. At an earlier time I don't think that was a high priority.'

'Hmmm, so maybe it's not that marriage is not for me, I'm just not ready – not old enough!' I chuckle to myself – tell that to the twenty-five-year-old spinsters of Convent, Louisiana. 'You know, I think the main fear for me is losing my freedom,' I confess.

Kathy totally understands. 'In my first marriage I found the relationship very confining so I thought that being involved with someone meant having to give up things and limit yourself. But when you find the right one it's the total opposite.'

'Really?' I still need to be convinced of this.

'Being a couple can enhance who you are and open everything up to you – it can get you doing things you didn't know you were capable of, show you things you never expected about yourself – it is uplifting and broadening,' she beams. 'And if you find somebody who will work with you to help you achieve your goals you can be better as a couple than you can ever be as two individuals,' Kathy insists.

'You're like the sales lady for love!' I laugh.

'Well, I have absolutely no patience with friends of mine who say, "I think I'm going to settle for this guy – he's making a decent living, he treats me pretty well . . ." I'm like, "What are you talking about? This is your life! This is your future! This is your happiness! You owe it to yourself to find bells and whistles and stars and magic. *It's there*,"' she enthuses. 'Really, I feel so

414

sad for women who either don't believe that exists or don't believe they are worthy.'

At which point Nina joins us, laden down with goodies from the supermarket. 'Twinkies! Ho-Hos! Ding-Dongs!' she holds up a series of synthetic sponges and cookies. 'Aren't they cute?'

I roll my eyes at her.

'Sorry!' she says, shoving the bag under the table. 'Have I missed the advice bit yet?'

'We're looking for tips on how to woo a North Carolina man,' I explain.

'Why would you two have any problems meeting any man that you wanted?' Fletcher shakes his head. 'I mean, if you were three hundred pounds, unkempt and missing a tooth I'd understand.'

'Trust me, if we walk into a bar in England, we don't turn a single head,' Nina insists, taking a slurp of my Chai tea.

'Well then the women in England must look a lot different than they do in America,' Kathy laughs, adding: 'If that happens here I'll be shocked.'

'I'm shocked anyway,' Fletcher tuts. Bless him.

'You know what,' a thought dawns on Kathy. 'I have lots of attractive female friends who don't get asked out. I think it's definitely harder now.'

Fletcher shudders. 'I'm just really glad I don't have to go out and try to meet someone, it's *work*!'

'Which is why we need a heads-up!'

'OK,' Kathy rises to the challenge. 'Firstly if you were going to woo a local man, someone born and raised here, it would be helpful if you went to college with them or were a friend of the family – this is really

415

traditional Southern Bible Belt country and it's hard to come in as an outsider and penetrate that. But Wilmington (the setting for *Dawson's Creek*) with its film industry or Asheville (home to the Biltmore Estate) with its spiritual arts community, are beautiful romantic places with far more outsiders resident, so your chances of meeting someone there would be much better.'

Hmmm, we may have to reconsider our itinerary.

Fletcher gives his twopenn'orth: 'Local men may have been babied by their mothers so they might want a little bit of taking care of but they are salt-of-the earth, trustworthy, 'manly' men – even the short ones!' he laughs. 'They can be brash and overbearing with women in general, but with the one woman that they love, they will idolise her and be incredibly chivalrous.'

'Which as a southern woman I really appreciate,' Kathy notes. 'It's very nice to be treated special, like a lady.'

I can certainly see the appeal of being pampered like a princess but after my experience with Cem, I'm not sure that's for me. It almost feels like role-play and I find myself at a loss for how to behave in response. Of course it's lovely to be cherished – and I'm definitely digging Troy's caring vibe – but instead of being put on a pedestal, I want to be an equal partner. I'm so glad we met Kathy and Fletcher – it's a good reminder that some relationships actually lift you up!

We hug them goodbye, hoping some of their love luck rubs off on us, and go in search of a love shack for the night, serenaded on our journey by Magic 96.1FM playing 'the Best of the Bridesmaids' – classic songs that only ever made it to Number Two in the charts.

Just as Van Morrison's 'Brown Eyed Girl' begins we spy the perfect place to stay: The Morehead Inn, where a little over £100 buys us a night in the sumptuous Hawthorne Suite. Set in a carriage house, our room has a large hardwood-floored lounge area with Indian rugs and Chinese accents, a bedroom with an 1820s brass bed and French windows opening onto the most darling patio – shame it's just started to tip down. As we dart out to the car to drag our cases across the bricked courtyard, we spy a forlorn wedding planner looking like she's ready to make some pagan sacrifice at the altar in order to win fair weather for tomorrow's ceremony. All the white wooden chairs are set out in a neat crescent but not even a speedily erected canopy could protect the guests from the every-which-way lashings of the rain.

'You know,' I start, 'when Kathy and Fletcher got married they had this outdoor ceremony overlooking the ocean and it began as this gorgeous sunny day then suddenly this nor'easter charged up and everyone's hair was blowing sideways and the wind drowned out all their vows on the video, but she didn't care.' (The woman got married in a pink suit with rhinestones so I'm guessing she was going to have a good time no matter what.)

'You really liked them, didn't you?' Nina looks quizzically at me.

'Yes I did,' I smile. 'Just seeing them so happy together makes me want to ring Trucker.'

'Well you do that, I'm going to read up on what's happening locally tonight.'

But before I can even dial Troy, my phone rings. My first thought is, 'Oh my God, he's thinking of me too!' but it's Cem – oozing TLC, eager for an update on my flu. I can't quite believe it – what with Troy's earlier talk of chicken soup, that's two men in one day genuinely concerned for my well-being. How odd. But whereas Troy is Mr Mellow, Cem is definitely more ardent, more jealous, more French. He asks me if he's the Only One. I fudge a reply. (After Paul I'm not interested in making any hasty, unsubstantiated pledges.) He calls me his angel and lots of *hon-he-hon* things I don't understand. I'm touched but I'm still a little in the dark as to why he's so keen on me – it's as though he's hopped aboard the love train but I'm still on the platform.

He says he wants to speak daily while I'm on the road but I tell him it's not really feasible. The last thing I want to feel is that nagging obligation. Hmmm, rather like I would if I had a full-time boyfriend. Every now and again I do question if it's what I really want. Anyway, I need to give the men of North Carolina a fair chance and I can't do that if I'm billing and cooing down the blower to him at every opportunity (says she, about to call Troy). Not that I tell him that, I simply say that it's unrealistic logistically. I can't believe I'm being Ms Cool. Normally I fall over myself trying to please but this Mr Right mission has changed all that – I have become The Bachelorette! But then isn't that the American way – aren't you supposed to have a number of suitors on the go initially? I feel spoiled at having both Troy and Cem be so sweet to me but assure myself that I'm not doing anything wrong – it's not like I've even

418

kissed either of them. I'm just getting to know them.

'Red Hot Chili Peppers! Red Hot Chili Peppers!' Nina comes tearing into the bedroom. 'They're playing down the road tonight! Give me the phone!'

She snatches it out of my hand and dials feverishly, pressing an interminable number of buttons to get through to a real-live sales bod.

'Two, that's right. Uh-huh – *YES!*' she squeals, dancing around then comes to a sudden halt. 'You do like them, don't you?'

'I like "Under The Bridge".'

'Good enough. We've got an hour. Woah – message.' She hands me back my buzzing phone.

This time it is indeed Troy – instant glee!

'I hope you pick this up in time – I want to come and see you. It's just a ten-hour drive from Florida to North Carolina. Do you want to meet?'

Oh my God! He'd drive a twenty-hour round-trip for me! Now you're talking! I laugh out loud and then suddenly panic. I'm so into the fantasy of him, do I really want to risk losing that by meeting up? Plus I wouldn't even grant Cem a phone call so isn't it somewhat breaking the rules to have an out-of-state visitor? I quickly switch off my phone. I'm having a wobble. I can't possibly speak to him now. I'm just not ready. We can talk tomorrow.

I flump back on the bed, trying to figure out why I'm freaking out so much. I think it's because I know with Troy it could be a big deal. Something about the instant chemistry between us, and the way our conversations make me feel; I sense he's not someone I could shrug off like Ricky. One of the ways I know he's getting

419

under my skin is whenever I see or hear something interesting or quirky, I find myself instantly wording the description in my head, ready for our next conversation. Right now I'm torn. I like him a lot but I'm scared – scared there's a chance it could actually work out between us. I know I'm jumping the gun but suddenly I don't know if I want things to change that much. I'm happy as I am. And anyway, chances are it'll end in tears. I think I'll just leave it for a bit.

The next morning Nina wakes me with the words, 'Nobody puts Baby in the corner.'

Yayyy! It's DD-day.

Within two hours we'll be at Lake Lure – the spot where Baby and Johnny practised that legendary lift.

Before we leave we check on the progress with the Morehead courtyard wedding – as the rain is still sloshing down like innumerable upturned bathtubs they've shifted the ceremony indoors to the hotel drawing room and, through the crack in the double-doors, I can just see the bride making her entrance down the grand staircase. There it is again – that love thing. I can't help feeling that both bride and groom are being incredibly brave putting so much faith in another human being. There are so many things that can go wrong, so many ways your heart can get obliterated and yet there they stand, looking into each other's eyes, willing to take that chance. Am I just being a coward about Troy? Am I potentially missing out on something wonderful?

'Come on,' Nina urges me. 'We should get going.'

The rains keep on coming, the roads get more

swervy-curvy and the greenery just keeps getting greener. It's as though every leaf has reached its full potential – if trees can be happy, these are happy trees.

'Can you imagine how incredibly beautiful this place must be in the autumn – all the reds and golds and oranges as far as the eye can see.'

'Gorgeous.'

'I mean, even when it's all pretty much one shade of green I still love it.' And I do. This place gives me a good feeling. So much so that when we stop off at a low-rent Waffle House staffed by waitresses with comedy-sketch Southern accents, I decide to leave my full $20 bill and not wait for any change.

'Oh ma gosh!' the waitress cries, incredulous. 'Those gals just left me an eight dollar tip!'

I step out the door feeling like a millionairess! Shortly after, we're gawping at the major moolah properties that trim Lake Lure, including one Italianate villa with its own private manmade beach.

'Isn't that gorgeous?' I sigh, gazing across the green waters that reflect the abundance of mimosa, crab apple, ash, mulberry, sycamore and dogwood trees that surround us.

'Even the junky looking houses are worth around $400,000 because of their position on the water,' our personal lake guide tells us. 'A new buyer would just tear it down and build a new one.'

We're sat aboard what is known as the Love Boat, though as it has four seats I'm not exactly sure what kind of loving they had in mind. As the boat is electrically powered we glide as silently as a swan, only disturbing the peace with our conversation.

421

'So this really is where they filmed the lake scene in *Dirty Dancing*?' Nina requires official confirmation.

'Yup, and it was November so they had to spray-paint food colouring on the leaves and they couldn't get the cameras too close to the actors cos their lips were blue and their noses dribbling!' he chuckles as he directs the boat to a picturesque bay with a clearing showing traces of old cement foundations. 'This is the site of the old Boys' Summer Camp they rented to film the staff quarters scenes.'

We sit up, eagerly conjuring a plimsoll-clad Baby venturing off-limits.

'Up until 1996 the revue you're going to tonight was held right here in the barn where they filmed the dance sequences.'

'Oh no – why did they stop?' I wail.

'Lack of business initially. The place lay fallow for a while and then it became a hangout for teenagers – there was vandalism, general screwing around and then one night someone lit a campfire inside and the whole thing burned down.'

'That's terrible – all those amazing memories, gone!'

'Not exactly,' our guide gets a certain glint in his eye. 'Just recently they took down the last cabin and the demolition guy called to see if there was anything our boss wanted so we went over and collected a whole bunch of wood from Johnny's cabin. I could give you a piece if you like?'

We practically upturn the Love Boat in our enthusiasm. 'Are you serious?'

'Yeah,' he shrugs, like it's no big deal.

'Oh my God – an authentic bit of Johnny's cabin!' I

fall into a swoon, barely able to comprehend the possibility of having a splinter of movie history in my hands.

This jubilation lasts for a whole thirty minutes, after which point irritation dominates our emotions – we're having the most infernal time trying find our accommodation for the night. I thought it would be a straightforward loop around the lake but there's all sorts of tricksy offshoots and different levels and we repeatedly find ourselves back at a rickety shack labelled Thelma's Mountain Store.

'I'm going in!' I announce tiredly, third time round.

It's everything you'd want a mountain store to be – rammed to the rafters with liquor, crisps and baccy, and staffed by a woman with grey hair plaited to her waist, surrounded by photos of her innumerable grandchildren. She couldn't look any less pleased to see me.

'I've lived here my whole life and I've never heard of it,' she grunts when I ask her for a clue to the location of the Ivivi Lodge.

'I'm not making it up!' I feel like bleating, though I will admit it's an unusual choice – the Lodge actually has a South African theme but I fell in love with one of the rooms on the Internet on account of its incredible panoramic views of the Blue Ridge Mountains. Not that there's going to be anything to view by the time we get there – the mists are descending and the sky is darkening.

'No luck?' Nina sighs.

I shake my head, getting increasingly vexed. We're seriously running out of time – the revue kicks off in ten minutes at Chimney Rock Park, it's at least a twenty minute drive from here and we're already an hour late for check-in. Naturally my phone has no reception. Stress!

We find another store owner a bit further on and follow their directions via Bill Creek then Buffalo Creek but somehow we miss the crucial 'Nobblit' turn and continue on up and up, clawing steeper and steeper until we get altitude anxiety. There only seem to be private houses up here and I'm convinced if we keep going we'll end up balanced on the pinnacle of some mountain until the snows come. Finally a half-moon of gravel to pull into. We pause, awaiting divine intervention, then a motorcycle rounds the corner and I fling my arm out the window to flag him down, practically smacking him in the face in the process. As he steps off his bike and approaches us, I busily jabber apologies and beg for clues on our whereabouts until Nina points out that he can't hear a word I'm saying because he's still wearing his helmet. Once his ears are liberated I run through it all again.

'I've been up and down this stretch of road four times in the past hour and I haven't seen any signs for the Ivivi Lodge,' he shrugs.

My heart sinks. I'm a little curious as to why he's been up and down the road four times but Nina distracts me with a Plan B suggestion.

'What if we go straight to Chimney Rock now?' she asks, then leans across to address the biker. 'Can you direct us there?'

'Sure!' he brightens.

Great! That means dirty dancing in sticky humidity

clothes with rain-frazzled hair, then returning to these unfathomable roads in inky darkness hoping that the Ivivi – Zulu for Invisible, I'm beginning to think – will step from the shadows and present itself to us. But what else can we do? Just at the point where we're resigned to our miserable fate we stumble across the Ivivi's sister hotel – the Lodge on Lake Lure – all dressed up with reams of white taffeta ribbons.

'Must be another wedding,' I deduce, leaning forward for a better view only to inadvertently blast the peace with a resounding honk on the horn. I shrink down, mortified. 'Oh God, imagine if that was just the point at which the priest said: "If any persons here present know of a reason why these two may not be joined in holy matrimony . . ."'

We creep out of the car, greeting every person we pass with an apologetic expression and a whispered 'sorry' just in case.

Fortunately the woman on reception is actually the Ivivi's manager doing a bit of moonlighting so she assures us that it's fine for us to check in after hours and promises us we can't possibly go wrong with the map she gives us. We'll see.

Back in the car, the road suddenly takes us into a whole new world with a darling marina and a convoy of Harleys, one with a sign on the back saying, 'If you can read this, the bitch fell off!' They all pull into a bar called Margaritaville but we continue onward, passing a row of the kind of crafty, touristy-trinket shops I used to love as a child on holiday then, finally, the grand grey-stone gate heralding the park entrance – we're nearly there!

We weave up the mountain, ploughing through the damp foliage until the road unexpectedly opens out into a muddy field.

'Is this it?' Nina frets, eyeing a cluster of elderly folk carrying folding seats.

'Can't be,' I assure her, though it doesn't bode well.

'You don't think it's been cancelled because of the weather?'

My heart sinks. It's perfectly possible but I'm not ready to let go of the dream just yet. I step from the car, desperate for some kind of indication of what to do next.

'There aren't even any signs,' Nina complains, now by my side. 'Where are we supposed to go?'

I look down at the clods of squelched grass imagining myself to be a keen-eyed detective. 'I'd say there's been definite merengue activity here within the last hour,' I faux-deduce, 'and over here . . .' I move on to a slushier patch, 'mambo!'

'Oh no – I think we're coinciding with some kind of school trip,' Nina spies a yolk-yellow schoolbus grinding up the hill towards us.

I cock an ear towards it. No sound. There is no such thing as a group of quiet children so I'm about to come up with an alternative explanation when the faintest strain of 'Where Are You Tonight?' – appropriately enough – teases my ears.

'It's begun! Where is it?' I flounder around the field, drawn into the ghostly mists. 'It's somewhere up here.' I point into white oblivion.

'Come on – let's get changed, quick!' Nina coaxes me back to the car where we hurriedly yank a lucky-dip top from our respective suitcases and begin a little synchronised stripping.

'Oh God!' Nina exclaims, hurriedly reversing the process – the school bus has come to a halt right next to us.

'How long are you girls going to be?' the driver leans out of his window to hail us.

'Um, five minutes or so?' we volunteer, looking suspiciously like we've been caught mid-fumble.

'There's just one more bus after this, make sure you don't miss it!' he salutes us and then disappears into the mist.

It's only then it dawns on us that we need to be bussed up to the next level, as opposed to taking little tic-tac steps with our arms outstretched in front of us.

Any further beautification goes out the window as we flag down the next bus and slide onto the battered brown leather seats. The other passengers (mercifully more our age) seem unduly solemn until one girl ends a mobile phone conversation with 'I love you!' and is met with a chorus of 'We love you too!' from the back of the bus.

'Why do you think they're using school buses?' I ask Nina as my ears pop with our precarious ascent. 'I mean, I'd presume it's because some school was selling them off cheap. But why would a school sell them unless something was wrong with them and if something is wrong with them is that really the kind of vehicle you want to be traversing these hairpin bends?'

Nina gives me a 'not helping' look and grips the seat in front until the driver comes to a halt in a small clearing. The music is louder – 'Big Girls Don't Cry' now – but there is still no sign of a band or dirty dancers. Frankly this current eerie environment would be better-suited to that other Swayze classic, *Ghost*.

Not knowing whether or not we're about to step off a cliff-edge we follow our fellow passengers further up the slope until we finally reach civilisation. The crowd sits fifteen or so rows deep around a stage which, in a less murky climate, would be teetering on the brink of one of North Carolina's most spectacular lookouts, stretching all the way down to Lake Lure. The band are called the Common Saints but today should be renamed The Silhouettes, for they are nothing more than dark apparitions.

'Lights!' is a common plea from the audience but they're already on full-beam, for what it's worth.

'OK, just one more song and it's showtime,' the lead singer (I'm guessing) announces.

Hoorah! We haven't missed any of the dance numbers and we still have time to get a drink. Oooh, and is that a gift store over by the rock face?

'I can't believe we're halfway up a mountain and we can still shop!' Nina cheers as we make a swift purchase of some groovy retro drink coasters and a pair of matching red T-shirts with Chimney Rock Park printed in white college-style lettering. We don them immediately and down our merlot in one – a girl needs both hands free if she's going to 'mash potato' along to 'Do You Love Me?'

The time has come. Six dancers take to the stage. The three guys have kept it simple in black trousers and tight T-shirts whereas the girls look like a cross between Jayne Torvill and the 'modern' troupe from

Come Dancing in their royal-blue sequined leotard dresses. Not that it matters – they are all fantastic movers, especially the dreadlocked black guy currently sexing up 'Love Man'. Watching him bump-bump-grind makes me hanker for Troy. Who am I kidding – I'm hankering for the dancer himself, he's outrageously sexy! (Now I'm the one with 'Hungry Eyes'!).

They do a great version of Mickey & Sylvia's 'Love Is Strange', complete with the comic-saucy crawl across the floor, followed by a beautifully fluttery 'She's Like The Wind'. I'm totally enraptured and don't want to miss a second, least of all the song that accompanies the pinnacle moment in Johnny's cabin when Baby tells him, 'I'm scared of walking out of this room and never feeling the rest of my whole life the way I feel when I'm with you!' – but I'm desperate for a wee. When I emerge from the Ladies 'Cry To Me' has begun – *nooooo!* I squeal, pelting full-tilt, looking like I'm doing the hundred-metre hurdles as I leap over chairs/ tables/ prams to get back to our prime viewing spot. I haven't moved so fast in years. I can barely hear the singing over my own panting but it is some kind of wonderful! I feel my spirits lifting and lifting, swirling me up until I am lost in the music. And then I see myself from the outside – damp from the mist, sweaty from dancing, woozy from booze, and I realise I couldn't be any happier. Nina catches the look on my face then pulls me into a euphoric hug. Right here, right now, I'm having the time of my life and YES! They do the lift!

'Wooooohooo!' Nina and I cheer and stomp our feet in admiration.

For a moment it's us up there, body taut, arms outstretched, a pair of strong hands supporting us at the waist.

No sooner have the performers taken their bows, we rush up to congratulate them. Then we put on our own show, dancing to every tune the Common Saints can throw at us. We're just re-creating the slo-mo opening sequence to 'Be My Baby' when we realise a hicky-looking guy with staring eyes and a hint of a moustache is copying our every move.

Nina gives him an encouraging smile and asks, 'Do you come here often?'

'Nina!' I scold.

'What? Oh God!' She sniggers. 'I can't believe I just said that.'

'Especially considering this event only happens twice a year and we're halfway up a mountain!'

'Good point!' she chuckles. 'So what star sign are you?' she asks him, carrying on regardless.

He's clearly never had this much attention from two British girls in matching T-shirts and when his time comes to leave he gives us both a scrap of paper with his phone number, delivered with repeated, emphatic 'call me' hand motions. Bless! For someone who's a few high-kicks short of a chorus line, he was a lot of fun!

Next we befriend a couple of pre-teen girls and their grannies. Everyone here is so pally and smiley, it feels a lot like a wedding reception only with a noticeable absence of eligible groomsmen. (To a man, each musician and dancer sports a wedding band, if not the wife herself.) Nevertheless, I can categorically say that this has been one of the best nights of my life.

As we descend back down the track in the school bus, the mood is positively riotous with goodwill.

'Faster, faster!' the passengers chant as the driver makes the already perilous journey now in pitch-black darkness.

'Roll it!' The heckles continue. 'I wanna see those hands off the wheel!'

It's hilarious! The couple next to us are laughing hard and clearly not yet ready to call it a night, urging us to join them at the local Tiki Bar.

'Yay! I love Tiki!' I cheer.

Once back in our own car we follow their directions, pausing in a motel car park to ingest a couple of bags of crisps in lieu of dinner.

'Do you still want to go?' I ask Nina, mouth crammed with crunchy salt and vinegar.

'I don't mind, what do you want to do?'

'It's just . . .' I pause to clarify my thoughts. 'I've already had the perfect evening.'

'Me too,' Nina smiles. 'Let's call it a night.'

When we awake the next morning the sun has overpowered the rain and we get to appreciate the full benefit of having expansive floor-to-ceiling windows looking out onto a lush, plunging panorama. Our room – named Ndlovu – is the premium space in an architecturally ingenious property (all bold angular wood) and we love everything about it: the creamy carpet, the three steps up to an enormous boxed-in bed, the pine-cube headboard-cum-room-separator, the chrome bowl-style sink . . . it's one of the freshest and most inspirational environments I've had the pleasure to pad around. I just wish we had more time to spend in it but we have to hurtle ever onward, next stop Memphis, Tennessee.

'I definitely want to come back here,' Nina decides over our all-too-brief (but excessively delicious) terrace breakfast of fruit salad, cinnamon rolls and eggs Benedict. 'Next time we could include a side-trip to Virginia and go to the resort they used as Kellermans' in the movie.'

'Oh, that would be great!' I agree. 'And we could do Asheville and Wilmington like Kathy and Fletcher recommended.'

'Maybe we should come here every year and do a different aspect?' Nina suggests. 'It could be our girlie retreat.'

'Deal!' I reach across and shake her hand. If it wasn't for the effect the humidity has on my hair I'd be happy to move here tomorrow.

'So, I hate to bring this up,' Nina tops up her herbal infusion, 'but what are you going to do about Trucker?'

I feel a twinge of guilt. It's two days since he offered to drive ten hours to see me and I haven't even had the courtesy to reply. Am I really going to let him slip through my fingers due to nerves? He calls me his 'soul throb'. He tells me, 'You make me smile, inside and out.' Even when we're not in contact, I feel like I'm carrying him with me. Maybe because I've had the chance to get to know him without the physical stuff getting in the way I feel like I'm glimpsing the man within and, with him being so open, I feel like he's someone I can trust. Ordinarily any kind of romantic

432

situation brings out the worst in me, I get jealous and suspicious and forever feel on edge, but with Troy it's like we have an unspoken understanding that it's just me and him. Cem and Ricky have already faded into the background – I like them but they are no longer registering in my heart. Troy's definitely my Number One. Maybe I should start treating him that way?

'I'll call him when we get to the airport,' I decide as we set down our napkins and give a farewell wave to the Ivivi Lodge, well worth the effort it took to locate it!

On our way back to the main road we do a commemorative drive-by of Thelma's Mountain Store and then, just a few curvy corners on, I yelp at Nina to 'Stop the car!'

'Oh my God – what is it?' Nina gasps, quickly checking that we haven't sent any other vehicles into a watery grave on account of our sudden swerve.

I go to let myself out of the car but she stops me.

'You're freaking out that we haven't found a man in Weddington, aren't you? Look, perhaps going Dirty Dancing wasn't the best choice – it's probably a bit girlie for the men round here – but I wouldn't change what we did for the world.'

'Me neither,' I assure her. 'It's not that – it actually hadn't occurred to me that we were missing out until you said that . . .' I pause for a moment to register that thought – that need in me that used to yell and stamp its feet has been mighty quiet of late.

'What is it then?' Nina looks confused.

I point off to a roadside fruit 'n' veg stand. 'I've got to get a picture.'

'What?' Nina frowns, looking at me like I've lost my mind. 'I don't get it.'

I step out of the car, march over to a heap of giant green ellipses, hoick one of the ten-pounders into my arms and cheer, 'I carried a watermelon!'

It had to be done.

Checked-in, scanned and in possession of a freshly blitzed smoothie, we still have an hour to spare before boarding. There's no more excuses – while Nina peruses the knick-knacks in the shops, I take out my phone and dial Troy.

For the first time in our telephone courtship his voice doesn't whoop in recognition of me. He sounds cautious, separate. Uh oh. Part of why I may have been so carefree about not finding anyone in Weddington is that I've had Troy in the back of my mind – my sure-thing secret weapon. Now things are suddenly different and I feel uneasy. We make small talk for a few minutes but I can't bear the sudden unfamiliarity and dare myself to ask him what's wrong. He just sighs heavily.

'Is it because I haven't been in touch?' I venture, needing to get to the bottom of this.

'Lately . . . I'm not feeling you,' he says.

I tell him he's right. I have been distant. I've been trying to get on with my life as if he's not a part of it.

'I feel like I'm being a fool, thinking there's definitely something between us,' he murmurs.

I admit that I'm trying not to get involved but something keeps pulling me back to him. We talk some more and gradually the warmth returns to his voice.

'Here I go again!' he laughs. 'It didn't take much to win me over, did it?'

I laugh too. He's just adorable. I feel really bad for not calling back, for hurting him, but I don't have to do that any more. Having had a couple of days to sort through my emotions, I'm ready to meet up. Better yet, he's offering to come to me in LA after the last leg of the journey is done. I feel a little naughty for sealing the deal before I've properly seen this quest through but I can't help it – I really want to see him and find out whether our fabulous conversations can translate into a potential relationship.

'Now I'm nervous!' he confesses. 'You're the first person in three or four years that's made me feel anything like this intense.'

I tell him it's the same deal for me.

For a moment we just breathe each other in. I can picture his face smiling, those highly decorated arms reaching for me. I feel light-headed with longing.

'Are you really going to do it – come to LA?' I can't quite believe it – we met for twenty minutes in a shop, now look at us!

'Do you want me to?' His voice is low and steady.

'Yes,' I say, totally sure. 'I really do.'

After our goodbye, I gaze besottedly into the

middle-distance, imagining being with him, imagining actually touching him . . . Long-dormant desires start to swirl to the surface but then I tell myself to get a grip – there's still one more trip to go.

Just a few more days and I can fall madly in love!

DARLING, MISSISSIPPI

& GUYS, TENNESSEE

Graceland was always a given – Nina loves Elvis and I love retro kitsch – but our dilemma is whether we choose to drive one hundred miles east across Tennessee to Guys or drop sixty miles south, venturing into Mississippi for Darling.

'I say we do both,' Nina concludes after intensive study of the map. 'They've each got a population of under five hundred, so based on the disappointment factor of Valentine and Weddington, I think it would be good to have back-up.'

I concur – we'll do a neat little loop taking them both in, then conclude back in Memphis for our very last night. Sounds like a plan.

'Bus!' Nina yanks me away from my worryingly frothy Blue Suede Shoes cocktail, bundling me onto the Graceland shuttle.

One face stands out a mile from the middle-aged fans with their poodle-perms and XXL T-shirts –

there's no mistaking those ice-blue eyes, jet black hair and cool shades. Yup, it's soap starlet Jessie Wallace aka Kat Slater from *EastEnders*! (Looking dead glam with a designer scarf knotted around her torso revealing a bare, tanned back.) Nina and I elbow each other excitedly as we slot into the seat two rows behind. She's with fiancé Dave Morgan, the police officer she met when charged with drunk driving. (Now that's a great love story!) She is clearly a major fan (Nina tells me she has a cat called Elvis) and lingers poignantly in the Meditation Garden overlooking Elvis's garlanded grave.

I love everything about this tour – the commentary by Lisa-Marie, the memorabilia collection (including his infamous gold lamé suit and innumerable platinum discs), the crazy facts (did you know that the broadcast of Elvis's *Aloha from Hawaii* concert was watched in more American homes than man's first walk on the moon?) but above all the Austin Powers décor.

I get my biggest thrill in the Jungle Room. I'm just thinking, 'This is so my taste!' as I gawp at the abundance of faux fur, chunky Polynesian furniture and green shag carpet (floor and ceiling), when suddenly I grab Nina's arm.

'I've got that lamp!' I gasp, pointing at a pineapple formed from a cluster of amber globes sprouting plastic foliage. 'I got it from the Rose Bowl flea market in LA for three dollars – I can't believe I own something that's in Graceland!'

I had thought the property would be overrun with Elvis impersonators but there's only one – a young lad with pimples, poorly applied fake tan and pushy parents.

'Heeey!' His dad corners us as we're posing for pictures by the white lions at the front of the mansion. 'Why don't I get a picture of you two ladies with my son – go on, cuddle up now.'

'Oh honey you look great!' Mom encourages her son as Nina writhes away in disgust.

'He looks nothing like Elvis,' she sneers as the Dad foists a card on us offering his son for hire.

Dad doesn't care, he's now in full Herb Ritts mode insisting on art-directing Nina and I in a series of porch shots. The one benefit to all this is that, thanks to the fact that he stands so far back, we actually innocently acquire a picture of us with Jessie and Dave in the foreground. Result!

Having learned of a *Blue Hawaii*-themed party to be held at the legendary Peabody hotel that night, we go the whole hog booking tickets to the do *and* a room at the hotel. (Well, is there anything better than being at a party when you know the journey home consists of nothing more than nine floors in an elevator?)

'Hey, did you know that Tom Cruise filmed several scenes of *The Firm* in this hotel?' I nudge Nina as we gawp in wonder at the Peabody's high-ceilinged marble lobby, twirling 360 degrees to take in the intricate wraparound balcony at mezzanine level.

'I thought it looked familiar. Oh my God – Lansky's!' Nina rushes over to a gentleman's outfitters, pointing out the man known as 'Tailor to the King' – still taking inside leg measurements in his eighties. 'What was that?' She turns to me.

'I didn't say anything.'

Nina frowns. 'I thought I heard a quacking noise.'

'That'll be the ducks in the fountain,' I offer, trying to sound casual. It's the biggest tourist draw in the hotel – every morning at 11 a.m., five plucky fellas take the lift down from their rooftop penthouse, waddle down the red carpet to the lobby fountain and spend the day paddling and posing for photographs. The ritual is repeated in reverse at 5 p.m.

Nina used to have a duck as a pet so she's particularly delighted at this. We enjoy a piña colada in their company and then, after an hour's beautification and costume-change, we approach the Aloha-fied Grand Ballroom where we're presented with a lei, albeit a scrumpled plastic affair as opposed to a string of dewy frangipani. And that's pretty much as good as it gets. I had thought this event would attract hula babes of both sexes but I was So Very Wrong. The majority of people staring gormlessly at the *Blue Hawaii* movie backdrop are American women in their sixties. (It does of course make perfect sense – they are the ones who have been in love with Elvis since their impressionable teens.)

'Is that a dwarf or a child?' Nina directs me to a mini Elvis in a gold satin suit with a black rug on his head, jiving like his life depended on it.

'Child,' I assert. 'And before you ask, that's a wig.'

We join him for a brief dance to the remix of 'Rubberneckin'' then Nina says, 'I think we're scaring him, shall we go?'

'Do you mean actually leave? As in Elvis has left the building?'

'Yes,' Nina confirms.

I'm surprised. I know there's not one potential hunka hunka burnin' love but she's such a big Elvis fan, I would have thought she'd want to stay with 'her people'.

'OK this next tune is very popular with our English fans,' the DJ cuts in. 'Let's see if you remember the moves . . .'

I watch with disbelief as everyone around us breaks into an identikit routine – kind of like 'The Macarena' meets 'The Birdie Song'.

'It's like Butlins!' I cry in horror.

'Welcome to the weird world of Elvis conventions,' Nina winks. 'Let's go.'

At least the legendary Beale St is guaranteed to rock our socks off.

Or is it? There's really only two bars exhibiting signs of life – the first, 152, has a great R & B band called After Dark but they send us running when they launch into a riff with lyrics that basically run: 'You've got a big ole ass, I've got a big ole ass, she's got a big ole ass.'

The second is Alfred's. For a venue that could easily hold four hundred it's rattling but then it's karaoke night, which is always good for a laugh. We take a seat near the stage intending to out-Simon Cowell each other with scathing remarks but instead we're instantly blown away by the vocal panache of an unassuming black guy sauntering through 'I'm Just A Gigolo'. I look around the room, desperate for an agent to spring up and offer him a life-changing contract. How can it be possible to be that good at something and not be doing it professionally? Next up is a large secretary-

445

dressed woman singing Patsy Cline's 'Crazy'. She's no oil painting but oh my Lord *can she sing*! Normality is swiftly resumed when two young guys get up and slaughter Neil Diamond's 'Sweet Caroline'. No great singers ourselves, Nina and I yodel along at the top of our lungs in a vain attempt to drown them out. Our hearty 'wo-wo-wo's don't go unnoticed and after they're done, the guys stagger over to our table to express their gratitude at our enthusiastic response.

'I'm Forest by the way,' the dishier of the two announces.

Nina can't believe her ears. 'Your name is Forest?' she gapes, mercifully sparing him the 'As in Gump?' addendum he must get all the time.

'Yes ma'am.'

'He called me ma'am,' she turns to me, giving me an 'I guess I'll have to snog him now!' look.

'And what do you do for a living?'

'I'm a Navy SEAL.'

Again she turns to me, this time upgrading to an 'I guess I'll have to shag him now' look.

'Do you know there's not a single British person named Forest?' she tilts her head, taking in his classic American chiselled jaw.

'Are you kidding me?' he marvels, pulling up a chair.

As the two of them rattle away and his friend shuffles back to his gang I sit back in my chair, free from the need to engage. In the past, situations like this could have left me feeling rejected or left out. I would have imbued them with far too much significance – look at me, all alone again – but somehow I

446

don't feel so self-conscious now. And knowing Troy is thinking of me is a pleasing comfort – it's almost like having an imaginary friend with me.

Before we left the hotel I picked up an e-mail from him, one he'd written directly after we'd committed to meeting up in LA . . .

'Can one feel composed and exhilarated at the same time?' he asked before launching into a stream-of-consciousness speculation on every possible way our upcoming rendezvous could go. It was both insightful and amusing – he seems to have a good sense of humour about the human condition. And I like the way he invites me into his head – I don't have to deal with any fretful 'what's he thinking?' worries because it's all out in the open. It's good – it makes me feel like we're in the game together.

He concluded by saying, 'Colours are skittering and notes are zinging. I don't have to be a rocket scientist to figure this one out – I want to ravish you something fierce, honey!'

As a consequence, as I sit here in a bar on Beale Street, I'm not hoping a stranger will come along and justify my existence; I'm not feeling like an unwanted gooseberry. There's a Troy-shaped stopper where that gap used to be and I'm just happy to sit here and watch Mr Bojangles tap his spats on the dance floor. I feel delightfully dignified and self-contained. Is this what being loved does for a girl? Or am I just happier in myself? I somehow suspect my change in attitude isn't all down to Troy, but either way, this feels good.

Seconds later the smug smile is wiped off my face. Over in the far corner is the man of my dreams –

straggly goatee, mid-length ponytail, questing brown eyes, the kind of caramel-knotted arms that spin waltzers at the fairground and I've-been-wearing-the-same-clothes-for-the-past-week dress sense. Everything I've always gone weak at the knees for. He is my first love Christian come back to haunt me. Catching me staring, he smiles and I know this is the Last Temptation of Belinda Jones. Though I try to rein my thoughts back to Troy I am powerless. My feet are walking towards him before I'm even aware that I've stood up.

'You're so beautiful, can I take your picture?' My words come out unapproved, embarrassing both him and me.

'Maybe I want a photograph of you,' he retorts, giving me a quirky look.

I stumble, unsure of what vibe he's projecting, then decide to get back to basics. 'What's your name?' I ask, trying to get a grip.

He looks at the tattoo on his forearm as if seeking a reminder then says, 'Ryan.'

And that's the straightest answer I get from him all night. Whatever I ask him, however innocuous, he's extremely evasive, talking in riddles and jumbled dialects – sometimes rough, sometimes refined, like a twenty-first-century Dean Moriarty. I can't figure out whether he's taking the piss or being deliberately mysterious. Then, for no apparent reason, he decides to take my pulse. We stand there in silence, him holding my wrist mouthing numbers, me trying not faint at the sheer sensuality of the moment. (Though it also strikes me that to the half-cut onlookers we probably look like

Vulcans or some strange Star Trek race with our own peculiar method of courtship.) Now it's my turn to do his. I press my fingers onto his smooth skin and look into his eyes, losing count before I get to three.

'Let's dance,' he says as Kid Rock and Sheryl Crow strike up the plaintive duet 'I Put Your Picture Away'.

I haven't slow-danced since I was a teenager and find this experience excruciating – instead of a seductive sway, the best we seem capable of is an awkward out-of-time shuffle. I can't relax and contrary to what I had imagined, his body doesn't feel right next to mine. As we rotate he makes up different lyrics to fit the song, some of which are witty, others frisky. I laugh rather too hysterically and pray he'll need a beer break come the final verse. I'm now regretting having approached him. There's no denying his beauty but there is something a little disturbed about his conversation, especially when he mishears some remark I make about the dedication of Elvis fans and he bellows, 'I'M NOT MEDICATED!'

I decide it's best if I dilute him with some company and coax him over to the table where Nina is sitting with her Navy SEAL. I make a vague introduction to which he says dismissively, 'Oh yeah, I know him, I used to work with him.'

I open my mouth to point out just how unlikely this is but instead offer him a beer, eager to have a quiet moment at the bar to compose myself. I definitely need to nip this in the bud. I'll just give him the drink as a parting gift and be on my way.

Unfortunately, one sip in, Ryan starts pouring his heart out about his girlfriend who already has two kids by two different men and who is now expecting a third child that may be his, or possibly the offspring of the 'African American' who she's just dumped him for and shacked up with.

'Oh dear,' I say. 'Well, at least it'll be fairly obvious whose it is when the child is born.'

He then tells me that he grew up on a series of campsites and lost his tooth in a fight with the man who is most probably the father of his ex-girlfriend's first child.

Gradually it dawns on me that I'm talking to someone who should be on Jerry Springer. I try to convey to Nina that I need saving but she merely nudges me and grins, 'He's so good-looking! So you!'

'But—'

Ryan taps me on the shoulder.

'Yes?' I gulp.

'You know, with your . . .' he pauses to peer down my top which I now realise is a button too undone, '. . . exquisite talents and your radiance and excellence—'

'Yes?' I breathe, slightly thrown by his overblown line in compliments.

'You could make a lot of money as a stripper.'

My jaw hits the floor. 'Wha—?' I balk.

'I mean it, they make good money.'

'I don't think you understand,' I stammer. 'I don't have that kind of body for starters—'

'You're crazy!' he protests, double-checking me out.

'Besides, I've already got a job, I'm a writer,' I tell him.

'Well, I'm just saying you should think about it, that's all.'

I'm gobsmacked. There is no way on this earth I could make even a dime taking my clothes off. Unless I was selling the garments themselves.

'Shall we go?' I suggest to Nina, feeling increasingly agitated. 'It's nearly 3 a.m. and the bar's about to close.'

Nina looks reluctant to leave Forest. I'm reluctant to leave him too, thinking that his combat skills may come in handy should Ryan have an un-medicated turn.

'He can walk us back if he likes?' I suggest, trying not to sound too desperate.

'OK!'

So we make our way along Second Street, Nina with her Navy SEAL, and me with my pimp, only Forest keeps stopping and dilly-dallying on every corner. I suspect this may be a deliberate ploy to lose us so I take a deep breath and stride on – the one blessing to walking with a psycho is that he's a darn sight scarier than all the other fellas jumping out at us.

'Spare a dollar?' the first one growls.

Ryan gives him two quarters. 'That's my telephone money man – you'd better be there to call my lawyer if I get arrested later, that's all I'm saying.'

He limps on his way. Then a second approaches, open-palmed.

'Sorry brother, I just gave all I had to the last guy but if you run you can still catch him!' Ryan suggests, obviously down with the street banter.

And here's me, about to swan into the $200-a-night Peabody Hotel.

'I used to work there, you know,' Ryan tells me.

'Yes, yes,' I roll my eyes, dreading the farewell scene, wishing that Nina would hurry up. 'Look it's been lovely to meet you and I do wish you well with everything and if you want my advice, stay away from that girlfriend of yours and you'll be fine!'

'Oh come on, can't we get a room?' he pleads, taking my hand. 'I've got money.'

I hope he means money for the room, not for me.

'No, no, thanks for the offer but—'

'Look there's a reason we found each other tonight – we're supposed to be together!'

'That's a very nice sentiment but—'

'You've got no wedding band,' he says, toying with my fingers, 'I've just split up with my girl. We could offer each other some comfort.'

'I see your point—'

'No you don't,' he gives me a lascivious look and grabs his crotch, 'if you'd seen my point you'd see it was a good ten inches and then you'd—'

'Ryan!' I feign shock.

'Brian,' he corrects.

'What?'

'My name's Brian.'

'I thought you said Ryan.'

He shows me the tattoo he'd consulted earlier. Definitely Brian.

'Look. Brian. I do hope you don't think I've been a tease but I really have to go.' Oh please don't let him turn nasty, I pray. I'm nearly at the entrance.

'At least give me your room number,' he begs, hurrying after me. 'So I can call you.'

'No, sorry. Bye.' I make a sudden dart for the door,

hurtling across the lobby to the lifts.

That's what you get for chasing down the memory of Christian, I berate myself, still jittery until I'm safely in the room with locks fully activated and a pillow pulled onto my chest. I take a breath, inhaling a realisation – it's time I let go.

I've always said I'll never love anyone like I loved Christian and now I realise I wouldn't want to. It hurt too much. I always look back at our relationship with rose-coloured spectacles but there was a very good reason why we split up – deep down I knew that I would never get to live my life, the life I was meant to live, if I stayed with him.

Suddenly a *Sex and the City* scene plays in my head – the one where Samantha dumps womanising Richard in Atlantic City:

'I love you Richard,' she told him. 'But I love me more.'

That's exactly how it was for me. All this time I've been focusing on the loss of love and how much I miss him but now I see how much I gained in the trade-off. I chose me. I chose to be good to myself. I can almost hear my heart whisper, 'Thank you! Thank you – now I'm free.'

Suddenly there's a knock at the door.

'B! It's me!' Nina hisses.

'Are you alone?' I quaver, fearing a Brian reprisal.

'Not exactly . . .'

Gingerly I prise open the door, relieved to see it's Forest by her side. Until I realise the implication of his presence.

'Just give us a moment!' I smile, tugging Nina

inside. 'Do you want him to stay over?' I cut to the chase.

'Not if it's a problem for you,' she bites her lip, looking rueful.

'It's fine,' I insist. 'You were more than accommodating with me and Ricky in Arizona.'

'That was a big ole suite, this is a little more intimate,' she grimaces.

'All I ask is that you get started in the bathroom, giving me a chance to fall asleep.'

'If you're sure . . . ?'

I nod an affirmative, switch off all the lights then dive into a pitch black bed. Ten minutes later I'm disturbed by a blinding light. I look up and see an entirely naked Forest backlit by fluorescent bathroom light.

'Oh my God!' I gasp, shocked by his neck-to-ankle tattoos.

'Sorry!' he hisses, quickly shutting the door behind him and scurrying across to Nina's bed.

'Blimey, that was quick!' I think as I squeeze my eyes closed, begging sleep to take me.

Five minutes later a body crawls onto my bed. It's Nina.

'What is it?' I hiss.

'He fell asleep! I asked him to step out of the bathroom so I could go to the loo and he's crashed out.'

She looks at me expectantly.

'I think you're waking up the wrong person,' I tell her. 'There's not a lot I can do.'

Her head falls into her hands. 'Do you think he took

454

one look at me naked and decided he didn't want to go through with it?'

'You think he's pretending to be asleep?' I gasp.

'Do you?'

'No, absolutely not. When you hear him snoring you'll be certain too.'

She sighs heavily and climbs into her own bed.

Next thing I know it's morning, and Forest has gone but not without putting an out-size smile on Nina's face.

'He was soooo flattering,' she kneels up in bed, excessively perky. 'He kept calling me a sexy bitch!'

'How delightful.'

'He said he noticed me as soon as I walked in. Said I had class!'

'You do, darling, you do,' I smile. 'Will you be keeping in touch?'

'Nope!' she chirrups, perfectly happy to accept the morning-after thrill for what it is. 'Anyway what happened with Ryan?' she propels herself onto my bed.

'Don't ask,' I shut the subject down.

'But he was so you!'

'No, he was so *Christian*,' I correct her.

'Same thing, isn't it?'

'Not any more.'

'What do you mean?'

'I've decided that Brian was Christian coming back to me one last time to show me that pale imitations won't work and to tell me goodbye.'

'Wow,' Nina falls back onto the headboard. 'That's big, as Oprah would say.'

'Huge,' I acknowledge.

'I think that's actually worthy of a room-service breakfast.'

Two hours later we're in Darling, Mississippi.

I knew it was but a cheek-pinch on the map so the odds of us finding Bo and Luke Duke weren't great, but I was hoping they might stretch to a few bobbly cotton fields and a spiky-chinned OAP with a banjo. But no. The surrounding land is flat and unengaging, the roads seem to be littered with more than their fair share of exploded tyres and furry fatalities and as for the village itself, well, I'm guessing it didn't get its name from a passing society dame exclaiming, 'Isn't it *darling*!'

The first building we encounter is a clapped-out Food Mart with a wonkily scrawled sign offering HOT FOOD (a little too hot judging by the fire-blackened smudges reaching up from what were once windows). There is an open door and signs of life but we suspect we won't be finding any freshly prepared mint juleps awaiting us inside. Besides, we daren't leave the car as we're being watched by four hefty black men in holey vests, sunk deep into a sofa, shading under an old oak tree. Though they appear to be sedated by the sweltering heat we're too nervous to make any attempt at socialising, having been warned that certain Mississippi locals aren't too fond of the unfamiliar and two giddy girls speaking in foreign tongues might push them over the edge.

'At least we can be fairly certain they're not KKK,' Nina looks on the bright side as we swing the car around to get back onto Highway 3.

The remaining mile of Darling consists of a handful

of pristine bungalows with a couple of new cars parked in the driveway. I can't imagine who might live there but I doubt they're Food Mart regulars.

'Wreaths, Balloons and Gifts.' Nina reads a sign tacked to the side of the last house in the village. 'Maybe we should get a multi-pack of wreaths so we can honour all the roadkill we pass.'

What a sweet girl she is.

We had thought of bowling straight on to Guys but decide we should allot at least one night to Mississippi. The question is where?

'We could go to Clarksdale, home of jook-joints, Muddy Waters and the Delta Blues Museum,' Nina reads from the guidebook. 'Or Indianola, that's where BB King was born. Apparently they have the largest catfish processing company in the world.'

'Do you know we're within an hour or two's drive of Aberdeen, Dublin, Rome, Paris, Verona and Brazil!' I marvel at the map.

'What?' Nina laughs.

'Look,' I hand her the road atlas.

'Hey, Oxford!' she jabs the page. 'I seem to remember reading that's some kind of award-winningly picturesque town . . .' she switches back to the guidebook, hustles through the index. 'Yes, here it is, home to John Grisham, William Faulkner's Rowan Oak and the "Ole Miss" University, aka the Harvard of the South.' She looks up at me. 'Shall we?'

'Just give me the directions and we're there.'

Forty minutes down the 278, Nina tells me to take a left and suddenly the landscape makes a dramatic change from open fields and the occasional swamp to a leafy dell. As the road dips down, the trees crowd in creating a shady corridor that leads us to an elegant town square with a white wedding-cake of a courthouse as a centrepiece. There's even an old-fashioned British red-gloss phone box on one corner.

'Isn't it *darling*!' we coo.

Judging by the quality of merchandise in the chichi boutiques and ra-ra department store, this is one monied enclave. The neighbouring houses are highly 'des res' with generous verandas boasting non-chip rockers and proud US flags. Forced down a series of one-way streets, we're despairing of ever getting our bearings when our eye is caught by a busty black woman sweeping down the steps of a grand, dark red building fronted by five white pillars and a string of hanging baskets. Admittedly the woman is wearing a T-shirt and leggings rather than a bustling dress and pinny but we feel the Oliver-Britt House will provide a more authentic Mississippi experience than the Holiday Inn alternative and brave the heat to enquire after a room.

Eleanor tells us there's just the smallest room available but when we see the bright white bedspread sprinkled with violets and the freestanding bathtub, we're sold. Minutes later we're reclining on veranda wicker enjoying cheese and crackers and a glass of chilled chardonnay. Despite our shiny faces and wilting hair we decide to take the short walk to the square and do a restaurant recce before we get dollied up for our night out.

'Not that there's going to be anyone to get dollied up for,' I predict. 'The university crowd are probably still on holiday and I don't suppose there's much else going on here.'

Wrong!

The first restaurant we come to – The Venice Pizza Company – is as tightly packed as pimento in an olive. I look at my watch. It's not even 6 p.m. We peer in the window of the fancier City Grocery next door – not a table to be had. Always concerned about where our next meal is coming from, we grab the first empty table we find, which happens to be across the street in Proud Larry's. One pizza and eight vodka-cranberries later we concede that there's no going back to get changed, we're just going to run with the sweaty look – judging by the rest of the clientele, it seems to be a pretty casual town.

Wrong again.

It's nearing 9.30 p.m. when we find ourselves back on a square now twittering with immaculately attired Pippa dolls in handkerchief-hemmed skirts, halterneck tops and kitten heels. Though nine out of ten of these girls are absolute stunners and could get away with a ponytail and a slick of lipgloss, each and every one is exquisitely made-up with painstakingly straightened hair. Nina and I assess our humidity-kinked locks and cover-all-sins skirts (one combat, one denim) and wonder how we're going to compete. Fortunately we're just one drink away from not caring and besides, as Nina points out, 'It's good to be different.'

The first bar we peer into (Longshots) seems to be ninety per cent women whereas next door at Parrish it's ninety-five per cent men. Hmm. How strange.

459

'Do you think they have a His and Hers drinking policy here?' Nina ponders before heading swiftly into Parrish.

'Heyyyy!' a dark-haired guy accosts us before we even get to the bar. 'I'm Madison the Fourth,' he extends a hand. 'I saw you two girls in Proud Larry's.'

'You did?' We like the idea that we stood out enough for him to notice, so much so we offer to buy him a drink.

'Cheers!' Nina chinks his glass, but before I can reach across it dawns on me that I promised to call Trucker tonight. It's strange – back at home I would have been aware of every hour in the countdown to call time, it's so different when you're on the road, everything is topsy-turvy. I have to say it's doing me good not to live in such a linear manner, my priorities have been shaken up and appear to be re-settling in a different order.

'Back in a mo!' I nudge Nina, darting out onto the street, tapping his number as I go.

He answers straight away but sounds faint so I dart up an alleyway hoping it'll be quieter there, only to get chased out again by a fast-moving Land Rover.

'Hold on!' I bleat, striding up an adjacent street but finding myself outside a shop churning out hot noisy air. I take another turn and crunch over broken glass. 'Youch! Hold on!'

I've only caught half of what he's been saying but I'm pretty sure the last thing was, 'I'm on my way.'

'What?' I shriek, setting a couple of garden dogs a-barking as I spin around, half-expecting an eighteen-wheeler truck to thunder into view.

'I've booked my flight to LA,' he tells me, coolly.

'Oh my God. *Oh my God!*' The full impact of what he's saying hits me. He's really done it – his word is good! I've finally met a man who thinks highly enough of me to pay several hundred dollars of his hard-earned cash and travel across the country to spend time with me.

'I have a good feeling about this,' he tells me.

Amazingly, so do I. I worried I might feel burdened if I committed to meeting up again but in actuality I feel quite bold and grown-up. I'm ready for this – ready to road-test Mr Right!

'I'm going to give you such a hug when I get there,' he growls.

My stomach flips. 'And the rest!' I tease, beating him to the inevitable innuendos.

He laughs. 'Now you're talking!'

I glance back at the bar to check on Nina and see she is now sitting alone in a window seat. 'I have to go.' I cut our flirtations short. 'Sorry this is so brief.'

'That's OK, soon we'll be able to talk for hours and hours. Face to face.'

And mouth to mouth, I can't help thinking.

His voice lowers another notch. 'You have a good night.'

'You too.'

'Actually, I'm already in bed,' he says, temptingly.

'Lucky you,' I sigh, shuffling back to the bar in a daze only to find Nina has ditched Madison and managed to impale herself on a sofa spring.

'Look!' she says, lifting her bottom to show me the exposed coil. 'Even those guys in Darling had a better

461

sofa than this!' She sits back down on it all the same and we survey the men in the bar.

'They're all a bit college-laddish for us, wouldn't you say?' I observe, trying to sound focused on the job in hand though my mind is still racing from my conversation with Troy. (I'm not going to tell her that I have a sure thing lined up in case she thinks I'll be copping out from now on.)

'Far too young,' she agrees. 'Shall we move on?'

Next up is Sneaky Tiki. This new bar may be just a few strides down the street but it's a whole different world – whereas Parrish was bookish and dark, this is an open-air raffia affair with sun umbrellas, fairy lights and Tiki torches. However, our brief thrill of anticipation is extinguished upon entry. The girls here are even younger, prettier and perter than the ones in the square. They are also a good deal more plastered.

'It's like a posh version of eighteen to thirties,' I lament.

'Or, more accurately, seventeen to twenties,' Nina corrects.

When we mention this sad fact to the cute blond barman he shrugs. 'What can I say? This is the number one pick-up joint in Oxford.'

He then amazes us by revealing that the majority of clientele are in fact law students from Ole Miss, just like Sandra Bullock's character in *A Time To Kill*.

'So if Sandy's character would have come drinking here, where would Matthew McConaughey have imbibed?'

'Burgundy Room, back on the Square. That's where all the qualified lawyers go.'

'Hmmm, I think a little light prosecution might be in order,' Nina decides.

We're just downing the last of our cocktails when a couple of 'mature' students approach the bench.

'Heyyyy!' The barman greets what turns out to be his two flatmates, Jay and Biff.

'Heyyyy!' we echo, equally delighted to see them on account of them being all of twenty-eight and twenty-six respectively.

They're probably the oldest guys in the place but there's something else that sets them apart – they're both male cheerleaders.

'What?' we splutter, trying to suppress images of them in kick-pleat skirts rustling pom-poms.

'You've never heard of male cheerleaders?' Jay returns our incredulous look.

'We're the guys who throw the girls in the air and twirl them round,' explains Biff who, coincidentally, is built like a quarterback. 'Did you know that Ronald Reagan and George W Bush were both male cheerleaders?' he adds.

Nina shakes her head. 'I think they may have deliberately kept that quiet.'

'Shots?' A girl carrying a tray of liquid pink testtubes makes a timely intervention, and Biff wastes no time purchasing an Alabama Slammer for each of us. I can't face mine so I pass it on to Nina who downs it while Biff's head is tilted back.

'So are you guys both from Mississippi?' Nina asks, clearly interested in one of these fellas but I can't yet deduce who.

Jay shakes his head. 'No ma'am, I'm from Arkansas.'

'Ahh, Bill Clinton!' Nina sighs. 'Now that's one good-looking man.'

Jay can't believe his Southern ears. 'You know, we were glad when he became president because it got him the hell out of Arkansas!' he growls.

The three of them then get into a big political discussion. For a while I phase-out thinking again of Troy but find my ears pricking up at the mention of the Ku Klux Klan, who happen to have their headquarters in Arkansas.

'So do you actually know any members of the KKK?' I ask Jay, feeling nervous just saying the words.

'Sure do,' he nods.

I expect him to denounce them as a horrifying embarrassment to the state but he says he actually has sympathy for their original motives, which he claims had more to do with the civil war and the North/South divide than Black/White issues. It's a pretty dicey area to get into and he doesn't endear himself to me any when he peppers his conversation with phrases like, 'I'm not going to apologise for being white!' 'That women's lib shit' and 'I'm proud to be heterosexual.'

Whereas I'm on the verge of asking, 'Is that a large white sheet in your pocket?' Nina (now quite visibly pie-eyed) seems to be hearing the humanity between the outbursts – how today's middle-class whites resent being made to feel bad for their ancestors' predilection for slavery and how affirmative action makes them feel discriminated against.

Just when I think it can't get any more contro-versial, Biff – quite out of the blue – tells me how he despises the women on *Sex and the City*. He says that Samantha is a 'ho' and Carrie is 'devious and mani-pulative'. Now this I can't take.

'I'm going to get something to eat,' I announce, sliding off my bar stool.

'The only thing available at this hour is chicken-on-a-stick at Exon,' Jay cautions me.

Gas station cuisine – my favourite.

'OK, back in a mo,' I put a brave face on it.

'Do you want me to walk you?' Jay offers.

'But then I'll have no one to talk to!' Nina protests.

I raise a knowing eyebrow. Biff would clearly be happy to talk her ears off so I suspect she might be taking a shine to Jay's shaved head. (He seals the deal by mentioning that he's in the National Guard.)

'You chaps stay put,' I say, hurrying on my way. 'I'll be fine.'

The square is now even more overrun with pretty rich girls. (And a few college guys who just can't believe their luck.) As I wade through them, utterly invisible, I find a restaurant that is still open but the banner sign outside saying 'Tastes Like Chicken' puts me off so I continue on to the gas station for salt and vinegar crisps and a dried-up donut. I feel strangely separate to the rest of the groomed revellers as I find a street bench on which to picnic and half-expect to get moved on by one of the roaming police cars. Once done munching, I sit awhile in quiet contemplation. I don't seem in any hurry to get back to the bar. In fact, I wonder if I ever will again. Am I done with all that? Am I finally grown-up?

One of the reasons my friends and I go to bars is to meet men, so now I've met one does that mean I'm saying goodbye to drunk-in-a-dive and hello to dinner-à-deux?

I don't know how many Alabama Slammers Nina's knocked back in my absence, but by the time I return she is positively hyper.

'*Allo Allo!*' she yelps, grabbing Jay's arm.

'Herr Flick!' he rejoins.

'*Are You Being Served?*'

'Mrs Slocombe!' he cheers.

I jiggle my ears in disbelief but it turns out that the two of them are now involved in a lively British TV retrospective. I wish I had the strength to join in but I don't. It's official. I've lost the will to flirt. Is it just that these guys aren't my type or has my heart made some secret pact with Troy's?

'*Friends* is my favourite TV show,' Biff tells me, making an effort despite my blank face. 'I'm like Chandler, a smart-ass but tender-hearted.'

'Really?' I try to sound like I care.

'Yeah. Most girls want to marry me.'

'Sorry?' I look around for doe-eyed admirers but find none.

'It's true. I'm The Guy. But a lot of the girls here are just interested in this . . .' He grabs his wallet pocket.

Could have been worse, I suppose.

'What I want is a girl who's been married before,' he continues. 'That way she'll know what she's letting herself in for.'

I'm genuinely taken aback. 'Gosh! I think that's the first time I've heard that.'

'I mean it. She'll have a better idea of what marriage is all about.'

'It's a theory!' I concede. In fact the more I think about it, the more it makes sense. So many single girls believe that their life will take on a magical sparkle at 'I do' when the reality is that it's a lot of work and compromise. Besides, you've got to admit someone who gets married for the second time is one of life's true optimists.

At 1 a.m. we're cajoled out of the bar. Being with Southerners 'n' all I didn't really expect to get away with walking home unescorted but I'm counting the steps till I can flop into bed and quit talking. Not that I'm having to yap too much, Biff is one of the chattiest men I've ever met. He's also an absolute gentleman, more keen to boast about his beloved Oxford than trying to make any last ditch attempts at pulling, despite the fact that such intentions are hanging heavy in the air between Nina and Jay.

'You know there's a lot more to this town than the square,' Biff tells me as I attempt to unlock the B & B's front door. 'I could show you around tomorrow if you like.'

'Yes, yes, that sounds lovely,' I say, rattling the lock with increasing fervour.

'Here, allow me.' Biff steps forward and gets equally purple-faced with frustration at not being able to open the door. 'I'm gonna call the manager. What did you say her name was – Eleanor?' he announces finally.

'You can't do that – it's the middle of the night!' I protest.

'But you can't get in,' Biff reasons.

'It must just be a matter of . . . urgh!' I humph and grunt, jiggling the key every which way, still to no avail.

Biff makes that call, Eleanor emerges looking understandably bleary then goes to demonstrate the correct technique only to find herself struggling too. Finally she gives me a new set of keys and we bid each other good night. It's only when I get up to the room that I realise I'm missing someone. I clomp back down the stairs and out onto the veranda calling, 'Nina!' into the balmy night.

No reply.

Oh God, it's like Kerry and Vista Verde all over again.

'Nina!' I call again.

This time I sense movement in the car park and as I approach, her head pops around the side of a minivan with a very clear 'Don't come any further!' in her eyes.

'I just need to leave you the key,' I explain my intrusion.

'That's fine – just drop it on the ground,' she says, trying to sound as though leaving a tiny bit of a metal on an unlit sprawl of tarmac in the dark of night is the most logical thing in the world.

I start to warn her that the lock may be a little tricky but her head has already returned to from whence it came.

For the next three hours I keep sitting up in bed, convinced I can either hear my name or the whole house rattling from the exertion of someone trying to open the front door. Finally, at 5.30 a.m. Nina stumbles in.

'You wouldn't believe the trouble we had with the front door!' she blurts.

'Please don't tell me you've been trying it for the past four hours.'

'Oh no, when we couldn't get in the first time we went down to the lake.'

'What lake?'

'Lake Sardis, it's about ten miles from here. There's a beach and everything.'

'How the hell did you get there?' I object, suddenly feeling wide-awake.

'In Jay's car. He's customising this Chevrolet Camaro – you know, putting in race-style bucket seats, leather interiors and a five hundred-horsepower engine – but at the moment it's a work in progress so it's making some funny noises . . .'

'You got in a car with a strange man from Arkansas?' I sound utterly outraged despite having done exactly the same myself in a number of other states.

'Oh it was fine!' she tuts, kicking off her shoes, then suddenly freezes. 'Oh my God – my toenail!'

'What's happened to it?' I gasp, scrabbling to her side of the bed.

'It's gone!'

At this point I should mention that as a result of some surgery, Nina lost the big toenail on her right foot and has been sporting a glued-on acrylic one ever since.

'Imagine if it's hooked itself to the blanket we were sat on and when Jay goes to pack it away he finds it hanging there!' she whimpers.

I can't help but snicker at the image.

469

'Oh don't!' Nina looks ashen.

'I'm sure it's just in the undergrowth,' I assure her. 'All the same, he must have been good if he made your toenail drop off . . .'

A broad smile fills Nina's face. 'He's a beautiful, beautiful man.'

'Really?' I say, taking a moment to bask in her happy glow. Forest was for kicks but she looks genuinely smitten with this guy, rapturising about their sparky banter and sexual chemistry.

'Oh Nina!' I say, embracing her, 'I want to hear every detail!', adding a stern: 'In the morning . . .'

The morning comes and goes with barely a re-squishing of our pillows. By the time we do rouse ourselves and make it to 208 Café in town it's gone 1 p.m. and there are no breakfast foods on the menu. Instead I opt for a watermelon and spinach salad with a treacly balsamic dressing, followed by a crab cake set on cheese grits. It's absolutely delicious and I polish off the lot. Nina, however, is too lovesick to eat even half her BLT soup. Last night's delirium has been replaced with morning-after anxiety.

'He must think I'm a right slapper,' she frets.

'Don't be silly!' I protest. 'That was pure passion! Does he know you've only slept with two guys in the last five years?'

'No,' she shakes her head.

'Well maybe you should tell him.'

'That's if I see him again.'

'I thought his parting words were "See you tomorrow"?'

'They were, but what if he's had second thoughts? What if we bump into him and he ignores me or runs in the opposite direction?'

'Why would he do that?'

'Maybe he didn't really like me.'

'How many times did you say you did it?'

'Three.'

'You're right. He obviously doesn't fancy you at all.'

Nina heaves a sigh. As do I. Oh the curse of being a woman! The self-doubt and the hang-ups that conspire to ruin our pleasures. Why do we let them win? Why do we feel so guilty when we 'give in' to our sexual desires? It feels so good to be spontaneous but then you have to deal with the payback the next day. I feel her pain. It's just so irritating when you think you've had a one-night stand, to wake up and realise that you want to see him again.

'Now I know I'm not going to see him again,' Nina grumbles as she emerges from the Ladies.

'What makes you say that?' I frown.

'My hair's gone right today.'

'It doesn't look that good,' I try to reassure her but she's having none of it.

We decide to have a quick look in one of the boutiques on the Square before we head off to Guys but the pretty blonde shop assistants can't get over the fact that a couple of Brits are rifling through their rails . . .

'What're ya'll doing in Mississippi?' they frown. 'Did your plane break down?'

We tell them we've come looking for love.

'Well, you've come to the right place – Southern men are the best!'

'And the cutest,' her friend chips in before adding, 'Do ya'll know Prince William? He's so hot!'

Suddenly I feel bad about dismissing all the girls we saw out last night. Maybe if I'd made the effort to talk to any of them I'd have found they weren't the snooty Southern princesses I presumed but absolute peaches like these two.

We've barely set a toe (with nail or without) back on the street when we sense a scurrying behind us and turn to find a grinning Jay gaining upon us. Nina does an involuntary Tim Henman fist-pump and I nearly kiss him, I'm so pleased on her behalf.

'You look lovely!' I blurt, though it's not really my place to be making such comments. Yesterday he had on a shabby brown-and-beige long-sleeve T-shirt, today he's sporting what he tells us is his favourite red check shirt, handed down through generations and fresh from the dryer.

'I've been doing laundry all day!' he laughs. 'And it's still not done.'

'A lot of white sheets, huh?' I mutter.

'What's that?'

'Nothing!' I pip.

By his own admission Jay 'doesn't go much on sweet-talking' but he looks pretty lit up around Nina. He even suggests meeting up with us for our last night back in Memphis. Nina is delighted and eagerly gives him my cell phone number.

'We'll either be there tonight or tomorrow night,' she explains, choosing to lop off the 'depending on whether we get lucky in Guys' factor.

I leave the two of them for a farewell smooch, still

472

not quite understanding the attraction on Nina's part but hey, as long as she's happy . . .

KEEP GUYS BEAUTIFUL. That's what the sign says and who are we to argue? Armed with various hair-styling pomades and pore-refining potions, we prepare to meet the guys of Guys, a small farming community just ninety miles east of Memphis.

'Uh oh,' Nina shrinks back as we spot our first candidate chugging around his garden on a ride-on lawnmower.

Though his puce complexion suggests he is in desperate need of a soothing gel mask he glowers so fiercely in our direction we fear he'll use us as target practice if we come any closer. Further down the lane we spy four pairs of hands in need of a manicure – elbow-deep in engine grease, grappling with an outsize carburettor.

'Keep going,' Nina recommends, still optimistic that we'll find an Ashton Kutcher-type lurking beneath a grubby trucker cap.

I'd be happier still to find another Grand Canyon Ken (he was from Tennessee after all) but the closest we get is three shirtless youths riding up front in a pick-up truck. They slow to gawp at us but then continue on their redneck way.

'You know, it's funny,' I decide, 'were it not for the inhabitants and these porch-and-rocker-style homes, we could be in the English countryside.'

There's rolling fields with newborn calves and foals, prickly hedges fluttering with butterflies, even a village green. I'm almost surprised to find that Guys'

Grocery doesn't stock Refresher chews and Palma Violets.

'Do you think they serve afternoon tea here at Family's Café?' Nina plays along, peering in the window of the adjacent shack and pretending she hasn't noticed the two thunking-great truck cabs in a neighbouring driveway. 'You know, if we leave now we could still make it to that Elvis Tribute baseball match – Memphis Redbirds versus the Las Vegas 51ers,' Nina appeals. 'First five hundred through the gate get a commemorative Elvis baseball.'

I take a last look around Guys – short of elbowing a child off her trampoline there's not much in the way of entertainment here and besides, I've never really wanted to date the kind of man who could skin a rabbit with his bare teeth. But a man in knickerbockers with a big bat . . .

'Let's do it!' I cheer, deciding it will be a fittingly Yankee ending – I started with cowboys and will conclude with that most American of sports, and a hot dog.

On the way back to Memphis, Nina lets Jay know our plans – we'll be checking into the hip Madison Hotel (it's Saturday night and our beloved Peabody Hotel is fully booked), catching the game, dining at Automatic Slim's Tonga Club and then hitting Beale Street till the wee small hours.

I find myself flinching slightly at this last bit – I don't know if I've got another night of partying in me. I am, quite frankly, pooped.

'Are you going to call Trucker?' Nina hands me the phone.

I decline – no need, I'm on the home-straight now.

'I can't believe there's a whopping great baseball stadium slap-bang in the middle of town!' Nina gapes up at the vast redbrick empire known as Autozone Park.

It's hard to believe that this was once the stage for the race riots sparked by Martin Luther King's assassination here in 1968. That tragic event marked the beginning of downtown decline and this whole area became synonymous with X-rated movie theatres and low-lifes, but then in the year 2000, $80 million of private cash transformed it into the best minor-league facility in America. And it really is impressive – a clean, proud, state-of-the-art structure with every imaginable need catered for, especially if you're peckish – we explore the vendors busily touting Barbecue nachos, Polish dogs, Delta dogs, burgers, peanuts, cracker-jacks, candyfloss, ice-cream, ice-cold beer, foot-long frozen margaritas . . . It's a fast-food fiesta! There's such a buzz in the air and I'm surprised how many attractive young people are swarming in – I thought it would just be die-hard old coots and Elvis fans after that commemorative baseball. If I wasn't feeling so distracted with thoughts of Troy, this would be a great place to guy-watch though the players themselves look more like cute little figurines from this distance. There they go – lifting that bat, taking a swipe, sending the stitched leather ball deep into the bluest of skies. It really is such an American sight we get chills. Then a real-live six-footer walks by in his bright white, scarlet-trimmed kit, complete with box-like shoulders and a geometric jaw.

'WOW!' He takes our breath away.

'Come in number sixteen!' I coo after him.

'Let's talk to him!' Nina dares me.

We hurry over with a view to sidelining him for two minutes but as he's a reserve today and coincidentally went to school in Oxford, we end up having a full-on heart-to-heart about Southern life and love. He tells us how the dedication of a Southern man to his woman can sometimes border on ownership, how more and more women don't like to have doors opened for them (seeing it as an affront to their independence), how he's tried Barbie girls but that's not working for him and the biggest shocker of all – he's yet to find his perfect Southern Belle.

'I'm twenty-eight and still single – professional ball player, you'd think I would have found The One,' he sighs.

We'd have thought so too – he's funny and cheeky as well as real pin-up material – so we ask if he has a theory as to why She has eluded him.

'Oh I have a theory!' he chuckles. 'First of all, it's hard to meet someone who can deal with this way of life. It's like the military really (*steady, Nina*) – you don't know where in the country you're going to get stationed. But for me personally the main obstacle has been money.'

'Money has stopped you finding love?'

He nods. 'Last year was the first time I made it up to the Major Leagues so from a financial standpoint up until then I didn't know if I was going to make a living out of this game, therefore I didn't want to get involved – it's back to the Southern male thing: I never wanted to get married until I knew I could give my wife a good life. Even if she has a job I wanted to be able to take care of everything.'

'So even if you met someone you liked, you didn't pursue it?' we check, amazed.

'That's right. And there were girls along the way that would probably have made great wives and mothers but I was so intent on making it to the major leagues I passed them by.'

Gosh. We can't help wondering whether he couldn't have just opted for a long courtship rather than miss out on Miss Right but it just goes to show, even for sports pros there are no guaranteed wins in the game of love.

'So!' he breezes, directing our gaze back to the pitch. 'Are you girls familiar with the rules of baseball?'

'It's basically rounders, isn't it?' Nina sounds blasé.

Five minutes later it becomes apparent we have No Clue what's going on. The crowd aren't particularly demonstrative and at certain crucial points we can't even tell who's winning.

'Was that in? Whose point was that? What does it mean?' we frown.

Matt patiently explains the basics to us and for a moment we think we've got it. Then we try and apply what he's said to what we're seeing and we find ourselves straight back at befuddled.

'It's too hot,' I complain, flapping at the clammy air, wishing I hadn't had that second daiquiri.

'I can take you upstairs to an air-conditioned box if you like,' he offers.

'Do you mean that?' we gasp.

'Sure.'

'What are we waiting for?' I leap to my feet, my thighs unsticking from the plastic chair a few seconds later.

Now this is more like it – lovely and cool and what a vantage point: we're in the front row in a balcony box overlooking the entire stadium.

'Watch out!' I scream as the ball gets wopped in our direction.

Nina and I duck and then feel foolish.

'As if it's going to get all the way up here!' Nina tsks as she sets herself back upright.

'I could have sworn . . .' I cringe, embarrassed for overreacting.

The next hit takes the ball directly into the press commentary box next door, cue tinkling of glass.

'Oh my God!' we gasp. 'You could get killed round here!'

'That's why we put a disclaimer on the back of every ticket,' Matt informs us, sounding matter-of-fact about the dangers of being a spectator.

We're just about to ask if we can borrow a couple of cage-fronted helmets when he beckons over his team's mascot to meet us.

'I have to go now but this guy will take care of you!' Matt hands us over to a man in a giant fluffy red bird costume. Hmm, not the best trade-off.

We try to make polite conversation but he just shrieks at us in a strange high-pitched voice, mercilessly taking the piss out of our accents and blowing raspberries every time we try and look away. Then comes a break in the game, and while the sprightly wee cheerleaders do their thing to 'You're The Devil In Disguise' (which seems disturbingly apt considering our current company) the Redbird starts crowing at the audience below. Once they realise he's about to throw free T-shirts at them they all get to their feet and wave and whistle and cheer up at us.

'Oh my God! I feel like Evita!' I say, just as Nina says, 'Robbie Williams.'

He throws three T-shirts then Nina snatches the fourth from him and hurls it at a little girl in a green top. It goes sailing past and into the hands of a middle-aged man.

'Oh no!' she laments.

The Redbird screeches his disapproval then flaps on his way.

'What a hoot!' I reel.

When the time comes to exit the gates I feel so fully entertained I'd happily call it a night, but Nina's energy levels are now going through the roof in anticipation of seeing Jay.

For me, this feels like New Year's Eve – one in which I'd happily forgo the champagne and madness in favour of quiet contemplation of all that has gone before and all that lies ahead. But then I inhale the aromas wafting from the kitchens at Automatic Slim's and decide I'll stay sociable a while longer.

'The coconut mango shrimp is wonderful,' a stunning blonde cross between Ursula Andress and Meryl Streep advises us as we study the menu at the bar. 'And you have to try the tobacco onion rings.'

With her looks she should be every woman's

nightmare but she's so gabby and girlie we take an instant shine and quickly learn her name is Alexandra, she works for the tourism office, lives upstairs and so basically considers Slim's her own personal dining room and bar.

A couple of cocktails later she's joined by her pal Barry, a single divorcé who has made a rather unusual pact with himself: 'I'm going to date one hundred women before I marry again,' he tells us.

'Gosh!' we gasp, impressed at his ambition. 'What number are you at?'

'Sixty-one,' he says.

'Do we count?' I ask.

'Yeah, can we be sixty-two and sixty-three?' Nina cajoles him. 'It gets you a few steps closer to your goal!'

'Why not?' he grins, toasting us.

We've now retired to the zebra-print window booth and are chatting happily to Alexandra and Barry, oblivious to everyone else in the bar, when a guy walks up to Nina and says: 'You need to get a tit job or wear a bra – that top's not working for you.'

For a moment there's a stunned silence then, as the words register, I become *incensed*. I couldn't even tell you Nina's reaction because I'm too busy scrabbling to get past the table to get at him. How dare he?! It's not even like he was chatting her up and she knocked him back – there was zero provocation. Propelled by an overwhelming urge to tear his head off I blast through the crowd to get to him. He's now sitting back over with his gang of mates but this doesn't deter me – heart hammering at the injustice I forcibly infiltrate the group and loom over him like the angel of death.

'Can you take that kind of criticism back?' I seethe, just millimetres from his face, which, thank you Lord, gives me plenty of ammunition.

'What?' he blinks.

'I want to know if you can take that kind of criticism back because man your acne scars are hideous!' I taunt. 'I mean really, I can't *believe* how bad your skin is.' I shrink back in disgust. 'And ooo-eee are you *ugly*!'

'She needs a bra,' is the best he can manage in return.

'Maybe, but at least she's got a pretty face. I mean, seriously, have you looked in the mirror lately?'

I always find barbed sarcasm to be the most effective way to extinguish small fry.

'I can't go out with a bag over my head,' he complains.

'Well then maybe you shouldn't go out at all,' I toot.

'Heeey!' one of his friends goes to step in.

'WHAT?' I yell, breathing fire at him. 'This is *nothing*! Did you hear what he said to my friend?'

'I know, I know, I'm sorry, he's drunk, we're leaving,' he splutters, bundling his friend out the door.

I'm still raging. 'I can't believe that!' I rant to no one in particular.

Back over with the nice people Nina is putting on a brave face, laughing and looking down at her chest: 'They don't look that bad, do they?'

'He's not a Southerner, that guy, I guarantee you that,' Barry is still astounded.

'No way,' Alexandra agrees, embarrassed that such a nasty incident should take place in her home from home.

'I'm getting us martinis!' I say stomping to the bar, still shaking with outrage.

Seconds later one of his friends is back.

'Look, I just wanted to apologise for my friend but I can see both sides of the argument —'

'WHAT?' I roar, blowing his hair back. 'What do you mean BOTH SIDES?' I'm incredulous. 'He comes up and insults her – that's ONE side! One person in the wrong!' I bark.

'I just wanted to apologise—'

'Which I appreciate,' I cut in. 'But don't say it to me, say it to her!' I point at Nina who genuinely doesn't seem that bothered, I have to admit.

Before he can scuttle off, Barry corners him. 'Where are you from?' he demands.

'Colorado, sir,' he whimpers.

'And your friend?'

'Arizona.'

'I knew it!' Barry toots. 'I knew they couldn't be from round here!'

I take a deep breath. I am still fuming that some punk should spoil our last night but Nina convinces me that it's nothing that a trip to Alfred's won't put right, so we bid Barry and Alex farewell and head off to Beale Street for our grand finale.

En route the phone goes – it's Jay!

There follows a brief moment of hysteria when he tries to persuade Nina to get a bus to Tunica (a mini-Vegas forty miles south in Mississippi) and meet him at the Horseshoe Casino. (His car has packed up and this is as close to Memphis as he can get, tagging along with Biff.)

482

'Let me look into it,' she tells him. 'I'll call you right back.'

The best transport solution we come up with is a $300 round-trip limo ride but it's just as well we don't lose our minds and go for it because by the time we've called back he's already on his way back to Oxford – Biff lost all his money within half an hour and was so peeved he insisted on going straight home.

'Well, that was exciting for a moment,' Nina sighs, clicking off the phone.

'How disappointing,' I sympathise.

'Yeah,' she shrugs. 'But I'm not going to let it spoil our night.'

'No?' I don't mean to sound disappointed but I really am done. And the sight of weekend-style Beale Street nearly finishes me off altogether – last time we were the only people on the sidewalk and a novelty in the bars. Tonight there are police barriers set up to ID every person who even wants to walk the heaving street, let alone go clubbing, and the competition has gone through the roof with a zillion girls dollied up in their J-Lo-Ho finest. I'm definitely daunted – it's the busiest, rowdiest street I've ever seen and that's including Bourbon Street on Valentine's night. As I have second thoughts about whether I've got the energy to join the surge, Nina steps forward and joins the party people.

'My God, this is brilliant!' she raves, making a beeline for Alfred's.

All I can think is, 'Oh God, these places don't shut till 5 a.m. at the weekend!'

At 4.55 a.m. I'm leaning in Alfred's doorway nearly

in tears. I've lost count of the number of drinks that have been spilled on me, the music has been cranked up so loud my eardrums are punctured with pain and don't even ask about my feet.

Initially, despite the crush, it was fun because an award-winning Elvis tribute artist was performing on stage and though he was quite a fright visually, even Nina had to admit he had the voice spot-on. At one point, when we were trying to find somewhere to stand where we didn't get heckled for obstructing someone else's view, I caught his reflection in the window and it was indeed as if the ghost of Elvis himself was with us that night.

When he was done the DJ slipped on Justin Timberlake and the already crammed dance floor was stampeded. He's a local boy, JT. I remember watching him being interviewed once and he got on the subject of women's bodies and confessed, 'I like some junk in the trunk – I'm a butt man, I can't fight it. That's Memphis talking.' I love that quote. It made me happy for about a minute thinking about it and then the fatigue made its final claim on me. I remember Nina trying to lure me on the dance floor but I said I couldn't because my feet were too hot. She looked at me in despair. I looked at me in despair. I couldn't ask for a more fun crowd to hang out with but I was done. I wanted tonight to be over. I tried to suggest to Nina that I might be ready to go but she was having none of it: 'This is the very last night of the quest! You can't go! Have a shot of tequila!'

So I did and for a brief moment I felt better. Two minutes later I was stood outside by myself, willing Nina and her new friends to sup up and ship out. As I watched the human debris stumbling and spewing, two unsavoury youths skulked past and as one made a lunge in my direction, the other said, 'Don't do it, man!'

I immediately tensed and thought, 'Here we go!' but he just stepped a little closer and said, very sweetly, 'You look nice!' and then went on his way.

I blinked after him. You can't beat that Southern hospitality, I'm telling you.

By the time I've actually persuaded Nina to go back to the hotel it's 7 a.m. – 7 *a.m.!* – and I am in a horrible mood.

'Is it too much to ask to have hotel curtains that actually block out the light?' I grizzle, yanking the fabric this way and that before I settle on the time-honoured tradition of a pillow over the head.

As I lie there trying to tell myself, 'It's all over now, you can relax' I am instead tormented by the prospect of packing with a tequila hangover just four hours from now and book an alarm call for 11 a.m. to ensure we make our flight home.

At 10.57 a.m. the most almighty siren penetrates our skulls and amplifies in our ears.

Ye Gods – I startle upright and look for something to slam/muffle but then we hear the words: *This is a fire alarm. Please exit the room immediately, take the stairs to the ground level and continue out onto the street.*

'You've got to be kidding,' I croak, cranking myself upright. My tequila head in my hands, I dial reception to ask, 'Is this for real?'

'I'm not sure, ma'am, I'll find out and let you know.'

I put down the phone.

'We should probably go anyway,' says Nina, stepping unsteadily into her clothes.

I wait a few minutes. There's no call back from reception. Is no news, good news or does this mean she's frying?

'Are we really going to go down looking like this?' I ask. We are absolute frights – hair every which way and last night's make-up staining our puffy, munched-up faces.

'Sunglasses!' Nina puts on her heavy gold rims but the only ones I can find are my cat-eyed diamanté creations. I look like a junkie Dame Edna Everage. It occurs to me briefly that my priorities are out of whack – instead of trying to coordinate our outfits we should be running for our lives.

We proceed as fast as we can down fourteen flights of stairs. Even though it's downhill my legs jellify by floor eight and by three I am severely lagging behind as I can no longer judge the steps and have to tap each one with my toe before I plant my foot. When I finally exit the stairwell and emerge into the lobby we find that the panic is over – someone was having a sneaky ciggy in the stairwell and it set off the alarms. We see a pack of firefighters leaving but we're told that the elevators won't be functioning for 'some time'. I know we've got a flight to catch but I can't possibly scale fourteen floors.

'I can't do it,' I tell Nina, sliding down the wall onto the cold marble floor. Nina does the same and we take it in turns to emit sounds of suffering and discomfort. We're not the only ones waiting for the lifts, a few other couples are loitering and one sweet woman says: 'I love your sunglasses!'

486

I try to look pleased but in fact I'm mortified that I'm wearing something so eye-catching at a time when I'd really rather be invisible. I haven't even cleaned my fuzzy teeth and I'm desperate to sluice away last night's sweat. It's therefore all the more mortifying when a cheery surfer type bounces in and says, 'Hey Elvis girls!' and gives us a dynamically dishevelled smile.

Nina and I look at each other. If we had the strength we'd go, 'Phwoar!'

A minute later he's back. 'No lifts, huh? I was just on the tour bus and I woke up to find ten fire engines outside. I was like, "All this, for me? You shouldn't have!"'

'Tour bus?'

'Tom Petty & The Heartbreakers. I'm doing the lighting for the show at the Orpheum theatre. You girls hanging here for a couple of nights?'

'We leave in two hours.'

'Now that's a shame.'

I'm guessing that from our squeaky-hoarse voices and the fact we look like we've just been found under a table in a bar that closed three hours earlier, he's got us pegged as good-time girls – if only he knew I spent the whole night complaining that my feet were on fire and concluded the evening with my hands over my ears because the music was too loud.

'You English?' I frown, trying to get a handle on his distorted accent.

'I'm from Stafford originally but I've been living in LA for the past thirteen years.'

'Whereabouts?'

'Benedict Canyon.'

'As of tonight I'm Beachwood Drive,' I manage to grunt.

'Really? You should let me take you out to dinner when I get back. You like sushi?'

I hold up a STOP! hand. 'Don't!' I plead. 'Even the *thought* of raw fish at the moment . . .' Let alone another date – I just couldn't!

He laughs and changes tack. 'Ever seen inside a tour bus?'

'Yes,' I say wearily, ruining his chance to impress us.

'Uh oh – I think we're the floorshow,' Nina whispers under her breath, noticing that everyone is staring at us as we banter back and forth.

I'm too clapped-out to care. Fortunately he has energy to spare. We learn his name is Adam and he likes motorbikes, then his boss comes by and does a double-take. 'What are you guys all doing on the floor – playing spin the bottle?'

'It's a thought!' says Nina, draining the last of our Evian.

'Give me your phone number,' Adam says, getting to his feet. 'I know how you girls are about phoning guys.'

'She's not that kind of girl,' Nina tells him.

'Well, let me have it anyway, just in case.'

The man delivers every line with such joyous enthusiasm I can't resist.

As Nina and I finally struggle upright I get a head-spin and a revelation: It's the morning after the last night of a love quest that's taken me the length and breadth of America and I've ended up meeting a Brit who lives three miles from my door.

Just wait till I get my hands on that Cupid . . .

AND NOW . . .

It's time to make the call. I punch in fifteen numbers and wait to be connected to England.

'Hello?' a female voice answers.

'Emily?'

'Belinda!' she whoops. 'Where are you? I haven't heard a peep out of you in months!'

'I'm in California,' I laugh, excited to find her in.

'Please don't tell me you're living in a trailer with Gino the toothless can-collector!'

'Nooo,' I chortle. 'I'm subletting this girl's apartment in LA to see if I want to stay out here for a while. Which, incidentally, I definitely do!'

'You jammy bugger. It's tipping down here,' she grumbles. 'So what happened with the Mr Right quest, did you finish it?'

'Yup, got back from Tennessee a week ago.'

'And?'

Where do I begin? It's taken me the last seven days just to process all that has happened in my head.

'Tell me!' Emily urges. 'Did you find Him?'

'Well, I'm not sure but in a few days time I'm getting a visit from a hunky trucker from Kissimmee!'

'What?' Emily gasps. 'You actually did it!' she cheers. 'You pulled it off!'

'Can you believe it?' I chime. 'All that chasing around and I've finally learned to let them come to me!'

'You sound so calm about it!' Emily marvels.

'Well, it's weird – I am almost ambivalent,' I admit. 'Troy is being wonderful and I am really psyched about seeing him again but at the same time . . .'

'He's not The One?' she sounds disappointed.

'He could be. I just don't seem to mind either way.'

'I don't get it – what's going on with you?' Emily demands.

No wonder she's confused – she's speaking to a very different woman to the one she set off to Eden with last year.

Back then I was convinced that only Mr Right could fill the gap in my life – I was sure he was the missing link to my future happiness – but I see now that was a convenient cop-out. His absence gave me an excuse to stop trying in all the other areas of my life. *Why should I put any more effort into my work or my home or my friends? They're not the problem. It's just a man I need, everything else is fine.*

I had pretty much ground to a halt, despondent in all things, and I was waiting for love to jump-start me.

So off I went with a view to finding my one true love so we could serve our one true purpose together.

However, over the course of several weeks and twelve states, I discovered there are as many ways to love as there are people to love: you can love everyone, like the elfin hippy in Truth or Consequences or you can work on loving yourself first, like Gino the can-collector from Nice. You can make a living from your loving like Weddington's yournovel.com couple or you can prize your love of the land over the love of a girl, like Chris the Texan cowboy. You can choose one love for life like the Amish or to love the one you're with like ladies'-man Ricky. And you can seek love in romantic beauty spots but find it in Ross Dress for Less.

The options are limitless. There's no one way. I'd forgotten that. I thought I must be doing something wrong because I was in my thirties and I hadn't found that special someone. I would sob myself to sleep because I felt so detached from everything and everyone. Now I feel that love is everywhere and instead of watching from the sidelines, I am in among it. And the biggest shock is that it turns out I don't have to be in a relationship to feel that. Whether or not I have made any lasting connections actually doesn't matter – though I am still in touch with Ricky and Cem, and of course Troy – the fact is, I have rejoined the world! Who knew there were so many ways to be happy?

My other significant revelation was that I have been (secretly) choosing the single life all along. Whenever I hankered after romance it was always movie-love, i.e. an hour and a half in a darkened room. I didn't want it in my life full-time, that would have been way too invasive. This trip has given me a big reality check:

when I'm offered it on a plate – say with Cem – I don't necessarily want it.

'It's one thing wishing for it, another thing living it,' Emily opines.

'Exactly. Although I am really glad I met Cem – I never knew I could be one of those girls who inspires such devotion! Maybe next time I'll go for it!'

'Next time – hark at you!'

'I know!' I laugh, remembering how I thought I was down to my last love token. That's why I clung on so tight to Christian – I didn't think there would be anyone to take his place if I let him go. 'Now I'm much more optimistic about meeting someone,' I tell Emily. 'I'm just in much less of a hurry!'

'This is amazing!' She can't believe her ears.

'I'll tell you something else – you know all that time I wasted feeling sorry for myself when I was single?'

'Yes I do,' she affirms. 'I lived it too!'

'Well now I think I was deliberately kept single for a reason.'

'What reason?'

'To make me look beyond boyfriends!'

'Explain! Expand!' Emily is impatient to understand.

'Well, take this trip. If I was in some serious relationship I wouldn't have been so open to all the amazing experiences I had along the way.' I pause, searching for something Emily can relate to. 'Like our night with Mark and Bobby – if we'd had boyfriends we never would have gone to Mark's mansion and had one of the sparkiest, funniest, most heart-warming evenings of our lives.'

Emily sighs. 'Yeah, it was the best.'

'Or sat under the stars watching blood-spattered cowboys spitting chewing tobacco!'

Emily laughs.

'Maybe I'm single because I'm supposed to have experiences like that. I'm supposed to experience lots of different people, not just one. That's what makes me feel *alive*!'

And, let's face it, if I'd been snuggled up on a sofa watching TV and eating Thai takeaway with some guy – as was my former wish – I would never have lunched with a mayor, toured a funeral home, overnighted in a converted train caboose, watched a stock-car race, seen a rainbow at Niagara Falls, tailgated an Amish buggy, bathed in a seven-foot champagne glass, got drunk on Bourbon St, learned how to make an alligator fall asleep, rafted down the Colorado river, ridden a horse called Red through a field of yellow flowers, flown in a helicopter over the Grand Canyon, felt the magic of a Sanctuary sunset, sand-boarded on a dustbin lid, waddled alongside the Peabody duck parade, eaten a hot dog at a baseball match, visited Graceland with Kat Slater or, best of all, dirty-danced on a misty mountain top.

'Are you sure these things aren't just distractions?' Emily ventures.

I think for a minute. 'I see your point but no, I don't think so. I'm not deluding myself that everything is all right just because I'm keeping busy. If anything I've become more self-aware.'

I can see now that it was all about teenage lust with Cowboy Casey, that I'm not quite grown-up enough to date a Nice Mark but one day I hope to be, that Arizona Ricky's looks and charm worked like a dream on me in person (aside from the hanky-panky) but we had no connection on the phone – something I probably wouldn't have noticed if I hadn't had these easy, profound, sexy conversations with Trucker. I also learned the hard way that I have no sense of judgement in the presence of a goatee and ponytail (Paul in Cazenovia and a reminder with Ryan/Brian in Memphis) but hopefully that is now history. I'm certainly wide-open when it comes to looks now. I've spoken to so many interesting people I would never have ordinarily considered 'my type' and found something attractive in all of them. Now I'm going to focus on how I actually feel with them, as opposed to how I feel about how they look.

On a more superficial note, it didn't hurt my confidence any to pull a hottie like Kane.

'Was he the best-looking of the bunch?' Emily asks, eager for the juice.

'Actually I think technically it may have been Ricky. Or Tony from Gatorland. In terms of outright sex appeal and presence Trucker wins but oh, the one that really made me melt – still makes me light-headed just thinking of him now – is Ken from the Grand Canyon.'

'Ken?'

'If you saw him you'd get past the name. He was the best. But he had a girlfriend.'

'Curses!'

'Tell me about it. Still it does my heart good just to know that men like him exist.'

'Look at you all philosophical!' Emily cries, clearly

astonished by the new me.

'I am, aren't I!' I laugh. 'And I tell you the strangest thing – I went to this awards ceremony last night and I wore exactly the same outfit that I wore to last year's do, same hair, same make-up and yet I couldn't have had a more different response from the men. It was the same industry types, same high glamour factor but last year I just skulked around presuming no one would be interested in a non-celeb like me and then left early because I felt so invisible and insignificant. But this year all these men – four or five really attractive guys – came up to me! I never get that!'

'Tell me more! Tell me more!' Emily pleads.

'I don't want to sound vain—' I hesitate.

'Oh don't be silly!' Emily clips. 'You're talking to me – boast away!'

'Well, this one really dapper, witty writer kept cropping up wherever I went, resuming our conversation and getting flirtier with every instalment and he gave me his card, then this gorgeous, far-too-young TV presenter bought me a drink, then this guy I've known for years told me that I'm the most wonderful person he knows and that I light up a room, then this arty, angsty actor asked me to stay overnight with him in his suite—'

'You're kidding! Tell me you said yes!'

'Well, I was sorely tempted but then he got into a fight with the barman and it put me off.'

'Oh.'

'I'm not saying I was inundated by Mr Rights,' I clarify. 'I'm just saying I was inundated, which at this point is good enough for me!'

'From road trip to ego trip – I love it!' Emily cheers.

'I know!' I laugh. 'How is this my life?' I take a moment to breathe. 'The point is, something must have changed in me, don't you think? I didn't look any different so it must be my behaviour, my confidence . . .'

'It's your attitude,' Emily decides.

'Well, I've certainly lost that desperation I was carrying with me. Now I feel like I have *choices*.'

'I'll say!' Emily hoots. 'And first up is the trucker. I can't wait to hear how it goes!'

'Well, the way I look at it is this: if it's love, that's great. If it's not I get to spend two nights in a hotel suite with an ex male stripper – how bad can it be?'

'Hotel suite?'

'Well, I thought neutral territory would be best.'

'Anywhere nice?'

'Hotel Oceana, Santa Monica.'

'I like your style!' Emily grins down the phone. 'So what about Nina, any joy?'

'Yes, actually. She and Mississippi Jay are e-mailing like crazy. She says it's mostly platonic chit-chat but I wouldn't be surprised if she went back to visit him.'

'Wow. So it really works!'

'In ways I never expected!' I acknowledge. 'Anyway,' I change the subject, 'how's your boy?'

'Lovely,' she says warmly.

'Good,' I tell her, meaning it. 'I know that's what you want.'

'I suppose that's the key,' Emily decides. 'Finding out what is right for you.'

'Exactly,' I confirm. 'I love my freedom. I know it

doesn't suit everyone but that's what's right for me.'

'Yeah, yeah, I'll call you after the weekend and find you hopped on a plane to Vegas and married Trucker! Or any of the myriad men you met last night!' she tuts.

'You never know!' I laugh, getting to my feet. 'And if they don't work out there's always Boys Town, Nebraska; Sacred Heart, Minnesota; Love, Oklahoma; Manly, Iowa . . .'

Emily chuckles down the line.

I'm walking over to the window to let in some California sunshine when I stop in my tracks. 'Remember that old song, "I left my heart in San Francisco"?'

'Of course.'

'Well,' I sigh, leaning on the ledge, 'somewhere between Eden, Texas and Guys, Tennessee I found mine.' Now brimming over with happiness at my new life, I add: 'I went looking for love and I found my heart.'

ON THE ROAD TO MR RIGHT
WEBSITE

Visit www.belindajones.com for a full bonus chapter (Loveladies, New Jersey), exclusive photos from the road trip and a multitude of out-take anecdotes!

You can also peruse sample chapters from DIVAS LAS VEGAS, I LOVE CAPRI and THE CALIFORNIA CLUB and e-mail the author.

**What are you waiting for?
Get your motor running and head out on the highway of love!**

DIVAS LAS VEGAS

A tale of love, friendship and sequinned underpants . . .

Jamie and Izzy, friends for ever, have a dream: a spangly double wedding in Las Vegas. And, at twenty-seven, they decide they've had enough crap boyfriends and they're ready for crap husbands – all they have to do is find them. So where better than Las Vegas itself, where the air is 70% oxygen and 30% confetti?

But as they abandon their increasingly complicated lives in sleepy Devon for the eye-popping brilliance of Las Vegas, their groom-grabbing plan starts to look less than foolproof. And those niggling problems they thought they'd left behind – like Izzy's fiancé and the alarming reappearance of Jamie's first love – just won't go away . . .

I LOVE CAPRI

Sundrenched days, moonlit nights and Italian ice cream. What more could a girl ask for . . . ?

Kim Rees became a translator for the glamorous jet-set lifestyle. So, five years later, how come she's ended up in a basement flat in Cardiff translating German computer games in her dressing gown? Fortunately her mother has a plan to extract her from her marshmallowy rut: a trip to the magical isle of Capri.

At first Kim refuses to wake up and smell the bougainvillea, but as she starts to succumb to the irresistible delights of cocktails on the terrace and millionaire suitors, she's surprised to realise she's changing. And when she meets a man who's tiramisu personified, she finds herself falling in love. But how far will she go to win her Romeo?

THE CALIFORNIA CLUB

What's your dream . . . ?

When Lara Richards jets off to glamorous California, the last thing she's expecting is to find her old friend Helen transformed from a clipboard-clasping frump into a shimmering surf goddess. The secret of her blissful new life? The mysterious California Club.

So the offer of guest membership – one wish, guaranteed to come true by the end of their stay – is one Lara and her friends can't resist. Could this be Lara's chance to win her best friend Elliot's heart after ten years of longing? Or does the fact that he's travelling with his brand new fiancée mean that Lara will have to come up with a new dream . . . ?

Praise for Belinda Jones

'A glitterball romp' *Glamour*

'A cut above most romantic comedies . . . a gem'
Woman's Own

'This will get you in the holiday spirit' *Company*

'The perfect uplifting beach read' *B*

'Deliciously entertaining' *heat*

'A wise and witty read about the secret desires deep within us' *Marie Claire*

'As essential as your SPF 15' *New Woman*